279.+
KEN

who is worthy?

The role of conscience in restoring hope to the church

D1450406

Ted Kennedy

Pluto Press

First published in 2000 by
Pluto Press Australia Limited
Locked Bag 199, Annandale, NSW 2038
http://media.socialchange.net.au/pluto

Copyright © Ted Kennedy 2000

Cover design by Justin Archer

Photograph of Ted Kennedy and Duane Captain courtesy of
Palani Mohan/*Sydney Morning Herald*

Edited by Val Noone and Lliane Clarke

Typeset by Chapter 8 Pty Ltd

Printed and bound by McPherson's Printing Group

Australian Cataloguing-in-Publication Data

  Kennedy, Ted
  Who is worthy?: the role of conscience in restoring hope to the church

  ISBN 1 86403 087 9.

  1. Catholic Church — Controversial literature.
  2. Catholic Church — Doctrines. 3. Aborigines, Australian — Social
  conditions. 4. Racism — Religious aspects — Catholic Church.
  5. Homosexuality — Religious aspects — Catholic Church. I. Title.

282.94

*In loving and grateful acknowledgment of the
parishioners of St Vincent's Church, Redfern,
and of many, many friends who have participated
in the unfolding authorship of this book.*

Father Ted Kennedy with Duane Captain

Contents

About the cover

Luke the Evangelist, according to legend, was a painter. Certainly he wrote with an artist's eye for symbolism. The poet James McAuley provides us with the image of 'Luke's woven cloth (threaded) so finely that the eye must prick the weave to catch its gold meander'.

It was similarly so in the work of Rembrandt. These two masters of intense imagery — Luke with words, Rembrandt with paint — show themselves capable of pushing the boundaries of imagined human feeling to hitherto unheard-of heights. They conspire in their accounts of 'The Return of the Prodigal Son.'

Both relate a parable of extravagant compassion. The story of the prodigal son is told only in Luke's Gospel. It carries a uniqueness in that it was first directed towards a unique readership. Luke the Greek wrote in the Greek language for a Greek-speaking audience, shocking them by pointing to a God who weeps, and bends low. The Greek gods were unbending, incapable of feeling. Not only would they not show any capacity to care. They could not; otherwise they would not be divine. It was summed up in one word — apatheia. Apathy comes near to it — unmoved, motionless, immovable, unmoving.

Luke was introducing them to a new kind of God, the God in Jesus; and he found a word[1] to describe how Jesus felt towards human frailty — σπλαγηνισομαι, literally 'to spill one's guts out'. Luke reserves the word to describe the profound heartfulness of Jesus, the one exception being where Jesus himself is seen describing certain parable figures. One such is the father of the prodigal son. With eloquent power of imagery, he describes the father sighting the son a long way off, running out to meet him so as to shield him from the community's taunts, and from social stigma. In various ways the father forgoes what were thought to be the requirements of patriarchy and adopts what was deemed the less dignified role of mother.

In this cover,[2] Rembrandt takes over with the portrayal of the Father's embrace, one hand male, the other female. The clearly male-gendered hand, emphatically veined and sinewed, traditionally assigned to the dominant 'dexterous' right side, is placed on the left. Whereas the female hand, slender, elegant but traditionally subordinate and even malignly 'sinister', is now on the right and accorded an equal if not leading role. Moreover, both hands now embrace the son, one with a soft caressing hold, the other with a strong protective clasp — each a form of reassuring and restorative touch, for here touch is all important, words are not needed.

The father's embrace is that of a love extending beyond gender expressed through both genders, and cannot be confined to the stodgy power-prone rules of patriarchy. Between God's love and those who turn to it, let no-one place an obstacle.

Perspectives

Danny Gilbert

TED KENNEDY entered the seminary at sixteen, and he has been a Catholic priest for almost fifty years. His ministry has been entirely pastoral, serving believer and non-believer alike. Ted's early years were in middle-class parishes. There followed a period in the 1960s as Catholic Chaplain at the University of Sydney. In 1971 he moved to Redfern, and so began his life among Australia's indigenous people.

Ted is stirred by recent examples of the Church's rejection of gay and lesbian people and his smouldering anger at the failure of his Church to fully face up to its role in the colonisation of Australia's Aborigines. He challenges the Church to fully embrace the glorified humanity of Christ, on which his faith is centred. In this book he discusses the understanding of this tenet in the early Church, and its subsequent diminishment, if not abandonment. His simple but powerful point is that this failure of the Church is at the very heart of its inability to celebrate all that is human. Consequently, Ted sees a Church which for the most part has defined humanity in terms of negative sinfulness rather than positive glory, a church concerned with control rather than compassion, a church more exclusive than inclusive, and a church more concerned with policing than embracing a diverse humanity.

No Australian priest who has stood for most of his life alongside Aboriginal people in their fight for justice could write about the Catholic Church without reference to them. Ted's discussion of the exclusion of Aboriginal people from the life of the Australian Church is damning. If any further evidence is needed of the consequences of a theology which excludes, then here it is, in all its destructive tragedy.

Ted's vision is plainly for a truly catholic Church — a Church that hears the voice of Conscience even when that voice is discordant. He sees little hope for a church where conscience is trivialised and sidelined, believing when this happens that the very *raison d'etre* of Church authority is undermined. Ted's demand is that all the faithful be allowed to participate, imaginatively and creatively, in the living tradition of the Church. If this can occur, then Church authority will be enriched and individual conscience reasoned and informed. Young people, in particular, will, as they have in the past, refuse to follow the dictates of Church authority where it is uninformed by such involvement. Unless the Church can face up to this challenge, many young people will continue to feel that there is no place for them in it.

Minorities and the marginalised are the people Ted sees as central to the Church. Here his vision is for a church that nourishes, and is nourished by, society's rejects.

This book is a plea for an open heart. With steadfast determination, Ted reproaches the Church where it is proud and unrepentant. With words of grace and love he reminds us of the promise of Christ's gospel and the sacredness of all humanity. He is a powerful advocate for the relevance of the gospel today, and profoundly concerned to see it in safe hands. He believes those hands were at work in the early Church and in the second Vatican Council. He believes he saw the shape of those hands in such figures as John Henry Newman, Gerard Manley Hopkins, Thomas Merton, Oscar Romero, Pope John XXIII and Shirley Smith. But for Ted, these are fading figures in a still clericalised Church, too preoccupied with law and dogma.

Ted's views will be of interest to many people. They are an uncompromising reminder of how the power of the institution can be used to crush and stifle the individual it exists to serve. The institution in point is the Catholic Church. Ted's preoccupation and love is for this Church, to which, after almost seventy years, he remains obstinately devoted.

DANNY GILBERT
Managing partner of Sydney law firm, Gilbert & Tobin,
member of the St Vincent's Church community
and long-time friend of the author

Tony Coady

IN THIS REMARKABLE book, Father Ted Kennedy describes himself as 'a sample of that endangered species — an Australian Catholic priest'. He is that, but he is more and even rarer. For what speaks to the reader in this book is the authentic, singular voice of prophecy, a voice seldom heard in the Australian Church.

Like all prophets, Kennedy is discomforting. He calls us back to the paths of true orthodoxy, exposing our cosy certainties to the light of the Gospel and the early Church, but also illuminating the questions he addresses with the words and experiences of poets, theologians and the oppressed.

The tone is biblical, scholarly, scathing, confrontational and, at times, unaffectedly Australian ('conveying the unlabelled "sly-grog" of moral acts into the sanctuary'). The specific topic is the Australian Church's failed response to homosexuals and Aborigines, but more generally its theologically impoverished reaction to the contemporary world. A primary target is Melbourne's Archbishop George Pell and his defective theology of communion, but as with many memorable polemics the substance of Kennedy's case transcends the occasion that prompted it. Not every reader will be persuaded by every argument, but it will be few readers who do not find their horizons widened and their assumptions challenged by this powerful *cri de coeur*.

PROFESSOR TONY COADY
Director of the Centre for Philosophy and
Public Issues and Professorial Fellow
at the University of Melbourne

Veronica Brady

IT IS THE NATURE of grace, it has been said, to fill spaces that have been empty. In the Church in Australia many of us feel there has been a great emptiness as far as the feminine aspect of the divine mystery is concerned, the gracious, merciful and inclusive nature of God's love for us and for all creation. As Ted Kennedy puts it: 'male force and dominating power have developed a "one-sided shape" to society in general and to the Church, allowing racism, sexism and all kinds of bigotry to flourish. But there is another way, another kind of church which will give life and hope to "warm flesh and blood human beings", not rules made in an age long gone, or ill-fitting principles which were never made to measure anyhow.'

This book explores this way, and is in effect a meditation on the story of the prodigal son and on Rembrandt's painting of it, which implies that the merciful father is also mother God. Drawing on the long tradition which has been obscured by a patriarchal church preoccupied with sin and judgment, Kennedy gives us a vision of God which is deeply 'feminine', maternal even, insisting, to use Hopkin's words:

> ... that we are wound
> With mercy round and round.

Kennedy insists that there is a place for everyone, not just those like the elder son in the parable who regard themselves as virtuous, and a special place for those who are marginalised, poor or oppressed, such as Aboriginal people and the gay and lesbian community.

SISTER VERONICA BRADY

David McKenna

ON PENTECOST SUNDAY in 1998 and 1999, gay and lesbian Catholics and their friends, families and supporters, wearing rainbow sashes, presented themselves for Communion to Archbishop George Pell at St Patrick's Cathedral in Melbourne.

The proclamation of their purpose was set out in their 'Letter to the Church':

> In wearing the 'rainbow sash' we proclaim that we are gay and lesbian people who embrace and celebrate out sexuality as a sacred gift.
>   In wearing it we call on the Church:
> ● to honour the experience and wisdom of lesbian and gay people;
> ● to enter into open dialogue with us;
> ● to work with us for justice and understanding.
> Together let us seek a new appreciation of human sexuality in all of its diversity and beauty.

Each time, Dr Pell refused the Eucharist to all those wearing the sash. On the first occasion, he delivered a statement from the altar, notable for its harsh tone and lack of pastoral dimension.

On the second occasion, Dr Pell announced to an astonished media group that homosexuality was a greater health hazard than smoking. He also suggested that discouraging homosexuality amongst the young might reduce the number of youth suicides.

Dr Pell is now supporting the promotion in his diocese of the American-based fundamentalist group, Courage. His Vicar-General has recently circulated a document to the priests of the diocese commending this group to them. The document states that: 'Courage offers hope in circumstances where men and women believe there is no hope for change and control of their homosexual behaviour or orientations.'

Courage, and in particular its founder, Father Harvey, promotes the view that homosexuals can be turned into heterosexuals with 'prayer, group support and sound therapy'.

The psychiatrists who attempted to cure homosexuals earlier in the twentieth century have been harshly judged by history. The treatment was fueled by myth, prejudice, ideology and often downright scientific dishonesty. In short, it was a disgraceful experiment on human beings.

It is almost beyond belief that such an experiment should now be tried again. It is deplorable that the Church should involve itself in any way in such a venture. The lives, welfare and happiness of gay and lesbian people will be placed at grave risk.

My involvement in the Rainbow Sash Movement has been a salutary experience. It reveals an extraordinary level of fear amongst Catholics, especially those employed by or closely associated with the Church, about offering any public support for the Rainbow Sash Movement or, indeed, the cause of gay and lesbian people generally. It also shows just how constricted and apprehensive these people are. Given the claims made by the Catholic Church about itself, this is a scandal.

Gay and lesbian people still lead lives of loneliness, unhappiness and despair. Suicide is often how these damaged lives end, especially for the young, as it is also for Aboriginal people.

In Australian history, the two most oppressed groups have been the Aboriginal people and gay and lesbian people. The case of the Aboriginal people is, of course, much worse. I do not wish to underestimate it in this context.

For reasons which, I suspect, reflect this atmosphere, no theologian or priest (with the possible exception of Father Claude, the national co-ordinator of Acceptance Australia) has offered any direct public criticism of the performance of Dr Pell on these issues.

No doubt the recent operations of the Congregation for the Doctrine of the Faith in destroying the pastoral ministry to homosexuals of an American priest and a religious sister have not encouraged public discussion by the religious on sensitive issues. Dr Pell is said to be an influential member of that institution.

Further, there is the recent example, as if any more were needed, of the distinguished Australian Jesuit moral theologian, Father Bill Uren. He has been 'silenced' for making critical public comments on the

Vatican's ruling against the provision of drug injecting rooms by Catholic hospitals and institutions.

Now Father Ted Kennedy, a priest notable for his courage and compassion, has decided to speak out. Who better? He is one of those priests whom Catholics readily identify as 'the real thing'. His pastoral work and devotion to the Aboriginal community in Sydney is legendary. He understands oppression.

Father Kennedy presents a sharp and well-founded criticism of Dr Pell's responses and pronouncements on the Rainbow Sash Movement and homosexuality. He also provides angry and passionate responses to the Archbishop's statements on Aboriginal issues.

Father Kennedy's response is timely. The Catholic Church is in a highly authoritarian and repressive phase. Its restoration to what it should be — a genuinely open, growing and tolerant community — depends on honest discourse and critical but constructive comment. Will others now follow?

DAVID MCKENNA
President of the Rainbow Sash Movement

Who is Worthy?

Time for plain words

Some time ago I suffered a stroke which triggered in me a decision to live the rest of my life as if I were already dead. I am now more inclined to state things as they are, or as I see them, without fear or compromise. That decision extends to any kindly bids to protect me from my own uncircumspect self.

In what I am about to write, I am concerned for two groups, each marginalised, each oppressed — gay people and the Aboriginal community. I suggest that, as a Christian leader, Archbishop George Pell of Melbourne is called to offer a public apology for the treatment that both groups have suffered and are still suffering.

Archbishop Pell, a prominent figure in the Australian Catholic Church and an official of a key Vatican policy body, has on a number of occasions refused Communion to several people wearing rainbow sashes who approached the altar in his cathedral. Later, in an interview with a national magazine, he justified his action this way:

They came up with the sashes wishing to go to Communion. I said I can't give you Communion, would you like a blessing? In the early times most of them took the blessing, later fewer of them did. I said it's not because they're homosexually oriented; it's because they believe they have a right to homosexual activity.[1]

To understand Archbishop Pell's position it is important to understand his related position on the 'primacy of Conscience'. A decade ago he told a university seminar in Melbourne:

The doctrine of the primacy of Conscience should be quietly ditched, at least in our schools, or comprehensively restated, because too many Catholic youngsters have concluded that values are personal inventions, that we can paint our moral pictures any way we choose.[2]

In Sydney on 4 August 1999, when giving the inaugural Acton Lecture, he returned to the same theme:

Catholic teachers should stop talking about the primacy of Conscience. This has never been a Catholic doctrine … such language is not conducive to identifying what contributes to human development. Sometimes primacy-of-Conscience advocates also insist that the Church apologise for the crimes against freedom committed by Christians in, for example, the Crusades, the Inquisition or against Aborigines. But against what standard might these deeds be judged? Who is to say our Conscience is superior to theirs?[3]

In the remarks quoted above, Archbishop Pell reveals a gut feeling of discomfort with the concept of the supremacy of conscience, a grudging acknowledgement of unfamiliar territory, and an inability to describe in specific terms what conscience might be about. Archbishop Pell appears not to face the finer implications of conscience and so he seems to jettison the term from his personal lexicon.

As late as 27 February 2000 in the ABC *Compass* program, the Archbishop continued unrepentently and unashamedly to rewrite Church history by reducing the central place of conscience to something far less than it has been declared by the Vatican Council.

Conscience as the vicar of Christ

Let us compare Archbishop Pell's statements on conscience with those by one of the great Christian thinkers of the modern era, Venerable John Henry Newman (1801–90), a sensitive Anglican theologian who became a Catholic and later a cardinal. In marked contrast to Archbishop Pell, Newman said:

> Conscience is not a long-sighted selfishness, nor a desire to be consistent with oneself, but it is a messenger from Him, who, both in nature and in grace, speaks to us as behind a veil, and teaches and rules us by His representatives. Conscience is the aboriginal Vicar of Christ, a prophet in its informations, a monarch in its peremptoriness, a priest in its blessings and anathemas, and, even though the eternal priesthood throughout the Church could cease to be,

in it, the sacerdotal principle would remain and would have a sway.[4]

It does appear to me quite unimaginable that Archbishop Pell, who studied in Oxford a hundred years after John Henry Newman wrote his famous words on conscience, seems not to have imbibed a skerrick of what lay deep in Newman's soul. As we shall see, Archbishop Pell has not understood what the words of Cardinal John Henry Newman might mean. Indeed, Archbishop Pell's concept of conscience appears to coincide with a 'miserable counterfeit' which Newman lampooned.

On the other hand, we can be grateful that Newman's commanding intellect has left its mark on the Second Vatican Council (1962–65). That gathering of all the bishops of the Catholic Church issued a remarkable declaration which stated:

> Conscience is the most secret core and sanctuary of a person. There a person is alone with God, whose voice echoes in the depths in that person ... for God has willed that each person be left 'in the hand of their own counsel' (cf. *Ecclesiastes* 15:14) so that each can seek their own creator spontaneously.[5]

In the special section on conscience in the Catechism of the Catholic Church, Newman's placing of the supremacy of conscience is certainly given prominence, where his letter to the Duke of Norfolk is invoked.[6] Furthermore, by a solemn declaration of Pope John Paul II, Newman has now been given the title of 'Venerable', the present Pope himself accepting Newman's authority when he wrote in his address for the World Day of Peace in 1999:

> People are obliged to follow their Conscience in all circumstances, and cannot be forced to act against it.[7]

In claiming that the primacy of conscience has never been a doctrine of the Church, Archbishop Pell flies in the face of this declaration of the Council. (Is it that he regards as infallible only a doctrine personally defined as such by a Pope?) Newman, who used to become quite exasperated with such thinking, reduced to absurdity such limits on what can be called a doctrine of the Church in his comment:

> In the first place, [the Church] says that the Pope has the Church's infallibility, but that infallibility has never been defined or explained. Then it says that the Pope is infallible when he speaks ex cathedra, but what ex cathedra is has never been defined.[8]

Again and again, Newman called such limits on Church teaching tyrannical and desperately anti-pastoral.

Newman's remarks about conscience are finely honed, with distinctions sharply made and propositions neatly jointed. They had been chiselled out of his experience of thirty years of misunderstandings, mistrust and sanctifying pain.

In his *Apologia pro Vita Sua*, a book which he wrote to defend himself against public slanders, Newman admitted that he had not succeeded in stating a proof for the existence of God that satisfied his mind. However, he often indicated that were he ever to do so, it would take as its starting point the fact of conscience.

In the end Newman could attest that the concept of Papal Infallibility was meaningless unless the concept of conscience was seen to provide its very foundation: that concept had become part of his personal 'credo'.

How traditional is Archbishop Pell?

Behind Archbishop Pell's actions and comments lies an understanding of sin, of conscience and the sacrament of penance in Catholic theology which, despite his avowals to the contrary, at best can be said not to reflect the primary insights of the Catholic faith. For we belong to a church whose proudest tradition lies in its capacity to stand high above any particular monolithic shape or form. Yet its lowest history has seen its leaders consumed with sheer power to the extent of crushing countless little ones.

I ask myself does Archbishop Pell know what the prospect of life continuing might look like from the perspective of the underside of life? Does he realise the sheer unregulated social force he possesses in an atmosphere still imbued with the power of ongoing colonisation and patriarchialism? It is so easy to walk away from one's Christian responsibility to enter into the pain of alienation and stay behind the ramparts, to bluff, to stickle and to enforce, refusing to recognise that we are all humans together, united in our common weakness.

Deathly silence can be the aftermath of the bully's outrage; suffocating silence the result of the bully's bluff by which he has blocked up all the exits, allowing no fresh air to blow. I have decided to break the silence, just in case it might be thought that his bullying tactics could ever succeed in extinguishing the problems related to his actions.

Has the Church changed significantly in the past?

In 1991, on the ABC television program 'Couchman', George Pell, then an auxiliary bishop, claimed that there was very little evidence of change from the institutional Church of the second and third centuries to the Church of the Constantinian era. No proof whatsoever for his completely gratuitous claim was given other than that he himself had gained his Oxford Doctorate in that area. In fact, the historical record shows that the change was profound, its effects on the Church disastrous and long.

Confession of sins once rare

In contrast to Archbishop Pell's position, two leading theologians of our century, Karl Rahner and Herbert Vorgrimler, men also well versed in the history of their tradition, make the point that the essential difference between the ancient Church and the modern Church in the use of the sacrament of penance is not the transition from so-called 'public' to 'private' penance (as many suppose — quite unhistorically), but from what was generally an end-of-life experience to a frequently repeatable experience. 'In Christian antiquity, from the second to the sixth century, the sacrament of penance could be received only once.'[9] In other words, in the primitive tradition the Church reserved the use of sacramental penance as a sort of theological 'tool-kit' which Christians used to carry them across the proverbial Great Divide — through the portals of death into everlasting life.

Thus anointing of the sick became known as 'Extreme Unction', and Communion in time of critical illness was called 'Viaticum', a Latin word meaning 'food for the journey'. Special rules grew up about the absolution of sins for those who were at the moment of death, 'absolution (in articulo mortis)'. It was the earliest form of what the Church has always regarded as 'the last rites', something that even daily communicants today seem to hope for at the end.

Josef Jungmann SJ, who still stands today as the greatest Catholic scholar of the history of forms of worship and prayer, wrote:

> Throughout the whole of Christian antiquity, the sacrament of penance was conferred only when necessary — that is, when notorious mortal sins were to be forgiven, such as the sins which exclude from the kingdom of heaven. For in the early centuries it was presupposed that the Christian, once having received grace in Baptism, should never be guilty of such sins. The majority of the faithful never received the sacrament of Penance, throughout their whole lives.[10]

This view can be seen in Tertullian (c.160–225 AD), who, while still a Catholic, wrote:

If somebody was once shipwrecked on the sea and was then saved, such a one, as a rule, does not think any longer of ships and sea-faring. So it must also be with one who, having sinned, has found forgiveness through God's mercy in Baptism.[11]

The one thing that remains certain is that human nature does not change. Sin in St Paul's day would have been as common as sin is today; notoriety as common as notoriety is today. When the shiver of fear or the sensation of alarm so shocks a community, then there is call for repentance to allow healing.

The early Church: a 'zone of enticement'

It must be remembered, of course, in that infancy period of the life of the Church, that the background of Christian social identification was in terms of the colonising presence of the Roman Empire. The ever-present danger and fear of martyrdom to a large extent set the tone and context in which the early Christian's life was played out.

In 1855 John Henry Newman made a brilliant attempt in his novel *Callista* to 'imagine and express the feelings and mutual relations of Christians and heathens' of the third century. Newman's heroine is portrayed as subject to the pressure of worshipping idols but finally responding to the voice of God in conscience:

You may tell me that this dictate is a mere law of my nature ... it is the echo of a person speaking to me. It carries with it its proof of its divine origins ... An echo implies a voice; a voice a speaker. That speaker I love and I fear.'[12]

By this imaginative expression Newman showed that conversion of conscience precedes faith, not the other way round. Rather, heeding one's conscience is essentially part and parcel of being open to faith. Conscience is determinative of faith. It is, therefore, a vexatious thing to suppose that 'faith' can suppress personal conscience, because that would be to produce a dysfunctional personality.

As such, martyrdom represented, not only the field of Christian triumph, but also the 'zone of enticement' which was the subject of Saint John's warning in the Apocalypse (or Book of Revelation) at the end of the first century. In our day, theological writers such as William Stringfellow, Thomas Merton and Daniel Berrigan have helped to revive this aspect of the Church's theology.[13] They remind us that, then as now, Christians face a powerful temptation to succumb to empire.

The rigorist excesses of the second and third centuries, as exemplified in Montanism and Novatianism, grew out of this seductive background. They forbade all compromise with the Roman Empire.

Apostasy

In this situation, the early Christians were faced with the occasional cases of lapse into apostasy. These usually took the form of reverting to worship of idols, adultery (a metaphor for apostasy[14]) and membership in the Roman army, for no soldier could become a Christian, no Christian a soldier. Each of these acts, in one form or another, was what constituted 'lapse of the renegade', a public scandal within the community, involving the reverting to pagan practices, earning a defector's stigma. These actions were deemed to involve a collapse of the very faith upon which all the sacraments are built. Such public offences came to be known as 'capital' offences, but they should not be confused with crimes of the Roman state (from which Christians kept an anonymous careful distance).[15] Nor are they to be confused with the 'sins of the believer', which in this context meant sins of a more or less personal, private nature which of themselves did not affect the community.

Where there was evidence of such notorious scandal, the community was obviously the first to be affected: community penitential exercises were required. In the highly exceptional case of the once-lapsed applying to re-enter the Church, the community had to come to terms with fears by requiring tests of faith. Formal exclusion from the Eucharist was hardly appropriate for those who had contracted out anyhow. The reapplicant had to be content with the natural suspicion and fears of the rest of the community expressed in postponement and delay.

The Eucharist brings healing

In the case of private sins not so affecting the community, the Eucharist itself was regarded as the all-sufficient primary sacramental healing factor in the ordinary Christian's life. Moral theologians to this day refer to a function of the Eucharist as healing venial sins. Yet the same logic applies to personal, or what might be considered private, mortal sins. It is possible for Church practice to revert to the primitive tradition where ordinarily people will receive the sacrament of penance only on limited occasions; with the one exception when the Church calls openly for signs of penitence from the real perpetrators of crime — those who have created victims by notorious crimes (often in the name of 'legitimate' government) and have forfeited the name of 'faithful'.

Indeed, I would predict that it will so change, for short of a massive intake of vocations from some other planet, trained in the Roman method, we are going to find it quite difficult to maintain staffing levels. Return to primitive Church practice can be more than a nostalgic journey into an antiquarian world; it can be a restoration of the implications of belief in the glorified humanity of Christ.

Christ present among us

The overwhelming realisation that Christ lives among us was the first belief of the primitive Church in the Risen Christ — in those very early years before the Gospels were even written and before the Apostles had died, when Christians were effervescent in celebrating the secret that had been kept hidden for ages: *'that Christ is present among us'*. In the early exuberance of that experience, Paul wrote it down and was able to acknowledge, with an immediacy and a brilliant clarity, the implications of the glorified Humanity of Christ, of the Mystical Body of Christ in the Church, of the Church's emancipation from the sterile letter of the law.

The early realistic penitential liturgy

We must remember that in the very early Church the most proximate and readiest image of the living glorified Christ that was to hand was the Christ alive and present in the community. That provided cause for realistic penitential liturgy. Sin was therefore naturally seen as first and foremost transgression against Christ in the community — public acts that were seen as scars on the Mystical Body, material for public repentance and public acceptance back into the community. That was the Christological background to liturgical practice.

> I say more: the just man justices;
> Keeps grace: that keeps all his goings graces;
> Acts in God's eye what in God's eye he is —
> Christ — for Christ plays in ten thousand places,
> Lovely in limbs, and lovely in eyes not his
> To the Father through the features of men's faces.
> GERARD MANLEY HOPKINS[16]

The practice of Resurrection-faith exemplified by the infant Church seems to have taken place spontaneously as the tangible experience of Christ's enduring presence in their midst changed people's lives. St Paul, the first Christian theologian, first observed and participated in the experience that was described in the Acts of the Apostles, and then he formulated in depth the meaning of the convergence of Christ into the community, of the community into Christ.

For Paul, it was always a meeting at eye level, a grounded earth experience, because Christ, our earth-brother, lived still among us. His central doctrine of

Christ's Mystical Body fairly sprang out of the pages of his epistles, signifying the jubilant certainty which Christians might experience — living in Christ because Christ lives in each and every human being.

There were two further unshakeable truths which flooded the sense of inner worth of every Christian: first, a positively radiant sense of being called saints, and that followed on from an unquenchable presence of Christ given in Baptism; and second, the spring-in-heel rejoicing that the iron-clad letter of law was now abandoned in favour of the Spirit glowing through.

Out of these primary experiences, linked like pearls on a string, were born the three original contributions of Pauline theology: a) Christ is present and alive; b) we are elevated and sanctified; and c) legalism is deathful to the soul — all held together in the unified belief in the enduring presence here on earth of the glorified humanity of Christ.

In those first three centuries the Church had not yet experienced the 'conversion of Constantine' nor the Arian heresies, nor indeed the massive anti-Arian reactions that followed.

The fourth century — seduced by empire

When hostility towards Christianity changed with the conversion of Constantine in the fourth century, both the internal and external shape of the Church changed dramatically. The Church was caught up in a tidal wave of change that swamped Pauline theology and Johannine theology to the point where they became meaningless because they were unintelligible. At the same time hitherto unheard-of ingredients like power and control began being absorbed into the Church. No longer did Christians feel obliged to assume a subversive attitude towards empire; they thought they had to accommodate it. Within the Church, what had been seen earlier as 'capital offences' were gradually rendered obsolete; the beginnings of the 'just war' theory began to be elaborated by Augustine. But even then, when St Augustine accepted that the state had a right to kill in warfare, he still never allowed the individual to kill in self-defence.

In addition to the emperor's conversion, during the fourth century the Church experienced the heresy of Arius and the massive anti-Arian reaction which followed. Arius, who emphasised the human aspect of Christ, also taught that the Son of God was not eternal.

In its reactions to Arianism the Church allowed its theological pendulum to swing away from its previous clear focus on the humanity of Christ, and in particular on the glorified humanity of Christ working within creation. After Arius its focus moved towards an all-eclipsing divinity of Christ, from an emphasis on the consoling presence of Jesus in the community to an awesome and forbidding sense of God in Christ.

The effect on the Church was disastrous and long

Is it any wonder that those two voices of the first century, the Pauline Epistles and the Johannine Apocalypse, so profoundly spiritual yet so profoundly down to earth, in the fourth century would be shouted down by the noise of empire? Those two classics of the Christian faith, written at white heat and with such superfine clarity, once they were downloaded into an alien culture lost their fire over the centuries and evaporated into unintelligibility. Poetic realism became construed as vague allegory.

Social and political morality, the dominant morality of the early Church, gave way to a privatised moralism, for it suited the powers-that-be that both Christ and the Church should be gentrified. The new Babylon, symbol of power and colonising destruction, was euphemised into the sweet-sounding Pax Romana; the screams of war on the first Christmas night ultimately to be translated into the unstressed lullaby of Silent Night.

Such a mentality had — and still has — its own in-built power to falsify facts. It goes hand in hand with Archbishop Pell's attempts to 'Vaticanise' the ancient Church, narrowing the terms of salvation in such a way as to poison the streams of the wide-open mercy of Christ.

Christ detached from frail humanity

From the fourth century, the deeper text of Pauline theology, the finely tuned doctrine of the glorified humanity of Christ, fell into obscurity. What was left was the memory of a Christ whose coming to earth was restricted to his performance of redemptive work, including his death. The Incarnation was but a historical past event in memory, not a present event. His Resurrection became reduced to the proving of his divinity and therefore a handy piece of apologetics to use as a polemic in argument. The Ascension was seen as a happy final departure before the ultimate Second Coming.

As the concept of the glorified Humanity of Christ was being smothered, the devotional and penitential practices which flowed from it lost their meaning.

Having sloughed off his humanity as no longer required, Christ ruled from heaven as an absentee landlord, leaving the male magisterium of the Church to govern on his behalf. The magisterium took on Christ's vice-regency, but as the agent of an offended — angry — God, not an ever-present, consoling one. As a result, the role of the laity was reduced to impotence; the role of priesthood was elevated to an absurdly discarnate position of divine power, largely exempt from accountability to the world. Clerics were assumed to possess a right akin to the divine right of kings.

The Church was deemed to be acting on Christ's behalf rather than He, in His glorified humanity, acting on behalf of frail humanity from within it. Later the doctrine of the Mystical Body of Christ would be condemned in the Council of Basel (1421–1439) as 'offensive to pious ears'.

Even as late as 1953, our seminary rector at Manly College was advising that we avoid in our preaching, reference to the doctrine of the Mystical Body as being confusing to the simple faithful. Ten years later, a lobby of bishops at the Second Vatican Council was pressing for the banning of the same term on the grounds that it favoured modernism. They could not conceive of a Christ acting on behalf of and within poor frail humanity.

The two natures in Christ: a balance in belief

The balancing of belief in the two natures of Christ — the human and divine — has always been delicate. Even within the bounds of strict orthodoxy, it can be as when the twin spires of a cathedral are viewed so closely that one is obscured. So it was that the massive anti-Arian reaction was so vehement that for many centuries it eclipsed the finer points of belief in the humanity of Christ, and particularly in the glorified humanity of the continuously incarnate Christ.

Another consequence of this post-Arian reaction was that the whole of the New Testament text was seen as heavily literal. What could not be pressed through the sieve of literalism was therefore blocked out. Pauline theology was largely ignored and the infancy and passion narratives took on tableau form in the Christmas crib and the Stations of the Cross, because they were seen as the most apprehensible of what the incomprehensible God had allowed human beings to share. Theologian, Karl Adam, describes what happened:

> The sacramental objective and social elements recede[d] in favour of the moral and subjective. The real basis of this veiled semi-Pelagianism lies in a secret detachment from the Mystical Body of Christ.[17] [Pelagius taught that people could pull themselves to salvation by their own bootstraps.]

Almost lost from the consciousness of the faithful was the sense of reliance on our elder-Brother-in-the-flesh, the first-born of Creation, the one so near at hand that he stands efficiently and effectively to plead our

44

cause, without whom we stand bereft of any power to contribute to our salvation. The insight of all the New Testament writers, that we can depend on nothing of ourselves but only on the free gratuitous mercy of Christ, for all intents and purposes was lost to sight. The Church was effectively back in Mosaic times worshipping a Unitarian God. Sin was seen as an offence against Christ as God. As such, it required the multiple 'apologies', declarations of sinfulness, that found their way into the Eucharistic liturgy in the early Middle Ages.

Of sin and unworthiness

When sin becomes the dominant element defining our relationship with God — a minus rather than a plus — when we no longer think of ourselves as positively and permanently graced, no longer entitled to call ourselves sons and daughters and equal members of God's family, we will undoubtedly lose heart; we will become disheartened and demoralised and imagine that unworthiness is something that disqualifies us.

However, a sense of unworthiness is itself a condition of life for us, because it allows us to see that only Christ's love and mercy are effective — not anything we do can bring about our salvation. Only this sense of emptiness and unworthiness will lead us to see that, in Christ, we are each and all worthwhile. And we must be forever on our guard against any brother or sister, priest or prelate who is driven by a sense of insecurity, to disguise his or her own lack of self-esteem by bombast or power and therefore distract us from owning our birthright.

Throughout doleful centuries, the laity found themselves back in the Old Testament relying on the sterility of law, where life was highly moralistic and spiritually problematic — the bright guardian angel of personal conscience not allowed to make her appearance to them in any central way. The immediate and vibrant impact of the living Word of God had been denied them, locked as it was in a dead language for their liturgy. Even as early as the fourth century, the simple faithful beyond their youth were deprived throughout their whole lives of the staple food of the Eucharist. St John Chrysostom (347–407AD) could complain, 'We stand idle around the altar; there is none who partakes.'[18] In the Middle Ages a general council found it necessary to command reception of the Eucharist at least once a year.

The people could no longer be assured by the Church's own ancient and consistent teaching that nothing can erase the indelible character that marks us, even when we inevitably remain sinners, as participating members of Christ's Body.

A central teaching of Jesus

Even when decadence crept into pastoral practice, the Catholic Church at the conciliar level of its teaching always remained cautious in her formulations of what might be considered obstacles to the conferral of sacramental grace.

> Suffer the little children to come unto me, and prevent them not, for it is to such as these that the Kingdom of God belongs.
>
> JESUS (*Mark 10:14*)

History is undoubtedly on the side of giving free, unrestricted access to the sacraments. It is important to realise the context in which these words of Jesus are seen. It seems that the phrase 'prevent them not' was part of an earlier baptismal formula which contains the solemn warning that no-one has the right to prevent the Baptism of anyone. St Augustine used the phrase 'non ponentibus obicem' — i.e. 'not placing a hindrance' regarding the Baptism of children, and that phrase was extended to all the Sacraments by the Council of Trent (Sess. VII Canon 6, Denz. 849) establishing the principle, as Godfrey Diekmann OSB says, 'that it is not the personal merit of the recipient that causes the grace received'.[19] We are no more capable of securing for ourselves saving grace than others are entitled to block it or withhold mercy from us.

The laity's loss

The loss of that central piece of the theology of Christ in the fourth century, of which we have already spoken, had a huge impact on the lives of the laity and especially on the poor, just as it did on the theology of the sacraments. With Christ now securely returned to his Father's side in the highest heavens and the Pope safely ensconced as His Vicar or substitute here, more and more the Church now lived in a world of negativities. Lay people were deprived of the living presence of Christ in the sacrament of the Eucharist because the Eucharist was seen as itself needing protection from sinful humans. Christ was now too 'godly' to be associated with sinners. It was again back to the doldrums and 'do-nots' of the Mosaic law and to a profound 'wowserism'. A creeping frown extended even over married life, so much so that from St Augustine to St Alfonsus Ligouri it was the common teaching of the Church that to enjoy sex in marriage was a sin.[20] It was as if a prurient 'pelvic' theology had become the order of the day. The greatest tragedy was the loss in practice of the sanctifying and healing power of sacramental grace. For all of sixteen centuries the vast majority of Christians were deprived of frequent use of the Eucharist.

A focus on the sins of others

It is not really something to be wondered at that when we become reduced to the language of negativities, of human beings defined as sinners not saints, as under the law, not free, then we will inevitably impose those negatives on others as well as ourselves. We will feel secretly dirty and unclean but at the same time ready to accuse others of filthiness. It is amazing how ready we then are to devise liturgies to make satisfaction for other people's sins, not our own.

In 1859 the loveable French sculptor monk, John Gorbeillon OSB, was found to have pulled up a French-speaking prostitute through his bedroom window at St Mary's Cathedral, Sydney. (She had coughed indiscreetly throughout the night and so was discovered). Archbishop Polding angrily defrocked his priest and sent him off penniless to God knows where, but inaugurated the *Quarantore* — the Forty Hours devotion —

to make reparation for Gorbeillon's sin. So millions of the faithful for more than a hundred years traipsed dutifully to their local Church to make reparation for him. In the same spirit there are in the year 2000 several parishes in the Archdiocese of Sydney advertising an invitation to make reparation for sodomy and adultery by way of Exposition of the Blessed Sacrament.

In contrast Thomas Merton, the famous twentieth-century American monk, writes:

> In the long run, no one can show another the error that is within him, unless the other is convinced that his critic first sees and loves the good that is within him. So while we are perfectly willing to tell our adversary he is wrong, we will never be able to do so effectively until we can ourselves appreciate where he is right. Love, and love only, love of our deluded fellow human-being as he actually is in his delusion and in his sin: this alone can open the door to truth.[21]

Testimony of a confessor

Time after time as confessor I encounter homosexual persons possessing a transparent gentleness and a finely tuned nobility born of pain; then my conscience insists that I must respect theirs and honour their freedom. When I find that violence is totally missing, when there is no evidence whatsoever of hatred or anger or bitterness or rancour or power or force, then I must conclude that the gracefulness I see before me can only be described as Grace. 'Where there is charity and love, there does the God of love abide.' What is more, I frequently find myself accepting their own testimony, based on their personal experience, that as they came to acknowledge to themselves their own sexuality they found the acknowledgement to be a therapy in itself, but also it allowed for a giant step in spiritual growth.

At that I seem to hear an indignant protest: 'What right have you to believe them?' We are close here to a central question in the life of the Church today — the question of mutual trust.

So many homosexual people of both sexes, and so many women who, after all, represent half of the Church, keep complaining: 'We cannot trust the *apparatchiks* of the Church because we ourselves have felt untrusted from the start.' These people claim the right of self-definition; it is surely the height of arrogance coming from these killers of hope to attempt to deny them that. All the casuistry in the world will finally fail.

When mutual trust breaks down we take to empty posturing.

We do not probe the wounds of our nature thoroughly; we do not lay the foundation of our religious profession in the ground of our inner man; we make clean the outside of things; we are amiable and friendly to each other in words and deeds, but our love is not enlarged, our bowels of affection are straitened and we fear to let the intercourse begin at the root; and in consequence, our religion, viewed as a social system is hollow. The presence of Christ is not in it.

JOHN HENRY NEWMAN[22]

Erotic desire and Christian faith

Desire, even erotic imaginative thought, can obviously be a seed of sin. But it can also be a seed of contemplation, of fostering sacramental faith and devotion. The shining and erotic poetry of St John of the Cross is there to remind us that to ignore this is to risk a stunted faith.

What does seem to be happening in the lives of present-day youth is that an immediate and urgent withdrawal from Mass attendance occurs coincidentally with the development of testosterone or oestrogen. Yet on the other hand, when they are allowed to participate in determining the world's shape, when initiative for compassion is given into their hands, when words have lost their meaning and only actions speak, there is one thing I must acknowledge too, that often such youth seem to be expressing a deep spiritual hunger for the Eucharist, a craving 'to lick the mealy bowl of heaven dry'. I wonder who am I to stay deaf to that hungry scream?

Francis Webb's poem deserves to be quoted in full:[23]

Song of Hunger

I lie extended on my canvas bed
Blowzed sun squats on his hunkers overhead
To lick the mealy bowl of heaven dry.
Soon in the town's back-streets I must be dead,
But not while one cloud is loafing in my brain
As that fragrant unleavened Bread
Which may not die.

Who Is Worthy?

Carbohydrate, sugar, fat protein
Are finite but as crucial as tropic rain;
So the sacked larder of manhood hazards mice
Of memory, infant voices: foetal grain
Puts on a blossom's child-cajoleries;
And the grey skinflint plain
Is lost in rice.

Mistake not, lives are in me, mysteries
Of throbbing corn and spectral orchard trees.
To empty bowels and airy compunctions give
Daylight one thousand thousand calories.
I loom at nightfall, surfeited with grace.
Fall on your knees, your knees,
For, man, I live!

So carouse with charity, hurry to this place,
My splayed eternity for your embrace:
Hold up the anna's fiery Host, and call,
See life's spotless calligraphies, crease my face
While rickety skeleton shanks work up above
Canvas, space platitude, race
To His tiny stall.

O my love, O my love!

It is a matter for consolation that far fewer parents of homosexual children are now willing to exclude them, but instead remain supportive of them as still and always their children. It is now a fact that can't be ignored that many a devout Catholic mother whose habit it had been to provide a packed lunch for her school child accompanied by a St Christopher medal, has now, when she has faced the reality that her child is actively homosexual, made the simple transition of encouraging the use of a condom with the same trusty medal.

Hunger has its own rules. In itself it can be enough to overturn the normally appropriate rules of protocol. Voracious hunger that is exacerbated by authoritarian regulation, exclusion and prohibition is yet another thing. That can be enough to call up a Christ-endorsed imperative to steal. 'Have you not heard that when David and his followers were hungry, they went into the temple and snatched the bread that was reserved for the priests?' This is recorded in all three of the Synoptics so should be regarded as the more central in the Gospel message, while Matthew adds the moral: 'I want compassion, not sacrifice.' Here Christ shows real contempt for putting rules before human needs.

> How shall I search, who never sought?
> How turn my passion-pastured thought
> To gentle manna and simple bread?
>
> GERARD MANLEY HOPKINS[24]

Ancient non-judgmental practices

In the thirteenth century, St Thomas Aquinas still presumed that the faithful would gather at the Eucharist with 'the right disposition', with 'faith and devotion'. That view is echoed in the *Memento of the Living* verses in the old Roman Canon (a prayer used at the central parts of the Mass): 'Remember your servants and handmaidens and all here present whose faith and devotion are known to you [Lord]'. Thus it remained unquestioned that the Lord accepted their personal act of faith and submission to God's redeeming love. That, after all, is why they were gathered.

While there has always been provision in the liturgy to ascertain public suitability for episcopacy and ordination, and the banns of marriage were once proclaimed canvassing public information regarding eligibility for marriage, there has never been such for the reception of Communion. The Church has been more concerned for the protection of the confessional seal and the sacrosanctity of the internal forum. It has always steered clear of any public judgment on the state of soul of any human being.

When you think of that long cycle of decline over a period of sixteen centuries when, for the little people, the Church became a church without hope, it is surely a matter of great jubilation that now there are positive signs that the swing of the pendulum back has begun to take place. It is basically a reinstatement of the crowning glory of God in humankind.

As Thomas Merton says:

The Cross is the sign of contradiction — destroying the seriousness of the Law, of the Empire, of the armies ...

But the magicians keep turning the Cross to their own purposes. Yes, it is for them too a sign of contradiction: the awful blasphemy of the religious magician *who makes the Cross contradict Mercy*! This, of course, is the ultimate temptation of Christianity! To say that Christ has locked all the doors, has given one answer, settled everything and departed, leaving all life enclosed in the frightful consistency of a system outside of which there is *seriousness and damnation*, inside of which there is the intolerable flippancy of the saved — while nowhere is there any place for the mystery of the freedom of divine mercy which alone is truly serious and worthy of being taken seriously.[25]

Roman policies lack compassion

A case in point is the recent contretemps with Rome entered into by Bishop Reinhold Stecher, the retired Bishop of Innsbruck (the university town in the Austrian Alps). His impassioned complaint is that Rome's bureaucratic choice for clerical celibacy has, in effect, overturned the once jealously guarded Thomistic principle — *sacramenta propter homines* — the sacraments are for human beings. And so millions of people have been deprived of their right to the sacraments.

Bishop Stecher's cry is that Rome, instead of being subject to the laws of love and compassion and forgivingness, now sees itself exempt from those laws. When bureaucratic power is used to mutilate and upturn the very meaning of Christ's gospel, it is understandable why vast numbers will turn elsewhere to march to a different drum, capable of producing the authentic sound of the Gospel.

With a hide as thick as St Catherine of Siena's in confronting papal power, Stecher reminds the Pope that he is risking the judgment of God by postponing for ten years the pleas of ten thousand priests who have married, for validation of their marriages.

It is to be noted that what Christ specifically required of St Peter as the first of the Popes was the flowing on of forgivingness and suppleness of heart to unimaginable depths. It was also an appeal to the no-nonsense fisher-man in Peter, the taking up of the strain and the letting go on the ropes, the mutual 'forgiving-ness' of the enter-prise, the give and take, on the nets; all this speaks of an underlying pliancy in Peter's life providing the flexible sinews of a living church, as against his dusty, brittle bones, upon which the Vatican is built.

A twentieth-century surprise

In the late twentieth century, against all odds and against the prevailing mood of theological thought, Fr L. Durrwell CSsR, a Redemptorist scholar, published his book on *Resurrection Theology*.[26] Suddenly the almost forgotten theology of Paul came alive again. The great encyclicals of Pius XII, *Mystici Corporis* and *Mediator Dei*, together with Paul VI's *Mysterium Fidei*, gave new emphasis to the life of sacraments and of the Spirit. The Second Vatican Council took up the reform with what was mind-blowing to the pre-conciliar mentality — the universal call to holiness which put an end to the totally false, usurping claim of perfection for priests and religious but not for the laity.

The subsequent reforms of the Liturgy published by Paul VI in 1972 were in direct line with a progressive re-emphasis on the doctrine of the exalted humanity of Christ. Who would have thought that Rome, after that long corridor of theological and scriptural decline, would have given a moment's attention to approval of the Third Rite of Penance, which recognises the pro-foundly communal nature of sin and forgiveness? (This rite relies on the whole congregation acknowledging its sin and celebrating forgiveness together. It does not require individual confession of sin to a priest.)

The fact is that Paul VI did reinstate the Third Rite of Penance in certain circumstances, dispensing with private auricular confession and personal absolution. The reasons given for approval of the Rite are clearly extraneous as to whether sins are deemed inherently grievous. This does show some slight progress towards returning to the traditional belief that all sin is forgiven within the Eucharistic reception, rather than in some necessary prior liturgy rendering people 'worthy of the Eucharist', as if 'worthiness' could ever be achieved!

The officially sanctioned circumstances for the approval of the Third Rite include the shortage of priests. This can surely be extended to shortage of *qualified* priests. Homosexual people are surely entitled to protection from homophobic fumes steaming out of some confessor's nostrils (because of an abhorrence of what homosexual people are deemed to be) well before their acts are examined, just as racism is usually based on a skewed perception of what persons are deemed to be well before they have been found to have done anything at all. It is a matter of some irony that the persistence of such warped stereotypes remains unquestioned by those who point judgmentally to warped sexual orientation.

The central issue: who is worthy?

The recent scene at St Patrick's Cathedral, Melbourne, showed Archbishop Pell refusing Communion to a group of 'unrepentant' gay people, making the point and ramming it home that it was an insolent open act of confrontation with the Church's authoritative ruling. What was completely disguised in the roar of the clapping he received from most of the Cathedral congregation was that many of those applauding the Archbishop were in the same boat: that among the young married a high proportion had long set their consciences in unspoken confrontation with the same authority in regard to birth control, that among teenagers and others a large proportion had settled for a similar unspoken conclusion in regard to masturbation, and, among actively heterosexual unmarried youth, conscience had been called on to determine their entitlement to sex, including frequent use of artificial means of contraception. The evidence for this, of course, comes directly from the Research Institute of the Bleeding Obvious.

Archbishop Pell appears to have grabbed the high moral ground and used his 'victory for a day' to put off facing the far-reaching and overwhelming reality which has already gained such mammoth proportions. Indeed its magnitude can only be rivalled by the profound depth of denial that Archbishop Pell is capable of entering. So this minority group of homosexual people are essentially no different from the throng of Catholics who, though readily identifiable to the survey-taker, remain adamant in keeping mum before His Grace, but nevertheless are equally deliberate in their defiance of the Roman decrees.

Archbishop Pell seems quite resigned to the scene where communicants remain tight-lipped and undisclosing regarding their state of soul, although one would have thought that their choice in conscience should worry him: 'If a person comes up anonymously we presume they're in good faith and we leave them to work it out with God.'[27] But shall we all be reduced to keeping our privacy to the extent of becoming 'smugglers' of undeclared acts, the closet holders of unnamed contraband, moonshiners conveying the unlabelled 'sly-grog' of moral acts into the sanctuary? That trend, as it has been noted, has already begun to take hold. But it could leave us all strangers to each other, cloaked in the protective armour of anonymity. In the words of John Henry Newman:

> Perhaps the reason why the standard of holiness among us is so low ... our beliefs so unreal ... is that we dare not trust each other with the secret of our hearts. We have each the same secret, and we keep it to ourselves, and we fear that, as a cause of estrangement, which really would be a bond of union.[28]

The Eucharistic miracles in the Gospels are not to do with Christ creating bread loaves out of nothing; they make no mention of the multiplication of loaves. But they do promise dailiness of our spiritual bread and unrationed plenitude and sufficiency.

When it comes to the sacraments, 'worthiness' offers no advantage at all. It offers no marks or credits whatsoever. In fact, claims made on the title of worthiness would certainly be rejected by Jesus Christ on the grounds of parading good works.

There was a time, not long ago, when the sodality system was regarded as the very life-blood of the

Australian parish, with its rigorous, often ruthless regimentation. Banners, emblems, medallions, insignia such as cloaks were the order of the day. People were relied on to wear them almost in triumphant display in the *Corpus Christi* Processions. Up the parish aisle they filed at the monthly sodality Mass, having made a good confession the night before, announcing to the world that they were free of sin, an announcement that was perilously close to 'strutting one's spiritual stuff'.

My first parish priest in 1953 had a ritual at each nuptial Mass, where the bride wore her Child of Mary cloak over the bridal dress. Then at the solemn moment of the pronouncing of vows, the president of the sodality would remove the blue cloak, a constant reminder to us all that virginity is best. Such a teaching was itself the cause of some Catholics breaking into strains of the popular Marian hymn: 'Oh Mother, I could weep for mirth.'

The whole regime behind the display of insignia in the parish sodalities came close to 'parading good works'. And that also is why any authoritarian attempt at excluding anyone from receiving Communion can be on the verge of requiring a state of worthiness in the recipient when that can never be. This is, I believe, the crux of my argument — the axis on which all the underlying issues turn — our preparedness or otherwise to accept as an admissible factor the so-called judgment of worthiness. It is so important because on it rests the possibility of bringing our practice into line with the Gospel practice of Jesus.

Memories of past male clerical behaviour

The story of the bully bishop (or parish priest) who refuses Communion to some of the faithful keeps reappearing in every generation. The memory of them seems to fade with a finality proportionate to their penal severities. Who now can put a name on Bishop Sheil, who was the man responsible for excommunicating Blessed Mary MacKillop? Who now as much as remembers Monsignor Joseph Cusack, the parish priest of Mosman, a man who took himself very seriously, whose practice it was to pass over the kneeling women with lipstick at the altar rails? Who now remembers the name of the priest who passed over the young Aboriginal woman at the altar rails — Mum Shirl — presuming that she could not give a guarantee that she had received her First Communion? Who now can call to mind the name of the parish priest, Father Shannon on the Gold Coast, whose practice it was to deny entry into the Sunday Mass of any woman wearing slacks or shorts? He ambushed one young woman in the church vestibule, insisting that she would be allowed in only if she wore a skirt. She apologised profusely as she undid a zipper, removing her slacks completely, then proceeded to make unrestricted entry into the church, wearing her mini-skirt. Who will remember George Pell, Archbishop of Melbourne, who, as late as 1999 was refusing Communion to a group of the homosexual faithful? It does seem, then ,that there are still bishops and parish priests who need to learn that Christ is not waiting for them to protect Him; that even they stand under the awful warning: 'judge not'.

It is to be noted that each of these dominating acts was marked by male clerical power and control and that expenditure in Christian courage was nil. It is for me a tragedy to find that the hand that ought hold the humble Shepherd's pastoral crook now should squeeze itself into a traffic policeman's powerful forbidding glove. Pastoral theology, which should of its very nature exude the fragrant aroma of compassion, is now wrenched from its roots and twisted into a forensic exercise which has the effect of 'slandering Our Lord Jesus Christ as merciless' (St Cyprian of Carthage).

In the words of the Australian poet Bruce Dawe:

> And so, until we learn to love what moves
> to other rhythms than ours,
> our lives will be most insecurely held,
> since history proves tyrants are never free.
>
> BRUCE DAWE[29]

That sort of high-handedness contains a built-in underside of exclusion and exclusivism and therefore is a far greater threat to the symbolic meaning of the Eucharist than any use of the foundational biblical symbolism of creation-unity, inclusion and inclusivism. After all, a sensitivity to that form of unity must underpin any derivative in the form of Church unity. It does not — cannot — work the other way round. That is why the vast theological fields of feminist theology, creation and environmental theology remain uncharted and subject to desperate jealous control, and we are left with a largely constipated spirituality in the mainstream Church.

Archbishop Mannix's suggestions

It is a matter of some desperate irony that forty years ago, the elderly Daniel Mannix, Archbishop of Melbourne, offered to Pope John XXIII's May 1958 ante-preparatory Commission for the Vatican Council his suggestions for items of agenda. These included the question of the relationship between Church and state, the concept of justice, communism and the role of the laity. Under this last heading his positive suggestions (just two) were inclusivist rather than exclusivist:

1. He thought that any person should be allowed to receive Communion at every Mass he or she attended, no matter how often on any one day; so recognising membership in the multiple communities of the modern Catholic.

2. He also advocated the abolition of Book 5 of the Code of Canon Law, that would have laid to rest all forms of excommunication, penalties and sanctions.

Pope John XXIII seemed to agree with him. On 11 October 1962, in his opening speech at the Second Vatican Council, the Pope showed himself unworried and philosophical when it came to repressing errors in the Church. He reflected that these errors often vanish as quickly as they arise, like fog before the sun. He admitted that the Church had 'frequently condemned [errors] with the greatest severity. Nowadays, however, the Spouse of Christ prefers to make use of the medicine of mercy rather than that of severity. She considers that she meets the needs of the present day by demonstrating the validity of the teaching rather than by condemnation.'

Rainbow as a sacred symbol

A few months ago I picked up a friend at Moss Vale Station, a friend who happens to be homosexual. We passed by a house displaying a little flag, which he recognised as the sign of the rainbow, that very basic sign of covenant which God set as a bow in the heavens, a sign to all that we are all equal under God — 'black, white, yellow, brown, or brindle,' as Mum Shirl, the Aboriginal woman famous for comforting the afflicted and afflicting the comfortable, was never tired of insisting. I, to my shame, had driven past that house a thousand times inadvertent to the symbolism, yet my friend was able to pick up a signal of hospitality and encouragement.

And it makes me ask why such a silent word of welcome is not displayed in every Church, including my own, because if the Churches are not able to give that assurance, what are we about? The holding out of that little lantern, that flickering flame that can give such welcome on a bleak and lonely night, has a primary symbolism that is rooted first in the world of fragile hope and dreams, designed to encourage the timid and frightened. Its secondary symbolism can be confrontational, a sharp reminder to the institutional Church of the Covenant sign that the Church should have embraced in the first place.

The superimposing of one Covenant symbol on the other, the rainbow on the Eucharist, insisting on their inner relatedness in that one undergirds the other, suggests that such stridency is warranted and seems to lift a sleepy liturgy onto a new level of potency. It can help to remind us that the Last Supper was enacted in the electric atmosphere of the night of Passover — Liberation — a sharp point of stridency that we have allowed to go blunt.

An Australian classic

Francis Webb's poem 'Homosexual'[30] stands as a piece of classic Australian literature. It carries the pain and the poignancy of the Catholic Australian boy, his parents becoming aware of his homosexuality, where the poet finds himself (or places himself) in a state of self-hatred, confronting gibes and jests and the prospect of suicide. He finds his own way through ugliness and agony, but also finds the assurance that God is loving all his compatriots and him, and, indeed, has found more.

Homosexual

To watch may be deadly. There is no judgment, compulsion,
And the object becomes ourselves. That is the terror:
We have simply ceased, are not dead, and have been
And are; only movement — our movement — is relegated,
Only thought, being — our thought, being — are given
Over; and pray God it be simply given.
So, at this man's ending, which is all a watching,
Let us disentangle the disgust and indifference,
Be all a thin hurried magnanimity:
For that is movement, our movement. Let us study
Popular magazines, digests, psychoanalysts:
For that is thought, being, our thought, our being.

WHO IS WORTHY?

I shall only watch. He is born, seized by joy,
I shall not speak of that joy, seeing it only
As the lighted house, the security, the Beginning.
Unselfconscious as the loveliest of flowers
He grows — and here we enter: the house stands yet,
But the joists winge [whinge] under our footsteps. Now the God,
The Beginning, the joy, give way to boots and footmarks.
Pale glass faces contorted in hate or merriment
Embody him; and words and arbitrary laws.
He is embodied, he weeps — and all mankind,
Which is the face, the glass even, weeps with him.

The first window broken. Something nameless as yet
Reists [Resists] embodiment. Something, the perennial rebel,
Will not rest. And this, his grandest element,
Becomes his terror, because of the footsteps, us.

I shall not consider sin beginning, our sin,
The images, furtive actions. All is a secret
But to us all is known as on the day of our birth.
He will differ, must differ among all the pale glass faces,
The single face contorted in hate or merriment.

Comes the day when his mother realises all.
Few questions, and a chaos of silence. Her thin eyes
Are emptied. Doors rattle in the house,
Foundations stagger. The Beginning becomes us;
And he is mulcted of words, remain to him only
The words of sin, escape, which is becoming all of life.
Easier, the talk with his father, rowdy, brief
Thank God, and only the language of the gutter,
He watches the moth pondering the gaslight, love-death,
Offers a wager as to her love or death or both.
His father stops speaking, fingers some papers on the desk.

And now he is here. We had him conveyed to this place
Because our pale glass faces contorted in hate or merriment
Left only sin as flesh, the concrete, the demanded:
He does not speak or hear — perhaps the pox.
But all his compatriots in sin or in other illness
Are flesh, the demanded, silent, watching, not hearing:
It is all he ever sought. Again I am tempted, with the Great,
To see in ugliness and agony a way to God:
Worse, I am tempted to say he has found God
Because we cannot contort our faces in merriment,
And we are one of the Twelve Tribes — he our king.
He has dictated silence, a kind of peace
To all within these four unambiguous walls,
Almost I can say with no answering scuffle of rejection,
He is loving us now, he is loving all.

Styles of authority

It is abundantly clear that the Catholic Church's present problems have nothing to do with the existence of authority as such, but everything to do with how individual holders of authority see their role and exercise it. Pope John XXIII, Bishop Willem Bekkers in Holland, Archbishops Helder Camara and Oscar Romero have all been spectacular in the way they have perceived their role and felt obliged to live it out. The word 'liberate' seems to sum it up. They were each both liberated and liberating. On the other hand, the faithful are faced in case after case with men who are basically unfree and insecure, who are desperately fighting to keep afloat, colourless, afraid of life and jealous of those who live it. They seem to look out on their world as through a prism.

And what they seem to see is indeed a cramped, distorted vision. What becomes manifest is dimly experienced by themselves, but often clearly recognised by those around them. The prospect of self-acknowledgment often terrifies them into a state of denial or evasion. They also have the capacity of bringing to the surface of the community people with similar inhibitions or neuroses, whereas those fascinated by Christ's promise of freedom often lose heart in the stifling environment.

Two Popes can hold up the same piece of legislation, the one with an enlightened mind and a liberating bent to place a humanising interpretation on it, the other with a closed and confining mind so that the same law is read with a constricting and inhibiting interpretation. The difference lies in simple pastoral open experience redolent of Christ's general bias — towards mercy, not sacrifice, towards giving hope to the timid, never bruising the reed in danger of being crushed.

Sin is social

But this demands of us a new openness in every aspect of the Church — from our conception of the way authority is exercised to our understanding of sin. We need openness to a redefining of the very nature of sin, away from thinking of sin disconnected from its social roots, but rather finding its very definition there. All sin that is to be taken seriously is social sin, sin that is victim-producing. Insights hammered out on the anvil of human experience can help interpret the cold principles that have their place but must always be set against the final arbitration of mercy, not sacrifice.

The very thought that there exist degrees of pardonability is itself obnoxious, yet that is how certain Pauline texts have often been misrepresented. But to insist that acts of injustice call for acknowledgment, recompense and reconciliation is to show the only way to being truly humanised and contributing to genuine peace.

Willem Bekkers, the Pope John of the Netherlands, said:

> Authority belongs to those who can authoritatively say something. And this does not mean those who can say something in the sense of giving the last word. It is much more than that. It is the power to say something that is worth saying, something that convinces by its very significance. We see the remarkable phenomenon of the authority enjoyed by someone who openly and honestly admits his own failures and shortcomings. We can also recognise the very different phenomenon — those who through a pose of importance try to give themselves an air of authority, but who fail miserably in the effort. It is clear that authority is not a matter of making impressions, or of tyranny or of domination. An authority relationship exists only among men who are worth trusting and who consequently can be trusted by others ... A genuine personal life is impossible without Conscience, that is, without conscious choice. It is a voice in each of us that speaks so imperatively that it cannot be silenced.[31]

The Gospel tells us that people saw that Jesus spoke with authority, not like the scribes. He *authored* what he had to say, as against mouthing words slavishly.

Effective liturgy

Effective liturgy must reflect the multifaceted responsibilities implied in the mutuality of personal relationships that go to make a Church. Ecclesial relationships are by no means one-sided. The old imperious model of chiefs and Indians should have gone forever. The prime undertaking of bishop to people is to contradict overlordship in favour of servitude without power or privilege. Off with the gold rings, the flim-flam, the glad-rags, the gorgeous lacy brocades, the sumptuous mitred displays of might. They are not going to be helpful in doing the real work of a bishop in introducing the different and differing elements of the faithful to each other, of opening up Jack and Mary to Pedro and Agatha, to Manfred and Alan, and revealing the inner soul of each to the others. For the real human tapestry is a multi-hued cloth and not one variant colour, tone or shade should be lost. And that is where a bishop should come into his own, in drawing out the fullest potential in every individual, in the unequivocal right of every individual to be, but always seeing that the littlest and the last participates fully.

To again quote Gerard Manley Hopkins:

Each mortal thing does one thing and the same:
Deals out that being indoors each one dwells;
Selves — goes itself, *myself* it speaks and spells;
Crying *What I do is me: for that I came*.

GERARD MANLEY HOPKINS[32]

Now, when the really hard questions continue unabated but unresolved, I find myself more and more calling conscience into life — what Cardinal Newman could describe by the elevated title 'the aboriginal Vicar of Christ.'

A change in priorities: sex or justice first?

There seems to be a number of contributing reasons for the 'going quiet on sex' phase that our Catholic faithful has now entered. One is natural attrition, a natural pulling away from extremes — away from flogging dead horses. It has allowed for more important responsibilities, like justice, to gain a foothold in our consciousness; like responsibility for the degraded state of our planet; for our having allowed male force and dominating power to develop a one-sided shape of human society, including the Church; for our having allowed racism and sexism to pervade core institutions in our society.

It is in that context that the event in the Melbourne Cathedral must be placed. Considering the sacredness of their sash-symbol — of the primeval Covenant, which underpins both Church and Eucharist — the urgency of their plea must be seen as positive. It might be conceived of not as a direct loggerhead confrontation with authority, but as an indirect supplement, a welcome reintroduction of a hitherto neglected bottom-shelf human right. An emphasis on Covenant symbolism can profitably underpin, protect and expand other strands of Eucharistic theology. Robert McAfee Brown notes:

> ... what can happen when the familiar melodies of Scripture confront us in (what seems initially to be) strident resettings. We discover that stridency is part

of the Biblical message itself, which, freed from the safe interpretative shell in which we had encased it, speaks to us in fresh, albeit threatening fashion, in ways with which we are forced to come to terms. We hear things we had not heard before, even though the words are the same as they always were.[33]

The sash therefore need not be regarded as a threat, but rather as a friend.

The basic unit of society: the human person

In 1989 Gordon C Zahn, biographer of Franz Jaggerstater and author of *German Catholics and Hitler's Wars*, in response to some American bishops, wrote an article in *Commonweal* on 'The human rights of homosexuals'. He recalled the 'night of the long knives' of 1934 and Hitler's dramatic attempt to justify his 'sanitising' the German nation of its homosexual minority (where ultimately a conservative estimate of 50,000 persons were exterminated). The bishops had argued that extending gay rights could undermine the rights of the family as the basic unit of society. Zahn reminded the bishops of a point of Catholic traditional theology which they should have known in the first place — that the basic unit of society is not the family but the human person. Upon this single rock, the human person, should the Church be basing its defence of the rights of every person to free choice, to decent and available housing, to a job suited to his or her interests and qualifications, and any of the other privileges and responsibilities of citizenship.

The gay people in St Patrick's Cathedral were making the hardly contestable point that the Church is weak in taking up this basic cause, and so continues to be part of the problem. Their decision to wear a multi-coloured symbol of the Covenant, insisting on human rights for all, was directed at a local church that to all intents and purposes acts as if they never existed and don't exist.

But they do exist. And their very existence and the public stand they are taking in the Melbourne Church is one reality among many which are forcing us to confront issues about ourselves, about the nature of the Church, about the nature of human love and sexuality for too long in our tradition locked in legalism.

Thomas Merton on the real purity of love

In his mature years Thomas Merton, unimpeded by the massive denial mechanisms of the Church he had entered, wrote that:

> ... the purity of love will be discovered not by the mechanical application of merely external norms but by the wise and even inspired integration of personal freedom and objective demands, so that the act of love will flower into a more fruitful and creative expression of life and truth. Such purity must, of course, be judged objectively, not merely by the subjective needs and desires of the lovers, and the standard of objective judgment will be, for instance, the wholeness of the act of love. That act will be pure which in all its aspects can be said to respect the

truth and integrity, the true needs and the deepest good of those who share it together, as well as the objective demands of others, of society and so on.

By this standard, certain casuistical interpretations which would permit an unhealthy and truncated sexual activity as still legally 'pure' will be seen as an affront to the authentic wholeness and purity of man. Others which might from a certain point of view shock and scandalise conventional minds may nevertheless meet a profoundly authentic and spiritual demand for inner purity and wholeness. But we cannot say that the individual person is left entirely to his own judgment in each case. The last court of appeal is not subjective freedom, which can easily become arbitrary and lead to just as many appalling truncations as legalism does. The mark of love is its respect for reality and for truth and its concern for the values which it must foster, preserve and increase in the world. Such concern is not compatible with fantasy, willfulness or the neglect of the rights and needs of other people.

In this new approach to purity, the emphasis will be not so much on law as on love, not so much on what happens to nature or to the parts of the body, as to what develops in the person (though in this case the two are manifestly inseparable). We must consider not so much what is acceptable in a social milieu as what will truly provide a creative and intimately personal solution to the questions raised in each special case.

This concept of purity is, therefore, not one in which two people seek to love each other in spirit and truth in spite of their bodies, but, on the contrary, use all the resources of body, mind, heart, imagination, emotion and will in order to celebrate the love that has been given by God, and in so doing, to praise Him![34]

Rules are one thing; facts, and love, another

The patterns of human conduct run on inexorably. In many, many cases we find that though we call on moral imperatives expecting human behaviour to be steered in a given direction, the facts of life remain resistant. Rules are one thing. Facts are another thing altogether. Over the long years we veteran confessors have had to recognise that. We were told in our youth about recidivism, how it might diminish moral responsibility. But we knew little of the mechanism of compulsion or addictiveness. We even advised penitents to tighten up the screws of willpower with futile, even damaging, results. Alcoholics Anonymous has introduced us to a new way of thinking. We have come to realise that moral theology must be played in a new key, that we must find a new way of thinking when it comes to Christ's language of love not law, compassion not sacrifice.

Karl Rahner has argued:

> It is part of the tragic and irreducibly obscure historicity of the church, that in both theory and practice it used bad arguments to defend moral maxims based on problematic, historically conditioned preconvictions, 'prejudices' ... This dark tragedy of the church's intellectual history is so burdensome because we are dealing here, in all or very many cases, with questions that penetrated deeply into the

concrete lives of human beings, because such false maxims, which were never objectively valid ... place burdens on people ... that from the standpoints of the freedom of the gospel were not legitimate.[35]

In an unpublished poem, Jeremy Nelson writes:

The Catechumen

The rules forbad you Christ;
yet called by Love, one day
at Mass, you took the host

in secret, so you thought,
but a tight-lipped woman armed
with Canon Law reported

you to the Parish Priest.
That pierced so much you wept
for days, and when you ceased

you found forgiveness
hard but in your heart forgave
as best one can those marred

by cold self-righteousness.
A letter to your friend
disclosed your shocked distress

to me, and I was moved.
If any man refused you Christ,
I'd not approve,

and were I standing next
to you to see your face
shamed and your love perplexed

I'd break the Sacred Bread
I had received, and that
your deepest need be fed

I'd share Love's meal with you.
Like idols, rules of stone
would execute the true

heart whom the Spirit draws,
but Love can counter them
beyond the man-made laws.

The danger of power in any relationship

There is no denying that all human relationships can be fraught with danger of sinfulness. Partnerships, whether sexual or otherwise, whether heterogenital or homogenital, can carry the possibility of turning in on themselves through selfishness or embittered hurt or unforgivingness or overbearing pride, suffocating life for the other partner, stifling growth, annihilating development through sheer power or greed.

Included in all such equations, the clerical-lay relationships are to be found. The very distance in altitude of pulpit towering over pew should be a reminder to us all that power and control can themselves go out of control to become a serious rupture in the Body of Christ. In the grades of seriousness of sin, the sexual factor must be found to make a relatively minor contribution in the matter of doing violence to the other person, the clerical factor of abuse often being far worse because what is at stake is the sheer crush of unconscionable, unregulated power over tender and sensitive souls.

In the history of the Christian Church there have been at least two grotesque excrescences on its life: the emergence of the prince-bishop, and the theological concept of excommunication. From these two developments comes the leadenness that defies the Spirit, and the consequent inability to rise above opulence, panoply and power.

There is the story of the young priest on a cathedral staff, being tired from hearing Saturday afternoon confessions, turning up for tea at the bishop's table, remarking that he'd been put in a quandary because a Protestant woman had appeared in the confessional, requesting Absolution. The bishop showed instant alarm as the priest impishly drew out the pros and cons of his dilemma, the bishop moving ever closer to the edge of his seat to gain more purchase in case he needed to spring. 'I finally decided,' said the priest, 'to do what Christ would have done.' The bishop did spring: 'You did NOT!'

Who is the sinner, who is the sinned against?

Jesus exemplified that the true pastor of souls has a sharp eye for discerning where people have been sinned against rather than sinning. For the Good Shepherd wards off the wolves and is not concerned for nitpicking. He or she is concerned to fan the flickering flame of faith. The real call to courage is to stand with the forsaken.

Any scripture scholar worth his or her salt now recognises that it was the undoubted practice of Jesus to enjoy table-fellowship with those whom society called sinners, the reprobates, the nobodies. He did this because by including first the sinned against, He could best proclaim comprehensively the Kingdom of God. It is also clear that this sort of maverick hospitality offered by Jesus was the very model adopted by the early Church community to give liturgical expression to the Eucharist. What is more, the early Church built the invitation of Jesus to the betraying Judas into all the Gospel Eucharistic accounts. That image was used as the template to impress on the Eucharistic community the dangerous memory of Jesus, a memory forever pointing us towards, and leading us into, a clear sense of what real social justice demands of all of us.

Such a sense of urgency for social justice is caught rather than taught. It springs out of the Gospel. It is felt as a movement in the pace and urgency by which the Christian is carried. General Pinochet, the former dictator in Chile, for instance, ought have no heart for the Church in the first place. If he makes an appearance at Mass, you can bet that the Church in that place has gone wrong; that it is offering him not the Gospel, but power; and that a specious co-dependency has begun to operate. If the Church were faithful to the Gospel, Pinochet wouldn't be able to keep up the pace; by natural attrition, he would drop out.

Jesus proffered Communion to all

An Irish theologian working in the Philippines, Brendan Lovett, has recently presented a strong case

for offering Communion to all, based on the teaching
and practice of Jesus and Paul. He says:

> And what is unavoidably and scandalously the case in
> the praxis of Jesus is the overthrow of a presumption
> clearly operative, even in the action of John the
> Baptist: first repentance, then communion. For
> Jesus, proffering communion to all is true proclama-
> tion of the Kingdom of God. This overthrow is clear-
> est in the pervasive tradition of the eating habits of
> Jesus, the record of those with whom he habitually
> ate. He ate with sinners.
>
> Israel had no problem with forgiveness of sin:
> well, no more than Christians seem to have. There
> was a welcome to the repentant sinner. There would
> have been no scandal if Jesus met with people who
> were repentant. A repentant sinner is not a sinner.
> Jesus is said to have eaten with sinners.

It has also become clear that Paul's frown on those
who receive the body of the Lord unworthily refers to
the rich who set up their own table ignoring the poor.

> [The Corinthian communities] apparently wanted
> to celebrate the Eucharist in a way that was not
> marked by death ... Whatever they may think, Paul
> tells them, in coming together it is not the Lord's
> supper that they eat. Paul knows this because of the
> exclusion of the poor.[36]

By and large in the Australian Church, all attempts
to tie the issues of social justice to the mainstream
Church will fail if conventional forms are maintained
and protected. It will continue to vomit out what it

finds uncongenial. A sense of social justice cannot coex-
ist with a powerful or rich Church. That is why a fresh
inner dynamic must be allowed to grow; tired old structures must be allowed to die. Otherwise the voice of
Vatican bureaucracy will continue to usurp the role of
Peter and Church and warrant the protest of the
Mothers of Plaza de Mayo Association to the Pope for
his seeming plea for Pinochet's release (Buenos Aires,
23 February 1999).[37]

Sins of injustice and private sins

The sins of injustice all bear a delineated identifiable
shape; their undeniable tracings remain like scars in
their social effects. These are the public acts which call
for personal acknowledgement in truth, personal apology, and personal recompense in the spirit of reconciliation. They are to be distinguished from private sins
which are analogous to 'victimless crime'. We are for-
tunate in having had placed before us the model of the
South African Truth and Reconciliation Commission,
which might teach us a better way to face a true moral
evaluation of our lives. In the Church, by contrast, we
have inherited unfortunate ways of attending to 'exam-
ination of Conscience' so that victimless sins are
accented at the expense of victim-strewn acts which are
often hidden in institutional processes of denial.

Such has been shown to be so in many cases of religious paedophilia. It is surely then an absurdity to most
minds to hear Archbishop Pell indiscriminately lump-

ing victimless acts between consenting adults with acts
of massive social consequence:

> If somebody came up with a sash and said they were
> an adulterer or running a string of abortion clinics or
> were a robber in a big way and they believed the
> Church should legitimise these activities, we couldn't
> give them Communion either.[38]

It is cart-before-horse thinking, as is his most recent
statement: 'Homosexuality is a greater health hazard
than smoking. Haven't you heard about the spread of
AIDS?'[39] The Archbishop, unencumbered by any sense of
responsibility to make fair distinctions, puts homosexuality as the killer, not unsafe sex. He finds no need to con-
textualise, and so extend his concern to places like Africa
where unsafe heterosexual sex is rife and the prime dev-
astating cause of death. We are not far here from the
skewed thinking of the Inquisition which was responsible
for the agonising deaths of homosexuals, equating homosexuality with what the Inquisitors called 'heresy'.

I am reminded of the famous interview a young
enthusiastic journalist had with Cardinal Gilroy on one
of his frequent returns from Rome. As his ship was
being tied up at Circular Quay, he was asked what he
considered the most fearful danger facing the modern
world. His reply was equally enthusiastic and met with
wide smiles (his and the journalist's). It was unhesitat-
ingly: 'Mortal Sin'. Undifferentiated mortal sin then
comprised missing Mass on any one Sunday, eating
meat on Friday, sewing enough buttons on Sunday,
embracing a 'girl' beyond a certain mathematical limit

— all these came in as an equal tie — yet the allowing of world hunger or the killing of millions in war were not considered sins. In Gilroy's Church there was no call for Aboriginal rights before the 1967 referendum, no scream for women's rights. Such a fundamentalist attitude to sin has the inevitable effect of reducing levels of sin to a single plane, and of ultimately trivialising the enormity of sin as a whole.

A cluttered Catechism has a way of domesticising and pedanticising sin, of ironing flat all contours, as the polite withdrawal of the younger generation of Catholics from church-going seems to attest.

A 'seated' conscience, or a 'creative' one?

Fr Bernard Häring CSsR is regarded as one of the most renowned moral theologians in the modern Catholic world. He was a professor of moral theology at the Lateran University in Rome for twenty-five years. Towards the end of his life he wrote about 'the criteria of any person who should preside at the Eucharist'. Having placed those criteria within the context of the Gospel he considered them 'more weighty than the highly questionable biological issue of sex':

> Christ bids us rest but does not require us to become *seated persons*, ie those men and women who are forever tired, devoid of ideals and inspiration, who are unable to enlist the power of the Spirit to encourage others. The seated person is the one who is incapable of internalising Jesus' invitation, 'Up, let us go forward'. Most especially if going forward implies the

risk of potential suffering, change and temporary insecurity. The seated person is static and self-satisfied, ever confident to celebrate past triumphs and achievements while ever avoiding the courageous responsibility that risk-taking involves. In a word, the seated person is cowardly. Ordinarily, the self-satisfied are fundamentalist in their thinking, eschewing new and creative formulations of doctrine while ever clinging to the norms and imperatives of the past. They are hard-and-fast traditionalists, and, if gifted with energies, they use them strenuously to promote the restorations of a past order. Seated persons are those perched on self-made thrones unwilling to move forward with the times because such a move would mean renouncing the glamour and privilege of clericalism in all its forms at every level.[40]

In 1989 when Häring was already seventy-seven years of age, he wrote an article appealing for a recognition of 'consensus seeking' which rests on the mystery of love and life, which is written in the heart and echoes in the core of conscience.[41] (He instances the use of coitus interruptus, the ancient form of contraception, practised throughout Africa, which protects the life of the unborn, though the practice is outlawed by the Church.) He also appealed for a recognition of the concept of 'creative conscience' (and this will not be pleasing to Archbishop Pell, as indeed it has failed to please Monsignor Carlo Caffara of the Holy Office) that exists for all who have understood what Paul said in the Baptismal lesson: 'You are not subjects of a rule of law, but rather are of grace' (*Romans 6:14*).

Creative conscience involves the discovery of an authentic, open ecumenical base which gathers in the consciences of many who have grown through struggle to embrace the non-violence of the Beatitudes, including the best representatives of Protestantism, Taoism, Confucianism, Hinduism, Judaism, Islam. Such people are Mahatma Gandhi, Nelson Mandela, Nugget Coombs, Simone Weil (none of them Catholic) and so many Aborigines who hold depths of Aboriginal spirituality. Each of these has been able to provide a releasing of spiritual insight, which the Church so sorely needs. And of course, such a reservoir can hold the voice of women unconstricted by the multi-shaped forms of gender bias with which the Church is loaded.

Father Häring tried patiently to explain to his bureaucratic, clerical detractors that his notion of creative conscience had nothing to do with nose-counting (determining moral truths by numbers) or theological logrolling (trading concessions for an inauthentic unity; here there are reverse shades of the momentously tragic influence on Paul VI by Cardinals Ottaviani and Pizzardo in the *Humanae Vitae* 'debate'). Creative Conscience is not the entering into an academic dispute over fine points of methodology in ethics, but rather has to do with basic attitudes towards the world and the very meaning of human life. Such a comprehensive notion of creative conscience has the enormous advantage of relying on the initiative and insights of both men and women, regardless of gender, denomination or non-denomination.

The concept of creative conscience was already adumbrated in the Second Vatican Council, which pointed to the Church's mutual reliance on the rest of the human family:

> By faithfulness to Conscience, Christians are con-
> nected with other people in the search for truth and
> for a truthful solution to all the many problems aris-
> ing in the individual's life in a society with others.[42]

As Newman himself quoted in this context the thought of St Hilary of Poitiers, 'the ears of the common people are holier than the hearts of the priests'.

Collective conscience — the *sensus fidelium*

Which brings us to one of the core concepts in Cardinal Newman's writings on conscience: the *sensus fidelium*.

I must confess to a deep despondency which has descended since reading the article about Archbishop Pell (*The Bulletin*, 27 April 1999). He appears to have painted himself into a corner when it comes to offering hope in the future Church. If he cannot accept the imperial nature of individual conscience, he cannot accept the role of collective conscience in the Church.

This concept figures in Newman's writings as the *sensus fidelium*, the consensus of the faithful, which is to say that within the body of Christian men and women is the experience of truth, and that this sense has something to say about new ways, both diverse and different, of experiencing and expressing faith. Archbishop Pell need go no further than his own cathedral congregation to uncover it. It is as essential an ingredient in the life of the Church as hierarchy or papacy, for each relies on the other. When the one ignores the other it does so at its own peril. But it is a consensus of the faithful which is never adequately indicated by the clapping of hands or the waving of palm branches.

Newman wrote to Lady Simeon at the end of the First Vatican Council (1869–70):

> We have come to the climax of tyranny. It is not good for a Pope to live 20 years. It is an anomaly and bears no good fruit; he becomes a god, has no one to contradict him, does not know facts, and does cruel things without meaning it.[43]

In these most uncertain times within the Church we need to go forward and trustingly allow the laity to take a clear lead. The *sensus fidelium* has learned to live underground and latently, through 'dungeon fire and sword' as during the Inquisition or the British subjugation of Ireland. It has also remained curiously impervious to Vatican knuckle-rapping. Cardinal Newman reminds us that:

> The Nicene dogma was maintained during the greater part of the fourth century, not by the unswerving firmness of the Holy See, Councils or Bishops, but by the consensus fidelium. There were untrustworthy councils, unfaithful bishops, there was weakness, fear of consequences, misguidance, delusion, hallucination, endless, hopeless, extending itself into nearly every corner of the Catholic Church.[44]

> Each constituent portion of the Church has its proper functions, and no portion can safely be neglected.[45]

> It is a great evangelical lesson, that not the wise and powerful, but the obscure, the unlearned, and the weak constitute the real strength [of the Church].[46]

Catholic brands of racism

Recently, the former prime minister of Australia, Malcolm Fraser, appealed to the decency of fellow Australians to reject Pauline Hanson's One Nation Party on the fundamental grounds of racism. 'It is anti-Asian, anti-Jewish and anti-Aboriginal', he said. In the face of such a serious warning, I would like to think that Australian Catholics would have pricked up their ears. But I have to admit sadly that that is not the case. I suspect that Pauline Hanson's appeal is shared by roughly an exact proportion of Australian Catholics as would be reflected in the rest of the population. That is a pretty frightening thought.

I've been saying for years — and there appears to be no forthcoming disproving evidence — that our Catholic school system has been for decades producing its full share of racists, that it fully blends in statistically with the rest of society. And that, I suggest, is the most powerful indictment of all — for today the Catholic Church stands spiritually crippled and dysfunctional, bereft of any power to recognise, let alone speak for, those being oppressed in our society.

In some ways the Church appears to be the victim of its own making. How else can we explain the wimpishness of so many bishops and clergy who, when faced with the racist attitudes of so many of their own 'faithful', revert to tongue-tied confusion, and then into a predictable silence. Similarly, how else can we explain the topsy-turvy nature of a church which claims to cherish the Gospel, but allows sentiments spectacularly

absent in the Gospel to delineate its public legal attitude to gay people in the Church?

Conscience and Aboriginal rights

On Aborigines, Archbishop Pell is quoted in *The
Bulletin*: 'I have spoken on occasion but we don't have
a big number of Aborigines in this State.'[47] In that single short sentence the Archbishop says far more than
what he admits. He reveals that he is part of the great
white conspiratorial lie that Aborigines have never
ventured here in any numbers. So there are very few
Aborigines here in Victoria and the evidence of fewness in numbers means that they do not warrant his
serious attention.

The fact is — and it is a pity that he does not
acknowledge it — the territory now known as Victoria
has a history of savagery hardly equalled anywhere.
The white squatters of Gippsland had learned from the
Myall Creek murder verdict. They were outraged that
whites could be found guilty of killing blacks. So, from
the so-called 'Warrigal Creek' massacres of 1843 on,
the squatters saw to it that not one evidential skull or
bone lay on the surface of the earth.

Aboriginal history in Victoria

The whole of the Gippsland was won (colonised) by violence and chicanery. Many, many whites have been
seduced by the great white tranquillising drugs, the
dirty secret of silence and the downright lie. The con-

tinuance of this vicious subterfuge, up to this very late hour, carries its own abhorrency.

By the 1850s it was true that the once proud Kurnai nation had been reduced from thousands of men, women and children to a pitiful 126 ragged beggars. The denial mechanisms in Henry Lawson's lines still are allowed to flourish:

> They needn't say the fault is ours
> If blood should stain the wattle.[48]

The lovely silver and gold Snowy River Wattle that grows in Gippsland has been drenched with gallons of Aboriginal blood.

To the 19,000 Aborigines who are indigenous to the state today, those words from the man who holds the Metropolitan See in Victoria, about fewness, must seem insensitive, dismissive, crass and unashamedly cavalier.

And not only in Gippsland. In the Western District, too, the story is the same. On 12 September 1876 the editor of the *Hampden Guardian* asserted that the history of the Western District could never be written 'for it would be such a long record of oppression, outrage, wrong and coldblooded murder on the part of "the superior race" that it dare not and therefore never will be written'. There is something deeply sinister here — ethnic cleansing without a name and unrecorded.

It is not easy to find anyone who remembers the name Coranderrk. The name is associated with an extraordinary political figure in the Aboriginal world, William Barak, one of a surviving group of Aborigines who squatted on a traditional camping site at Coranderrk, forty-five miles from Melbourne.

A deputation from the people asked the government for land to be handed back for their use and they were granted 930 hectares in 1863, extended to 1,960 hectares in 1866. By 1875 the community was showing a lot of success in self-determination and self-reliance, in clearing the land and building their own housing. But the dreaded BPA (Board for the Protection (!) of Aborigines), influenced by white avarice and jealousy, decided to sell the land and relocate the people to arid, rubbish-tip land north of the Murray.

The people refused to go. Barak and two young Aboriginal men, Robert Wandin and Tom Dunolly, continued a long battle of resistance against the Board, forcing a royal commission in 1877. Barak had been quoted in *The Leader*, a Melbourne newspaper, in February 1875, as to why he and his people did not want to move: 'The Yarra is my father's country. There's no mountains for me on the Murray.'[49]

The Board, which could not believe that the people could manage their protest so successfully, hired a detective to uncover the identity of the suspected white sympathisers, who turned out to be the very black Tom Dunolly! In March 1882 the Coranderrk people marched to Melbourne to publicise and promote their case.

In the face of such political success, there was nothing more for the whites to do but to change the law (as John Howard decided after the Wik High Court decision), which then became the *Victorian Aborigines Act*, and Aborigines found themselves being redefined into full-bloods and half-castes, not the first expression of the divide-and-conquer rule and of the politics of pauperisation. For the half-castes were sent away from Coranderrk and the community was disempowered and demoralised. In 1893 half of the land was seized and leased out to whites. In 1923 the residents were relocated to Lake Tyers Aboriginal Reserve and the rest of the land was then sold.

By that time the eyes of Melbourne Catholics were focused on Michael Collins' assassination and the freedom-fighters of Ireland. It is a pity that they did not see the intimate connection with the freedom-fighters of Australia. The story of the proud political history and the very name of Coranderrk seem now to have been expunged from the consciousness of whites; the district now goes by the name of Healesville.

The story of the cruelly dashed hopes of the Aboriginal people of Coranderrk has been told as one of the true but grim stories by Inga Clendinnen in the 1999 Boyer Lecture. A similar story is told of the Yorta Yorta people from the Shepparton area, whose claims for traditional rights were rejected in a one-minute delivery of judgment by Judge Olney in Melbourne on 18 December 1998 — case closed.

Why not be an outspoken supporter?

So the Archbishop continues in his interview: 'I'm neither a frequent nor an outspoken supporter of Aboriginal issues.' 'Why not?', we shout hoarsely; 'there are 19,000 reasons for demanding an answer. If you said nothing during the Wik debate, how can Aborigines begin to trust you? If you claim to specialise in issues of moral leadership, where are you now?'

And finally, from the Archbishop: 'I'm certainly in favour of their proper place in Australian society.' These are uncommitted, meaningless words, such that John Howard might throw away. Many of us would like to see an unceasing zeal for the cause, not pusillanimous clap-trap. Aborigines are entitled to far more than hollow words. Orthodoxy means nothing unless it is proven by orthopraxis, which is simply what the Apostle James said: 'I will show you my faith by my actions.'

There are many now who have lived in fear of embarrassment of what might eventuate if Archbishop Pell were to open his mouth again. And, of course, he has.

An aside: the Lord Acton Inaugural Address

On 4 August 1999, when Archbishop Pell addressed the Centre for Independent Studies in Sydney, he began by offering a misquotation of Lord Acton's famous aphorism. What the Archbishop said was 'Power corrupts, and absolute power corrupts absolutely'. The actual historical quote is 'Power tends to corrupt, and absolute power corrupts absolutely'. The Archbishop then went on to add some 'contemporary cynic's' parody (and that still in terms of his own misquote), 'Power corrupts and the loss of power corrupts absolutely'. One is tempted into the suspicion that his anonymous parodist just might well be his own very self. The correct version stands out in contrast to the misquotation in that it highlights the utter corruption of absolute power, averse to any attempt to make a joke of it.

The Archbishop's lecture also failed to provide the context in which the famous words were written by Lord Acton — in a private letter to the Anglican Bishop Creighton of Peterborough on 5 April 1887. Acton was angrily accusing Creighton of what he regarded as the paramount heresy of falsely deferring to rank: 'There is no worse heresy than that the office sanctifies the holder of it ... I cannot accept your canon that we are to judge Pope and King unlike other men, with a favourable presumption that they did no wrong.'[50] (It is my feeling that much of the present clerical reticence in the face of the misuse of power is due to timidity based on such deference to rank, and therefore warrants Acton's scathing derision.)

It is also somewhat alarming that the Archbishop refers to Acton as a 'devout Catholic', considering that Acton never made a public act of submission after Papal Infallibility was defined in July 1870, and that he risked excommunication in 1874 and again in 1875 by deliberately evading a declaration of assent being pressed home by Manning, the Cardinal Archbishop of Westminster.[51]

But then it is not so surprising when we find him sailing close enough to the wind as to reject certain propositions contained within decrees of a General Council of the Church. It is a matter of some irony that John Acton is now the best-known advocate in modern times for the sovereignty of individual conscience, the very concept with which Archbishop Pell has so much difficulty.

His Sydney lecture, entitled 'Catholicism and the Architecture of Freedom', is a medley of opinions of indifferent value and importance, none of which springs directly from the thoughts of Lord Acton, or can be even shown to relate to them; none of which has been 'defined by the Church' as it has no direct theological content. With one exception. There is a sudden return to his old hobby-horse, the denial of the primacy of conscience (quoted earlier). For some reason which the Archbishop does not make clear, this preoccupation keeps floating to the surface of his mind like a piece of free-floating flotsam, unconnected with the environment around it.

The thinking of Archbishop Pell is undoubtedly marked by the intransigence of Ultramontanism, which historian Eamon Duffy describes as 'a form of absolutism revelling in what Cardinal Manning called "the beauty of inflexibility".' Denial of the primacy of conscience, which has become a permanent fixture in the ecclesiastical wardrobe of his mind, is in the end, it seems, a cloak that hides insecurity and fear of loss. But at the same time it can bluff the unwary so that whole lives can be locked into cramp, a paralysis, from which they are entitled to Gospel freedom.

The demand for defining an evident truth smacks of the Apostle Thomas's condition for proving the wounds of Christ.

When confronted with such inflexibility in the mind of an Australian Archbishop one is tempted to look for causes, to ask how it has come about that his like has been produced in this day and age. What makes him tick as an Australian, a Catholic, a priest and an archbishop?

Perhaps history can be of help and provide some clues as to why an ethos of detachment has developed in the Australian hierarchy.

Columbus Fitzpatrick

Columbus Fitzpatrick is an example of a very early white Australian-born son of an Irish convict, a devout Catholic indeed, whose recollections covered the era of Fr O'Flynn, Fr Therry and Archbishop Polding. His published evidence shows that he was seduced by the great white myth in relation to Aborigines, the result of the galvanising together of Church and Crown in Polding's time:

> Only for the blacks, we should have been happy; but the blacks had commenced a war of extermination with the poor defenceless settlers and nothing but the firmness of the governor saved whites from utter ruin.[52]

Fitzpatrick, of course, was an early imbiber of the white folkloric stereotypes; he showed no outrage at the injustice, no sense of compassion for those killed in the Myall Creek massacre of 1838.

Archbishop Polding

On 26 January 1838 the Waterloo Creek massacre of hundreds of Aborigines occurred. That was the fiftieth anniversary of the founding of white Australia, and

Archbishop Polding was celebrating in St Mary's Cathedral his thanks for the Queen and the blessings God had shed on this land. But he issued no pastoral Letter sharing any anguish over the massacres in 1838 when the Sydney daily papers were crammed with the debate as to whether blacks were simply vermin or not.

On 18 December 1838, seven convicts were hanged for the Myall Creek massacre. Of those, Catholics had their full representation. Edward Foley, Jemmy Oates and John Russell were Catholics, and Fr Francis Murphy gave them the last rites at the scaffold. Perhaps embarrassment explained Polding's public silence? However, he did offer a low-profile opinion published in the *Australasian Chronicle* on 5 November 1839, signed with the simple initials +JBP, where he deplored the tone of a society where the extermination of Aborigines was accepted. Yet this was a whole year after the public furore had risen in the newspapers and had already died down.

Seven more years were to elapse before he was invited to give the replies, only recently made famous, to the Parliamentary Committee on Aborigines. This was behind closed doors and in the safe, polite company of his social peers. His words, now rescued from the protection of that privileged, panelled room, seem strong and form the basis of the Pope's reference to Polding in his 1986 speech to Aborigines in Alice Springs:

> From the earliest times men like Archbishop Polding of Sydney opposed the legal fiction adopted by European settlers that this land was terra nullius — nobody's country. He strongly pleaded for the rights

of the aboriginal inhabitants to keep the traditional lands on which their whole society depended.[53]

Certainly, judged in contrast to all later Catholic episcopal performance they seem pioneering, even brave. When recontextualised, however, Polding's words tend to pale, particularly when we know of his 1843 efforts to establish an Aboriginal mission on Stradbroke Island.

The story of Stradbroke Island[54]

All of Polding's missionary projects started with the British Empire. So in June 1841 he personally approached Lord John Russell in London with a plan which involved the financing not of a mission but a monastery on Stradbroke Island. It was rejected. However, he returned from England in 1843 with four Italian Passionists. He did secure from the Colonial Office at the local level a lease on a property on Stradbroke Island and, though he had invited the Passionists to the Mission, it became clear almost immediately that he planned to replace them. From very early in his episcopate it had been clear that Polding was overly interested in gaining recruits for the Benedictine Order. Within a month of their arrival, on 9 June 1843, he was writing from Moreton Bay to the monks of Downside Abbey in England:

> I want to have a regular supply of Benedictine Missioners for the Aboriginal and Colonial service ... The Government have allowed me for two years a

place which with small expense may be changed into an excellent monastery, with the understanding that on application, leave will be continued as long as the place is used for missionary purposes ...

I have distributed slight dresses amongst them (the Aborigines) selecting the principal warrior amongst them as Chief, and giving him and his wife a distinguishing dress. Before, they were all as Adam and Eve before fig leaves came into fashion. Don't be shocked. It is a fact. Some of them speak English a little. I feel that our Italian friends will be but bunglers ... They cannot express themselves in English even now for the commonest purpose.[55]

(One's imagination can easily take flight, conjuring up the slight apparel Polding had in mind for Aborigines — flimsy negligees in the shape of the Benedictine habit.)

In a rare and invaluable piece of Aboriginal oral history, Oodgeroo Noonuccal (Kath Walker) records the amusing story that follows, providing a sharp contrast with the coloniser's story:

Now when the Roman Catholic missionaries came to the island in 1838, they saw no hope in bringing Christian salvation to the people if they were to continue wandering about the island, fishing, hunting and gathering food for themselves. The missionaries told them they must choose one area that would become their permanent place for living. The people chose Moongalba's sitting-down place, and it was here (just north of Dunwich) that the mission established a church, a school and a cemetery.

The priests told the people that they were living in sin and insisted that they wear European clothes and go through a marriage ceremony with their partners and say prayers every day. So every day the Noonuccal people gathered at the mission church and one of the prayers they said was the Lord's Prayer. Some of the older women began to ask questions about 'daily bread' and wondered where it would come from. From Heaven they were told. But no bread came, however hard they prayed. Eventually, some of the elders called a 'big-talk' at a midden-site about a mile south of the mission, and they decided the missionaries were not telling them true things. The old men told the women to discard their clothes and throw away their wedding rings and soon the people drifted back into their old familiar habits and dispersed over the island.[56]

Oodgeroo's father was one of a group of young men who later decided to settle at One Mile, as it became known, and it was here that he subsequently built the family house. She would tell how her parents kept digging up the gold-plated wedding rings that the women had discarded (a belated lesson in missiology).

The story of the Italian Passionists on Stradbroke Island is told by Fr John Hosie in his excellent book *Challenge*. He tells how Polding failed in his commitment to support them; how the Aboriginal people supported them with food; how they returned to Sydney dispirited, hungry and in tattered clothes, to receive warm hospitality from the French Marists at Church Hill. Polding was quite unjustifiably annoyed to receive a direction from

Rome that since he no longer needed them, they would be released to take up work where they were, in fact, wanted.

Twenty-six more years were to elapse in Polding's episcopate before we hear any more of a Catholic mission to Aborigines in Eastern Australia.

The death in custody of John David Murra

Despite his talk of separating Aborigines from the corrupting white world, right from the start Archbishop Polding was taking Aboriginal children to St Mary's Monastery in Sydney, imposing on them outlandish European names and force-feeding them with frightening foreign ideas.

In February 1850 the Archbishop of Sydney kidnapped (at least that is how his father felt) a little black boy of seven or eight years. The monks kept him hidden, while waiting to despatch him to Rome, for, as Bishop Charles Davis wrote to Downside Abbey on 1 March 1850:

> We got him naked from the bush and we have not kept him longer, for if the Blacks were to find out where he was, they would be sure to steal him away. His father gave him up to the Archbishop quite cheerfully, but we have to understand that he is already sorry for having done so, and is longing to have him again.[57]

On the same day — 1 March 1850 — Polding wrote to Benedictine Abbot PF Casaretto in Italy: 'finally I have found an opportunity to send your Most

101

Reverend Excellency a native-born Australian boy',[58] and further intimating that there were many more such boys to come.

Just four days later, on 5 March 1850, a lonely, terror-stricken little black boy sailed out of Sydney Heads on HMS *St George* in the care of a complete white-stranger, Captain Jones. He died soon after in Genoa. He was, even then, probably not the first black death in custody.

Polding was never charged with the kidnapping or death of John David Murra, the little Aboriginal child with the Latinised surname and the broken heart whose unmarked grave is on foreign soil. But I am sure that St John the Baptist, another death in custody victim, was there to welcome him to paradise. It is likely that he was the first of the long list of stolen Aboriginal children who remain the shame of white Australia.

Even allowing for the accepted practices of the white world at the time, Polding's behaviour stands as an appalling atrocity and a warning to us all of the evil effects of clericalism, patriarchalism and monasticism *pro seipso* (for its own sake).

Roman pressure on Australian bishops

As late as 1869, at the second Provincial Council of the Australian Bishops, held in Melbourne, the silence on Aboriginal rights was broken by words that appear somewhat brave: 'The stain of blood is upon us ... shall we not protest against this?' But then how enlightening it is to find that what really stirred the bishops into words was pressure from the Roman Congregation for the Propagation of the Faith. The commitment did not last.

Forty-four years were then allowed to elapse while the Australian hierarchy remained silent about Aborigines. In 1914 Rome fired another bullet in the person of Archbishop Ceretti, the first Papal Delegate to Australia, who informed the Bishops that he had received special orders from the Congregation of Propaganda Fide to press for more concern for Aborigines. He appeared relentless. He sent out questionnaires, first individually then collectively. If the reply of Bishop Patrick Dwyer of Maitland to the battery of questions sent out by his Excellency was typical, the Delegate would not have been much enlightened. The Bishop answered just one of the questions: 'As a matter of fact, I have not succeeded in finding even one Catholic Aborigine in this Diocese and I doubt if even one exists.'

The Delegate proposed, on behalf of the Congregation, 'the formation of an inter-diocesan society of priests, drawn from the ranks of the secular clergy and supported by contributions from each diocese'. The proposal was ignored. When the Delegate presided over the episcopal meeting in April 1919, he was advised cynically that 'great difficulty has been experienced in doing anything for Aborigines' and the bishops left it to the Delegate to report back 'after he had personally visited the Missions in Australia and the Pacific'.

One could perhaps be forgiven for thinking that the culture of denial had so entered the episcopal psyche that every new bishop appointed to Australia subsequently was affected by it.

The 'Great Slumber'

The bishops then re-entered their 'Great Slumber' — the period longer than the snooze of Rip Van Winkle — when nothing was said for half a century about Aborigines, except maverick cries like that of Duncan McNab (Blessed Mary MacKillop's cousin) in the 1870s and her brother Donald MacKillop SJ in the 1890s.[59]

The bishops' cynicism was reflected in their grudging parsimony about releasing personnel and funds for Aboriginal causes. They were content to leave that responsibility to foreign overseas Orders. The Spanish Benedictines of New Norcia, the Austrian Jesuits, the German Pallotines, the French MSCs, the Indian sisters of Mother Teresa were relied on to provide the cheap task force and the funds. And while each year one third of the Society for the Propagation of the Faith takings was held back in Australia, ostensibly for the home missions, Aboriginal missions missed out (the Bishops' Conference Centre at Kensington was paid for in the 1970s from this fund, as also was the holiday house for a Victorian bishop in an exclusive Victorian seaside resort).

In a letter to Archbishop Kelly of Sydney on 29 November 1930, Monsignor Joe McGovern could complain, 'Except for one Sacred Heart Father on Bathurst Island, there is no Australian, Irish, English or Scottish priest working among the Aborigines.'[60] Around that time Archbishop Daniel Mannix gave some support to the rights of Aborigines in the face of punitive expeditions in the Northern Territory. On Social Justice

Sunday in 1940, Archbishop Mannix made a further reference to the rights of Aborigines.[61] Throughout those years, particularly between 1940–1966, when the bishops issued special 'Social-Justice Statements' — originally directed by BA Santamaria — there was no mention of Aborigines at all. And the 1967 referendum was put and carried without any official interest from the Catholic Church.

Awakening the conscience of the Australian Church

In 1970 Rome began to intervene again. The voice of Pope Paul VI on his visit to Australia was like a great bell booming, using words to Aborigines that the Australian Church seemed not to be able to get its tongue around, and to say things which heartened their spirits:

> We know that you have a lifestyle proper to your own ethnic genius or culture — a culture which the Church respects and which she does not in any way ask you to renounce.[62]

His words inspired Shirley Smith (Mum Shirl) and Gary Foley, two prominent Aborigines, to lead a delegation to the Apostolic Nuncio in 1974, asking Archbishop Gino Paro to present to the Pope a petition that was very much in line with the suggestions made by Archbishop Ceretti fifty-five years before. His Excellency showed the petition to the Australian bishops at their next sitting. Bishop O'Loughlin of Darwin moved that it be sent on. He seemed to know that nothing would come of it. And that was true. (This was told to me by Archbishop Guilford Young immediately after the meeting.)

Papal interventions have continued. After the visit of Pope Paul VI in 1970 came Pope John Paul II in 1986:

> Let it not be said *that the fair and equitable recognition of Aboriginal rights to land* is discrimination. To call for the acknowledgment of the land rights of people who have never surrendered those rights is not discrimination.[63]

As late as 1999, while the paralysis of tongue of Bishops like Archbishop Pell remains fixed, the Pope's recent call to white Australia is even now resounding in our ears:

> Who can forget the painful history of the first inhabitants of Australia and the need now for reconciliation and healing?[64]

In the early decades of the eighteenth century the goldrush fever on the Ballarat diggings crowded out the tragic news of the massacre of the Aborigines. Something akin to that same fever under its many different guises seems still to be responsible for blotting out 'the painful memory' to which John Paul II here referred.

Spiritual treasure from Aborigines

It would be quite wrong to imagine that I am here alerting Archbishop Pell to 'think welfare' — to activate the St Vincent de Paul machinery to take on more

Aboriginal cases, so to extend the long cold arm of welfare. On the contrary, I offer the hope that he would one day see what spiritual treasure the Aboriginal people can offer him, that his own inner liberation is bound up with theirs! When all is said and done, Catholic theology needs the impetus of creative conscience, of accepting the sacredness of the earth in a new and fresh way, and of our responsibility to protect and nourish it with new insights and energy.

Rudolph Bultmann has said that real loyalty does not involve repetition, but carrying things a stage further. Catholic theological thought, however, will be pushed into an even deeper impasse of suppression if Archbishop Pell, unchanged, has anything to do with it. Newman's thoughts on change and conscience are entwined:

> In a higher world it is otherwise, but here below to live is to change, and to be perfect is to have changed often.[65]

To accept change is to accept a new way of thinking.

There is a season for everything

There is a season for everything under heaven. There is a time for picking up stones — like the age-old but ever-new stones of knowledge which Aborigines hold about saving the earth — and there is a time for throwing away stones — the dead-weight stones, the many prejudices and smug complacencies of white supremacy.

The Real Australian Story

I mourned again for the Murray Tribe
Gone too without a trace,
I thought of the soldiers' diatribe,
The smile on the Governor's face.
You murdered me with rope, with gun
The massacre my enclave,
You buried me deep on McLarty's run
Flung into a common grave.
You propped me up with Christ, red tape,
Tobacco, grog and fears,
Then disease and lordly rape
Through the brutish years;
Now you primly say you're justified,
And sing of a nation's glory.
But I think of a people crucified —

JACK DAVIS[66]

It comes as no shock that the Archbishop does not understand the seasons, that he should prioritise the 'minimum rules' for a practising Catholic today simply as 'the basic commandments of 2,000 years', when 2,000 years ago was the very time that Jesus Christ abrogated the Mosaic Law. Jesus's command to love God and neighbour rather should insist that the Archbishop start from an acknowledgment of, and an identification of, the victims in his own backyard of Victoria, and from a Christian leader's unambiguous declaration of their innocence. Then, he might be able to take up the challenge in the recent words of Pope John-Paul II:

Reconciliation with Aboriginal people will not be resolved except on the basis of an unambiguous

108

vision of the dignity of every human being and a firm
sense of human-rights, which no individual, group or
Government can claim either to concede or deny,
since these are transcendent rights, innate to every
man or woman.[67]

Looking back, looking forward

Now I am sure that I would never have come to write
these words had I not lived so long.

The Catholic Church, despite its seemingly
immutable outer surface, is forever undergoing changing moods like the ever-changing seasons. If we live
through successive papal times, we will certainly feel
the climates change. Yet at any given moment we may
not have had words to describe what was happening.
The historian was yet to appear to add perspective and
interpret context.

Time to shout, danger!

There is something clearly recognisable in Archbishop
Pell's way of thinking which tells me that I have passed
through this country before, and it makes me want to
shout danger! I am a sample of an endangered species
— an Australian Catholic priest — and, rarer still, I am
old enough to predate Vatican II when it was still com-
pulsory for humble priests or eminent Cardinals, on
taking new office, to recite the anti-modernist oath
which had been in place since September 1910. This
was part of a veritable 'Roman Inquisition', most

remarkable in that it was carried out in complete secrecy away from the eyes of the non-clerical world. It was an attempt at enforcing faith, a theological absurdity. It contained an intransigence of mind which, according to the Eamon Duffy, became the 'required mark of the good Catholic'.[68] 'Real' Catholics were 'integralists', accepting as a package deal everything the Pope taught, not picking and choosing in the 'pride and curiosity' of their intellect.

I still hold vivid memories of being required to take what Eamon Duffy called the lengthy and ferocious oath against modernism which was still in force in 1952. It was a grim reminder to us that, almost fifty years before, a former rector of Manly College, Dr Thomas Hayden, had been reported to Rome for teaching progressive ideas on the teaching of Scripture. The ensuing vituperously inspired investigations, conducted in the utmost secrecy, left Dr Hayden permanently cautious, and the quality of teaching at Manly bereft of theological energy or imagination, and distinctly shallow. The result was to produce generations of theologically bankrupt priests, incapable of preaching anything but the flat 'party line' and boring their congregation into unspeakable numbness.

In theory, the Church is catholic in that it can embrace equally all cultures, all races and colours, all modalities of sex. As anyone and everyone can claim to be favoured by God, so they can take particular pride in being their own individual selves. To exclude the different or to control diversity is uncatholic, because it suggests a narrowing of the terms of salvation. When the

110

Apostles with Jesus' mother were huddled together in a confined space in an upper room in Jerusalem, there was the Church truly catholic. To be catholic has nothing to do with geographical size but everything to do with the capacity to point to universal eligibility in the Kingdom of Heaven.

I have lived long enough to remember that climates can change dramatically in the Church, to recall that Pope John XXIII as a young man became suspect of heresy; long enough to be able to name present forms of obscurantism for what they are. For I find the public utterances of Archbishop Pell to be every bit as intransigent, as high-handed and Church-serving, as depreciative of the poor, as given to excluding the simple faithful from active participation and from decision-making in the Church, as those behind the pre-Vatican II purges.

Contrition follows from the forgiveness of being loved — not the other way round.

Those whose sole language is 'Pellspeak' seem at a loss to see why Jesus had a fondness for prostitutes and tax collectors. They have a need to edit in 'former sinners who have now made a good confession'. But Jesus found in such people a contriteness of heart and a capacity to believe, even in their 'sin', unlike the papyrus and hide-bound scribes and the law-for-law's-sake Pharisees.

Jesus saw them as having learned in the places of social destitution a pliant suppleness in their capacity to 'think better', which the scribes and Pharisees, in their rigid moralism could not do:

> I tell you solemnly, tax collectors and prostitutes are
> making their way into the kingdom of God before
> you. For John came to you, a pattern of true right-
> eousness, but you did not believe him, and yet the tax
> collectors and prostitutes did. Even after seeing that
> you refused to think better of it and believe in him.
>
> (*Matthew*, 21:31–32)

As I grow older and yet older, and memories crowd
in from the past, I think with shame of common practices in the Australian Catholic Church which public
inquisitorial figures such as Paul Brazier and his ilk
now wish to see revived. I think of those green census
books which Sydney curates were obliged to fill in with
noughts and crosses, indicating whether parishioners
had fulfilled their Easter Duty etc, and the occasional
Ne Tem tick, noting a candidate for the Redemptorist
priest to visit at the next parish mission. That *Ne
Temere Decree*, that went out from Rome across the world
nullifying all attempts of marriage of a Catholic before
a state registrar or a non-Catholic minister, was as
good as dynamite when it came to splitting families,
often for a lifetime. Marrying outside the Church was
like a premature dive into hell, and any attempts to
live in harmony with other faiths held out no premium
at all. And the bigotries became entrenched. Is it any
wonder that the Irish Bishop Willie Walsh should have
received such Protestant applause when he acknowledged recently that the *Ne Temere Decree* had been
responsible for much of the bitter sectarianism of modern Ireland, when all roads to inter-faith dialogue
remained firmly closed.

I think of the school confessions before every First Friday (the arbitrary yet 'finite nine' that became the 'perpetual nine', just in case) when thousands of often grudging school children were dispatched from school-room after school-room and marched to the parish Church where they were ranked before the confessionals until they were all 'done'. There was the relentless marshalling reminiscent of lamb-marking or sheep-dipping and a definite hint that the sacramental principle *ex opere operato* (the principle of the inherent power of sacraments) had gone horribly wrong.

Then I think of those Saturday evening confessional lines and the silence of the cold half-lit Church broken by the occasional cough or the dropping of a kneeler; the penitents reciting their spiel, with an overly familiar ring, remarkably reminiscent of the sample formulas which some catechist had provided for their first confession, but with little comprehension of what goes to make adult moral and social responsibility in this day and age.

There is another way

It is now that I tend to stand back and take stock and say to myself that there must be another way. Like the lengthening shadows of the late afternoon light in my life, the whole of life seems cast in a new and more realistic translucent perspective. The crimson glow of the setting sun which I now see as not so distant, reminds me that life is made up of warm flesh-and-blood human beings, not rules made in an age long gone, or ill-fitting principles that were never made-to-measure anyhow.

The Jesus I know is no cold, hard Iron-Christ; nor does Jesus deserve to be reduced to smug, glib and uncompassionate irrelevancies when the real meaning of His love is what people need so desperately. I stand inspired by the towering figure of the martyr-bishop Oscar Romero, who, like Christ, was murdered for resisting social sin, not private sin.

> It is in practice illegal to be an authentic Christian in our environment ... precisely because the world around us is founded radically on an established disorder before which the mere proclamation of the Gospel is subversive.[69]

Appendix I:
Statements by Archbishop Pell
on conscience

They came up with the sashes wishing to go to Communion. I said I can't give you Communion, would you like a blessing? In the early times most of them took the blessing, later fewer of them did. I said it's not because they're homosexually oriented; it's because they believe they have a right to homosexual activity. If somebody came up with a sash and said they were an adulterer or running a string of abortion clinics or were a robber in a big way and they believed the Church should legitimise these activities, we couldn't give them Communion either. If a person comes up anonymously, we presume they're in good faith and we leave them to work it out with God ... I'd be quite certain there'd be a number of [homosexuals who are practising catholics] but I'd say their situation is incongruous. There are a lot of people who are sinners but accept that it's wrong and regret their situation.

Archbishop George Pell,
Bulletin, 27 April 1999, p.29

The doctrine of the primacy of conscience should be quietly ditched, at least in our schools, or comprehensively restated, because too many Catholic youngsters have concluded that values are personal inventions, that we can paint our moral pictures any way we choose.

Bishop George Pell,
Seminar on the Sociology of Culture,
La Trobe University, 12 May 1988

[Of primacy of conscience] ... I think it's a dangerous and misleading myth. In the Catholic scheme of things, there's no such thing as primacy of conscience. We stand under the truth, under the word of God, we have no right to violate the rights of others simply because my conscience says I can. Conscience is a faculty we have to recognise the truth — it can be like a watch: if you set it wrongly it can be a minute or an hour out. In one of the recent encyclicals of the Holy Father, he spoke of conscience as the proximate norm for the truth — in other words, we have to use our own reasoning capacity, our conscience. We've got to be sincere but there's always the possibility that you might be mistaken and there's always the possibility that you might be culpably mistaken because it's just not in your interests to pursue the truth. There's even the possibility that you've become spiritually blind in a way that you don't recognise.

Archbishop George Pell,
Bulletin, 27 April 1999, p.29

Appendix II:
Statements of Cardinal Newman on conscience

THESE SUPERB PASSAGES taken from the work of John Henry Newman, *Certain Difficulties Felt by Anglicans In Catholic Teaching*, (Vol. II. London, Longmans, Green and Co., 1885), reveal his depth of soul, where 'heart speaks to heart'. They stand at variance with the words of Archbishop Pell in his ram-rod conservatism.

So little does the Pope come into this whole system of moral theology by which (as by our own Conscience) our lives are regulated, that the weight of his hand upon us as private men is absolutely unappreciable. I have had a difficulty where to find a measure or gauge of his interposition. (p. 229)

It seems, then, that there are extreme cases in which Conscience may come into collision with the word of a Pope, and is to be followed in spite of that word. Now I wish to place this proposition on a broader basis, acknowledged by all Catholics, and, in order to do this satisfactorily, as I began with the prophecies of Scripture and the primitive Church, when I spoke of the Pope's prerogatives, so now I must begin with the Creator and His creature, when I would draw out the prerogatives and supreme authority of Conscience ...

I say, then, that the Supreme Being is of a certain character, which, expressed in human language, we call ethical. He has the attributes of justice, truth, wisdom, sanctity, benevolence and mercy, as eternal characteristics in His nature, the very Law of His being, identical with Himself; and next, when He became Creator, He implanted this law, which is Himself, in the intelligence of all his rational creatures. The Divine Law, then, is the rule of ethical truth, the standard of right and wrong, a sovereign, irreversible, absolute authority in the presence of men and Angels ... (p.246)

This law, as apprehended in the minds of individual men, is called 'Conscience' and though it may suffer refraction in passing into the intellectual medium of each, it is not therefore so affected as to lose its character of being the Divine Law, but still has, as such, the prerogative of commanding obedience ...

This view of Conscience, I know, is very different from that ordinarily taken of it, both by science and literature, and by the public opinion, of this day. It is founded on the doctrine that Conscience is the voice of God, whereas it is fashionable on all hands now to consider it in one way or another a creation of man. (p.247)

... I observe that Conscience is not a judgment upon any speculative truth, any abstract doctrine, but bears immediately on conduct, on something to be done or not to be done. 'Conscience', which says St. Thomas, 'is the practical judgment or dictate of reason, by which we judge what hic et nunc is to be done as being good, or to be avoided as evil.' Hence Conscience cannot come into direct collision with the Church's or the Pope's infallibility; which is engaged on general propositions, and in the condemnation of particular and given errors.

Next I observe that, Conscience being a practical dictate, collision is possible between it and the Pope's authority only when the Pope legislates, or gives particular orders, and the like. But a Pope is not infallible in his laws, nor in his commands, nor in his acts of state, nor in his administration, nor in his public policy. Let it be observed that the Vatican Council has left him just as it found him here. (p.256)

Conscience is not a long-sighted selfishness, nor a desire to be consistent with oneself; but it is a messenger from Him, who, both in nature and in grace, speaks to us behind a veil, and teaches and rules us by His representatives. Conscience is the aboriginal Vicar of Christ, a prophet in its informations, a monarch in its peremptoriness, a priest in its blessings and anathemas, and, even though the eternal priesthood throughout the Church could cease to be, in it the sacerdotal principle would remain and would have a sway. (pp.248–9)

But, of course, I have to say again, lest I should be misunderstood, that when I speak of Conscience, I mean Conscience truly so called. When it has the right of opposing the supreme, though not infallible Authority of the Pope, it must be something more than that miserable counterfeit which, as I have said above, now goes by the name. If in a particular case it is to be taken as a sacred and sovereign monitor, its dictate, in order to prevail against the voice of the Pope, must follow upon serious thought, prayer, and all available means of arriving at a right judgment on the matter in question. And further, obedience to the Pope is what is called 'in possession'; that is the *onus probandi* of establishing a case against him lies as in all cases of exception on the side of Conscience. Unless a man is able to say to himself, as in the Presence of God, that he must not and dare not, act upon the Papal injunction, he is bound to obey it, and would commit a great sin in disobeying it. Prima facie it is his bounden duty, even from a sentiment of loyalty, to believe the Pope right and to act accordingly. He must vanquish that mean, ungenerous, selfish, vulgar spirit of his nature, which, at the very first rumour of a command, places itself in opposition to the Superior who gives it, asks itself whether he is not exceeding his right, and rejoices, in a moral and practical matter, to commence with scepticism. He must have no willful determination to exercise a right of thinking, saying, doing just what he pleases, the question of truth and falsehood, right and wrong, the duty if possible of obedience, the love of speaking as his Head speaks, and of standing in all cases on his Head's side, being simply discarded. If this necessary rule were observed, collisions between the Pope's authority and the authority of Conscience would be very rare. (pp.257–8)

...did the Pope speak against Conscience in the true sense of the word he would commit a suicidal act. He would be cutting the ground from under his feet. His very mission is to proclaim the moral law, and to protect and strengthen that 'Light which enlighteneth every man that cometh into the world'. On the law of Conscience and its sacredness are founded both his authority in theory and his power in fact.

Certainly, if I am obliged to bring religion into after-dinner toasts (which indeed does not seem quite the right thing) I shall drink — to the Pope, if you please — still to Conscience first and the Pope afterwards. (p.252)

If either the Pope or the Queen demanded of me an 'Absolute Obedience' he or she would be transgressing the laws of human society. I give an absolute obedience to neither. (p.243)

Newman's words are so finely honed, distinctions so sharply made, propositions so neatly jointed. They had been chiseled out of the experience of thirty years of misunderstandings and mistrust and sanctifying pain. In the end he could attest that the concept of Papal Infallibility was meaningless unless the concept of Conscience was seen to provide its very foundation — it had so become part of his personal 'credo'. He admitted in his *Apologia pro Vita Sua* that he had not succeeded in stating a proof for the existence of God that satisfied his mind. But often he indicated that were he ever to do so, it would take as its starting point the fact of Conscience.

In 1855 John Henry Newman made a brilliant attempt to 'imagine and express the feelings and mutual relations of Christians and heathens' of the third century in his novel *Callista,* where the heroine is portrayed as subject to the pressure of worshipping idols but finally responding to the voice of God in Conscience:

> You may tell me that this dictate is a mere law of my nature ... it is the echo of a person speaking to me. It carries with it its proof of its divine origins ... An echo implies a voice; a voice a speaker. That speaker I love and fear. (*Callista, A Tale of the Third Century,* Longmans Green, New York, 1893, p.315)

By this imaginative expression Newman showed that conversion of Conscience precedes faith, not the other way round. Rather, heeding one's Conscience is essentially part of being open to faith. Conscience is determinative of true faith. It is a vexatious thing to suppose that 'faith' can suppress personal Conscience, because that is to produce a dysfunctional personality.

Appendix III:
Twenty-Five Years At Redfern

TED KENNEDY delivered the following address on 24 November 1996 to mark the twenty-fifth anniversary of the beginning of his ministry with the Catholic parish of Redfern. It was originally published in *Eremos* Magazine Essay Supplement No. 23 of November 1997.

Part One: Formation and disenchantment

When to the sessions of sweet silent thought
I summon up remembrance of things past,
I sigh the lack of many a thing I sought,
And with old woes new wail my dear time's waste:
Then can I drown an eye, unus'd to flow,
For precious friends bid in death's dateless night,
And weep afresh love's long-since cancell'd woe,
And moan the expense of many a vanish'd sight.
Then can I grieve at grievances foregone ...

Sonnet 30, SHAKESPEARE

I remember the years leading up to my arrival in Redfern twenty-five years ago as carrying the pain of loss and bitter disillusionment and loneliness. They were the six years following Vatican II. So many of my friends had left the priesthood; few of the officials had as much as asked why. They just fell, with all their talents, with all their profound pastoral, committed experiences, into an ecclesiastical abyss of accusatory silence. Josef de Schmedt, the Bishop of Bruges, screamed out from the Vatican Council in 1963 the clarion call, 'Let us rid the Church of clericalism, juridicism and triumphalism.' It seemed to set the euphoric agenda that could centre our very lives. Yet just three years after the Council, it was becoming clear that some of the powers-that-be were incapable of hearing the stirring challenge of de Schmedt.

Let me give just one example. One day in 1968 I received a phone call from the Cathedral — the voice of the archdiocesan secretary informing me that my application to allow a mixed marriage was incomplete. Though I had requested the Protestant party to sign that he would not interfere with the religious belief of his future wife, I had failed to ask him to sign the further promise that he would allow the children to be brought up Catholic. 'But', I said, 'that's ridiculous. He's seventy-five and she's sixty-seven years old.' 'Doesn't matter', he said with the unmild manner of a snappy Pomeranian. 'It is an assurance of his good faith.' Aware that if I were to press for this signature, the elderly gentleman would be entitled to request an assurance of my sanity, I then, with an embarrassed chuckle, told him about the phone call. And he, with admirable courtesy and tolerance, said: 'Please tell the good father, that if it were possible for me to be a father I would be delighted to have the child baptised Catholic.' I then resubmitted the application with his assurance, but still without the actual signature. Another phone call, the stern voice again: 'Not good enough', Monsignor barked. I had never until that day forged a signature.

It was also the day that I made my final departure from the Catholic Church — if the bureaucrats were right in insisting on its form and shape. But of course they are quite wrong and so I have stayed within its deeper reality. Clericalism, legalism and triumphalism have a way of stifling life, crippling the mind and breaking the heart. There was a terminal quality about that decision every bit as definitive as James Joyce's decision to leave Ireland forever. And the reasons were roughly the same, for in the face of pretentiousness, arrogance, downright cruelty and suffocating unfreedom, we have the obligation to claim our God-given birthright to freedom. And when it came to the clericalised world, with all its toxic potential, I found for myself Joyce's own three points of escape — exile, silence and cunning.

I must say I cringe when I remember, well before the crisis of *Humane Vitae*, those old pious women, their rosary beads rattling against the confessional grille, desperately anguished over what were really the man-fabricated clerically controlled 'sins' like sewing on Sundays. Judith Wright talks about that in her poem, 'Eli, Eli':

To see them go by drowning in the river —
Soldiers and elders drowning in the river,
the pitiful women drowning in the river,
the children's faces staring from the river —
that was his cross, and not the cross they gave him.

...

He watched, and they were drowning in the river;
faces like sodden flowers in the river,
faces of children moving in the river;
and all the while, be knew there was no river.

I then joined up with fourteen other Sydney priests who felt the same way. We tried to express our anguish to Cardinal Gilroy but he seemed consistently to miss our meaning. On January 12, 1969 I wrote a letter of seven closely typed pages to him. The letter is here reproduced in part:

Catholic Presbytery Punchbowl,
12 January 1969

I have been a priest of this Archdiocese for fifteen years. At my ordination, I could not have felt a stronger sense of belonging. Most of the priests of the Archdiocese were known to me personally. They had been in my home, receiving hospitality and honorary medical attention from my father. My priest-uncle had been honoured among them. Today, all sentiment such as I held for the Archdiocese is as good as dead, although I have a large number of close priest-friends in it. It might be said that it was through my own fault I let it die. Whatever truth there is in that, I believe that, in the main, it was trampled to death, and I am certain that a similar drop in morale has been experienced by many other priests.

For what it is worth I shall attempt to describe something of my sense of priestly vocation which finds me so out of accord with the stated policies and the unstated but heavy expectations for the style of life of Sydney priests. Much of it depends on the values and priorities I saw in my own father. He was recognised as a good and holy man, patient, loving and kind, responsive to people in need. Yet he shrank from pretty well all of the parish activities so often seen as indices of holiness. He was a most prayerful man, but never said the family rosary. He had a love for the Eucharist, but could never see the point of joining the Holy Name Society. He never attended a Novena in his life, never encouraged his children to join the Catholic Youth Organisation or the Legion of Mary. My mother was much the same. They saw Catholicism in far more liberal and less regimented terms than its standard image in this Archdiocese. The vision they gave me of the priesthood was never one of being an almost full-time agitator for the above activities. If that is what is expected of me, I am a failure from the start. My heart was never in these things.

Since entering the ecclesiastical world of the seminary and the Archdiocese, I have been hearing a stress on the structuring of priorities which runs counter to my parents' emphasis. With the notable exception of a few priests, the mentors set up to teach authoritatively ascetical and spiritual values have, to my mind, been ill-chosen. They have achieved a ring of phoneyness about their words. I have felt that their 'piosity' has been used as a slick coverup for the genuine ingredients in Christian growth in love.

There seems no denying that there has been a glaring lack in our formation, so that certain defects emerge in our conduct because of the training rather than despite it. Since I believe these to be serious and fundamental defects, endemic to us clergy as a group, the problem must be tackled specifically. When authority is used to make power and anger appear legitimate, then there is need to change the manner in which it is used. If restrictive control is exercised to disguise ignorance or fear, then there is need for education and formation.

To scatter earnest and idealistic young men throughout the diocese so that each receives his share of the frustrations contained within the system can only produce a uniform mediocrity. Episcopal imperatives will continue to be ignored. The foundations of religious orders in every age of need indicate a consistent pattern of movement away from established structures, to remain firmly within the Church. This must happen to avoid a mass movement out of the Church. I am in no way interested in sitting at table where a bell summons a housekeeper, where an interview room is furnished so uncomfortably that all business (mostly paper work) is expedited as soon as possible (but the rest of the house is lavishly furnished).

Alongside the clerical world, there is the world of the artists and the intellectuals and countless other people in this city who, to the last person, feel alienated from the ethos of this Archdiocese. I yearn to be a member of a community which would be a liturgical centre for these people. Can it honestly be said that the Church in Sydney indicates that literature and the arts are important to it, as the Vatican Council says they are? I know a large number of people who are nauseated and disgusted by the insecure and anti-cultural attitudes exemplified by a large proportion of the clerical body, creative people whom the Vatican Council says the Church should be attracting to herself. They consistently tell of a negative reaction from men in authority: safe, colourless, authoritarian, afraid of life and jealous of those who live it.

One of the indications of this failure in appropriate 'formation' is the reaction of the large number of young men who have left the seminary in recent times. I know literally dozens of these men, and know well the depth of youthful love and generosity they had for the Church. I know too the depth of anguish they have experienced when their motives were consistently mistrusted, their visionary ideals frustrated, and the intense hurt which they felt when they were finally told that the Church had no use for them at all.

I can only say that I stand fairly and squarely with these young men. I feel an undivided sense of unity with them, and I trust them. Therefore it would be both illogical and dishonest of me not to admit that, if these men are not wanted in the priesthood here, then I am not wanted either. One of the final factors in determining my present position is that, one by one, the altar boys and students whom I have come to know and love as they face priesthood, have almost all been rejected, or have left with great regret.

There comes a limit to what one can stand in this regard. How now can I summon the enthusiasm to encourage vocations to the diocesan priesthood here?

It seems that our seminary is producing pro rata more atheists and agnostics than any other tertiary institution. It is idle to suggest that the confusion of faith which so many of these men end up in is only an indication that they were not fit candidates in the first place. Until there are priests in the seminary who carry no vestige of external authority, who can act thereby simply as priests and receive the students' trust, the formation will be defective; further tragedies must result.

The main point that I was making in the letter to Gilroy was to do with the disease of clericalism. The position I took up then, I would with much more urgency take up today. I believe that the mass exodus from the Church, which has taken on stampede proportions, has been in essence claustrophobic. And I would offer the advice of Alice Walker:

> While love is unfashionable
> let us live
> unfashionably
>
> Let us be poor
> in all but truth and courage
>
> While love is dangerous
> Let us gather blossoms
> under fire

Looking back now through an incubation period of nearly twenty-eight years, I am deeply convinced that one of the inevitable side-effects has been the rash of clerical paedophiles, the news of each case exploding as regularly and as frequently as a time bomb. Psychologists insist that paedophilia is a phenomenon of psychosexual developmental arrest. It is not necessarily tied to an institutional factor but for religious and clerics there is a social and gendered political context. When you look at the ingredients that make up the male-dominated clericalised world — the drawing off from family at a young age, during a critical phase of sexual development, for entry into a male-dominated world where power, control and privileged secrecy are the norm, you certainly have the right climate for the phenomenon to show itself. In that infantile world, where grown men remain little boys, psychosexual development, and indeed other important emotional areas of human adult maturity, were put on hold. There still remain many men trapped in a clericalised lock, impeding them from facing, as an adult, not only the demands of mature sexuality but of equal importance the adult demands of critical social justice issues facing the modern Church. The concern of the real Church, as opposed to the fantasy Church, should be for the formation of psychosexually mature adults. Sexual maturity does not take account of sexual orientation, whether activated or not, but should be deeply concerned about sexual social responsibility.

Bruce Dawe, in his poem 'At Mass for Peter Phelan' put his finger right on it in that same year of 1969:

Snap frozen in some seminary, the Word,
secured
against the ubiquitous shock of honest air
or breath,
rots as it thaws

The seminary system was indeed designed to keep us in short pants forever; and there are many bishops to this day who can relate to their priests only in the schoolmaster-pupil relationship mould. There in that closed-circuit world, the language used is private, encumbered by deep denial mechanisms, miserably prosaic (while at the moment undergoing in secret a desperate loss of morale). Still there are any number of clerics who have been seduced into that club by delicious enticements and clerical rewards, and a subtle warranty against growing pains! They live in a theological climate characterised by an unspeakable lack of energy, profound prosaicism, offering a faded, dog-eared image of *ecclesia pro seipsa* — a Church for its own sake.

In the words of Vincent Buckley:

> Their noisy dying world
> Deafens them like the last lapse of blood.
> Corpses which, in other days,
> Would have greened their crops
> Block the city's drains.
> Their public speeches dwell on private morals,
> Neither hating or approving evils.
> Surprised in attitudes of prayer
> They struggle to remember which they chose,
> a scorched earth policy or
> The laying-on of hands.

In the Veech Lecture of 1994, Morris West expressed the impassioned hope that the Church will return to a true fidelity to her founder — 'the only answer is a continuous dispensation of love and the tolerances of love'.

Part Two: Redfern — 'A terrible beauty is born'

AND SO JUST THREE of us arrived here twenty-five years
ago out of the original fifteen who had by then dispersed: John Butcher, Fergus Breslan and myself. In
some ways we were the ragged remnants who straggled
in from the mountains after a long guerrilla war —
three links in a fifteen link chain, sad that most of our
friends had dropped out of the priesthood, frustrated.

But now the new Cardinal Freeman was offering us
Redfern. It was the end of a chapter of struggle and the
beginning of a totally uncharted course. Sure enough,
there was the redoubtable foot-bell under the dining
room table to summon a panting, frazzled housekeeper
who left immediately. Auntie Helen Waters was our first
visitor, an unforgettable Aboriginal woman, who came
timidly requesting some food and stayed for several
years. She remains in death for me a symbol of the love
affair I have had with Aboriginal people as a whole ever
since. It was in the days when there were no Aboriginal
hostels, no Aboriginal housing of any kind, and the numbers quickly built up to about a hundred on cold wet
nights. Today I am glad and somewhat proud to say that
in those twenty-five years I have never called the police,
even to the stickiest and most dangerous situations. For
what young athletic drunken Koori wanting to pick a
fight was not reduced to a respectful meekness before
the commanding Herculean figure, with rippling mus-
cles, of the twenty-eight-year-old Bob Bellear?

For most of those years, Mum Shirl was at the helm.
No-one was ever quite sure that she did not carry in her

handbag those two revolvers; but I did often see the handbag itself being wielded as a very efficient retaliatory weapon. The Police Force itself was and remains a major problem for Aboriginal people. Things have not perceptively changed. Aborigines are seventeen times more likely to be arrested than other Australians. The incarceration of Aborigines increased by 61 per cent between 1988 and 1995. Aborigines are nearly seventeen times more likely to die in jail than non-Aborigines.

We as a parish in March 1992 wrote the following letter to several newspapers:

> Let us not mistake the reality of what is now being revealed regarding the manners of our Police Force. Give it its proper name — institutional racism, the very same in essence and potential as that which brought about the extermination of six million Jews.
>
> In this the fiftieth anniversary year of the Holocaust, let us honestly recognise elements here which are genetically related. What we have here is not just a set of attitudes faithfully reflecting those of society at large. Beyond that, we have a predominantly male system with a force capacity far exceeding the sum total of its members, with long-standing traditions geared to protect and perpetuate themselves. It is a closed system with its own private language and has the power to initiate and control members' attitudes. It jealously contains a smelting process whereby existing poisons are distilled and transformed exponentially into more virulent and lethal forms. Even now the ever-enduring and unanimous registration of pain by the Aboriginal people is being 'set in context' by the blithering 'only a joke' theory of Tony Day (Police Spokesman).

Here there are haunting resonances of Australian massacres of black men, women and children in the name of jolly white sports. Aboriginal people know from the sly wink and the cupped hand-over-mouth that real danger lies ahead. These are matters not being acknowledged or addressed by superficial staff adjustments or the consigning of an apologetic letter. We are each irresponsible, not just for our individual attitudes of race, but for our failure to eradicate a brutality and blinding virus in the system they euphemistically call 'The Force'.

I tell you that this is a savage moment in the history of Australia, and I feel obliged to mark it. Our young Aboriginal people at this moment are carrying a humanly impossible burden laid on them by white society. The problem is not that we white people are unaware of this. The facts are overwhelmingly sufficient as they come to us through the media.

The problem is rather to be found in the way we manage the facts so clearly presented to us. It is not a question of more information. It is really a question of understanding. The word 'understanding' is, I think, what Aborigines themselves use to pin-point the almost despairing problem they have with us whites. We simply don't understand. We don't know them, we don't understand them. Yet they remain in a strategic position which has allowed them to observe us with remarkable accuracy. They know us well and often make the crucial observation that, not only do we not understand them, but we don't understand ourselves. We desperately need a new way of looking at ourselves so that we might come to recognise that we ourselves are in need of liberation and that our own liberation ultimately is bound up with theirs.

Over recent years I have been performing or attending the funeral of young Aboriginal persons frequently. Some of them appear to have suicided. It forces me to reflect on some of the differences between Aboriginal and non-Aboriginal Australians. The pride and pain of their race is transmitted directly to them. The pride and pain of their race is being held almost in a sacred trust, but always unfiltered and undiluted. Nothing is blocked out. It is humanly unbearable to hold that sort of fire in one's heart. Without promise, they can only lose all hope.

We white people, on the other hand, are ordinarily well equipped with the defence mechanisms of denial. Selective hearing of truths is an understandable, even necessary, psychological device for use in the face of bitter realities, particularly basic human survival. One would like to think that Aborigines could resort to such safety devices when it is they who are fighting to live at the harsh edge of survival. Yet it seems one of those cruel ironies that they are the ones who do not possess any alleviating mechanism for their pain. In contrast, we whites tend to keep safe control of our personal environment; we exercise reserve powers of manoeuvrability. As things get tough, we can move to safer ground. And whereas we can do this to keep on top, they have a desperate need just to keep afloat.

There is yet another depth to the dismal irony. By poison and starvation they have so often been deprived of the physical means of survival. In individual cases at least, they are now deprived of the psychological means of continuing to live. And this only points out more sharply the miracle of their survival as a race. The individual deaths can be truly seen as a protest of the race itself. What we are failing to recognise in ourselves is that what we seem to perceive as safer ground turns out to be our tomb. We bury ourselves under our denials as we blind ourselves to the inner spirit of other human beings. That also is a kind of suicide.

Throughout forty-three years of priestly ministry, I have had much to do with cases of suicide, where it is a common thing for the person to leave an explanatory note. The horrible thought has now come to me, as I look back on my experience with so many Aboriginal suicides, that not one of them left such a note. They felt no need to leave a note, because they knew that their loved ones would understand. They felt it was no use in leaving any message for the rest of us, because we would not understand. It is surely a grim and silent sign of the tragic sufferings of their race.

As Paul Keating said in his memorable speech at Redfern Park on December 10, 1992:

> We took the traditional lands and smashed the traditional way of life. We brought the diseases, the alcohol. We committed the murders. We took the children from their mothers. We practised discrimination and exclusion. It was our ignorance and our prejudice and our failure to imagine these things being done to us. With some noble exceptions, we failed to make the most basic human response and

enter into their hearts and minds. We failed to ask 'How would I feel if this were done to me'. As a consequence, we failed to see that what we were doing degraded all of us.

As I stood there in the open-air gathering in Redfern Park in that gala, summery atmosphere, I saw what I had never yet seen in all my years — the tears welling up in the eyes of countless Aborigines who had believed that they would never hear a prime minister of Australia say that.

But look what has happened with a change of government since then — and in so short a time! We can ignore Pauline Hanson but when Prime Minister Howard and Minister for Aboriginal Affairs Herron can each be capable of uttering such a collection of gauche, insensitive, uneducated and plainly insulting remarks about Aboriginal people we must protest. It is possible for a white person to hold respect and credibility in the eyes of Aboriginal people; witness Nugget Coombs. Measuring them against his stature, these two forlorn, pathetic figures get no marks at all, not even for trying. Why should the Aboriginal people be required to tolerate this empty posturing, this clumsy pretence, this masquerade of solutions pulled arbitrarily from the air, when they themselves were not consulted? I refer in particular to Howard pillorying the so-called black armband view of history, evading the admission of shame, and Herron calling in the army to provide Aboriginal housing as if that were a new idea.

For us whites, reconciliation starts not with guilt but with the acknowledgement of the truth. Unspeakable atrocities were perpetrated. Guilt is a wasted emotion; it cannot be passed down, for Christ has taken guilt away. Guilt is unproductive, indeed harmful, but shame is another matter. We do share the shame. Whether our ancestors came on the First Fleet or we are new migrants who came on the last plane, we all share the shame. We must all remember that not one of these good things which we non-Aboriginal Australians enjoy today — benefits which are the envy of the world, which seem to sparkle the more in the Australian sunlight — not one of these good things has been attained without the wrenching distress and grieving, starvation and dying of Aboriginal people in the past.

There was denial and fantasy and there was white self-delusion in Henry Lawson's lines in 1891:

> They needn't say the fault is ours
> If blood should stain the wattle

The real truth should be reflected in our shame that the golden Australian wattle had already been drenched in blood. Unacknowledged truth has a way of setting iron bands on the soul. The paralysis chokes. And unacknowledged truth also has one of those perverse ways of imposing a sadness and a false guilt on the victim's heart. As a child can carry the hounding guilt of a father's abusive betrayal of trust, so many Aboriginal people can carry a false internalised image of themselves, one that the perpetrating coloniser has created for them. It is true that shame brings its own embarrassing confusion. But there is a single exit from that confusion.

The way out lies in letting go of the grand, deluding myth, so pervasive in the white psyche as to cause us to brandish hollow sounds of what we call 'Australian pride', so invasive of the Black world as to assure them that the invasion is still going on.

When Aborigines notice that we non-Aborigines are beginning to see that our liberation is bound up with theirs, the healing power of truth will begin to set each of us free:

> You murdered me with rope, with gun,
> The massacre my enclave,
> You buried me deep on McLarty's run
> Flung into a common grave.
> You propped me up with Christ, red tape,
> Tobacco, grog and fears,
> Then disease and lordly rape
> Through the brutish years.
> Now you primly say you're justified,
> And sing of a nation's glory,
> But I think of a people crucified —
> The real Australian story.
>
> JACK DAVIS, *Aboriginal Australia*

There have been two grotesque excrescences on the life of the Church: the emergence of the prince-bishop and the theological concept of excommunication. They represent, in my view, the greatest derailments in the history of the Christian Church. Scripture scholars are concurring that it was the undoubted practice of Christ to enjoy table-fellowship with the reprobates, the sinned-against, the nobodies, those deemed socially undesirable. It is also becoming clear that this sort of table-fellowship was the very model adopted by the early Church community to give liturgical expression to the Eucharist. The early Church built the invitation of Jesus to the betraying Judas into all the Gospel Eucharistic accounts. That image was used as the template to impress on the Eucharistic community the dangerous memory of Jesus. It has also become clear that Paul's frown on those who receive the body of the Lord unworthily refers to the rich who set up their own table ignoring the poor. We are beginning to understand that the Eucharist was designed for the broken, sinful ones of this world. We are beginning to hear the hoarse voice of Christ shouting over the glum control-mongers. 'Come to me all you who labour and are overburdened and I will give you rest.' It is perhaps a classic ultimate irony that the heavy exclusionists are finding that this rediscovered piece of Pauline theology is ricocheting back on their own heads.

I want to point to four groups whom the clerical world jealously excludes from its liturgy, its ministry and from its administrative structure. Their absence represents a massive lacuna in the life of any faith community which needs that wealth of creative vision and spiritual luminosity found among them.

(1) The poor who, as such, possess the lens which allows them to see God most clearly. That capacity to point to God is the unique contribution the poor have to offer the wider Church. We need to turn up the volume of the distant melody, the lives of the poor, so long hidden.

Was God bored, as men are with the poor?
Christ Lord hears in the voices of the meanly poor
Homeric utterances, poetry sweeping through.

PATRICK KAVANAGH, *Lough Derg*

The poor should be given first place in consultancy in the functioning of a living Church. At this very late hour, it is to the discredit of the Australian Church in those dioceses where Aborigines are not selected as prime consultants in policy making, and puts into question the Conference on Poverty that is being held in Sydney this very weekend [23–24 November 1996].

(2) Women in the Church, the religious who for too long have been regarded as 'consecrated' coolies, or women in general who are now unwilling to accept imposed servitude. Women too should be given a place of primacy in the functioning of a living Church. When women do take their rightful place in the Church, it will mean a resetting of the imbalance created by male clerics who have taken the stage since the sixth century AD, so eclipsing the full implications of the glorified humanity of Christ.

(3) Homosexual men and women who were assured by the clerics as infants that they were full members of the Church and children of God. Later they were made to feel that their Baptism was like an inoculation that didn't take, so that they must go back behind the line. Now they are beginning to claim with rightful confidence that it is the nature of this flower not to wither but to bloom. Homosexual men and women too should be given a place of primacy

in the functioning of a living Church — simply, unapologetically — because the Gospel directs us to prioritise and enfranchise the sinned against.

(4) All the clerical and religious dropouts, the kind of women featured in the 'Brides of Christ' mini-series and the hundreds of seminarians and brothers and priests like them: you who gave your lives so whole-heartedly to the Church. It was you who had the foresight to see the storm clouds forming and the thick fog rolling in. It was you who had the imagi-nation to suggest ways of coping with the coming storm and were willing to pledge your young lives to act accordingly with courage. And when you were made to drop out, the clericalists desperately tried to cover over the holes, to pretend that you never existed in the first place. From Morris West to Tom Keneally, to Brian Crittenden to Julian Miller, to Pat Dodson to Michael Crosby, to Kevin and Margaret Walsh, to Dick Buckhorn, Barry Bell, Brian McMahon and Grantley Farqueson, to Graham English and Erin White, to Bernice Moore to Narelle Lickiss and Germaine Hearst, to John Butcher, Terry Fox, Peter and Eileen Willis, Steve and Paula Hyndes, Chris Geraghty, Val and Jo Rogers — the list could go on and on. I want to say, to all you brave and wonderful drop-outs so beloved to me, a simple word of admiration and thanks.

I want today to salute all you Koories each and every one, alive, but also the dead, for your profound indomitability of Spirit. I once, in a private conversation, expressed to Garry Foley my wide-eyed admiration of the way Koories handle life, the continuous unfolding of the story of inner strength in weakness. His eyes glistened and he said with immense Aboriginal pride: "Yes, mate, it's facing adversity that does it".

In the glory of that deep human mystery, for those with eyes to see it, "a terrible beauty is born".

And so, today, I can offer the one lesson gained through the enduring years, the poet Keats' own:

> I am certain of nothing but the holiness
> of the heart's affections, and the truth
> of the imagination.
>
> *Letter to Bailey*, November 22, 1817

Dom Helder Camara was advised in his youth to mistrust imagination as it could compromise his priesthood: 'But' he said, 'I am not afraid of imagination. Imagination is like a sister, a sister that can help us immensely. It helps me to see things, to understand creation, to understand God.'

Our Church will remain dysfunctional while ever it remains lop-sided. When the people of imagination take up their rightful voice, then it will be revealing fidelity to a true incarnational focus. A spirit of imagination and adventure will be required in the future for the paradigm shift to centre our theology on a wholesome environment for the whole of humanity. It will have entered into that deeper ecumenism calling us all to denounce as perfidious those fatal technologies poised to 'pull out the very soil from under the feet of humanity' (Ivan Illich).

In the words of Ezra Pound:

Go, my songs, to the lonely and the unsatisfied,
Go also to the nerve-wracked, go to the enslaved-by-
convention,

…

Go as a great wave of cool water,
Bear my contempt of oppressors.

Speak against unconscious oppression,
Speak against the tyranny of the unimaginative,
Speak against bonds.

Endnotes

About the cover

1. 'Sequence' in *A Vision of Ceremony*, Angus and Robertson, Sydney, 1956, p10.
2. *The Return of the Prodigal Son,* in the Hermitage Museum, St Petersburg.

Who Is Worthy?

1. *Bulletin,* 27 April, 1999, p.29.
2. Bishop George Pell, 'Seminar on the Sociology of Culture', La Trobe University, 12 May 1988.
3. Archbishop George Pell, 'Catholicism in the architecture of freedom', Inaugural Acton Lecture, Sydney, 1999.
4. John Henry Newman, *Certain Difficulties Felt by Anglicans in Catholic Teaching,* Volume Two, Longmans Green, London,1885, pp.248–249.
5. '*Gaudium et Spes:* Pastoral Constitution on the Church in the Modern World', 7 December 1965, in Walter Abbot (ed.), *Documents of the Second Vatican Council,* Geoffrey Chapman, London, 1966, pp.213–214.

6. See *Cathechism of the Catholic Church*, St Paul's Libreria Editrice Vaticana, 1994, Pars.1778–1796.

7. Pope John Paul II, Address, World Day of Peace 1999.

8. Edmund Campion, *John Henry Newman, Letter to Alfred Plummer*, Dove Communications, Melbourne, 1980, p.107.

9. Karl Rahner and Herbert Vorgrimler, *Concise Theological Dictionary*, Burns and Oates, London, 1965, p.347.

10. Josef Jungmann SJ, *Public Worship Challoner*, London, 1957, p.77.

11. Tertullian, *Codex Agobardinus*, Bibliotheque Nationale, Paris.

12. John Henry Newman, *Callista: A Tale of the Third Century*, Longmans Green, New York, 1893.

13. I also recommend *Unveiling Empire, Reading Revelation Then and Now* by Anthony Gwyther and Wes Howard Brook, Orbis, New York, 1999.

14. 'In idolatry you are to see adultery and fornication. Every servant of false gods commits against the truth, since all falsehood is adulteration', Tertullian, *Codex Agobardinus*.

15. The Canons of St Hippolytus, in Gregory Dix (ed.), *The Apostolic Tradition*, SPCK, London, 1937.

16. Gerard Manley Hopkins, *Early Poems*, No. 57, Oxford University Press, London, 1948, p.95.

17. Karl Adam, *Christ Our Brother*, Collier Books, New York, 1962, p.34.

18. St John Chrysostom, Homily VII in *Hebrews 9*, Nicene and Post-Nicene Fathers, Series 1, Volume xiv.

19. Godfrey Diekmann OSB, *Come Let Us Worship*, Helicon Press, 1961, p.32.

20. Ute Ranke-Heinemann, *Eunuchs for the Kingdom of Heaven*, Penguin 1990; Chapters vi, x and xxi.

21. While I have not been able to identify the source of this quotation, the tone is decidedly Mertonesque. The truth of the theological point stands.

22. John Henry Newman, 'Christian Sympathy', *Parochial and Plain Sermons*, Volume Five, Rivingtons, 1870, p.127.

23. Francis Webb, 'Song of Hunger', *Cap and Bells: the Poetry of Francis Webb*, Angus and Robertson, Sydney, 1991, p.208.

24. Gerard Manley Hopkins, *Early Poems*, No. 77, Oxford University Press, London, 1948, p.127.

25. Thomas Merton, *Raids on the Unspeakable*, New Directions, New York, 1966, pp.32–33.

26. L. Durrwell CSsR, *La Resurrection de Jesus*, Xavier Mappus, Paris, 1963.

27 *Bulletin*, 27 April 1999, p.29.

28 *Parochial and Plain Sermons*, 'Christian Sympathy', Volume V, p.127

29 'Ode on the Science of Human Cruelty' in Bruce Dawe, *This Side of Silence: Poems 1987–1990*, Longman Cheshire, p.65.

30 Francis Webb, 'Homosexual', *Cap and Bells: the Poetry of Francis Webb*, Angus and Robertson, Sydney, 1991, pp.220–222.

31 Willem Bekkers, *God's People on the Way*, Burns and Oates, London, 1966, pp.129,123.

32 Gerard Manley Hopkins, *Early Poems*, No. 77, Oxford University Press, London, 1948, p.95.

33 Robert McAfee Brown, *Theology in a New Key*, The Westminster Press, 1978, pp.76–77.

34 Naomi Burton Stone and Patrick Hart (eds), *Love and Living: Thomas Merton*, Harcourt Brace Jovanavich, New York, 1979, pp.118–119.

35 Kart Rahner SJ, *Schriften zur Theologie*, 13, 1978.

36 Brendan Lovett, *It's Not Over Yet*, Claretian Publications, Quezon City, 1990, p.27 and p.40.

37 'Letter from the Mothers to the Pope in response to his support for Pinochet' (http://www.madres.org/ingles/index.html).

38 *Australian*, 24 May 1999.

39 *Bulletin*, 27 April 1999, p.29.

40 Bernard Häring, *Priesthood imperilled*, Triumph Books, Missouri, 1995, p.56.

41 Bernard Häring, 'Building a creative conscience: resisting moral rigor mortis', *Commonweal*, 11 August 1989.

42 *'Gaudium et Spes'*, 16 in Abbot, *Documents of the Second Vatican Council*, Geoffrey Chapman, London, 1966, p.214.

43 Edmund Campion, *John Henry Newman*, Dove Communications, Melbourne, 1980, p.105.

44 John Henry Newman in John Coulslon (ed.) *On Consulting the Faithful in Matters of Doctrine*, Geoffrey Chapman, London, 1961, p.77.

45 ibid. p.103.

46 ibid. p.110.

47 ibid. p.103.

48 'Freedom on the Wallaby', *A Campfire Yarn: Henry Lawson, Complete Works 1885–1900*, Lansdowne Press, 1988, p.146.

49 Michael Christie, 'Aboriginal literacy and power: an historical case study', *Australian Journal of Adult and Community Education*, Vol. 30, No.2, July 1990.

50 Lord Acton, *Essays on Freedom and Power, Acton-Creighton Correspondence*, Thames and Hudson, London, 1956.

51 Josef Altholz, *The Liberal Catholic Movement in England*, Burns and Oates, London, 1968, p.242.

52 Letters in *Goulburn Argus*, 1865.

53 John Paul II, Alice Springs, 29 November 1986.

54 John Hosie, *Challenge*, Allen and Unwin, Sydney, 1987.

55 'Polding to Heptonstall', Downside Archives MS 248, Australian National Library.

56. Kathie Cochrane, *Oodgeroo*, Queensland University Press, 1994.

57 'Davis to Heptonstall', Downside Archives MS 248, Australian National Library.

58 *Letters of John Bede Polding OSB to Abbot PF Casaretto OSB*, Volume 2, Fast Books, Sydney, 1996, p.151.

59 Kevin Livingstone, 'Voices in the wilderness: apologists for the Aborigines in the past', *Australasian Catholic Record*, April, 1979, pp.176–191.

60 ibid.

61 Patrick Dodson 'Daniel Mannix Memorial Lecture', Melbourne University, 4 September 1996, published in *Eureka Street*, October 1996.

62 Address to Aborigines by Paul VI at the Apostolic Delegation in Sydney, 2 December 1970.

63 John Paul II, Alice Springs, 29 November 1986.

64 *Catholic Weekly*, 13 June 1999.

65 John Henry Newman, *Essay on the Development of Christian Doctrine*, Pickering & Co, London, 1881, p.40.

66 Kevin Gilbert (ed.), *Inside Black Australia*, Penguin, Ringwood, 1988, p.58.

67 *Catholic Weekly*, 13 June 1999.

68 Eamon Duffy, *Saints and Sinners: The History of the Popes*, Yale University Press, 1997, p. 251.

69 Unpublished Address, 1979. See also: *The Church is All Of You: the Thoughts of Archbishop Oscar Romero*, compiled and translated by James R. Brockman SJ, Winston Press, Minnesota, USA, 1984, p.96.

Welcome to Pluto Press Australia

Pluto Press

We specialise in titles that place readers at the cutting edge of new ideas, research, new ways of reading, seeing and communicating.

Our specialty subjects include:

media and communication • gender • political economy • cultural studies • pop • politics • history • fine arts and film • the law • international relations • multiculturalism and identity • labour movement and the left • welfare studies • social work • urban and regional studies • activism • digital culture • Australian literature • ethics • environment

Visit our Website

media.socialchange.net.au/pluto

Our new web site includes a complete mail order catalogue and a new online magazine showcasing critical essays, interviews, chapter excerpts, conferences and launches.

• buy books at a discount • pitch us a publishing project • join friends of Pluto • join a discussion • find a conference speaker • read sample chapters • shop for course readings • author profiles

Recent Titles

Open Australia by Lindsay Tanner

White Nation, *The myth of white supremacy in a multicultural society* by Ghassan Hage

Playing the Man, *New approaches to masculinity* Edited by Katherine Biber, Tom Sear and Dave Trudinger

Goodbye Normal Gene, *Confronting the genetic revolution* Edited by Gabrielle O'Sullivan, Evelyn Sharman and Stephanie Short

Bizarrism, *Strange lives, cults, celebrated lunacy* by Chris Mikul

New Voices for Social Democracy, *Labor Essays 1999-2000* Edited by Dennis Glover and Glenn Patmore

Celebrities, Culture and Cyberspace, *The light on the hill in a postmodern world* by McKenzie Wark

Running on Empty, *'Modernising' the British and Australian labour parties* by Andrew Scott

Pluto Press Australia Locked Bag 199, Annandale NSW 2038
Website: media.socialchange.net.au/pluto
Ph: 61 2 95193299 • Fax: 95198940
Email: tmoore@socialchange.net.au

SO-CAD-972

Photoshop Elements 9

FOR WINDOWS

JEFF CARLSON

OFFICIALLY
WITHDRAWN

PALATINE PUBLIC LIBRARY DISTRICT
700 N. NORTH COURT
PALATINE, ILLINOIS 60067-8159

 Peachpit Press

Visual QuickStart Guide

Photoshop Elements 9 for Windows

Jeff Carlson

Peachpit Press
1249 Eighth Street
Berkeley, CA 94710
510/524-2178
510/524-2221 (fax)

Find us on the Web at: www.peachpit.com
To report errors, please send a note to errata@peachpit.com
Peachpit Press is a division of Pearson Education.

Copyright © 2011 by Jeff Carlson

Project Editor: Susan Rimerman
Production Editor: Myrna Vladic
Copyeditor: Liane Thomas
Indexer: Karin Arrigoni
Composition: Jeff Carlson
Cover Design: Peachpit Press
Interior Design: Peachpit Press

Notice of Rights

All rights reserved. No part of this book may be reproduced or transmitted in any form by any means, electronic, mechanical, photocopying, recording, or otherwise, without the prior written permission of the publisher. For information on getting permission for reprints and excerpts, contact: permissions@peachpit.com.

Notice of Liability

The information in this book is distributed on an "As Is" basis, without warranty. While every precaution has been taken in the preparation of the book, neither the author nor Peachpit shall have any liability to any person or entity with respect to any loss or damage caused or alleged to be caused directly or indirectly by the instructions contained in this book or by the computer software and hardware products described in it.

Trademarks

Visual QuickStart Guide is a trademark of Peachpit Press, a division of Pearson Education. Adobe, Photoshop, and Elements are registered trademarks of Adobe Systems Incorporated in the United States and/or other countries. All other trademarks are the property of their respective owners.

Many of the designations used by manufacturers and sellers to distinguish their products are claimed as trademarks. Where those designations appear in this book, and Peachpit was aware of a trademark claim, the designations appear as requested by the owner of the trademark. All other product names and services identified throughout this book are used in editorial fashion only and for the benefit of such companies with no intention of infringement of the trademark. No such use, or the use of any trade name, is intended to convey endorsement or other affiliation with this book.

ISBN-13:   978-0-321-74131-8
ISBN-10:   0-321-74131-5
9 8 7 6 5 4 3 2 1

Printed and bound in the United States of America

Dedication:

For Emma V.

And for Eliana, who waited.

Special Thanks to:

For their hard work and positive attitudes, my gratitude goes out to Susan Rimerman, Liane Thomas, Karin Arrigoni, Myrna Vladic, and Lisa Brazieal. They've been a great team on this edition of the book.

I'm also the grateful beneficiary of invaluable production help from Lisa Fridsma, Owen Wolfson, and Kim Carlson.

Thank you to Roman Skuratovskiy and Ginny Sidell at Edelman, and Roma Dhall and Bob Gager at Adobe for their assistance in providing the software and information I needed.

The content in these pages also owes a great debt to Glenn Fleishman, Agen G. N. Schmitz, Jeff Tolbert, and Laurence Chen, who assisted with an earlier edition just before the birth of my daughter.

Thanks to my officemates Kim Ricketts and Jenny Gialenes for camaraderie and support.

I also want to thank Craig Hoeschen for providing great material to work with: the editions prior to version 5.

My gratitude also extends to Parie Hines, Cindy Dorsey, Steve Horn, Jill Thompson, and Scott and Lisa Johnson for their permissions to use photos of their adorable kids.

Lastly, my appreciation and love to Kim and Ellie for making me a happy man.

Contents at a Glance

Table of Contents

Introduction

Welcome to Photoshop Elements, Adobe's powerful, easy-to-use, image-editing software. Photoshop Elements gives hobbyists, as well as professional photographers and artists, many of the same tools and features found in Adobe Photoshop (long the industry standard), but packaged in a more accessible, intuitive workspace.

Photoshop Elements' friendly user interface, combined with its bargain-basement price, has made it an instant hit with the new wave of amateur digital photographers lured by the recent proliferation of sophisticated, low-cost digital cameras.

Photoshop Elements makes it easy to retouch your digital photos; apply special effects, filters, and styles; prepare images for the Web; and even create wide-screen panoramas from a series of individual photos. And Photoshop Elements provides several features geared specifically to the beginning user. Of particular note are the Quick and Guided photo editing controls that make complex image corrections easy to apply.

Photoshop Elements 9 provides new tools and enhancements that not only help stretch the bounds of your creativity, but also help to make your quick photo corrections and creative retouching even simpler and more fun than before.

In the next few pages, I'll cover some of Photoshop Elements' key features (both old and new) and share a few thoughts to help you get the most from this book. Then you can be on your way to mastering Photoshop Elements' simple, fun, and sophisticated image-editing tools.

What's new in version 9

For most of its existence, Elements has been "Photoshop Light," a scaled-back version of Adobe's image-editing behemoth. Over time, Adobe has retooled Elements to be a powerful asset for digital photographers.

Photoshop Elements 9 continues Adobe's quest to make an image editing application that responds to people's real-world needs. There's a lot of power in being able to apply adjustment layers and clipping masks and filters, but that isn't always helpful when your goal, for example, is to just improve the exposure in a too-dark photo—and you don't have the time to learn all the science behind the tools. Here are a few standout items.

For touching up images, the biggest improvement is content-aware healing, the new default mode of using the Spot Healing Brush. Using technology borrowed from Photoshop CS5, the program is smarter about patching imperfections— it's so good, in fact, that you can use it to "paint out" objects, people, or other larger areas of a scene.

People familiar with Photoshop will appreciate that Elements now, at last, supports real layer masks. Although it's been possible to make clipping masks and even get a taste of layer masks by applying adjustment layers, version 9 now lets you mask anything you want in a layer, offering more control when compositing and editing multi-layer images.

If you've worked with Photoshop Elements in the past, you should feel right at home in version 9.

Personalizing Photoshop Elements

Because no two users work quite the same way, Photoshop Elements gives you the freedom to customize its tools and palettes to suit your own personal work habits, expertise, and aesthetic. You can create favorite sets of brush types, swatch libraries, and patterned fills, and you can set preferences for save options, transparency, ruler units, and grid color. Slightly more advanced options help you to set the ways the program manages memory, and the ways it works with your monitor and printer to display and print color.

Additionally, since it supports Adobe's plug-in file format, Photoshop Elements can be a constantly changing and evolving tool, as you add new plug-ins for everything from custom filter effects to digital camera image browsers.

Setting preferences

Preferences are settings that let you control and modify the way Photoshop Elements looks, works, and behaves. The Preferences dialog is divided into a series of windows, each one focusing on a specific aspect of the application: general display properties, file saving options, cursor display and behavior, transparency settings, rulers and units of measurement, grid appearance and behavior, cache levels for managing memory, display settings for the file browser, and more. You can change preferences at any time by choosing Preferences from the Edit menu.

How to Use This Book

This Visual QuickStart Guide, like others in the series, is a task-based reference. Each chapter focuses on a specific area of the application and presents it in a series of concise, illustrated steps. I encourage you to follow along using your own images. I believe the best way to learn is by doing, and this Visual QuickStart Guide is the perfect vehicle for that style of learning.

This book is meant to be a reference work, and although it's not expected that you'll read through it in sequence from front to back, I've made an attempt to order the chapters in a logical fashion.

The first chapter takes you on a tour of the work area and provides a foundation for the basics of importing photos and image editing. From there you dive into managing your photo library using the Organizer. Then you explore color, selections, layers, effects, painting, and typography, and move along to learn a variety of techniques for saving, printing, and sharing images, including special formatting options for distributing images over the Web.

This book is suitable for the beginner just starting in digital photography and image creation, as well as hobbyists, photo enthusiasts, intermediate-level photographers, illustrators, and designers.

Keyboard shortcuts

Many of the commands accessed from Photoshop Elements' menu bar have a keyboard equivalent (or shortcut) that appears beside each command name in the menu. Keyboard shortcuts are great time-savers and prevent you from having to constantly refocus your energy and attention as you jump from image window to menu bar and back again. When this book introduces a command, the keyboard shortcut is also listed. For example, the keyboard shortcut for the Copy command is displayed as Ctrl+C. You'll find a complete list of Photoshop Elements' keyboard shortcuts in the appendices.

1

The Basics

Before you start really working in Photoshop Elements, it's good to take a look around the work area to familiarize yourself with the program's tools and menus. The work area includes the document window, where you'll view your images, along with many of the tools, menus, and panels you'll use as you get better acquainted with the program.

In This Chapter

Understanding the Work Area

The Photoshop Elements work area is designed like a well-organized workbench, making it easy to find and use menus, panels, and tools.

The Welcome screen

When you first start Photoshop Elements, the Welcome screen automatically appears **A**. Click Organize to open the Adobe Elements 9 Organizer application, or click Edit to open the Adobe Photoshop Elements application. (You can bypass the Welcome screen by opening either of those apps by themselves.)

The Organizer and the Editor

Photoshop Elements is made up of two separate components: the Organizer and the Editor, which can be (and often are) open simultaneously. The conventions in this chapter primarily apply to the Editor; the Organizer's unique interface items are covered in Chapter 2.

TIP Click the Settings button at the upper-right corner of the Welcome screen to set how Elements starts up **B**.

TIP Click the Home icon in the Organizer or the Editor to return to the Welcome screen at any time **C**.

TIP If you have a Photoshop.com membership, go ahead and enter it at the Welcome screen—but it's not necessary at this point. I cover Photoshop.com integration later in this chapter.

A The Photoshop Elements Welcome screen provides a simple and fast way to start organizing and editing your images.

B Choose which parts of Photoshop Elements should launch at startup.

C The Home icon brings up the Welcome screen from anywhere within the program.

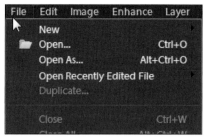

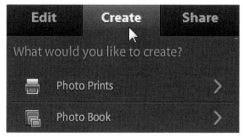

D The menu bar offers myriad drop-down menus, with commands you choose to help perform tasks.

E The options bar changes its display depending on the tool you select in the Tools panel.

F The Project Bin is a holding area where you can access all of your open images.

G Panels can be used from within the Panel Bin (as shown) or moved to your work area.

Menus, panels, and tools

The **menu bar** offers drop-down menus for performing common tasks, editing images, and organizing your work area. Each menu is organized by topic **D**.

The **options bar**, running above the work area, provides unique settings and options for each tool in the Tools panel. For instance, when you're using the Marquee selection tool, you can choose to add to or subtract from the current selection **E**.

The **Project Bin**, located at the bottom of the desktop, serves as a convenient holding area for all of your open images **F**. In addition to providing a visual reference for any open image files, the bin allows you to perform several basic editing functions. Click to select any photo thumbnail in the Project Bin, and right-click to display a pop-up menu. From the thumbnail menu you can get file information, minimize or close the file, duplicate it, and even rotate it in 90-degree increments.

The **Panel Bin** (also referred to as the **Task Pane** in the Organizer) groups common tasks and controls into the right edge of the window **G**. Clicking a heading displays the panels for editing, creating, and sharing. To temporarily hide this area and make more room for working, choose Window > Panel Bin.

When you're in the Full Edit interface, the Panel Bin contains the Effects and Layers panels, and any other panel you open (such as the Adjustments panel when you apply an adjustment layer).

You can also drag a panel's name to the main work area to display it as a floating panel. Panels can be grouped together or docked to one another, depending on your working and organizational styles (see "Working with Panels," later in this chapter).

The **Tools** panel may be the single most important component of the Editor's work area. It contains most of the tools you'll use for selecting, moving, cropping, retouching, and enhancing your images. The tools are arranged in the general order you'll be using them, with the most commonly used selection tools near the top, and the painting, drawing, and color correction tools toward the bottom.

The panel is docked on the left edge of the work area where the tools are displayed in a single, long column ⊕; if your screen doesn't accommodate all the buttons, the panel appears in a two-column format.

Tall or wide, the Tools panel can also become a floating panel: Drag the top of the panel away from the edge. Clicking the double-arrow button that appears switches between a one- or two-column layout.

Move (V)

Zoom (Z)

Hand (H)

Eyedropper (I)

Marquee (M)

Lasso (L)

Magic Wand (W)

Quick Selection Tool (A)

Type (T)

Crop (C)

Cookie Cutter (Q)

Straighten (P)

Red Eye Removal (Y)

Healing Brush (J)

Clone Stamp (S)

Eraser (E)

Brush (B)

Smart Brush (F)

Paint Bucket (K)

Gradient (G)

Shape (U)

Blur (R)

Sponge (O)

Default Colors (D)

Switch Colors (X)

Background Color

Foreground Color

⊕ The Tools panel contains the tools to edit your images.

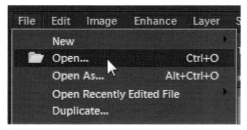

A Choose Open from the File menu to open an image file on disk.

B The Open dialog displays all files that match formats Elements understands.

TIP If several files are open, you can close them all at once by choosing **Close All** from the File menu or by pressing **Ctrl+Alt+W**.

Opening and Closing Files

Photoshop Elements provides several methods of opening photos, depending on whether you're working in the Organizer or the Editor. (If you need to import photos into the Organizer, see Chapter 2.)

To open a file in the Organizer:

- Select a thumbnail and choose Edit > Edit with Photoshop Elements; the image opens in the Editor. You can also right-click an image and choose the same item from the contextual menu.

- With a thumbnail selected, click the pop-up menu to the right of the Fix tab in the Task Pane and choose one of the edit options, such as Full Photo Edit.

To open a file in the Editor:

1. To find and open a file, choose Open from the File menu A, or press Ctrl+O. The Open dialog appears.

2. Browse to the folder that contains your images B.

3. To open the file you want, do one of the following:

   ▸ Double-click the file.

   ▸ Select the file and click the Open button.

   The image opens in its own document window.

To close a file in the Editor:

- Click the close button on the title bar for the active window.

- From the File menu, choose Close, or press Ctrl+W.

Saving Files

As you work on an image in the Editor, it's good practice to save the file to your hard drive regularly. When you save a file, you can choose from a number of file formats. (For detailed information on the formats, see Chapter 13, "Saving and Printing Images.")

If you're interested in posting your photos to the Web, you can choose the Save for Web option. Saving your images for the Web involves its own set of unique operations; these are covered in detail in Chapter 12, "Preparing Images for the Web."

To save a file:

From the File menu, choose Save, or press Ctrl+S.

To save a file in a new format or to a specific location:

1. From the File menu, choose Save As, or press Ctrl+Shift+S. The Save As dialog appears  .

2. Choose a destination for the file by browsing to a location.

3. In the Save As field, type a name for the file.

4. If you want to save the file in a different format, choose one from the Format drop-down menu.

   If you're not sure which format to use, choose either the native Photoshop format (PSD), which is the best all-purpose format, or the JPEG format, which works especially well with digital photos. When saving an image as a JPEG file, choose the highest quality setting possible (but be sure to review Chapter 13).

A The Save As dialog includes several options beyond just naming the new file.

Working with Version Sets

In the digital photography realm, the "negative" is the original image file captured by your camera. On the computer, you're working with those original files. So, for example, if you were to change a photo from color to grayscale and save it, then you've lost the color version forever.

To guard against that, Elements offers the ability to save the file in a version set when you perform a Save As operation. You're saving a new copy, but it's linked to the original image in the Organizer as a revision **B**; otherwise, the edited version would appear as a completely separate image. Click the expansion arrow icon to the right of the image to view or hide the version set.

B A version set tracks image edits.

Each image format has its own specific settings, such as those shown in this dialog for saving a JPEG file.

Choose how files are saved in Photoshop Elements' preferences.

5. If you want to be sure not to alter your original file, select the As a Copy option to save a duplicate. This selection protects your original file from changes as you edit the duplicate.

6. To include color profile information, make sure the Embed Color Profile box is selected. For more information on managing color in your images, see Chapter 7, "Changing and Adjusting Colors."

7. When you've finished entering your settings, click Save.

   Depending on the format you chose, you may be prompted to set other options, such as with JPEG files .

TIP Saving using the As a Copy option is a good idea if you're experimenting with various changes and want to ensure that you keep your original version intact. It's also handy if you want to save an image in more than one file format, which is useful if you want to save a high-quality copy for printing and keep a smaller-sized file to e-mail to friends.

TIP Photoshop Elements allows you to customize how files are saved. From the Edit menu, choose Preferences > Saving Files. In the Saving Files dialog you can control how file extensions are displayed, choose whether to include image previews with your saved files (image previews are small thumbnail images that appear in the Open dialog when you select a file), and specify under what circumstances you would like to be prompted with the Save As dialog .

Selecting Tools

The Tools panel contains all the tools you need for editing and creating your images. You can use them to make selections, paint, draw, and easily perform sophisticated photo retouching operations. To view information about a tool, rest the pointer over it until a tool tip appears showing the name and keyboard shortcut (if any) for that tool.

To use a tool, first select it from the Tools panel. Some tools hide additional tools, as indicated by a small triangle at the lower right of the tool icon **A**.

To select a tool from the Tools panel:

Click the tool's icon in the Tools panel.

When you move your pointer into the document window, the pointer changes appearance to reflect the tool you have selected **B**.

To select a hidden tool:

1. On any tool that displays a small triangle, either click and hold the mouse button, or right-click the tool icon. A menu of the hidden tools appears **C**.

2. Click to select the tool you want to use.

TIP For easier access to tools, just use keyboard shortcuts. You'll find them in tool tips, on the printed Quick Reference card included in the product box, and in the online help. For example, press T on your keyboard to activate the Type tool. (Note that when you press a letter to select a tool with a hidden tool group, Elements selects the tool from the group that was used most recently.)

TIP To cycle through hidden tools, repeatedly press the tool's shortcut key.

Other tools available

A A small triangle next to a tool icon indicates additional tools.

Lasso tool icon

B When the Lasso tool is selected, the mouse pointer changes to the Lasso tool icon.

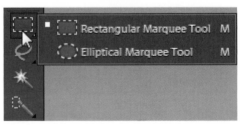

C Click and hold the mouse button or right-click to view the hidden tools.

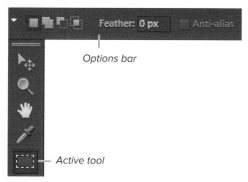

Options bar

Active tool

A Use the options bar to customize the tool you've selected, including selecting alternate tools.

Previous View/ Next View   *Rotate Image*

B The options bar in the Organizer contains commonly used tools.

Using the Options Bar

Think of the options bar as a natural extension of the Tools panel. After you select a tool, you can adjust its settings from the options bar. The buttons on the options bar change depending on the tool selected. If you're using the Brush tool, for example, you can use the options bar to select a brush size and opacity setting.

To use the options bar:

1. From the Tools panel, select a tool.

2. In the options bar, choose an available option for that tool **A**.

TIP In the Organizer, the options bar includes common tools such as Previous View and Next View, image rotation buttons, a slider for setting the thumbnail size, and others **B**.

Working with Panels

Although the Editor opens with just three panels displayed in its Panel Bin, a total of 10 panels are available from the Window menu. Each panel can be used entirely on its own or can be combined with other panels to help organize and streamline your workflow. All the panels feature handy drop-down menus that allow you to perform additional tasks or customize panel options.

A From the Window menu, show or hide any panel.

To display a panel:

From the Window menu, choose any panel to display it in your work area **A**.

To move a panel out of the Panel Bin:

1. Click the tab of the panel that you want to move from the Panel Bin.

2. Drag the tab until the panel is in the desired location in your work area **B**.

   The panel is now a floating panel on the desktop.

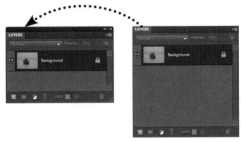

B To move a panel from the bin, drag the tab outside the bin; it becomes a stand-alone panel.

To use panel menus:

Click the More menu in the upper-right corner of any panel **C**.

To close a panel:

Do one of the following:

- From the Window menu, choose any open panel; open panels are indicated by a check mark.

- If the panel is open in your work area (outside the Panel Bin), click the close box on the panel title bar.

- If the panel is inside the Panel Bin, click the More menu and choose Close.

More menu   *Close box*

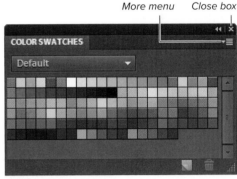

C The More menu includes more actions. To close a panel, click the close icon on the title bar.

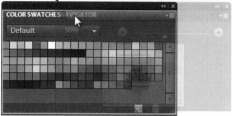

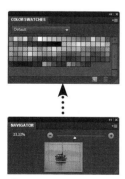

D Drag a panel tab into another open panel (top) to form a panel group (bottom).

E Docking one panel below another helps avoid clutter in your work area.

To return a panel to the Panel Bin:

Click the panel tab and drag the panel back into the Panel Bin. A horizontal blue line appears in the bin to indicate where the panel will end up when you drop it.

To group panels:

1. Make sure you can see the tabs of all the panels you want to group.

2. Drag a panel tab into the window of the target panel **D**.

   A thick line appears around the window of the target panel to let you know that the panels are about to be grouped.

   To ungroup a panel, simply drag the panel's tab out of the panel group.

To dock panels:

Drag any panel's tab to the bottom of any panel outside the Panel Bin. Drag the panel by its title bar to successfully dock it to another panel **E**.

To undock a panel, click on one panel's tab and drag it away from the other panel.

TIP Pay attention to the blue line that appears when adding panels to the Panel Bin. A horizontal line indicates that the panel will be stacked with the rest. An outline means the panel will be added to a panel group.

TIP If you choose to close a single panel residing in a panel group, the entire panel group will close. However, making one panel in the group visible using the Window menu makes the entire group visible again.

TIP To hide the Panel Bin and gain more workspace, choose Window > Panel Bin.

To collapse panels to titles:

Double-click the panel tab or title bar .
Double-click again to reveal the panel.

To collapse panels to icons:

Click the Collapse to Icons button at the top of a floating panel or panel group. This option gives you more additional workspace, at the expense of hiding controls. You can click the button again to expand the panels .

Clicking a panel's icon reveals the contents of only that panel.

To return panels to their default positions:

Click the Reset Panels button at the top of the Photoshop Elements window; or, from the Window menu, choose Reset Panels.

To hide the Panel Bin entirely:

From the Window menu, choose Panel Bin (so its checkbox goes away) to gain the most screen space for your image.

F Double-click the panel tab to collapse a panel or panel group.

G Click the Collapse to Icons button to reclaim workspace from panels and the Panel Bin.

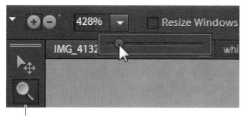

Zoom tool

A With the Zoom tool selected, adjust the magnification level using a slider.

Zoom In button

B To zoom in on an image, check that the Zoom In button is selected on the options bar.

Using the Zoom Tool

It's rare that you'll want to view your images at one magnification level—editing out dust, for example, requires a close-up view. The Zoom tool magnifies and reduces your view, which you can control using a variety of methods.

The current level of magnification is shown in the document status bar and, when the Zoom tool is selected, in the options bar above the document window. In the options bar you can adjust the magnification either with the Zoom slider or by entering a value in the Zoom text field **A**.

To zoom in:

1. In the Tools panel, select the Zoom tool, or press Z on the keyboard. The pointer changes to a magnifying glass when you move it into the document window.

2. Be sure that a plus sign appears in the center of the magnifying glass. If you see a minus sign (–), click the Zoom In button on the options bar **B**.

3. Click the area of the image you want to magnify.

   With a starting magnification of 100 percent, each click with the Zoom In tool increases the magnification in 100 percent increments up to 800 percent. From there, the magnification levels jump to 1200 percent, then 1600 percent, and finally to 3200 percent!

To zoom out:

1. In the Tools panel, select the Zoom tool, or press Z on the keyboard.

2. Click the Zoom Out button on the options bar, and then click in the area of the image that you want to zoom out from **C**.

   With a starting magnification of 100 percent, each click with the Zoom Out tool reduces the magnification as follows: 66.7 percent; 50 percent; 33.3 percent; 25 percent; 16.7 percent; and so on, down to 1 percent.

To zoom in on a specific area:

1. In the Tools panel, select the Zoom tool; if necessary, click the Zoom In button on the options bar to display the Zoom tool with a plus sign.

2. Drag over the area of the image that you want to zoom in on.

   A selection marquee appears around the selected area **D**. When you release the mouse button, the selected area is magnified and centered in the image window.

3. To move the view to a different area of the image, hold the spacebar until the hand pointer appears. Then drag to reveal the area you want to see. For more information on navigating through the document window, see "Moving Around in an Image" later in this chapter.

TIP You can also change the magnification level from the zoom-percentage text field in the lower-left corner of the document window. Double-click the text field to select the zoom value, and then type in the new value.

Zoom Out button

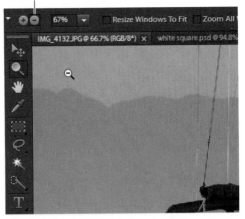

C To zoom out on an image, check that the Zoom Out button is selected on the options bar.

D Drag with the Zoom tool to zoom in on a specific area of an image.

E Clicking the 1:1 button on the options bar returns the image view to 100 percent.

F Entering 100 in the status bar also changes the image view to 100 percent.

To display an image at 100 percent:

To display an image at 100 percent (also referred to as displaying actual pixels), do one of the following:

- In the Tools panel, double-click the Zoom tool.

- In the Tools panel, select either the Zoom or Hand tool, and then click the 1:1 button on the options bar **E**.

- From the View menu, choose Actual Pixels, or press Ctrl+Alt+0.

- Enter **100** in the Zoom text field in the options bar, and then press Enter.

- Enter **100** in the status bar at the bottom of the document window, and then press Enter **F**.

TIP With any other tool selected in the toolbar, you can toggle to the Zoom tool. Hold down Ctrl+spacebar to zoom in or Alt+spacebar to zoom out.

TIP To change the magnification of the entire image, press Ctrl++ (Ctrl and the plus sign) to zoom in or Ctrl+– (Ctrl and the minus sign) to zoom out.

TIP Toggle the Zoom tool between zoom in and zoom out by holding down the Alt key before you click.

TIP You can automatically resize the document window to fit the image (as much as possible) when zooming in or out. With the Zoom tool selected, click the Resize Windows to Fit checkbox on the options bar. To maintain a constant window size, deselect the Resize Windows to Fit option.

Moving Around in an Image

When working in Photoshop Elements, you'll often want to move your image to make a different area visible in the document window. This can happen when you're zoomed in on one part of an image or when an image is just too large to be completely visible within the document window.

To view a different area of an image:

Do one of the following:

- From the Tools panel, select the Hand tool and drag to move the image around in the document window 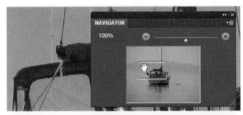 ⒶⒶ.

- Use the scroll arrows at the bottom and right side of the document window to scroll to the left or right and up or down. You can also drag the scroll bars to adjust the view.

To change the view using the Navigator panel:

1. Choose Window > Navigator to open the Navigator panel.

2. Drag the view box in the image thumbnail Ⓑ.

   The view in the document window changes accordingly.

TIP With any other tool selected in the tool-bar, press the spacebar to give you temporary access to the Hand tool.

TIP Drag the slider in the Navigator panel to adjust the magnification level in the document window.

Drag with the Hand tool...

...to move the image.

Ⓐ To view a different area of the same image, drag with the Hand tool.

Ⓑ You can also use the Navigator panel to view a different area of the same image.

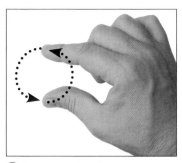

A Rotate your hand to turn an image 90 degrees.

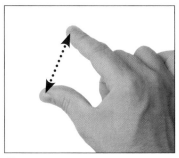

B Pinch out to zoom.

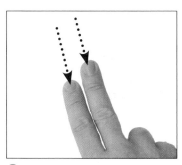

C Drag two fingers to scroll.

Using Multitouch Gestures

If you own a device that accepts touch input—such as a laptop's trackpad or a touch-sensitive screen—Photoshop Elements supports multitouch gestures that let you work in a more hands-on manner.

To rotate an image:

1. Place two fingers on the multitouch surface.

2. Turn your fingers clockwise or counter-clockwise, like you're turning a physical knob, to rotate the image 90 degrees in that direction **A**.

To zoom:

1. Place two fingers on the surface.

2. Pinch outward to enlarge the image (zoom in), or pinch inward to reduce the image (zoom out) **B**.

To scroll in an image:

1. Place two fingers on the surface.

2. Drag in the direction you wish to move the visible portion of the image **C**.

TIP Adobe calls the scrolling gesture a "flick," because the image continues to move after you've lifted your fingers, depending on how you made the gesture. The movement approximates physics and quickly comes to a smooth stop.

Accessing Photoshop.com

Photoshop Elements integrates directly with Adobe's Photoshop.com service, enabling you to publish photo albums directly (see Chapter 14). Recognizing the value of digital images, Adobe also added the capability to automatically back up your photos to Photoshop.com, so you have copies in case your computer or hard drive dies (see Chapter 2). And because your photos are online, you can view and edit them from any modern computer, not just the machine where Elements is installed.

A Basic Photoshop.com membership is free and includes 2 GB of online storage. Adobe also sells a Plus membership that costs $49.99 per year and includes 20 GB of storage, plus new ongoing tutorials, seasonal artwork, and templates delivered directly to Elements.

You can sign up for a Photoshop.com membership at the Welcome screen. After you've created an account, log in at the Welcome screen or by clicking the Sign In link at the top of the Organizer or Editor **A**.

Once you've signed in, Elements provides quick access to your settings and online photo gallery at the Welcome screen. You can also click the "Welcome, *your name*" link at the top of the Organizer or Editor.

A Sign in to your Photoshop.com account, or click Create New Adobe ID.

2

The Organizer

Digital photography can be a double-edged sword. Ironically, its greatest advantage to the amateur photographer—the ability to quickly and easily capture a large number of images, and then instantly download them to a computer—can also be its greatest source of frustration. Once hundreds of images have been downloaded, photographers find themselves faced with the daunting task of sorting through myriad files, with incomprehensible filenames, to find those dozen or so "keepers" to assemble into an album or post to the Web for friends.

The Organizer workspace comes to the rescue with a relatively simple and wonderfully visual set of tools and functions to help you locate, identify, and organize your photos. And once your photos are organized, you can import categories and collections of images that you assemble directly into projects like slide shows, calendars, flipbooks, and online albums.

Because we need some source material to work with, this chapter jumps right into importing photos from a digital camera and opening images already on your hard disk.

In This Chapter

Importing Images

Digital cameras have revolutionized photography and are a main force driving the need for products like Photoshop Elements. Typically, these cameras come with their own software to help you browse and manage photos—but don't bother breaking the seal on the disc's envelope. You can access your camera from within Elements and then download your images, or download photos from the camera to your hard drive and then open them in Elements.

To import images from a digital camera (Standard dialog):

1. Connect your digital camera to your computer using the instructions provided by the camera manufacturer.

   If the Photo Downloader launches automatically, skip to step 3. If you don't see the Photo Downloader dialog, continue to step 2.

2. If you're in the Editor, click the Organizer button to launch the Organizer **A**.

   If you're in the Organizer already, go to the File menu, choose Get Photos and Videos, and then choose From Camera or Card Reader **B** or press Ctrl+G.

   The Photo Downloader dialog opens in its Standard mode **C**. For more importing options, see "To import images from a digital camera (Advanced dialog)," just ahead in this chapter.

3. Your camera will likely be selected in the Get Photos from drop-down menu, but if not, choose your camera.

   Listed below the menu are the number of pictures, and their combined size.

A The Organizer button launches the Organizer, where you import photos.

B Choose From Camera or Card Reader to download photos from your digital camera.

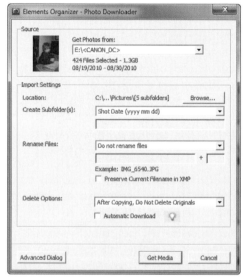

C The Photo Downloader's Standard dialog makes it easy to import all photos in one fell swoop.

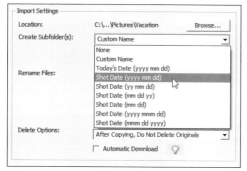

ⓓ To make it easier to find images on disk later, specify a custom name for subfolders.

ⓔ Choose a date format for naming subfolders with the images' shot dates.

4. By default, images are saved to your Pictures folder; hold your mouse pointer over the truncated path listed next to Location to view the full destination.

If you want to save the files to a different location, click the Choose button and select a folder or create a new one. Then click OK to return to the Photo Downloader dialog.

5. The Photo Downloader dialog is set to create new subfolders to store each batch of imported images, named according to the shot dates. From the Create Subfolder(s) drop-down menu, you can customize this behavior by choosing one of the following options:

- ▸ None saves the files in the folder specified by Location, normally your My Pictures folder.
- ▸ Custom Name creates a folder with a name that you enter **ⓓ**.
- ▸ Today's Date automatically creates a folder named with the current date.
- ▸ Shot Date creates folders with the date the images were captured; choose your preferred date format from one of the options **ⓔ**.

6. The Rename Files drop-down menu gives you the option of automatically naming the imported files something more descriptive than what your camera assigns. Choose an option from the drop-down menu.

For example, your camera's default naming scheme is probably something like "IMG_1031.JPG." With a Rename Files option selected, you can name and number a set of photos "Vacation," for instance. Then your photos will be saved and named "Vacation001.jpg," "Vacation002.jpg," and so on.

continues on next page

7. In the Delete Options area, choose what happens to the files on the memory card. Just to be safe, I like to leave the option set to After Copying, Do Not Delete Originals, and then erase the card in-camera later.

The Automatic Download option is useful if you want to offload pictures onto the computer without going through the Photo Downloader. Images download automatically when a camera or other device is attached. You can turn it off later in the program's preferences.

8. Click the Get Media button to download the selected images to your computer.

Your downloaded photos will first appear in their own Organizer window. Click the Show All button to return to the main Organizer window **F**.

To import images from a digital camera (Advanced dialog):

1. Follow steps 1 through 8 in the previous sequence, but click the Advanced Dialog button in step 2 to switch to the Advanced dialog **G**.

2. Click to deselect the checkbox under any photos you do not want to download.

By default, the Photo Downloader assumes you want to download every image.

3. In the Advanced Options area, choose to enable or disable the following **H**:

▸ Automatically Fix Red Eyes attempts to correct red eye problems in your photos as they're downloaded.

▸ Automatically Suggest Photo Stacks groups similar photos together for easy organization and review later (see "Using Stacks to Organize Similar Photos," later in this chapter).

To view your entire photo library, click the Show All button.

F Photos downloaded from the camera or memory card appear in the Organizer.

G Preview all photos on your camera before importing them in the Advanced dialog (left side of window shown here).

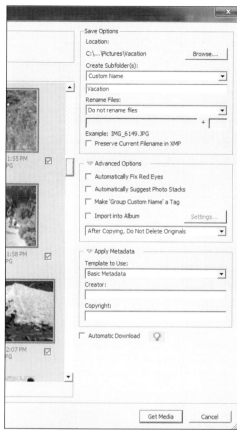

H Further customize the importing process in the Advanced dialog (right side of window here).

Rotate buttons

I Rotate images during import so you won't have to do it later.

▸ Make 'Group Custom Name' a Tag takes the name you specified in Step 5 two pages back and creates a keyword tag (see "Creating Keyword Tags," later in this chapter).

▸ Import into Album assigns the photos to a photo album you've previously set up (see "Using Albums to Arrange and Group Photos," later in this chapter).

4. Type your name (or the name of whoever took the photos) and a copyright notice in the Apply Metadata fields. This text is embedded with the image files.

5. If you want to rotate an image, select it and click the Rotate Left or Rotate Right buttons at the lower-left corner I. You can also press Control and the left or right arrow keys.

TIP For a fast way to select just a few photos for import, first click the UnCheck All button, and then click on the photos you want—don't worry about clicking their individual checkboxes. With the images selected, click just one checkbox to enable the boxes of your selections.

TIP Photoshop Elements can import photos stored in Camera RAW formats, which are the unprocessed versions of the captured images. RAW enables more adjustment possibilities than JPEG (which is processed and compressed in the camera). Elements brings RAW files into the Organizer without editing the image information. When you edit the photo, Elements first brings up the Camera Raw dialog to set initial edits before opening the image in the Editor. For more information, see "Adjusting Camera Raw Photos" in Chapter 7.

TIP The contents of the Creator and Copyright metadata fields are applied to all photos imported in that batch. If you want different authors for the pictures, for example, either import them in several batches or edit the metadata after they've been added to the catalog.

To import images from files or folders:

1. In the Organizer, go to the File menu, highlight Get Photos, and choose From Files and Folders.

   If you insert media that contains pictures, such as a CD, Windows may ask what action you'd like to take (if you haven't specified it already). Click the icon labeled Organize and Edit using Adobe Photoshop Elements 9.0, which opens the Get Photos from Files and Folders dialog.

2. Select the files you want to import 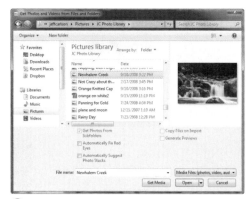; Shift-click to select a consecutive range of files, or Ctrl-click to select noncontiguous files.

3. If the images are stored on removable media and you want to import only low-resolution versions, disable the Copy Files on Import option and enable the Generate Previews option (see the sidebar for more information).

4. As in the Advanced dialog mentioned on the previous pages, select from the processing options below the preview.

5. Click the Get Media button to import the photos. If the photos already include keyword tags, you have the option to import them.

TIP Now that we've gotten those steps out of the way and you understand what's going on, here's a much quicker method: Simply drag image files from a folder on your hard disk to the Organizer's window. Elements imports them without fuss.

TIP If you know some photos exist on your hard disk but can't find them, let Elements hunt for them instead. Under the Get Photos submenu of the File menu, choose By Searching, enter criteria about the files, and click the Search button.

J Import images from other areas of your hard disk or from removable media such as CDs.

Working with Offline Images

With removable media, you have the option of importing just a low-resolution file to the hard disk. This feature can save hard disk space, especially if lots of files are stored on a shared network drive or on several CDs or DVDs. Importing them as offline images allows you to view and track your entire media catalog.

Offline images are designated with an icon in the upper-left corner of the image in the Organizer **K**. You can apply tags, build collections, and perform other tasks. However, if you want to edit the image, Elements asks you to insert the original media. If it's not available, you can still edit the low-res proxy, but the results won't look good. Once you make the original available again, Elements copies the source image to your catalog as an online image.

Offline icon

K Offline images are denoted by a corner icon.

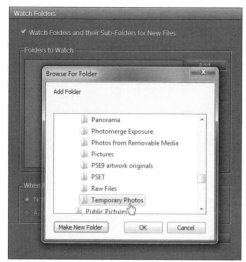

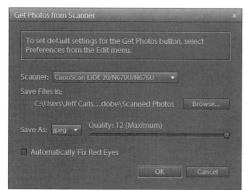

L Elements can keep an eye on one or more folders and import photos when they're added.

M Elements works with your scanner's software to import images.

To import images using Watch Folders:

1. You can specify one or more folders that Elements watches in the background for new files. In the Organizer, choose Watch Folders from the File menu.

2. Click the Add button and navigate to the folder you wish to watch L. Repeat for as many folders as you'd like.

3. Select an action under When New Files are Found in Watched Folders; Elements can notify you when files are found, or add them to the Organizer automatically.

4. Click OK when you're done.

5. When you add photos to your watched folder, Elements asks if you want to import them (if you opted to be notified in step 3). Click Yes to add the photos, which are moved from the watched folder to the directory where Elements stores your catalog.

To scan an image into the Organizer:

1. Connect the scanner to your computer using the instructions provided by the scanner manufacturer.

2. In the Organizer, go to the Get Photos menu under the File menu and choose From Scanner.

3. Select your scanner software from the Scanner pop-up menu M.

4. Choose an image format and quality level, and optionally enable the Automatically Fix Red Eyes checkbox.

continues on next page

5. Click the OK button. Elements hands off the actual scanning duties to the scanner's software for you to complete the scan.

6. When you complete the scan and exit the scanner's software, Elements imports the image to your catalog.

TIP If you're planning to use only part of an image, you'll save a lot of time by using your scanning software to crop your image *before* importing it into Photoshop Elements **N**.

TIP On the off chance that you want to scan an image in black and white (not grayscale), well, don't. Elements doesn't recognize bitmap images.

N Crop your images before importing them. In this figure, Canon's ScanGear software handles the actual scan, but the photo ends up in Elements.

O The Frame From Video dialog enables you to snag shots from video footage you captured.

P I grabbed three frames from the video clip, which appear in the Editor as three separate image files.

Importing Video Files

The Organizer accepts video files as well as still images, a necessity now that most still cameras shoot decent video. Double-clicking a video file's thumbnail lets you play the movie and assign keyword tags; press Esc to exit the player window.

To capture frames from video footage:

1. In the Editor, go to the File menu and choose Import > Frame From Video. (This feature appears only in the Editor, not the Organizer.)

   The Frame From Video dialog appears.

2. Click the Browse button to locate the file you want, and then click Open to see the video footage.

   The video clip appears in the dialog **O**.

3. To view your footage, click the Play button. When you see the frame you want, click the Grab Frame button.

   To grab the frame you want, you can also use the Pause button to stop the video at the desired frame. Another useful option is to simply move the slider to the correct frame in the video.

4. Grab as many video frames as you want, one by one, and then click Done.

   As you click the Grab Frame button, the images appear as new files in the Editor **P**.

5. Once you've captured the frames, you can save and edit them just like other images.

TIP Use the left and right arrow keys to view frames in the video one at a time.

TIP You'll likely encounter a greater variety of exposure problems with video frames than with the still shots you take with a digital camera. You can easily fix contrast and tonal problems with a few of Photoshop Elements' correction tools, which you'll explore more in Chapter 6 and in Chapter 7.

Understanding the Organizer Work Area

The Organizer is divided into two main components: the Photo Browser and the Organize Bin. The Photo Browser, along with its timeline, is used to find and view thumbnail representations of your photos. The Organize Bin contains the Albums and Keyword Tags panels you'll use to group and organize your image files **A**.

The Photo Browser

At the core of the Organizer is the Photo Browser. Every digital photo or video downloaded into Photoshop Elements is automatically added there. Resizable thumbnails in the Photo Browser window make it easy to scan through even a large number of images.

The Organize Bin

The Organize Bin on the right side of the window holds the Albums and Keyword Tags panels. You use these to identify, sort, and organize your photos **B**.

The timeline

An optional, but helpful, way to quickly navigate your photos by date is the timeline, located just above the Photo Browser. Choose Timeline from the Window menu, or press Ctrl+L. For example, when a Date viewing option is selected in the Browser window, the timeline uses date and time information embedded in each image to construct bars (month markers) to represent sets of photos taken within specific months and years. When a month marker is selected in the timeline, that month's photos are displayed at the top of the Photo Browser **C**.

Photo Browser   *Organize Bin (albums and keyword tags)*

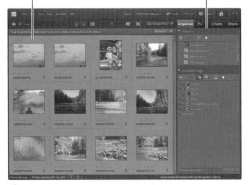

A The Organizer workspace makes it easy to browse your entire photo collection.

B The Organize Bin contains panels for albums and keyword tags.

C Click a month marker in the Organizer timeline to view that month's photos on the Photo Browser.

A A selected thumbnail appears with a light gray frame around it.

B Ctrl-click to select thumbnails that are not consecutive.

C Shift-click to select thumbnails that are consecutive.

Working in the Photo Browser

The centerpiece of the Organizer is the Photo Browser, a flexible workspace that provides a number of options for customizing the way you manage and view your image files. Throughout this chapter I'll cover a variety of ways to work in the Photo Browser to label, identify, and organize your photos. But first it's important to know how best to select, sort, and display the image thumbnails.

To select photo thumbnails:

Do one of the following:

- Click to select a thumbnail in the Photo Browser. The frame around it becomes light gray, indicating that the thumbnail is selected **A**.
- Ctrl-click to select several non-adjacent thumbnails at once **B**.
- Shift-click to select a group of thumbnails in sequence **C**.
- From the Edit menu, choose Select All, or press Ctrl+A to select every thumbnail in the Photo Browser.

To deselect photo thumbnails:

Do one of the following:

- Ctrl-click to deselect a single thumbnail.
- From the Edit menu, choose Deselect, or press Ctrl+Shift+A to deselect every thumbnail in the Photo Browser.

TIP You can tweak the appearance of the Photo Browser. From the View menu, you can choose to display details such as filenames, ratings, timestamps, and people recognition.

To sort photo thumbnails:

- From the Arrangement drop-down menu above the Photo Browser, choose a sorting option :

  ▸ Date (Newest First) displays the most recent photos at the top, judged by the images' creation dates.

  ▸ Date (Oldest First) displays photos in order, with the oldest at the top.

- Click the Display button to choose how photos are grouped:

  ▸ Thumbnail View (Ctrl+Alt+1) is the default grid of thumbnails.

  ▸ Import Batch (Ctrl+Alt+2) groups photos into the batches they were imported in. Included is information on when the batch was imported and from what source .

  ▸ Folder Location (Ctrl+Alt+3) displays photos grouped into the folders in which they're stored, and provides detailed file-path information to make it easy to locate the folder and original files on your hard drive.

To resize photo thumbnails:

- Above the Photo Browser, drag the thumbnail slider to the right to increase the size of the thumbnails, or to the left to make them smaller 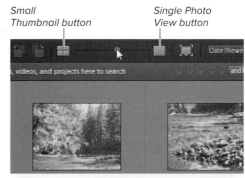.

- Click the Small Thumbnail button to the left of the slider to display the thumbnails at their smallest possible size.

- Click the Single Photo View button to the right of the slider to display just one large photo thumbnail at a time.

> **TIP** Double-click on any thumbnail to change to Single Photo View. Double-click the image to return to your most recent multiple thumbnail view settings.

D Select an option to sort thumbnails in the Photo Browser.

E When you select the Import Batch option, thumbnails in the Photo Browser are displayed in grouped batch sets.

*Small
Thumbnail button*

*Single Photo
View button*

F When you drag the thumbnail slider to the right, the thumbnails grow larger (top). When you drag the slider to the left, they become smaller (bottom).

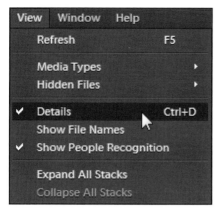

A The Details option displays title and date information in the Photo Browser.

Displaying and Changing Information for Your Photos

Images you import from a digital camera or scanner carry embedded file information— everything from the date and time a photo was shot or scanned to whether or not the camera's flash fired. The Organizer uses that date and time information to determine the display order of the photo thumbnails in the Photo Browser.

If your camera's clock wasn't set properly before shooting (a problem especially if the batteries die), the Adjust Date and Time dialog lets you substitute a new date and time for any image file. You can also easily adjust for time zone differences by shifting the time a set number of hours.

To adjust the date and time:

1. From the View menu, check that the Details option is enabled A to display date and filename information below the image thumbnails.

2. In the Photo Browser, click to select the thumbnails whose date and time you would like to change.

3. From the Edit menu, choose Adjust Date and Time (or Adjust Date and Time of Selected Items if more than one thumbnail is selected), or press Ctrl+J.

continues on next page

4. In the Adjust Date and Time of Selected Items dialog, choose one of the options and click OK 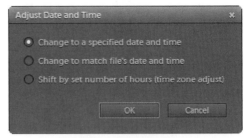:

- Change to a specified date and time opens the Set Date and Time dialog where you can set a specific year, month, day, and time **C**.

- Change to match file's date and time reverts the date and time information to what is embedded in the original image file.

    Remember, date and time changes you enter here are only for sorting and organizing your images within the Photo Organizer.

- Shift by set number of hours (time zone adjust) adjusts the time of selected images forward or backward by the number of hours that you specify **D**.

TIP A preference enables you to open the Adjust Date and Time dialog by simply clicking on the date in the Photo Browser. From the Edit menu, choose **Preferences > General**, and then select the **Adjust Date and Time by Clicking on Thumbnail Dates** option.

TIP You can view file names in addition to dates. From the View menu, choose **Show File Names**.

B The Adjust Date and Time dialog offers different options for changing an image's date and time information.

C The Set Date and Time dialog.

D Use the Time Zone Adjust dialog to set the time of your images backward or forward in one-hour intervals.

E Apply a rating to quickly identify your higher-quality photos.

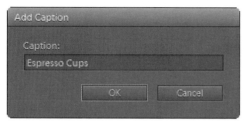

F The Add Caption dialog.

To rate a photo:

1. In the Photo Browser, position your mouse pointer over the gray star icons; they change to yellow depending on the pointer's location **E**.

2. Click to select the rating you wish to apply: One star typically denotes a low-quality photo, while five stars is excellent. (You can choose your own values, of course; this feature provides an easy way to separate good from bad photos, as you'll see later in "Using Smart Albums.")

To add a caption to a photo:

1. Click to select an image thumbnail.

2. From the Edit menu, choose Add Caption, or press Ctrl+Shift+T.

3. In the Add Caption dialog, type a caption for your image, and then click OK **F**. Although captions don't display with images in the Photo Browser, they do appear along with your photos when you create projects such as Web Photo Galleries and Photo Album Pages.

> **TIP** You can also add and edit captions in Single Photo View. In Single Photo View, click the Click here to add caption text. The text changes to a text field where you can type a new caption. If you've previously entered a caption, click on the text to edit or delete it.

> **TIP** You can add the same caption to multiple images at the same time. Select a group of images in the Photo Browser, and then from the Edit menu choose Add Caption to Selected Items. The caption you enter in the Add Caption to Selected Items dialog is applied to the selected images.

To rename a photo:

1. In the Photo Browser, click to select an image thumbnail.

2. From the Window menu, choose Properties, or press Alt+Enter to open the Properties panel.

3. Enter a new name for your image file in the Name field.

To add a note to a photo:

1. Select an image thumbnail.

2. From the Window menu, choose Properties, or press Alt+Enter to open the Properties panel.

3. In the Notes field, enter the text you want to include with your photo 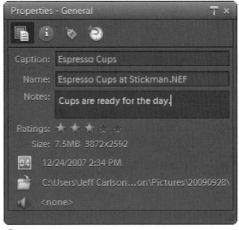.

G Notes entered for images are accessible only in the Properties panel.

TIP Notes can be viewed only in the Properties panel in the Organizer.

About the Properties Panel

The Properties panel may not look like much at first glance, but it contains a storehouse of information about every image in the Organizer. In the preceding steps you learned how it can be used to enter and record image data like captions, names, and notes—but what are those other icons for?

The icons across the top of the panel actually serve as buttons that allow you to view different property types.

The General area displays (and allows you to enter) caption, name, and note information. In addition, three buttons along the lower-left edge give you access to the Adjust Date and Time dialog; provide a jump directly to the folder containing your images; and allow you to record audio captions.

The Metadata area displays the detailed camera data (EXIF information) embedded in a digital photo file.

The Keyword Tags area displays any tags associated with an image and any albums to which it belongs. I'll discuss tags in the next section.

The History area displays date and time information for an image, as well as a general history of where the file has been and what it's been used for. For instance, you can see when the image was printed and if it has been used in creations like Web photo galleries or PDF slide shows.

Lastly, if you want to dock the Properties panel to the Organizer bin, click the T-shaped icon in the upper-right corner of the panel.

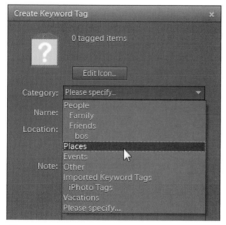

A Click the New button at the top of the Keyword Tags panel to create a new tag.

B All tags reside in categories. Define a category for your new tag in the Create Keyword Tag dialog.

C Tags appear nested below their categories in the panel.

Creating Keyword Tags

The humble little tag serves as the foundation for the Organizer's sorting and filing system. You can create a tag from scratch or create one based on a set of photos grouped within a folder. Use names that are descriptive, but not so specific that they apply only to a limited number of photos.

To create a new keyword tag:

1. Click the New button (the plus sign) at the top of the Keyword Tags panel.

2. From the drop-down menu, choose New Keyword Tag or press Ctrl+N **A**. The Create Keyword Tag dialog appears.

3. From the Category menu, choose the category or sub-category in which you want to place your new tag **B**.

4. In the Name text field, enter a name for your tag.

5. In the Note text field, enter information relevant to the photos that will have the tag applied.

6. Click OK to close the dialog.

   Your new tag appears in the Keyword Tags panel within the category you chose **C**.

TIP The first photo to which you attach a new tag automatically becomes the icon for that tag. This is an easy and convenient way to assign tag icons, so I'll ignore the Edit Icon button for now.

TIP You can associate a location with a tag (whether or not it's categorized as Places) by clicking the Place on Map button in the Create Keyword Tag dialog. See "Using the Map," later in this chapter.

To import tags from other images:

1. Using the steps outlined earlier, import photos from your hard disk that may already contain keywords (for example, if someone sent you the images or you used another program to assign tags).

2. In the Import Attached Keyword Tags dialog, choose which tags you want to add to your list. Click OK. The tags can be applied to any photos in your library.

TIP Click the Advanced button to access more options such as renaming the tags before they're imported **D**.

To create a tag using the Keyword Tags field:

1. Select one or more images in your library.

2. Type a keyword in the Tag selected media field **E**. (Note that the field moved from the top to the bottom of the panel between versions 8 and 9 of Photoshop Elements.)

   Better yet, type *several* keywords, separated by commas, to create and apply them together.

3. Press Enter or click Apply. The new tag is created and applied to the image.

TIP I'm happy to detail the different methods of creating and applying keyword tags in this chapter, but for me, the capability to do it from the Tag selected media field trumps the other methods. It's quick, and promises to make keyword tagging much less of a chore than in the past.

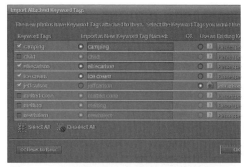

D When you import photos that already contain keyword tags, you can opt to add them to the list in the Keyword Tags panel.

E Type a word into the Keyword Tags field to create a new tag for it.

G Delete a keyword tag you don't want to use.

F Edit a tag's properties.

To change a tag's properties:

1. In the Keyword Tags panel, select the tag you want to edit.

2. Click the New button (the plus sign) and choose Edit **F**.

Or

1. In the Keyword Tags panel, right-click the tag whose properties you would like to change.

2. From the tag contextual menu, choose Edit (name of tag) keyword tag.

3. In the Edit Keyword Tag dialog, make the desired changes and click OK.

To delete a tag:

In the Keyword Tags panel, select the tag you want to delete and click the Delete button (the red minus sign) **G**.

Or

1. In the Keyword Tags panel, right-click on the tag you would like to delete.

2. From the tag contextual menu, choose Delete (name of tag) keyword tag.

3. In the Confirm Keyword Tag Deletion warning box, click OK **H**.

   The tag is removed from the Keyword Tags panel and from any photos tagged in the Photo Browser.

H The Confirm Tag Deletion warning box reminds you that when a tag is deleted from the Keyword Tags panel, the tags are also removed from the thumbnails in the Photo Browser.

Using Keyword Tags to Sort and Identify Photos

Tags operate independent of where photos are located on your computer, which means you can attach a tag to photos in different folders—even on different hard drives—and then use that tag to quickly find and view those photos all at once.

To attach a tag to a single photo:

- Drag a tag from the Keyword Tags panel onto any photo in the Photo Browser **A**.

- Type a term into the Keyword Tags field; if the tag already exists, click it from the pop-up list that appears **B**.

A category icon appears below the photo in the Browser window to indicate that it has been tagged; in the Keyword Tags panel, the tag assumes that photo for its tag icon **C**.

To attach a tag to multiple photos:

1. In the Photo Browser, Ctrl-click to select any number of photos.

2. From the Keyword Tags panel, drag a tag onto any one of the selected photos **D**.

   A category icon appears below all of the selected photos in the Browser window to indicate that they have been tagged.

TIP You can also drag a thumbnail to a tag in the Keyword Tags panel to attach it.

TIP Hover the mouse pointer over a photo's tag icon to view which tags are applied to the image.

A To attach a tag to a photo, drag it from the Keyword Tags panel to a thumbnail image in the Photo Browser.

B Existing tags appear as you type into the Keyword Tags field.

Keyword Tag applied   *Tag icon set*

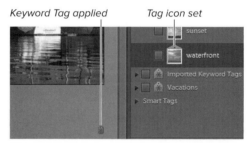

C When you use a tag for the first time, the photo you attach it to is used for the tag's icon.

D You can select multiple photos, and then tag them all by dragging a tag icon over just one.

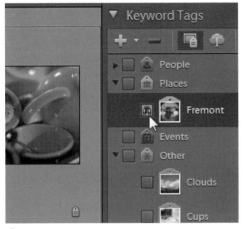

E When you click on an import batch or folder icon, all of the photos in that batch or folder are selected at once.

F When the binoculars icon is visible next to a tag in the Keyword Tags panel, only that tag's photos appear in the Photo Browser.

G Remove a tag from a photo with a single click on the category icon below the thumbnail in the Photo Browser.

To attach a tag to an import batch or folder:

1. From the Display drop-down menu, choose either Import Batch or Folder Location.

2. Identify the import batch or folder group you want to tag, and then click on either the import batch or folder icon at the top of the window for that group **E**.

   All of the photos in the group are automatically selected.

3. From the Keyword Tags panel, drag a tag onto any one of the selected photos.

   A category icon appears below all the selected photos.

To view a set of tagged photos:

In the Keyword Tags panel, do one of the following:

- Double-click a tag.
- Click the blank box to the left of a tag.

   A small binoculars icon appears in the box, and the Photo Browser will change to display just the photo or photos that carry the attached tag **F**.

   To view all photos again, click the Show All button, or click the binoculars icon in the Keyword Tags panel.

To remove a tag from a photo:

Select a photo thumbnail in the Photo Browser, and then do one of the following:

- Right-click a photo thumbnail; then, from the contextual menu, choose Remove Keyword Tag > (name of tag).
- Right-click on the category icon below the photo thumbnail and select Remove (name of tag) Keyword Tag from the contextual menu **G**.

To change a tag's icon:

1. In the Keyword Tags panel, right-click on the tag you would like to change.

2. From the tag drop-down menu, choose Edit (name of tag) keyword tag.

3. In the Edit Keyword Tag dialog, click the Edit Icon button.

   To assign a new icon image in the Edit Tag Icon dialog, you can select from any of the photos that the tag has been applied to, or you can import a completely new photo.

4. To select a different tagged photo, click the Find button **H**.

5. In the Select Icon for (name of tag) Keyword Tag dialog, click to select a photo thumbnail and click OK **I**.

   The new image appears in the preview window of the Edit Tag Icon dialog.

6. To crop the area of the photo that will appear on the tag icon, click and drag any of the four cropping handles in the image preview **J**.

7. To select a different cropped area of the photo to appear on the tag icon, click inside the crop box and drag it in the preview window **K**.

8. When you're satisfied with the look of your icon, click OK to close the Edit Tag Icon dialog, and then click OK again to close the Edit Keyword Tag dialog. The new icon appears on the tag in the Keyword Tags panel.

TIP If you'd like to use an image for your icon different than any of the photos you've tagged, click the Import button in the Edit Tag Icon dialog to browse your computer and select an image.

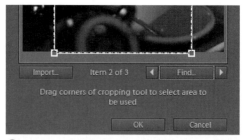

H Click the Find button in the Edit Tag Icon dialog to browse for a new photo to use as the source for your tag icon.

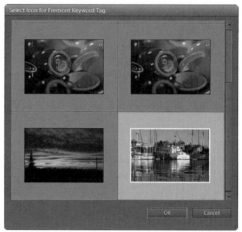

I The Select Icon dialog.

J Resize the selection rectangle in the Edit Tag Icon dialog to choose the visible area of the icon.

K Drag the selection rectangle to choose a different area of a photo to use for the tag icon.

Keyword Tag Cloud

Many photos include the keyword "jeffcarlson", as indicated by the tags' larger size.

You can edit or delete keyword tags directly in the Tag Cloud.

Using the Keyword Tag Cloud

In addition to the hierarchical display of tags, you can view keywords in a "cloud": All keyword tags are listed; terms applied more frequently appear in larger type. Click the Keyword Tag Cloud button in the Keyword Tags panel .

To view photos using the Tag Cloud:

Click a keyword in the cloud to view all photos to which the tag is applied.

To apply a tag from the Tag Cloud to a photo:

1. Ctrl-click one or more tags.

2. Drag the tag(s) to one or more selected photos in the library.

To edit or delete a tag using the Tag Cloud:

1. Double-click a tag to make it editable .

2. Change the tag's name in its text field and press Enter. Or, click the X button to remove it. If you decide not to do anything, click elsewhere in the Tag Cloud to deselect the tag. Deleting a tag removes it from all photos that possessed the tag.

Marking Photos as Hidden

If you have some photos you feel are cluttering up the Photo Browser, use the Hidden attribute to keep them out of sight until you need them. Select a photo and choose Edit > Visibility > Mark as Hidden (or press Alt+F2) to make the image disappear from view.

To view hidden photos, choose View > Hidden Files and choose either Show All Files or Show Only Hidden Files. A closed eye icon appears on the face of each photo thumbnail . You can hide them again by choosing View > Hidden Files > Hide Hidden Files. To make a photo permanently visible, choose Edit > Visibility > Mark as Visible, which removes the Hidden attribute.

Hidden files display a closed eye icon when you've chosen to view hidden files.

Auto-Analyzing Photos

The Organizer can help you tag images using its Auto-Analyzer feature. It scans your library and applies Smart Tags for characteristics such as High Contrast, Blurred, Pan Motion, and more. You can then locate images using those criteria by choosing Smart Tags in the Keyword Tags panel.

To analyze selected photos:

1. Select one or more photos in the library.

2. Choose Edit > Run Auto-Analyzer, or right-click on a photo and choose Run Auto-Analyzer from the shortcut menu.

3. After the Organizer analyzes the files, click OK.

The photos gain a Smart Tag icon; hold your pointer over the icon or right-click to reveal which tags were applied .

To analyze photos automatically:

1. Go to Edit > Preferences > Media Analysis to view controls for the feature.

2. Enable the Analyze Media for Smart Tags Automatically option 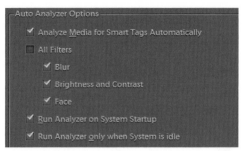.

   You can also choose which filters to apply; for example, if you don't store any audio or video files in the Organizer, you may want to disable the Audio filter. Click OK.

TIP Hover over the Auto-Analyzer status icon to check or pause the analysis .

TIP In the preferences, enable the "Run Analyzer only when System is idle" option to prevent the Organizer from monopolizing your computer's processors.

A The Organizer can apply tags based on its analysis of an image.

B Choose which attributes are considered in the image analysis.

C Auto-Analyze can take a while, but you can check its status.

TIP If you've installed only Photoshop Elements, just three filters are available in the preferences: Blur, Brightness & Contrast, and Face. With Premiere Elements also installed, additional filters appear in **B**.

A When the Organizer asks, click and enter a name in the "Who is this?" field.

B As the database of recognized photos builds, the Organizer attempts matches.

C The Organizer finds the face, but needs your help identifying it.

Using Face Recognition

The Find People for Tagging feature offers an easy way to sort, identify, and tag photos based on the people in them.

To identify a person:

1. Double-click a photo containing a person to view it full-size.

2. When the Organizer displays a "Who is this?" field, click it and do one of the following:

   ▸ Type a name **A**. If it's a new person, a new keyword tag is created under the People category and applied to the photo.

   ▸ Click the name of an existing tag that appears below the field.

   ▸ The Organizer will start to make suggestions as the database of faces grows **B**. Click the green checkmark button if the suggestion is correct; click the red button to enter a different name.

3. If a person is in the picture but wasn't identified, click the Add Missing Person button (in the lower right corner of the window), draw a box around their face, and then enter the person's name.

TIP If you want to identify faces in a large number of photos, choose Find > **Find People for Tagging**, or click the **Start People Recognition button in the Keyword Tags panel. The Organizer displays photos zoomed in on faces for faster labeling **C**.

Using Categories to Organize Tagged Photos

All tags must reside in either a category or sub-category. The Organizer starts you off with four ready-made categories, but you can create as many new categories and subcategories as you want. Tags can be easily moved from one category to another and also converted to a sub-category that contains its own set of tags.

To create a new category:

1. Click the New button at the top of the Keyword Tags panel.

2. From the New drop-down menu, choose New Category to open the Create Category dialog .

3. In the Create Category dialog, enter a name in the Category Name text field.

4. In the Category Icon area of the dialog, use the scroll bar or arrows to search for an icon you would like to use to identify your new category .

5. Click to select a category icon. The icon appears in the category preview at the top of the dialog.

6. At the top of the dialog, click the Choose Color button to open the Color Picker.

7. Select the color you would like to appear on all the sub-category and tag icons within your new main category and click OK .

8. If you're satisfied with your other category settings, click OK to close the Create Category dialog.

   Your new category appears at the bottom of the Keyword Tags panel.

Ⓐ Use the New menu in the Keyword Tags panel to open the Create Category dialog.

Ⓑ The Create Category dialog includes a variety of icons you can use to represent your new category.

Ⓒ The color you choose in the Color Picker appears on the icons for tags in your new category.

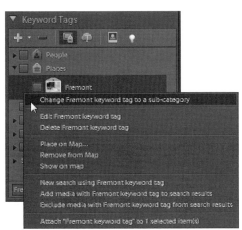

D Sub-categories can be nested within categories or other sub-categories.

E Convert a tag to a sub-category from the tag contextual menu in the Keyword Tags panel.

To create a new sub-category:

1. Click the New button at the top of the Keyword Tags panel.

2. From the New drop-down menu, choose New Sub-Category to open the Create Sub-Category dialog.

3. In the Create Sub-Category dialog, enter a name in the Sub-Category Name text field.

4. From the Parent Category or Sub-Category drop-down menu, choose a location in which to place your new sub-category **D**.

5. Click OK to close the Create Sub-Category dialog.

6. Your new sub-category appears in the Keyword Tags panel, within the category or sub-category you selected.

To convert a tag to a sub-category:

1. In the Keyword Tags panel, right-click on the tag you want to convert.

2. From the tag contextual menu, choose Change (name of tag) keyword tag to a sub-category **E**. The tag icon changes to a sub-category icon.

TIP An easy way to convert a tag to a sub-category is to drag the tag's icon to a category name.

TIP If you decide you'd like to convert a sub-category (that was formerly a tag) back to a tag, go to the Sub-Category contextual menu and choose the Change sub-category to a tag option. All the tag's properties, including its icon, are retained.

To assign a tag to a new category or sub-category:

1. In the Keyword Tags panel, right-click the tag you want to place.

2. From the tag contextual menu, choose Edit (name of tag) keyword tag.

3. From the Category menu in the Edit Keyword Tag dialog, choose the category or sub-category in which you want to place the tag **F**.

4. Click OK to close the Edit Keyword Tag dialog. In the Keyword Tags panel, the tag appears within the category and sub-category you defined **G**.

   If you've already applied the tag to a photo or photos in the Photo Browser, the category icons below the photo thumbnails will automatically update to display the icon of the new category.

TIP You can also move tags into new categories or sub-categories right in the Keyword Tags panel. With both the tag and the category or sub-category visible, simply click to select a tag and then drag it onto a category or sub-category icon. The tag will nest beneath the category or sub-category you choose. The disadvantage of this method (as compared to the one outlined in the procedure) is that you must be able to see the tag and category or sub-category in the Keyword Tags panel. Since the Keyword Tags panel can get filled with categories quickly, it may require that you do quite a bit of scrolling and searching, whereas the Category menu in the Edit Keyword Tag dialog gives you a list of every category and sub-category in one convenient place.

F You can easily move a tag from one category to another using the Edit Keyword Tag dialog.

G Changes you make to a tag's placement in the Edit Keyword Tag dialog appear instantly in the Keyword Tags panel.

H Delete a category or tag from the Keyword Tags panel by clicking the Delete button.

To view photos belonging to a category or sub-category:

In the Keyword Tags panel, do one of the following:

- Double-click a category or sub-category.

- Click the blank box to the left of a category or sub-category.

    A small binoculars icon appears in the box, and the Photo Browser changes to display just the photos in that category or sub-category set.

    To return to the main Photo Browser window, click the Show All button, or click the binoculars icon in the Keyword Tags panel.

To delete a category or sub-category:

In the Keyword Tags panel, click a category or sub-category, and then do one of the following:

- Right-click to display the category contextual menu, and then select Delete (category name) category.

- Click the Delete icon at the top of the Keyword Tags panel **H**.

TIP Before you delete a category or sub-category, bear in mind that you will also delete all related sub-categories and tags and will remove those tags from all tagged photos. In some circumstances, a better alternative may be to change a category or sub-category's properties to better match the content or theme of related tagged photos.

TIP Deleting a category does not delete the photos that belong to the category.

Using Albums to Arrange and Group Photos

Photos have gone digital, but we don't have to discard our analog thinking. Just as you store Polaroids and prints in a photo album, you can collect your digital photos in Elements albums.

An album can be composed of photos from several different tags or categories. Plus, the photos within albums can be sorted and reordered, independent of their date or folder structure—particularly useful when you're creating a project such as a PDF slide show or Web photo gallery.

To create a new album:

1. Click the New button at the top of the Albums panel.

2. From the New drop-down menu, choose New Album . The Organize panel fills with the Album Details dialog .

3. Leave the Album Category menu set to None (Top Level). You'll learn more about album categories later in this section.

4. In the Album Name field, enter a name for your album.

5. If you want to automatically back up the album, enable the Backup/Sync checkbox (see "Backing Up Photos Online," later in this chapter).

6. Drag the photos you want to add to the album to the Items field 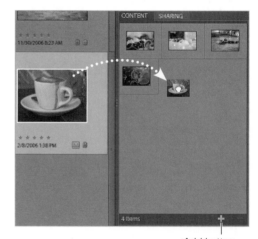. Or, select one or more photos and click the Add (+) button.

7. Click Done to close the dialog. Your new album appears in the Albums panel. By default, albums are sorted in alphabetical order.

Ⓐ Use the New menu in the Albums panel to open the Create Album dialog.

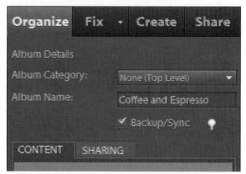

Ⓑ The Album Details dialog uses the entire Organize pane while you're creating an album.

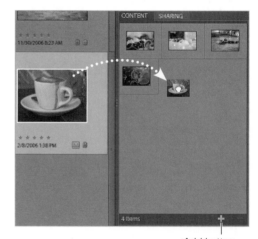

Add button

Ⓒ Populate the album by dragging photos to it or by selecting them and clicking the Add button.

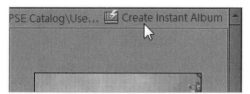

D Every folder group in the Photo Browser has its own Create Instant Album button.

E The album is given the same name as its source folder.

F Click an album name to view only its photos.

G One way to populate an album is to drag its icon from the Albums panel to one or more photos.

To create an album from a folder:

1. Click the Display button and choose Folder Location to display your photos in folder groups.

2. Identify the folder group you want and click the Create Instant Album button D.

   The album is created with the name of the folder E.

To view a photo album:

Click an album name in the Albums panel. The Photo Browser displays only the photos in that album F.

To view your entire catalog, click the Show All button.

To add photos to an album:

Do one of the following:

- From the Photo Browser, drag a photo onto the appropriate album in the Albums panel.

- From the Albums panel, drag an album onto a photo thumbnail in the Photo Browser G. An album icon appears below the photo in the Browser window to indicate it is part of an album.

Or

1. In the Albums panel, select an album and click the Edit icon.

2. Drag photos to the Items field; or, make selections in the Photo Browser and click the Add (+) button.

To rename an album:

1. In the Albums panel, select an album and click the Edit icon.

2. Change the Album Name field and click Done.

To arrange photos within an album:

1. In the Albums panel, click an album name.

2. In the Photo Browser, click to select a photo, and then drag it to a new location .

Or

1. In the Albums panel, select an album and click the Edit icon.

2. Drag to rearrange the photos in the Items field.

To remove photos from an album:

With an album displayed in the Photo Browser, select a photo thumbnail and then do one of the following:

- Right-click on the album icon below the photo thumbnail and select Remove from (name of album) Album from the contextual menu .

- Right-click inside a photo thumbnail, and then from the contextual menu choose Remove from Album > (name of album).

Or

1. In the Albums panel, select an album and click the Edit icon.

2. Select one or more photos and click the Remove (–) button.

To create an album category:

1. Click the New button at the top of the Albums panel.

2. From the New drop-down menu, choose New Album Category to open the Create Album Category dialog.

3. In the Album Category Name text field, enter a name ❶.

H To reorder photos within an album, drag a thumbnail to a new location in the Photo Browser. The numbers on the thumbnails indicate their order.

I Right-click a photo's album icon to remove it from the album.

TIP You can also right-click an album name and choose Sort the Album by Date (Oldest First) from the contextual menu.

TIP You can't drag an album out of an album category to take it back to the top level. Instead, click the Edit Album button, and then choose None (Top Level) from the Album Category drop-down menu.

J The Create Album Category dialog.

K Once you've created an album category, you can add albums to it from the Albums panel.

TIP It's possible to group one album category within another when creating a category. If you've already created an album category, its name appears in the Parent Album Category menu of the Create Album Category dialog. You then have the option of nesting your new album category within the existing one.

TIP Deleting a shared album also removes it from public view at Photoshop.com, although the photos remain online.

4. Leave the Parent Album Category option set to None (Top Level).

5. Click OK to close the Create Album Category dialog.

   Your new album category appears at the bottom of the list in the Albums panel.

To add an album to an album category:

In the Albums panel, drag an album icon onto the name of the album category K.

Or

1. In the Albums panel, right-click the album you want to include in the album category.

2. From the album contextual menu, choose Edit (name of album) album.

3. From the Group menu in the Edit Album dialog, choose the group in which you want to place the album.

4. Click OK to close the Edit Album dialog. In the Albums panel, the album appears within the category you defined.

To delete an album:

In the Albums panel, select an album and click the Delete icon.

Or

1. In the Albums panel, right-click the album you would like to delete.

2. From the album contextual menu, choose Delete (name of album) album.

3. In the Confirm Album Deletion warning box, click OK. The album is removed from the Albums panel, and the links to any images in the Photo Browser are broken.

Using Smart Albums

One of my grandmother's cupboards was filled with photo albums, organized roughly chronologically, along with a bunch of envelopes and stacks of free-floating pictures that weren't in any order. The problem with lots of photos is that there's only so much time you can spend sorting them.

But what if you had an assistant who could do the organizing for you? Not just once, but ongoing, changing the albums based on new photos or keyword tags or other criteria? Smart albums operate just like that (and they don't mind the workload).

To create a smart album:

1. Click the New button at the top of the Albums panel.

2. From the New drop-down menu, choose New Smart Album to open the New Smart Album dialog.

3. Type a descriptive title in the Name field.

4. In the Search Criteria area, choose an attribute from the first drop-down menu .

   The other drop-down menu and field change depending on the criteria. For example, choosing Keyword Tags presents a list of tags.

5. To add more criteria, click the plus button  and specify the attributes.

6. By default, the album picks up photos containing any of the criteria you specify. To view only photos that match every attribute, choose the radio button labeled All of the following search criteria [AND] .

7. Click OK. Only the images matching the criteria are displayed .

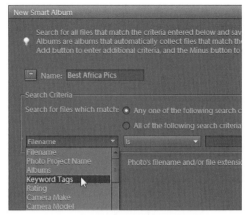

A Choose from several attributes to start building the smart album.

B Click here to add additional criteria.

C This smart album will display only photos marked with the Vacations keyword tag and having a rating of 4 or 5 stars.

D After the smart album is created, the pictures that match its criteria are displayed.

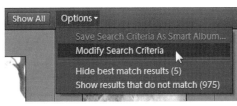

⒠ Choose Modify Search Criteria when you're viewing the contents of a smart album.

⒡ Make sure you mark the criteria as a smart album, or else Elements modifies the search for that instance only.

⒢ A smart album can be built using the criteria of a regular album.

To modify a smart album:

1. Select a smart album in the Albums panel to view its contents.

2. From the Options drop-down menu at the top of the Photo Browser, choose Modify Search Criteria **⒠**.

3. In the Find by Details (Metadata) dialog that appears, edit the attributes you set up originally.

4. To keep the new criteria, mark the checkbox labeled Save this Search Criteria as Smart Album **⒡**.

5. Enter a name for the album (see the tip below).

6. Click Search to save the settings. The images in the Photo Browser reflect the new criteria.

To create a smart album from search results:

1. Perform a search using the techniques described ahead in "Finding Photos".

2. From the Options drop-down menu, choose Save Search Criteria As Smart Album.

3. In the Create Smart Album dialog, give the smart album a name and click OK **⒢**.

TIP If you give a modified smart album the same title as the original album you're editing, Elements creates a brand new album instead of replacing the old one.

TIP To easily view all photos *except* those in the smart album, go to the Options drop-down menu and choose Show results that do not match.

TIP Although you can specify a keyword category or sub-category as criteria for a smart album, the Organizer only looks for media marked with that category tag, not the keyword tags that fall under the category.

Reviewing Photos Full Screen

When you're looking over a set of photos, you want to see the photos, not everything else around them. The full-screen reviewing option lets you see just your images, with a minimal set of controls for ranking and sorting, and even for applying basic edits.

To review photos full screen:

1. Click the Display button and choose View, Edit, Organize in Full Screen, or press Ctrl+F11. If you have a photo selected, it fills the screen; if not, the first item in your library appears **A**.

2. Use the navigation controls at the bottom of the screen to switch between files, play a slideshow, or hide or show the QuickOrganize and QuickEdit panels **B**.

3. Use the QuickOrganize panel to apply keyword tags and create new tags **C**. (See "Using the Keyword Tag Cloud," earlier in this chapter.)

   You can also use the QuickEdit panel to make basic adjustments if you're in a hurry.

4. Press Esc to exit full-screen mode when you're finished reviewing.

> **TIP** If you apply a QuickEdit to a RAW image, you're asked to save the edited version in a different file format, such as JPEG.

> **TIP** Click the tiny pushpin icon on the panels to toggle between remaining visible and automatically retracting to the edge of the screen.

> **TIP** To sort through your photos quickly, forget the panels and just type the keys 1-5 to apply ratings.

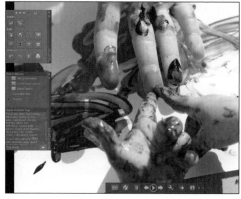

A The full-screen review includes panels that automatically hide when not being used.

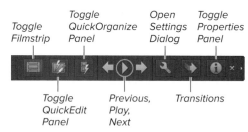

Toggle Filmstrip   *Toggle QuickOrganize Panel*   *Open Settings Dialog*   *Toggle Properties Panel*

Toggle QuickEdit Panel   *Previous, Play, Next*   *Transitions*

B The full-screen control bar.

C Tag your photo or add it to an album without leaving the full-screen view.

Full-Screen Slideshows

The full-screen review feature is good even if you're not reviewing. Use it to play quick slideshows, including background music and transitions. Click the Play button in the control bar (or press the spacebar) to start; adjust the settings by clicking the Open Settings Dialog button; and choose a transition by clicking the Transitions button.

A Type a word in the Search field to view photos that include that term.

B You can omit terms by specifying NOT in the Search field.

Finding Photos

In addition to locating photos using keyword tags and albums, the Organizer offers a host of other options for finding and viewing photos in your catalog. I'll touch on just a couple of the more popular methods here for locating photos by their embedded date information. For example, the text search capability takes advantage of the keyword tags you applied earlier.

To find photos using a text search:

- Type a term into the Search field in the Options bar. The Photo Browser searches the photos' metadata and displays matches as you type **A**.

- The Organizer is smart enough to understand the operators AND, OR, and NOT, which allow you to quickly narrow your search **B**.

- For more specific searching, enter any of the following search tags into the field. For example, typing `make:canon` (note the lack of a space after the colon) finds all photos in my library shot using a Canon camera. You can also group tags to narrow the results **C**.

  - ▸ `tag:`
  - ▸ `filename:`
  - ▸ `caption:`
  - ▸ `make:`
  - ▸ `model:`
  - ▸ `author:`
  - ▸ `notes:`
  - ▸ `date: ##/##` (month/day, depending on date preferences in Organizer)
  - ▸ `date: ####` (year)
  - ▸ `date:` (`today`, `yesterday`, `lastweek`, `thisyear`, or `lastyear`)

C Here I've used two terms to define a more specific search (photos shot with a Canon camera sometime in 2005).

To find photos using the timeline:

1. If the timeline isn't visible, choose Window > Timeline (Ctrl+L).

2. In the timeline, click on a bar corresponding to a specific month and year  . The Photo Browser automatically scrolls to display the photos for the month you selected.

To display photos within a date range:

1. From the Find menu, choose Set Date Range, or press Ctrl+Alt+F.

2. In the Set Date Range dialog, use the text fields and drop-down menus to enter your dates.

3. The timeline highlights just the range of dates you selected 🄴 .

To quickly search by attributes:

Drag keyword tags, albums, or other criteria to the Find bar at the top of the Photo Browser 🄵 .

TIP You can also move the date range markers on the timeline to view photos within that range.

TIP When you drag photos to the Find bar, Elements displays images with similar qualities such as color.

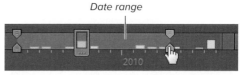

🄓 Bars (month markers) in the timeline represent sets of images shot or acquired in specific months. Click a timeline marker to view its photos.

Date range

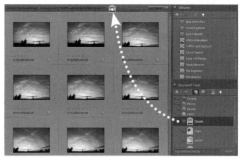

🄔 After you set a date range, only those photos that fall within the specified range are visible.

🄕 Dragging the "Clouds" keyword tag to the Find bar above the Photo Browser narrows the number of displayed photos.

G The date view offers three calendar layouts for viewing photos.

H Click a shaded date in Year view to see the photos associated with that day.

I The Day View window.

To find photos in the date view:

1. From the Display drop-down menu, choose Date View (Ctrl+Alt+D).

2. At the bottom of the Date View window, click to select a view option G.

3. Use the navigation buttons in calendar view to move from one year, month, or day to another.

   In Year view, dates shaded in blue indicate the days those photos were taken. A preview window to the right contains a thumbnail of the first photo in the set, plus navigation buttons to view the remaining photos in the set H. In Month view, thumbnails appear on the dates the photos were taken.

4. To view the complete set of photos for any given day, do one of the following:

   ▸ Double-click either a shaded day in Year view or a day thumbnail in Month view.

   ▸ Click to select a day in either Year or Month view, and then click the Day button at the bottom of the Date View window.

   In the Day View window you can see large, single-image views of your photos I. You can also add notes for a complete day's set of photos and enter a caption for individual photos.

TIP From the Find menu, you can search for photos to view by a number of different criteria. Some that you'll probably use most often are by caption or note; by filename; by history (imported on date, and printed on date, among others); and by media type (photos, video, audio, and creations). Just choose an option and then fill in its dialog (when applicable) to refine your search.

Using Stacks to Organize Similar Photos

You've spent a day on the valley floor of Yosemite shooting picture after picture, and when you return home in the evening and download all of those photos to your Photo Browser, you realize you have about a dozen shots of the same waterfall: some lit a little differently than others; some with different zoom settings; but all similar.

Stacks serve as a convenient way to group those related photos together. They not only save valuable space in the Photo Browser, they also make assigning tags much faster, because tagging a stack automatically tags every photo in the stack. When you're ready to take a careful look at all of those waterfalls and weed out the greats from the not-so-greats, you simply expand the stack to view all of the stacked photos at once.

To create a stack:

1. In the Photo Browser, Ctrl-click to select the photos you want to include in a stack **A**.

2. Choose Edit > Stack > Stack Selected Photos, or press Ctrl+Alt+S.

   The photos are stacked together, indicated by a Stack icon in the upper-right corner of the top photo in the stack **B**.

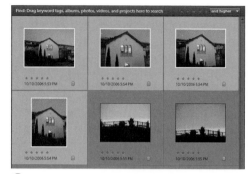

A Select similar photos to organize them into a stack.

Stack icon

B When stacked, the photos occupy just one thumbnail, and are indicated by the Stack icon.

C An expanded stack reveals the photos that have been grouped together.

D A warning box reminds you that you are about to delete all but the top photo in your stack.

To view all photos in a stack:

In the Photo Browser, click the arrow icon at the right of the stack. Or, choose Edit > Stack > Expand Photos in Stack; or press Ctrl+Alt+R. The photos in the stack appear **C**.

To flatten a stack:

1. If you're certain you don't want any photo in a stack except for the top one, you can "flatten" the stack and delete the others. Choose Edit > Stack > Flatten Stack.

2. In the warning dialog that appears, click OK to delete all of the photos except for the top photo in the stack **D**.

    You can also choose to delete the associated image files from your hard disk.

To unstack photos in a stack:

Choose Edit > Stack > Unstack Photos.

The stacked photos return to their original locations in the Photo Browser window.

> **TIP** While you're viewing the expanded stack, you can also remove specific photos from a stack, or designate a new photo to be the top photo (the photo that appears at the top of the stack in the Photo Browser). Just right-click on any stacked photo and then, from the thumbnail contextual menu, select an option from the Stack submenu.

Using the Map

Sometimes where you took a photo is as important as what's in the image. The Map feature lets you associate locations with your photos, using support from Yahoo! Maps .

To place a photo on the map:

1. Right-click one or more photos and choose Place on Map from the contextual menu.

2. In the Photo Location on Map dialog, type an address **B**.

3. Elements checks online for a match and displays the results; select the one closest to the location you're looking for and click OK.

   A red pushpin icon appears in the Map pane at the location you specified. Clicking the icon displays the photo **C**.

4. Use the Zoom, Hand, and Move tools to navigate the map.

A The Map view lets you plot photos anywhere on the globe.

B Enter an address, city, state, or country (or any of the above) to find the location.

TIP You can also choose Show Map from the Display drop-down menu to view the Map pane and then simply drag photos to a location on the map to place them. However, the steps above make it easier to find specific locations, versus dropping a bunch of pictures onto "North America" and calling it good.

TIP When creating tags, click the Place on Map button to specify a location in the Map pane. Any photo assigned that tag automatically appears on the map.

TIP The pop-up menu at the lower-right corner of the Map pane lets you display a traditional map, a satellite image, or a hybrid version (satellite with street names superimposed over it).

C Clicking a marker on the map displays a window containing thumbnails of the photos associated with that location.

Right-click a pushpin icon on the map to remove the photos from the map.

To move a location on the map:

Right-click a pushpin icon and choose Place on Map; follow the directions on the previous page.

Or

1. Click the Move tool in the Map pane.

2. Drag a pushpin icon to another location.

   All photos associated with that location are marked with the new location.

To remove a photo from the map:

In the Map pane, right-click a pushpin icon and choose Remove from Map .

TIP Placing images on the map can also be a convenient way for others to view your photos.

Using Catalogs to Store Your Photos

Catalogs are the behind-the-scenes backbone of the Organizer workspace, where all the information for tags and categories and albums are stored. When you install Elements, a default catalog (called My Catalog) is set up for you. That might be enough to work with, but you can also create additional catalogs—for example, if more than one person is using the same computer. You may want discrete catalogs for each person's photos: Bob's Catalog, Sara's Catalog, and so on.

To create a new catalog:

1. From the File menu choose Catalog, or press Ctrl+Shift+C.

2. In the Catalog Manager dialog, click a radio button to specify whether the catalog is available to all user accounts on the computer, just the current user, or saved to a custom location 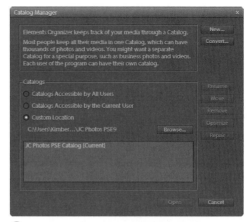.

3. Click the New button.

   If online backups are enabled for your existing catalog, a warning dialog appears stating you'll need to set the new catalog to be backed up in the Backup/Sync preferences (see the next section). Click OK to continue.

4. In the File name text field, enter a name for your new catalog .

   At the bottom of the naming dialog is the Import free music into this catalog checkbox. Leave this option selected so the music files you received with Elements (to use as background tracks for PDF slide shows and other creations) will be available in the new catalog.

5. Click OK to create your new catalog.

A Choose which users and locations the catalog belongs to.

B Make sure to name your new catalog differently than any existing catalogs.

Repair and Optimize Catalogs

If your library seems out of sorts—maybe not all thumbnails are appearing, for example—turn to the Catalog Manager for help. Select a catalog name and click the Repair button to scan for problems and fix them.

Clicking the Optimize button pares the catalog size and can also improve performance if the Organizer seems sluggish.

C Juggle multiple catalogs using the Catalog Manager dialog.

D Specify where your backup files are to be copied.

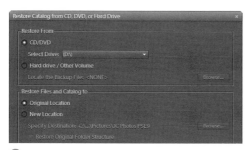

E If you need to reconstruct a catalog from your backup, use the Restore Catalog command.

TIP Restoring a catalog isn't just for when disaster strikes. If you need to move a catalog to another computer, create a full backup first, and then use the Restore feature in Photoshop Elements on the other machine.

To access saved catalogs:

1. From the File menu choose Catalog, or press Ctrl+Shift+C.

2. Select the name of the saved catalog you want to open **C**.

3. Click the Open button.

To make a backup of a catalog:

1. Since you obviously don't want to lose your photos, choose File > Backup Catalog to Hard Drive.

2. In the Backup dialog, choose Full Backup to make a complete copy of the catalog. On subsequent backups, you can choose Incremental Backup to copy only new and changed image files.

3. Click Next.

4. Select a destination drive from the list, and specify a location by clicking the Browse button for Backup Path **D**.

5. Click Done when you're ready. Elements copies the image files and catalog information to the drive.

To restore a catalog from backup:

1. In the event that your catalog becomes unreadable, choose File > Restore Catalog from Hard Drive.

2. In the Restore dialog, choose the media on which the backup is stored **E**; click the Browse button to locate the **.tly** file that accompanies the backup.

3. Choose where to copy the restored files: the catalog's original location or another location.

4. Click Restore. The images and catalog information are copied to the destination.

Backing Up Photos Online

The capability to back up your catalog to an external hard disk or removable media has one limitation: You need to actually do it. And speaking from experience, that's something easily forgotten or put off for another day. But hard drives don't fail on a schedule, and thieves don't wait to pilfer your laptop until it's most convenient for you.

I covered the basics of the integration between Elements and Photoshop.com in Chapter 1. With an account set up, you can direct Elements to back up your photos over the Internet in the background. Even if your computer perishes in a natural disaster, your photos are safe on Adobe's servers.

Elements also *synchronizes* your backup. If you make a change to a photo in your library or online, the change is reflected in both locations.

To set up Photoshop.com backups:

1. Sign in to your Photoshop.com account if you haven't already.

2. In the Organizer, choose Edit > Preferences > Backup/Synchronization.

   You can also click the synchronization status icon at the bottom of the Organizer screen and choose Open Backup/Synchronization preferences from the pop-up menu that appears 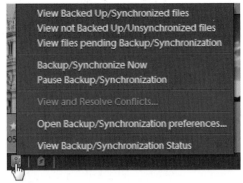.

3. Enable the Backup/Sync is On checkbox if it's not already active , and click OK.

A Access the Photoshop.com backup settings from the synchronization status icon.

B The master switch for enabling backups is in the Backup/Synchronization preferences.

Sync Photos Between Computers

Photoshop Elements and Photoshop.com enable you to keep backups of your photos on Adobe's remote servers (and optionally share them via the Web), but you can take advantage of the service to keep your library synchronized on more than one computer.

Use the directions in this section to log in to your Photoshop.com account on the machines you want to use, and make sure they're set to sync.

Depending on the size of your library, you can sync your entire catalog between machines (you may need to upgrade your account for more storage). In the Backup/Synchronization preferences, click the Backup/Sync Entire Catalog button.

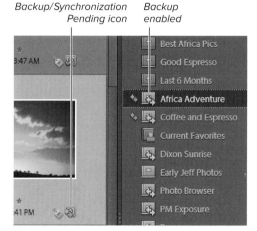

C Enable the Backup/Synchronize checkbox to copy the contents of an album to Photoshop.com.

Backup/Synchronization   Backup
Pending icon   enabled

D You can tell at a glance which photos and albums are getting backed up.

Backing up albums

Elements primarily organizes online backups by album. This approach cuts the amount of data transferred (since image files tend to be quite large) and lets you decide which photos are backed up.

To enable an album for online backup:

1. Create a new album, or select an existing album and edit it (see "Using Albums to Arrange and Group Photos," earlier in this chapter). The Album Details dialog fills the Organize panel.

2. Enable the Backup/Synchronize check-box C.

3. Click Done. The album icon displays a pair of icons indicating that it gets syn-chronized, and each photo in the album gains a pending synchronization icon D.

   Elements copies the images to the Photoshop.com servers in the back-ground while you perform other tasks.

To view the backup status:

Click the synchronization status icon and choose one of the first three items in the menu to display: files that have been backed up; files that are not set for backup; or files that are due to be backed up. The photos appear in the Photo Browser.

> **TIP** New albums are automatically set to be backed up. To turn off this behavior, disable the **New Albums Will Backup/Sync Automatically** checkbox in the Backup/Synchronization preferences under Advanced Backup/Sync Options.

To control when backups occur:

- Click the synchronization status icon and choose Pause Backup/Synchronization from the status icon pop-up menu to temporarily halt copying. Use this command when you want to maximize your Internet bandwidth for other tasks.

- Click the Elements Organizer menu bar item and choose one of the following options **E**:

  - Backup/Sync only when idle: Elements copies files only when you're not using the computer.

  - Backup/Sync Now: Synchronize immediately.

  - Pause Backup/Synchronization: Temporarily halts copying.

  - Stop Backup/Synchronization: Disables the Backup/Sync is On setting in the Elements preferences and ends the agent. You must go back to the preferences to restart the service.

To stop backing up an album:

1. Select an existing album and edit it.

2. In the Album Details dialog, disable the Backup/Synchronize checkbox.

3. Click Done.

   When you turn off backup/synchronization, Elements no longer communicates with Photoshop.com about the photos in that album. However, the images still remain online; if you want to delete them from Photoshop.com, you need to do so there.

TIP To see what's being transferred, choose View Backup/Synchronization Status from the synchronization status icon **F**.

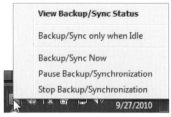

E The Elements Organizer menu bar menu controls when images are copied.

F In the Backup/Synchronization preferences, click the Sync checkbox for the albums you wish to sync.

Keep a Backup Backup

The best approach, of course, is to have multiple backups of your precious images. The advantage of an online backup is that it's performed automatically and the data is stored in a physically separate location. But that also means the backup is out of your hands—if Adobe's servers go down or become corrupted, your backup is gone. It's unlikely, but still possible. So make a point of keeping multiple backups: online, on external hard disks, on CD or DVD media, or whatever combination works best for you.

A In the Backup/Synchronization preferences, click the Sync checkbox for the albums you wish to sync.

B At Photoshop.com, the original version of the image at right was replaced by this version that was edited in Elements.

Synchronizing Photos with Photoshop.com

Communication between Elements and Photoshop.com goes both ways. When you edit a photo in Elements, the changes are automatically uploaded to your library at Photoshop.com and vice-versa. You can specify which albums are synchronized in the Backup/Synchronization preferences **A**.

Here's how synchronization works:

- Elements copies all files in an album to Photoshop.com. However, the online service only works with JPEG images, so if you want to edit a raw file, for example, Photoshop.com first converts the image.

- When you edit a file at Photoshop.com, the edited version is added to your Elements library as a new version; the original is still available.

- If you edit an image in Elements, only the most recent version of the file is uploaded to Photoshop.com **B**. The original version exists only in your Elements library.

- If your Elements album contains a version set, only the "top" version (the latest) is uploaded to Photoshop.com, not all versions in the set.

- Removing a photo from an album in either Elements or Photoshop.com does not delete the file; it's still available in the libraries at both locations.

- If you delete an album in Elements that you've shared (made public), the photos still reside at Photoshop.com but are no longer publicly available.

continues on next page

- If you delete a synchronized photo from Photoshop.com, Elements alerts you that a synchronization problem exists (see below). You can remove this confirmation step by disabling the preference labeled When I Delete a File Online, Ask Before Deleting It from My Computer.
- If you edit several different aspects of a photo—for example, adding a caption at Photoshop.com and applying keywords in Elements—those changes are merged so that each version is the same.

Resolving synchronization issues

Sometimes synchronization isn't straightforward. What happens when you add a caption to a photo in Elements and then accidentally add a different caption for the same photo at Photoshop.com? The synchronization status icon turns yellow to indicate a conflict.

To resolve synchronization issues:

1. Click the synchronization status icon and choose View and Resolve Conflicts from the pop-up menu 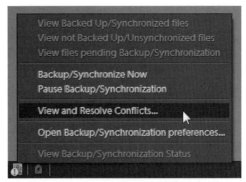.

2. In the Backup/Synchronization Resolution dialog, review the conflicts and choose the version you wish to keep .

    If you've deleted a file from the library (not just removed it from an album), as I mentioned above, the Deletions tab lets you confirm or reject the deletion.

3. Click the Apply Changes and Quit button to resolve the conflicts.

TIP Photoshop.com doesn't automatically update its library when you're viewing an album online. If you're expecting synchronized files to appear, click the Refresh button to update the library .

C The yellow synchronization status icon indicates you need to resolve a conflict.

D Elements details the sync conflicts and lets you choose which version to keep.

E Click the Refresh button to update the library.

Creating and Managing Images

So far, I've introduced Photoshop Elements and worked mostly in the Organizer, importing and arranging photos for manipulation later. But Elements is based on the code from Photoshop, the industrial-strength image editor used by the pros. As such, it's important to build a foundation of knowledge about digital images in preparation for editing them later.

This chapter offers some basic guidelines on adjusting image size and resolution. If you want to e-mail a photo to a friend, you'll need a small file size for easy delivery— so you'll want to create a low-resolution image, which means it contains a smaller number of pixels. If you're planning to print high-quality images on your ink-jet printer, you'll want to maintain as high a resolution as your printer can handle (meaning a greater density of pixels) to ensure a crisp, clear print.

I also cover creating images from scratch, the different methods for viewing additional information about your images, and working with window behavior in Elements.

In This Chapter

Understanding Resolution and Image Size

Resolution and image size are frequently used and often misunderstood terms.

Resolution simply refers to the number of *pixels*, or picture elements—tiny, square, building blocks—that make up a digital image. Today's computer monitors and LCD displays pack millions of pixels into the screen you're viewing; the more pixels, the higher the resolution, and in general the more detail you're able to see.

Image size refers to both the print size and resolution of an image. Depending on whether you want to print a photograph, post it on a Web page, or e-mail it to a friend, you'll need to adjust its image size and resolution accordingly.

Pixel basics

Everything you do in Photoshop Elements involves controlling and changing pixels. Pixels make up your entire image and are typically not visible as individual elements until you zoom in on your picture **A**.

Images are often described using pixels as the unit of measure. For example, a digital camera may shoot images at 1600 x 1200 pixels (the *x* is pronounced "by," just as in "3 x 5 photo"). Multiplying 1600 times 1200 gives you the total number of pixels in the image, which in this case is 1.92 million pixels.

Digital cameras often include preset resolution modes. These settings determine both the physical dimensions and file size of the image **B**.

A Pixels become more visible as you increase the magnification of your image.

3872 x 2592 pixels, 16.9 MB

640 x 480 pixels, 1.4 MB

B Examples of common digital camera resolutions and associated file sizes, all viewed at 100 percent (also referred to as actual pixels). Higher-resolution images, like the photo on top, provide a sharp, clear picture that's excellent for printing. Lower-resolution images, like the bottom photo, lack sufficient pixel information for printing purposes, but work fine for e-mailing or posting on the Web.

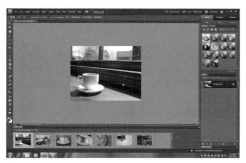

Displaying and printing images

Any discussion of resolution and output can be confusing, so you need to keep a few basic details in mind. Image resolution is described in *pixels per inch*, or *ppi*.

The ideal amount of detail and level of resolution depends on how you intend to use an image. If you're going to display your photos on the Web, keep in mind that large files take forever to download and view, so you'll want to choose a lower resolution like 72 ppi (72 ppi is the most common image resolution for monitors).

Three factors affect the way an image is displayed on a computer monitor: the number of pixels in the image, the screen resolution, and the screen size **C**. The size of each pixel is determined by the resolution and size of the monitor. For example, a 17-inch monitor set to a resolution of 1024 x 768 pixels would have 82 pixels per inch **D**. The same monitor set to a resolution of 800 x 600 would have fewer pixels per inch, so each pixel takes up more screen space **E**. If you change your monitor resolution to a lower resolution setting, the images and icons appear larger on your screen. It takes fewer pixels to fill the monitor, so the size of each pixel appears larger.

Print resolution is usually described by the number of *dots per inch*, or *dpi,* a printer is capable of printing. If you want to print a high-quality flyer or photo, you may want to use an image resolution as high as 300 pixels per inch, so that a maximum amount of image information is sent to the printer. Fortunately, a wide range of available image resolutions work well for different situations, and Photoshop Elements includes some automatic functions (such as the Save for Web command) that take the guesswork out of the process.

C The display of an onscreen image is based on the resolution of the image, the size of the monitor, and the monitor resolution.

D A monitor set to 1024 x 768 is a common setting, and allows program menus to be seen more easily.

E The same monitor set to 800 x 600 displays fewer pixels per inch, so less of the image is visible.

Creating a New Image

If you want to start with a blank canvas, use the New dialog to set up the basic dimensions, image resolution, and color mode. You can create your own work of art using Photoshop Elements' many painting and drawing tools, or you can assemble a collage of multiple images. But for now, I'll stick with the basics.

To create a new image:

1. To create a new image go to the File menu and choose New > Blank File, or press Ctrl+N.

2. In the New dialog, enter a filename; then enter dimensions for the width and height . The default size is 6 x 4 inches, which works fine as a starting point. You can always change it later.

3. Set the resolution and color mode. For more information, see Chapter 7, "Changing and Adjusting Colors."

4. From the Background Contents drop-down menu, choose an option for the background layer of the image.

   ▸ White is the default background option and creates a pure white background layer for the image. This option is just fine for most purposes.

   ▸ Background Color fills the background with the current background color—useful if you want a Web graphic that matches the background color of your Web page.

   ▸ Transparent makes the first layer transparent and results in an image with no background at all—a good choice if you're creating an image for the Web and want it to appear transparent on the page.

Ⓐ The New dialog lets you name your new image and set its dimensions, resolution, and color mode.

Don't Panic

Don't be intimidated by the sheer number of size, resolution, and transparency settings available when you first create a new image. All of these settings will be covered in more detail as you progress through the book. If you're brand new to Photoshop Elements, creating a new image can be as simple as pressing Ctrl+N and accepting the default settings.

Ⓐ This image was duplicated (top) then reduced 50% (bottom). Notice in the zoom views that the reduced image isn't as detailed as the original. That's because, even though both have the same number of pixels per inch, the reduced image contains fewer pixels overall.

Changing Image Size and Resolution

Pixel dimensions, image dimensions, and resolution are all adjusted using the Image Size dialog. You will often capture one image and then use it for different purposes, so it's important to understand how these adjustments affect your image file.

For the Web and other onscreen viewing, it's common to adjust the pixel dimensions, or number of pixels, to control the resolution and/or file size of the image. This is known as *resampling*. The Resample Image checkbox is probably the most important feature to understand. When this box is checked, the pixel dimensions change—that is, the pixels will increase or decrease in number as the image is resampled **Ⓐ**. When the box is *not* checked, the pixel dimensions are locked in, and no resampling can occur. You can change the *document* size (the size the image will print), but the number of pixels in the image and the size that the image displays onscreen will stay the same.

Recommended Resolutions

There are no absolute rules for the best resolution to use when working with images for the Web or for printing. The best approach is to try a couple of settings, using the following guidelines, and see what works well for your specific situation. Here are some typical situations and recommended resolution ranges:

- For onscreen viewing of Web images, 72 ppi is a standard and safe resolution.

- For color images printed on color ink-jet printers, a range of up to 150 ppi is often ideal. The exact resolution will depend on your printer and the type of paper on which you are printing.

- For color or high-resolution black and white images printed on photo printers, you'll want a resolution between 150 and 300 ppi.

If you want to create higher-quality professional projects, such as magazine or print design work, be aware that Photoshop Elements is not capable of producing CMYK files (the color-separated files used for high-end printing). If you need an image-editing program that can handle these kinds of jobs, consider buying the full version of Adobe Photoshop.

To resize an image for screen viewing:

1. From the Image menu, choose Resize > Image Size to open the Image Size dialog.

2. Make sure the Resample Image box is checked, and click the Resample Image drop-down menu **B**.

   When you resample an image, its pixels are transformed using a process known as an *interpolation*. Interpolation is a computer calculation used to estimate unknown values based on existing known values—in this case, pixel color values. So, when you resample an image in Elements, its existing pixels are changed using one of five primary interpolation methods **C**:

   ▸ Bicubic is the default option and generally produces the best results and smoothest gradations.

   ▸ Bilinear produces medium-quality results.

   ▸ Nearest Neighbor is the fastest method, but may produce jagged effects.

   ▸ Bicubic Smoother can be used when you're increasing the size of an image, or *upsampling*. Typically, I strongly advise against upsampling, because there is usually a noticeable loss of image quality and sharpness. But I've seen acceptable results with Bicubic Smoother, as long as I don't resize much above 120 percent.

   ▸ Bicubic Sharper can be used when you're reducing the size of an image, or *downsampling*. Its purpose is to help retain sharpness and detail. My success with this option has been mixed.

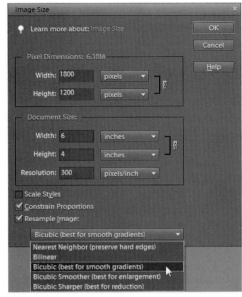

B The Resample Image drop-down menu includes five options for specifying how the resampling occurs.

C You can resample an image using one of three calculation methods: Bicubic (left), Bilinear (center), or Nearest Neighbor (right). Bicubic does the best job at retaining detail and anti-aliasing, whereas Nearest Neighbor creates images with a rougher quality.

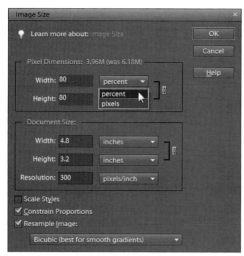

 Pixel dimensions can be entered as pixels or as a percentage.

3. To maintain the current width-to-height ratio, make sure Constrain Proportions is checked.

4. Enter new values in the Pixel Dimensions fields. You can enter values in pixels or as percentages ❶.

   If you choose percent, you can enter a percentage amount in either the Height or Width field to automatically scale the image to that percentage. The new file size for the image is displayed at the top of the dialog (along with the old file size in parentheses).

5. Click OK to complete the change. The image is resized larger or smaller, depending on the pixel dimensions or percentage you entered.

TIP When you change an image's size by changing its pixel dimensions, you also change its print size (you'll see the change in the width and height dimensions in the Document Size fields of the Image Size dialog). Although these images are acceptable for onscreen viewing or as quick test prints, you may be disappointed with their printed quality. That's because you discard image information by resampling, and so lose some sharpness and detail.

Downsampling vs. Upsampling

Downsampling, which is the term for decreasing resolution by *removing* pixels from your photo, is one of the easiest and most common ways to make your files smaller. If you take an 8 x 10 photograph of your grandmother and shrink it to a 4 x 5 image by reducing its pixel count, you've just downsampled it. Elements "throws away" unneeded pixels intelligently, with little visible impact on the quality of your image.

But *upsampling*, which is the term for increasing resolution by *adding* new pixels to your photo, should be avoided whenever possible. If you take a 4 x 5 photograph and try to enlarge it to 8 x 10, Elements must manufacture those pixels out of thin air. They tend to add a ghosted, fuzzy appearance to any hard edge—the overall effect is that your image can look out of focus.

Because downsampling rarely detracts from the quality of your images, you should capture all your original files at the highest resolution possible, whether you're scanning an image or snapping a digital photo.

To resize an image for printing:

1. From the Image menu, choose Resize > Image Size.

2. To maintain the current width-to-height ratio, check that the Constrain Proportions option is selected.

3. Uncheck the Resample Image box.

4. Choose a unit of measure (or a percentage) and then enter new values for the width or height in the Document Size portion of the dialog **E**.

   In the Document Size portion of the dialog, the resolution value changes accordingly. For instance, if you enter width and height values of half the original image size, the resolution value will double, and the image will print clearer and sharper. That's because you're compressing the same number of pixels into a smaller space. So, when scaled at 50 percent, an image 4 inches wide with a resolution of 150 pixels per inch (ppi) will print at 2 inches wide and at a resolution of 300 ppi.

5. Click OK to complete the change.

   The image's print size will be changed, but since it still contains the same number of pixels, it will appear to be unchanged on your screen. You can, however, view a preview of the final print size onscreen:

   ▶ From the View menu, choose Print Size. The image is resized on your screen to approximate its final, printed size **F**.

   ▶ From the View menu, choose Actual Pixels, or press Ctrl+1 to return the display size to 100 percent.

TIP To return the dialog to its original settings, press Alt to change the Cancel button to Reset, then click Reset.

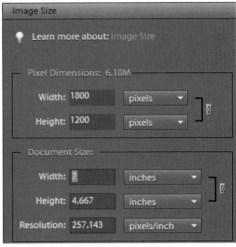

E Enter new width and height values to change an image's print size.

F An image can be viewed at an approximation of its final print size, even when its resolution differs from the computer's display.

Color information

A Any two sets of color information (RGB, HSB, Web Color, or Grayscale) can be viewed at once.

B Color modes (and other settings) can be changed from pop-up lists in the panel.

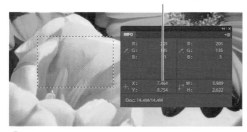

X and Y coordinates

C The x and y coordinates of the pointer are shown in the Info panel.

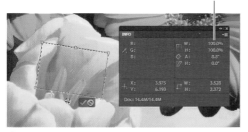

Transformations

D Any change in the scale or transformation of a selection or layer is visible in the Info panel.

Getting Information about Your Image

The Info panel displays measurement and color information as you move a tool over an image. In addition, you can customize the status bar at the bottom of the Info panel to display different file and image information.

To use the Info panel:

1. From the Window menu, choose Info to view the Info panel.

2. Select the desired tool and then move the pointer over the image. Depending on the tool you are using, the following information appears:

   ▸ The numeric values for the color beneath the pointer. You can view any two sets of color modes at the same time A. Information for different color modes can be displayed at any time by clicking either of the eyedropper cursor buttons in the Info panel B.

   ▸ The x and y coordinates of the pointer, and the starting x and y coordinates of a selection or layer, along with the change in distance as you move the pointer over your image C.

   ▸ The width and height of a selection or shape and the values relating to transformations, such as the percentage of scale, angle of rotation, and skew (which distorts a selection along the horizontal or vertical axis) D.

TIP It's usually quicker to change units of measure using the Info panel rather than by using the Preferences menu.

To display different Info panel options:

1. Click the More button on the Info panel to open the panel menu, and then choose Panel Options ⓔ.

2. Use the drop-down menus in the top three areas of the dialog to change the color and unit options you would like the panel to display ⓕ.

3. In the Status Information area of the dialog, click the checkbox next to the options you would like the panel to display ⓖ.

Here are descriptions of some of the most useful options:

▸ Document Sizes displays information relating to the file's size. The first number represents the approximate size of the file if flattened (all layers combined into one) and saved. The second number represents the current file size, with layers.

▸ Document Profile displays the color mode of the image.

▸ Document Dimensions displays the width and height of the image.

▸ Scratch Sizes displays the amount of memory needed to process the image. The first number represents the memory currently used to display all open images. The second number represents the total available RAM. If you think you're running into memory problems and need to add more RAM to your computer, viewing this information will help you evaluate the problem.

ⓔ Access Panel Options from the Info panel's More menu.

ⓕ You can control what type of information will be displayed for color modes and for units of measurement.

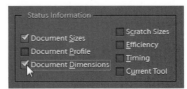

ⓖ The Info panel can display the status for up to seven different types of information, all at the same time.

Document tabs

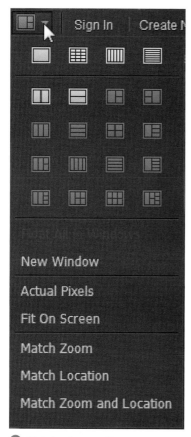

A Open documents occupy the main workspace and are only visible one at a time. Click a tab to bring a document to the front.

B Click the Arrange Documents button to set how multiple files appear in the Editor.

Arranging Windows

Photoshop Elements takes a different approach to arranging open file windows than many applications. Instead of windows floating on top of each other, they occupy the entire work area, with tabs that indicate open files **A**.

If you prefer overlapping windows, a preference enables them to float like traditional windows (or like Elements behaved prior to version 8) in Full Edit mode.

To arrange multiple windows:

1. Click the Arrange Documents button above the toolbar.

2. From the menu that appears, click a preset layout icon **B**.

To enable floating windows:

Go to Edit > Preferences > General and enable the option titled Allow Floating Documents in Full Edit Mode.

With that active, you can drag a window's title bar away from the workspace edge to make it appear as a free-floating window.

The options in the next section assume you've enabled floating windows; otherwise, many are not available.

Arranging Multiple Views

You can open multiple windows with different images, or, if you prefer, you can open multiple views of the same image. This is a handy way to work on a detailed area of your image while viewing the full-sized version of the image at the same time. It's especially useful when you're doing touch-up work, such as correcting red eye or erasing a blemish in a photo.

A Two windows are displaying the same image in the vertical 2 Up layout.

To open multiple views of an image:

From the Arrange Documents menu, choose New Window. The window appears as a new tab; you can also look in the Project Bin to see the new view.

To arrange multiple views:

Do one of the following:

- Click the Arrange Documents menu and choose one of the layout icons (such as one of the 2 Up orientations) **A**.

- To create cascading, overlapping windows, choose Float All in Windows.

- If the windows are floating, position them by dragging their title bars, or use the commands under Window > Images to tile or cascade them.

B Multiple image views let you work on a detailed area (left) while at the same time allowing you to see how the changes affect the overall image (right).

To close multiple view windows:

Do one of the following:

- To close a single window, click the close button on that window's title bar.

- To close all document windows, from the File menu, choose Close All or press Ctrl+Alt+W.

TIP To quickly switch from one open window to another, press Ctrl+~ (tilde).

TIP You can set different levels of magnification for each window to see both details and the big picture at the same time **B**.

TIP When you're working on a zoomed-in image, it's easy to get lost. From the Arrange Documents menu, choose Match Zoom to set all open windows to the same zoom level. Or, choose Match Location to make the same visible pixels appear in all windows. That's a quicker option than scrolling around looking for a match, or using the Navigator panel.

TIP To put all floating windows in tabs, choose Window > Images > Consolidate All to Tabs.

A The rulers' zero point establishes the origin of the rulers.

B Drag the zero point to a new location anywhere in the document window.

Using Rulers

Customizable rulers, along the top and left sides of the document window, can help you scale and position graphics and selections. The rulers are helpful if you are combining photos with text (in a greeting card, for example) and want to be precise in placing and aligning the various elements. Interactive tick marks in both rulers provide constant feedback, displaying the position of any tool or pointer as you move it through the window. You can also change the ruler origin, also known as the *zero point*, to measure different parts of your image.

To show or hide the rulers:

From the View menu, choose Rulers to turn the rulers on and off, or press Ctrl+Shift+R.

To change the zero point:

1. Place the pointer over the zero point crosshairs in the upper-left corner of the document window **A**.

2. Drag the zero point to a new position in the document window.

   As you drag, a set of crosshairs appears, indicating the new position of the zero point **B**.

3. Release the mouse button to set the new zero point.

To change the units of measure:

Right-click on either ruler. A contextual menu appears, from which you can choose a new measurement unit.

TIP To reset the zero point to its original location, double-click the crosshairs in the upper-left corner of the document window.

Setting Up the Grid

The nonprinting, customizable grid appears as an overlay across the entire document window. As with the rulers, it can be used for scaling and positioning, but it can be especially helpful for maintaining symmetry in your layout and design, or for occasions when you'd like objects to snap to specific points in the window.

To show or hide the grid:

From the View menu, choose Grid to turn the grid on and off .

To change the grid settings:

1. From the Edit menu, choose Preferences > Guides & Grid to open the Guides & Grid Preferences.

2. From the Color drop-down menu, choose a preset grid color, or choose Custom **B**.

   Choosing Custom displays the Color Picker, where you can select a custom grid color.

3. From the Style drop-down menu, choose a line style for the major grid lines **C**.

4. In the Gridline every drop-down menu, choose a unit of measure; then enter a number in the accompanying field to define the spacing of the major grid lines.

5. In the Subdivisions field, enter a number to define the frequency of minor grid lines **D**.

6. Click OK.

A Activate the document grid from the View menu.

B Choose a grid color from the list of preset colors or create a custom color.

C Examples of grid line styles.

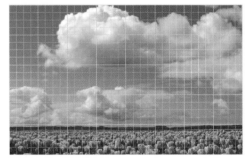

D This figure shows a document grid with major grid lines set every inch, subdivided by four minor grid lines.

Quick Fix Edits

As you'll discover in the rest of the book, Photoshop Elements is a sophisticated image editor, enabling anyone to make photo corrections that would have been absurdly difficult years ago. But sometimes you don't want to be an image expert. Let the computer do the work for you, analyzing photos and correcting them automatically.

When you don't want to mess with the particulars, or when you know that a photo needs just a bit of tweaking but you want a bit more control over the adjustments, turn to the Quick Fix features. You can experiment on your photo—ranging from slight tonal changes to radical tints and lighting adjustments—and then undo those changes if they seemed better in your mind's eye than they look on the screen.

The concepts behind the tools in Quick Fix, such as adjusting levels and sharpening, are dealt with later in the book. Use this chapter as a jumping-off point.

In This Chapter

Making Quick Fix Edits

When you want Elements to take over and make corrections according to its analysis of a photo, the speediest method is directly in the Quick Edit pane.

Using the Quick Fix editor

Quick Fix is a component of the Editor workspace and gives you a bit more control than the buttons in the Fix pane.

To edit photos in Quick Fix:

Open a file in Elements and then click the Quick option in the Edit pane. The Quick Fix workspace opens **A**.

To set view options:

- From the View menu located below the photo, choose whether you want to see the end result (After Only), the original (Before Only), or a comparison layout (both the Before and After options) **B**.

- Use the Zoom field and slider to specify how zoomed-in you want to be **C**. In the Before and After views, the zoom level applies to both versions.

  When the Zoom or Hand tool is active, you can also click the Actual Pixels, Fit Screen, or Print Size buttons in the options bar to switch to those zoom levels.

- If Elements did not rotate your image correctly during import, click the Rotate buttons to turn it clockwise or counter-clockwise in 90-degree increments.

A The Quick Fix workspace includes your image and a set of common photo manipulations.

B The Before and After options offer split-screen views of how fixes are affecting the photo.

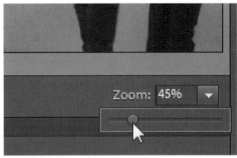

C Use the Zoom field or slider to view the photo close-up.

Walk Through Adjustments Using Guided Edit Mode

If you want to start with a little more hand-holding than what's offered by Quick Fix, try the Guided Edit mode; access it by choosing Guided in the Edit pane.

Clicking a task in this mode provides step-by-step instruction on performing common editing tasks .

When you've accomplished each step, click the Done button to apply the changes, or click Cancel to discard them. You can also click the Reset button that appears in each category to go back to the state before you applied those particular edits if you want to try a different setting.

Some Guided Edit options include:

- Basic adjustments such as Brightness and Contrast and Enhance Colors.
- The Guide for Editing a Photo, which walks you through all of the edit steps.
- Photomerge tools such as Scene Cleaner and Style Match (see Chapter 6 for more information).
- Photographic effects such as Old Fashioned Photo and Line Drawing.
- Fun Edits such as adding a reflection or making part of the photo pop out from the rest of the image.

The Guided Edit interface.

The Reflection guided edit created a lake where one didn't exist before.

Applying Quick Fixes

The following tools perform common image correction tasks, but we want to start with the most important command first: Reset.

To reset and undo changes:

- After making an adjustment using the tools described in this chapter, click the Cancel button that appears in the tool's title bar **F**.

- Choose Undo from the Edit menu to undo the previous command.

- If you've made several edits and want to revert to the original image, click the Reset button. This removes any Quick Fix adjustments.

To select areas for applying edits:

1. Select the Quick Selection tool from the toolbar.

2. Draw within an area that you want to select. Elements makes a selection based on the colors of the pixels you drew upon **G**.

To apply lighting, color, and sharpening fixes:

1. To apply fixes to a specific area of the image, use the Quick Selection tool to select an active area. Otherwise, skip to the next step.

2. Click the Auto button for one or more fixes in the Smart Fix, Lighting, Color, or Sharpness panels.

3. Drag the sliders for specific adjustments (such as Shadows) to fine-tune the settings **H**.

4. Click the Commit button (the check mark) to apply the fixes.

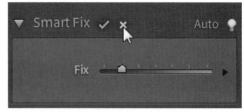

F Clicking the Cancel button restores the image to the state before you made the adjustment(s).

G Drawing with the Quick Selection tool creates a selection based on that area.

H Use the sliders associated with each type of fix to adjust the After image.

I The preview grid gives you an immediate sense of how the adjustment will appear.

J Drag a selection using the Crop tool to keep only that area and discard the rest of the image.

TIP It never hurts to play with the Smart Fix slider. Smart Fix adjusts lighting, color, and sharpening based on its algorithms. In some cases, this may be the only edit you need.

To apply fixes using previews:

1. Click the triangle icon to the right of an adjustment slider to reveal thumbnails of the range of that fix's settings.

2. Move your pointer over a thumbnail to preview the edit **I**.

   The slider is still available for fine-tuning, but there's a better way. Click and drag left or right within the thumbnail to make smaller adjustments.

3. Click the thumbnail to apply the setting.

To crop the image:

1. Select the Crop tool from the toolbar.

2. In the image's After version, drag to select the area you wish to keep **J**.

3. Click the Commit button (the check mark) that appears outside the selection to apply the crop.

To remove red eye:

In the General Fixes area, click the Auto button next to Red Eye Fix.

Or

1. Select the Red Eye Removal tool from the toolbar.

2. In the After version, drag a selection around the red-eye area. The fix applies when you release the mouse button.

To apply all edits:

1. Choose File > Close, or click the close button in the upper-right corner of the workspace.

2. When prompted, save your changes.

TIP See Chapter 6 for details on the settings offered by each tool.

Making Touch Up Edits

A few tools in the Quick Fix editor are designed to easily fix some specific situations. In the Quick pane, note the addition of four tools in the Tools panel: Red Eye Removal Tool, Whiten Teeth, Make Dull Skies Blue, and Black and White–High Contrast .

Unlike the other Quick Fix edits, which apply their adjustments to the entire image or to an area that you first specify using the Quick Selection tool, these Touch Up tools perform the selection and apply the edit in one step.

To make a Touch Up edit:

1. With a photo active in the Editor, click one of the Touch Up tool icons to select it.

2. Click and drag to define the area to be edited; for example, with the Make Dull Skies Blue tool active, drag in the sky area.

   Elements makes a selection and applies the effect Ⓑ.

3. Adjust the affected area using the selection tools Ⓒ.

TIP You can apply multiple Touch Up tool edits to the same image. When you click an icon, any adjustment you've already made is highlighted for further editing.

TIP The Touch Up tools are actually simplified versions of edits that the Smart Brush makes. You can apply one and then edit it further in the Full Edit mode later. See Chapter 6 for more information.

Ⓐ Touch Up tools.

Ⓑ The Make Dull Skies Blue applies a blue gradient to the selected area.

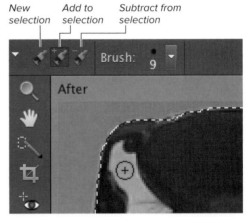

New selection   *Add to selection*   *Subtract from selection*

Ⓒ Use the selection tools to refine where the effect is applied.

Run Automated Actions with the Guided Edit Action Player

A The Action Player can run automated combinations of adjustments.

The Action Player is a feature found in the Guided Edit pane for applying preset effects such as creating captions or applying combination edits like changing a photo's colors to sepia and adding grain to the image. In the Guided Edit pane, click Action Player under Automated Actions to reveal a set of automated effects that ship with Elements **A**. Choose a set, pick a specific action, and then click the Play Action button.

That's not the whole story, though. The Action Player can run any action created in Photoshop CS. So, for example, if a friend of yours uses Photoshop extensively and has created an action that resizes an image and adds a border and photo credit, you could run that action in Elements instead of performing each step. (Elements can currently only *run* actions, not create them.)

Adding a new action isn't straightforward, however. Here's how to do it:

Take a Photoshop action file—it ends in the extension .atn—and place it in the following directory on your hard disk (each slash represents a folder; you may need to specify that hidden folders are visible by opening a Windows Explorer window and choosing Filder and search options from the Organize menu):

`\ProgramData\Adobe\Photoshop Elements\9.0\Locale\en_us\Workflow Panels\actions`

Relaunch Elements, go to the Guided Edit pane of the Editor, and you'll see the action set appear in the first drop-down menu.

5

Making Selections

Photoshop Elements offers many sophisti-cated options for enhancing and retouching your image. Those options include colors, filters, resizing tools, vignettes, and all sorts of special effects. But before you can start tinkering, you need to learn how to make selections. Once you select a specific area of an image, you can change its color, copy and paste it into another image, or change its size and rotation.

You can also use selections to create a protective mask for specific portions of an image. It's easy to select one area of an image, apply a change to the rest, and keep the selected area untouched.

In this chapter, you learn about all of the selection tools and when to choose one tool over another. You also learn how to use these tools in tandem to make the quickest and most accurate selections, depending on your specific needs.

In This Chapter

About the Selection Tools

Often, you'll want to make changes and adjustments to just a portion of an image. For example, you may want to eliminate a distracting element in your photo, change the color of a specific item, or adjust the brightness of the background. Photoshop Elements gives you a wide variety of selection tools from which to choose.

The selection tools are all grouped near one another at the top of the toolbar Ⓐ. You make rectangular and elliptical selections using the marquee tools. When you select one of the marquee tools, the selection area is indicated by a row of moving dots, like the sign outside an old-style movie theater—hence the name Ⓑ.

You select free-form, or irregularly shaped, areas using the lasso tools Ⓒ. These include the regular Lasso tool; the Polygonal Lasso, which is great for selecting areas that include straight sections; and the Magnetic Lasso, which can select the edge of an area based on its color or tonal values.

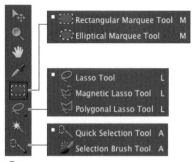

Ⓐ Access additional tools by clicking and holding on a menu item or right-clicking the selection tools in the toolbar.

Ⓑ A selection border is represented by a row of moving dots, called a marquee.

Ⓒ Each of the three lasso tools works best in a particular situation.

D The Magic Wand lets you select areas based on color.

E The Magic Wand also lets you set the tolerance, or range of colors selected.

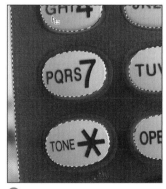

F Here, the black background was selected with the Magic Wand, and then the selection was inverted to capture the buttons.

The Magic Wand lets you select areas with the same (or similar) color or tonal value. This tool is probably the most difficult to master, but with a little practice it allows you to make selections that would be difficult to make with any of the marquee or lasso tools **D**. For example, if your photo displays a field of yellow poppies, you can select them all at once, rather than having to select each flower individually.

The selection tools work well on their own, but often the area you want to edit includes all sorts of angles and edges. In these situations, you can use the tools in combination to expand and change the selection area.

You can also expand or contract a selection area using the same tool with different settings. For example, the Magic Wand allows you to alter the range of your selection by adjusting the tolerance using the options bar before making a selection **E**.

When a photo includes an object surrounded by a large background area, it's often easier to select the background and then invert the selection to select the object. Once the selection is made, you can copy and paste it into another composition or make any other changes **F**.

continues on next page

With a selection area made, you can add to or subtract from it. Using one tool to make your initial selection and then editing the selection area using another selection tool is often easier than trying to make a perfect selection with a single tool all at once  G.

The Selection Brush allows you to make selections simply by dragging across any area or object in an image. Like the lasso tools, it works especially well for selecting irregular areas. Unlike the other selection tools, you actually "paint on" the selection using any of the brush shapes available in Elements' vast collection of brush sets H. This method of selection affords you great control and flexibility, although you need quite a bit of dexterity.

The Quick Selection tool works in much the same way as the Magic Wand tool—selecting areas based on similar color and tonal values. What distinguishes the Quick Selection tool from the other selection tools is the method you use to make the selections. By painting a series of scribbles and dots on the image, Photoshop Elements creates a selection area based on the color or tonal values below the painted marks I. Selections are additive: As you paint, the selection grows larger; use other selection tools to shrink the area.

G Here, the Elliptical Marquee tool was used to select the ladybug's main body, and then the Magic Wand tool was used to add the legs and head.

H The Selection Brush can be used in either Selection or Mask mode, selectable from the Mode menu in the options bar.

I When you "paint" through an area with the Quick Selection tool (a small area painted at left, and a larger area at right), any pixels similar in color or tonal value to those you brush over will be selected.

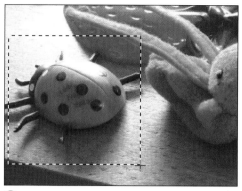

A After grabbing one of the marquee tools, just click and drag to make a selection.

B To select a perfect square or circle, hold down the Shift key while dragging.

C To draw a selection from the center outward, hold down the Alt key as you drag.

Using the Marquee Tools

The Rectangular and Elliptical Marquee tools are the easiest and most straightforward selection tools to use. You'll often want to move a selection area to align the area perfectly, and Photoshop Elements offers a couple of quick and simple ways to make these kinds of adjustments.

To make a rectangular or elliptical selection:

1. From the toolbar, choose either the Rectangular Marquee tool or Elliptical Marquee tool.

   The default setting on the options bar creates a new selection. See "Adjusting Selections," later in this chapter, for more information on other options when creating selections.

2. Click and drag to choose the selection area **A**.

TIP You can create a perfect circle or square selection using the marquee tools by holding down the Shift key as you drag **B**.

TIP You can draw the marquee from the center outward by holding down the Alt key **C**.

TIP To toggle between marquee tools, press the M key. In fact, this works for any tool with hidden tools—simply press the keyboard shortcut key repeatedly to toggle through all of the choices.

TIP To select all pixels on a layer, press Ctrl+A. This creates a selection around the entire image window, and is useful when you want to make universal color corrections or add special effects to your image. (See Chapter 8 for more on working with layers.)

To reposition a selection border:

1. Once you've made a selection, with the New selection icon active, position the pointer anywhere in the selection area.

   The pointer becomes an arrow with a small selection icon next to it . Note that if either the Add to, Subtract from, or Intersect with icon is active, the pointer indicates that choice and the selection can't be moved.

2. Click and drag to reposition the selection area.

   The pointer arrow changes to solid black as you move the selection **E**.

To reposition a selection border while making a selection:

1. Click and drag to create the selection area.

2. While keeping the mouse button pressed, press the spacebar. (The pointer arrow shows a set of cross-hairs whether or not the spacebar is pressed.)

3. Move the selection area to the desired location and release the spacebar and mouse button **F**.

TIP You can use the arrow keys on your keyboard to move a selection in 1-pixel increments. Holding the **Shift** key at the same time moves the selection in 10-pixel increments.

D To move the selection area, position the pointer within the selection boundary.

E Drag the selection border to a new location.

F To move the marquee during a selection, just press the spacebar while holding down the mouse button and adjust the border's location.

Ⓐ Select any area by tracing around it with the Lasso tool.

Ⓑ When you release the mouse button, the ends of the selection automatically join together.

Selecting Areas Using the Lasso Tools

Use the lasso tools to select areas with irregular shapes. The standard Lasso tool lets you draw or trace around an object or area freehand, much as you would draw with a pencil. This method takes patience, but with practice you can use the Lasso tool to make accurate selections.

The Polygonal Lasso tool is useful for selecting areas that include straight edges; you can toggle between the freehand and straight-edge modes when your object includes both irregular and straight edges.

As you trace around an area using the Magnetic Lasso tool, it automatically "snaps" the selection border to edges based on differences in color and tonal values in adjoining pixels. For this reason, the tool usually works best on high-contrast images. Experiment with the settings on the options bar to get the best results.

To select with the Lasso tool:

1. From the toolbar, choose the Lasso tool (or press L).

2. Keeping the mouse button pressed, drag all the way around an object or area in your image Ⓐ.

   When you release the mouse button, the open ends of the selection automatically join together Ⓑ.

TIP To keep a selection active without keeping the mouse button pressed, hold down the Alt key before releasing the button.

TIP Use the Alt key to switch between the Polygonal Lasso and regular Lasso tools.

TIP Making lasso selections is much easier with a pressure-sensitive drawing tablet.

To select with the Polygonal Lasso:

1. From the toolbar, choose the Polygonal Lasso tool.

2. Click points along the edge of the object to create straight-line segments for your selection .

3. Click back at the original starting point to join the open ends of the selection.

   You can also Ctrl-click or double-click anywhere to close the selection.

To select with the Magnetic Lasso:

1. From the toolbar, choose the Magnetic Lasso tool.

2. Click on or very close to the edge of the area you want to trace to establish the first fastening point .

3. Move the pointer along the edge you want to trace.

   The Magnetic Lasso tool traces along the selection border to the best of its ability and places additional fastening points along the way .

4. If the selection line jumps to the edge of the wrong object, place the pointer over the correct edge and click the mouse button to establish an accurate fastening point .

5. To close the selection line, click the starting point. You can also Ctrl-click, double-click anywhere on the image, or press Enter.

TIP Be warned: The Polygonal Lasso tool can sometimes slip out of your control, creating line segments where you don't want them to appear. If you make a mistake or change your mind about a line selection, you can erase line-segment selections as long as you haven't closed the selection. Just press the Backspace or Delete key, and one by one the segments will be removed, starting with the most recent one.

C The Polygonal Lasso tool creates a border of straight-line segments.

D To start a selection border with the Magnetic Lasso tool, click the edge of the area you want to trace to create the first fastening point.

E As you trace with the Magnetic Lasso tool, it places additional fastening points along the selection edge.

F Sometimes the Magnetic Lasso tool jumps to another edge (left). To correct the path, just click the correct edge to bring the border back to the right location (right).

Feather: 0 px ✔ Anti-alias Width: 10 px

Contrast: 10% Frequency: 57

G Look at the options bar while the Magnetic Lasso tool is selected; you'll find options that are unique to this tool.

H The Edge Contrast setting makes it easy to find an edge in high contrast areas (left, set to 80 percent) and low contrast areas (right, set to 5 percent).

I The Frequency option lets you determine how closely the fastening points are spaced. Top is set to 7. Bottom is set to 70.

To set Magnetic Lasso tool options:

1. Select the Magnetic Lasso tool.

2. Set any of the options visible on the options bar **G**.

    ▸ Width sets the size of the area the tool scans as it traces the selection line.

    You can set this option to a value from 1 to 40 pixels. Wide widths work well for high-contrast images, and narrow widths work well for images with subtle contrast and small shapes that are close to each other.

    ▸ Contrast sets the amount of contrast between shapes required for an edge to be recognized and traced **H**.

    This option is indicated by the percentage of contrast (from 1 to 100 percent). Try higher numbers for high-contrast images, and lower numbers for flatter, low-contrast images (just as with the Width option).

    ▸ Frequency specifies how close the fastening points are to each other.

    For Frequency, enter a number from 1 to 100. In general, you'll need to use higher frequency values when the edge is very ragged or irregular **I**.

    ▸ If you are using a stylus tablet, you can select Stylus Pressure to increase the stylus pressure and so decrease the edge width. That's right: With the button enabled, pressing harder on the stylus will yield a smaller, more precise edge.

TIP Press Alt and click to use the Polygonal Lasso tool while the Magnetic Lasso tool is selected. Press Alt and drag to use the Lasso tool.

Making Selections by Color

The Magic Wand and Quick Selection tools allow you to make selections based on a selected color or tonal value. These tools can seem truly magical—or wildly unpredictable—at first. When you select an area of an image with either tool, it selects all of the pixels within a color or tonal range close to the pixel you've initially selected.

The Magic Wand tool provides options for setting tolerance (the range of color or tonal values included in the selection around the pixel where you're clicking or dragging), anti-aliasing (smoothing), contiguousness (whether the pixels need to be connected to that first selected pixel), and whether to include all layers in the selection.

The Grow and Similar commands, found in the Select menu, can be used to expand the selection area. The Grow command expands the range of adjacent pixels, and the Similar command expands the selection based on the pixel colors.

Although the Quick Selection tool doesn't offer the options available with the Magic Wand, it will often make an accurate selection based solely on the areas you mark with the brush.

To use the Magic Wand:

1. From the toolbar, choose the Magic Wand (or press W) .

2. On the options bar, choose whether to create a new selection, add to or subtract from an existing selection, or intersect with an existing selection **B**.

   The default setting on the options bar creates a new selection.

A The Magic Wand icon is located just below the Lasso tool on the toolbar.

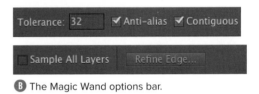

B The Magic Wand options bar.

C The Tolerance setting determines how wide a range of colors is included in the selection.

D Uncheck Contiguous if you want to select similar colors throughout the image.

3. Select the tolerance (a range of pixels from 0 to 255) to establish how wide a tonal range you want to include in your selection.

   The default tolerance level is 32 pixels. To pick colors or tonal values very close to the selected pixel, choose lower numbers. Entering higher numbers results in a wider selection of colors **C**.

4. If you want your selection to have a smooth edge, select Anti-alias.

5. If you want only pixels adjacent to the original pixel to be included in the selection, select Contiguous **D**.

6. If you want the selection to include pixels on all the layers, select All Layers (see Chapter 8 for more on working with layers).

7. Click a color or tone in the image. Based on your settings, a group or range of pixels will be selected.

TIP **When you make your original selection with the Magic Wand, it takes a color "sample" from your image. You can adjust the sample size with the Eyedropper tool. The options bar lets you sample 1 pixel, or the average of a 3-by-3-pixel area (9 pixels total), or a 5-by-5-pixel area (25 pixels total). Whichever option is active determines how the Magic Wand establishes the sample color.**

To expand the selection area:

1. From the toolbar, choose the Magic Wand tool.

2. Click a color or tonal value in the image.

3. From the Select menu, choose Grow to expand the selection of adjacent pixels.

   Each time you select Grow, the selection is expanded by the tolerance amount displayed on the Magic Wand options bar .

E Making a selection at left covers just part of the desired image. Choose Grow to expand the selection to adjacent, similarly colored areas.

To include similar colors:

1. From the toolbar, choose the Magic Wand tool.

2. Click a color or tonal value in the image.

3. From the Select menu, choose Similar to expand the selection of nonadjacent pixels.

   The selection is extended through the image to similar tonal values using the tolerance amount set on the Magic Wand options bar **F**.

F Choose Select > Similar to add pixels to your selection throughout the image.

TIP You can also access the Grow command by right-clicking after you have made a selection with the Magic Wand. A contextual menu appears in the image window, which includes the Grow and Similar commands plus a number of other useful selection options.

G The Quick Selection tool.

To use the Quick Selection tool:

1. From the toolbar, choose the Quick Selection tool (or press A) **G**.

2. In the options bar, choose a brush size.

3. In the image window, click—or click and drag—in the area where you want to make your selection. As you drag, the selection is created **H**.

4. To add to the selection, drag an area outside the current selection **I**.

5. To subtract from a selection, choose the Subtract from Selection button or hold down the Alt key, and click (or drag) inside the selection area **J**.

H Painting through an area with the Quick Selection tool creates a new selection.

I To add to a selection, paint in additional brushstrokes (Add to Selection is chosen by default).

J Use the Subtract from Selection button in the options bar to delete a portion of a selection.

Using the Selection Brush Tool

The Selection Brush tool lets you make a selection by painting over an error; it differs from the Quick Selection tool by selecting only the areas covered by the brush's "paint," instead of contiguous areas of similar tonal values.

The Selection Brush tool's options resemble those offered for the normal Brush tool. You can choose among a wide range of brush styles and sizes.

When you use the Selection Brush tool in the default Selection mode, simply click and drag through an area of your image to create a free-form, brushed selection. Unlike the other selection tools, the Selection Brush offers a Mask mode, which allows you to create a "protected" or unselected area. To work more easily with masked areas, you can control the opacity and color of the mask overlay. The two modes can be used together with great results. It's easier to make your initial selection in the default mode, and then switch to Mask mode to tune your selection.

To make a selection with the Selection Brush:

1. From the toolbar, choose the Selection Brush (or press A) .

2. Make sure the Mode menu on the options bar is set to Selection **B**.

3. Choose a brush style and optionally choose values for the brush size and hardness **C**.

    You can either enter values for the size and hardness, or drag the sliders **D** until you get the setting you want.

A The Selection Brush.

B To make a selection, choose the Selection mode.

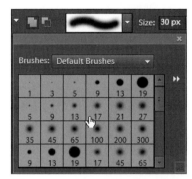

C Choose from a wide variety of prebuilt brushes.

D The brush size can be set from the options bar.

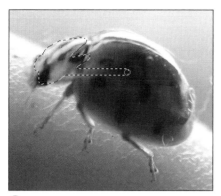

E To make a selection, just "paint" over your image with the Selection Brush.

F You can expand the selection by brushing around and through the original selection.

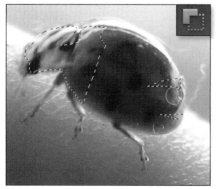

G Use the Subtract from Selection button in the options bar to remove areas of your selection.

4. Drag the brush tool over your image to make a selection E.

5. To expand your selection, brush on the edge of the selected area F. To make a selection in another portion of your image, click and drag away from the original selection.

6. To subtract from your selection, choose the Subtract from Selection button in the options bar, and then click and drag through any portion of the selection G.

TIP Like other brushes, the Selection Brush tool works well with pressure-sensitive tablets that let you paint more naturally.

TIP A quick way to change the size of the Selection Brush is to press the bracket keys on your keyboard: Press [to reduce size and] to increase size.

To make a mask with the Selection Brush:

1. Choose the Selection Brush tool.

2. From the Mode menu on the options bar, choose Mask .

3. Choose a brush style and optionally enter values for the brush size and hardness.

4. Set the overlay opacity with the slider, or enter a percentage in the text field .

5. Set the overlay color by clicking the Overlay Color box in the options bar, and then choose a color from the Color Picker.

   The default color is red, so if your selection area is also red it may be hard to see. Choose a color that works best for each image.

6. Drag the brush tool over your image to make a mask .

   As soon as you select another tool, the mask overlay area changes to a selection border. The area is protected from any changes you apply to the image 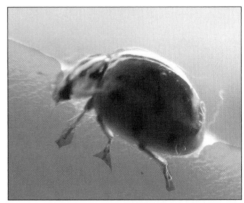. If you want to modify the mask, select the Brush Selection tool again. The mask will automatically appear over the image, and you can continue to paint in additional masked areas.

TIP The mask overlay is a very handy tool for inspecting your selections and can be used with any selection tool. Whenever you have an active selection, just click the Selection Brush tool and select the Mask option to see the masked area. When you're done viewing it in Mask mode, choose Selection from the Mode drop-down menu.

H To make a mask, first select the Mask mode option.

I The opacity of your mask overlay can be set with the slider or entered into the text field.

J When you paint with the Mask option on, the area becomes filled with the mask overlay.

K In Mask mode, you paint a mask through any areas that you *do not* want to be selected.

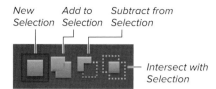

New Selection   Add to Selection   Subtract from Selection

Intersect with Selection

A To add to the current selection, either click the Add to Selection icon on the options bar or hold down the Shift key while making another selection.

B In this example, two selections combine to form a single selection.

Adjusting Selections

You can probably tell by now that a little fine-tuning is needed to make selections just the way you want them. For example, imagine you're using the Magnetic Lasso tool to trace the outline of a face, but then realize you didn't include the ear in your selection. Rather than start again from scratch, you can add to or subtract from your selection until you've included every part of the image you want. Photoshop Elements even lets you select the inter-section (or overlapping area) of two independent selections. This feature offers an effective solution for constructing inter-esting selection areas that would be difficult to create with a single selection tool.

To add to a selection:

1. Make a selection in your image with any of the selection tools.

2. With the selection still active, do one of the following:

    ▶ Using the same selection tool or after selecting another one, click the Add to Selection button in the options bar **A**.

    If the Add to Selection button is already highlighted, skip to step 3.

    ▶ Hold down the Shift key, and, if you want, select a different selection tool.

    A plus sign appears, indicating that you are adding to the current selection.

3. Make a new selection in your image. If you want to add to your existing selection, make sure your new selec-tion overlaps the original. If you want to create an additional selection, make sure you click outside of your original selection. The new selection area is added to your first selection **B**.

To subtract from a selection:

1. Make a selection with any of the selection tools.

2. With the selection still active, do one of the following:

   ▸ Select the Subtract from Selection button on the options bar, optionally choosing a different selection tool.

   ▸ Hold down the Alt key.

   A minus sign appears, indicating that you are subtracting from the current selection.

3. Drag the pointer through the area you want to subtract.

   The area you defined is removed from the selection .

To select the intersection of two selections:

1. Make a selection with any of the Marquee or Lasso selection tools.

2. With the selection still active, do one of the following:

   ▸ Select the Intersect with Selection button on the options bar and create a new selection that overlaps the current selection.

   ▸ Hold Alt+Shift and create a new selection that overlaps the current selection. An X appears, indicating that you are selecting an area of intersection.

3. A new selection area is formed based on the intersection of the two selections .

C A pie-shaped cutout is left where the rectangle selection has been subtracted.

D In this example, only the area of intersection remains.

A When you delete a selection, the selected area disappears, and your current background color shows through.

To deselect the current selection:

From the Select menu, choose Deselect, or press Ctrl+D.

To reselect the last selection:

Choose Select > Reselect, or press Ctrl+Shift+D.

To delete a selection:

Choose one of the following methods:

- From the menu bar, choose Edit > Cut, or press Ctrl+X.
- Press Delete.

  When you delete a selection, the portion of the image within your selection disappears entirely, leaving a hole in your image **A**. If you accidentally delete a selection, choose Undo from the Edit menu or press Ctrl+Z.

To hide a selection border:

From the View menu, uncheck Selection, or press Ctrl+H.

Sometimes, after you've made a selection, you want to hide the selection marquee while you edit the image; this prevents the selection border from obscuring your view. Be sure to press the same keyboard shortcut to display the selection once you're done—otherwise, you might lose track of it.

TIP You can deselect an entire selection at any time by pressing the Esc key.

Softening the Edges of a Selection

Selections often work best when their edges are smooth, instead of hard. Anti-aliasing adds blended pixels to create a smooth edge instead of a stairstepped or jagged edge 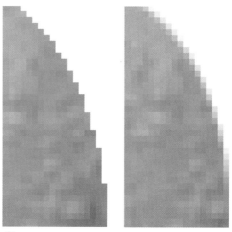. Most selection tools offer an Anti-Alias checkbox in the options bar. That option is usually checked by default, and you almost always want to leave anti-aliasing enabled. When compositing images (combining several pieces into one), anti-aliasing smooths the border between elements.

Feathering blurs the edges of a selection. Set the amount of blurring on the options bar in the Feather box. Unlike anti-aliasing, which affects just the very edge of a selection, feathering creates a more dramatic, soft transition or halo effect around an image. Depending on the image selection, you may want to experiment with different feathering settings, because some detail is usually lost around the edges of a feathered selection.

Ⓐ Anti-aliasing automatically smooths a selection edge by adding pixels that blend the color transition.

Refine Edge Combines Several Softening and Selection Tools

The Refine Edge dialog combines several softening and selection modification tools in one place Ⓑ. Refine Edge appears as a button in the options bar for several tools, but the dialog can be brought up via the Select menu for all selection tools as long as a selection has been made.

With the Preview button checked, changes are interactive as you combine Smooth, Feather, and Contract/Expand options. You can zoom in or out, or pan the image.

The red Custom Overlay Color button provides a mask; double-click the button to set the overlay color.

Ⓑ The Refine Edge dialog combines softening and selection options.

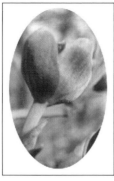

C Select Anti-alias on the options bar before you make a selection to create a smooth edge, even on curved shapes.

D The dogwood blossom at left was highlighted through the Quick Selection tool, and then Inverse was chosen from the Select menu. A 25-pixel Feather was applied, and the background deleted to create the image at right.

To smooth jagged edges with anti-aliasing:

1. From the toolbar, choose any selection tool other than the Rectangular Marquee tool.

   The Rectangular Marquee tool's edges are composed of straight right angles, so no anti-aliasing is necessary. A rectangle selection's edge can still be softened with the Feather option.

   Anti-alias is checked by default on the options bar. If you unchecked the option, check it before making the selection.

2. Make a selection using the desired tool.

3. Cut or copy and then paste the selection into a new file.

   The resulting selection edge is automatically smoothed, with no jaggies C.

To feather the edge of a selection:

1. From the toolbar, choose from any of the Marquee or Lasso tools.

2. On the options bar or in the Refine Edge dialog, select a value for the feather radius (from 0.1 to 250.0 pixels).

3. Make a selection.

   The resulting edge appears blurred, based on the number you entered for the Feather option D.

TIP You can apply feathering after you make a selection, unlike anti-aliasing. With your selection active, from the Select menu choose Feather or Refine Edge, and then enter a feather radius.

TIP You can also apply feathering effects to your image by applying the Vignette effect, available in the Effects panel. For more detail, see "Applying Filters and Effects" in Chapter 9.

Modifying Selection Borders

You can make subtle—or not so subtle—changes to a selection border. The Border feature lets you change the width of the selection border. The Smooth command smooths out a jagged or irregular selection edge. To increase or reduce the size of a selection, use Expand or Contract. (In the Refine Edge dialog box, Expand/Contract is a slider from –100% to 100%.)

To change the width of the border:

1. Make a selection in your image with any of the selection tools.
2. From the Select menu, choose Modify > Border or Refine Edge.
3. Enter a value for the border width.

   The selection border changes based on the number you enter .

To smooth the edge of a selection:

1. From the Select menu, choose Modify > Smooth or Refine Edge.
2. Enter a value for the radius of the smoothing effect.

   The radius values range from 1 to 100 and define how far away from the current edge the selection will move to create a new, smoother edge.

To expand or contract the selection area:

1. From the Select menu, choose Modify; then choose Expand or Contract.
2. Enter a value for the number of pixels you would like the selection to either grow (expand) or shrink (contract) .

A The Border command lets you control the width of a selection border. In this example, a 15-pixel border is selected at left, then filled with color at right.

B You can expand or contract the size of a selection border from the Modify menu.

Fixing and Retouching Photos

How often have you thumbed through photo albums and found images you wished were better composed or lit more evenly? Or maybe you've sorted through shoeboxes from the attic, disappointed that time and age have taken their toll on those wonderful old photographs of your dad in his high school band uniform and your grandparents honeymooning at the lake. Until recently, there was no simple way to correct or repair photographs regardless of whether they were out of focus, water damaged, or poorly composed.

Happily, things have changed. In this chapter, you'll learn how to perform a wide variety of photo fixes, from cropping and straightening to removing blemishes. I also discuss several clever and time-saving features such as the Photomerge Scene Cleaner, which removes unwanted objects from photos, the Smart Brush tool for painting effects on an image, and much more.

In This Chapter

Cropping an Image

Professional photographers almost always use cropping techniques to achieve that perfect composition. In spite of all the advances in film and digital cameras, rarely is a picture taken with its subjects perfectly composed or its horizon line set at just the proper level. More often than not, subjects are off-center, and unwanted objects intrude into the edge of the picture frame. Photoshop Elements offers two simple and quick methods for cropping your images.

To crop an image using the Crop tool:

1. Select the Crop tool from the toolbox (or press C) **A**.

2. In the image window, drag to define the area of the image you want to keep **B**.

   The image outside the selected area is dimmed to indicate the portions that will be deleted.

3. If you want to modify your selection, move the pointer over one of the eight handles on the edges of the selection; then drag the handle to resize the selection **C**.

4. When you're satisfied with your crop selection, double-click within the selection, press Enter, or click the Commit button on the lower corner of the selection **D**.

   The image is cropped to the area you selected **E**.

   If you're just not satisfied with your selection and want to start over, click the Cancel button.

> **TIP** In the options bar, click the **Clear button** to remove any entries in the **Width, Height, or Resolution** text fields.

A The Crop tool.

B Elements highlights the image that will be preserved and dims the portions to be deleted.

C You can easily move and resize the area you choose to crop by dragging the handles around the perimeter of the cropping selection.

D The Commit and Cancel buttons appear on the lower edge of the crop selection.

E The final, cropped image.

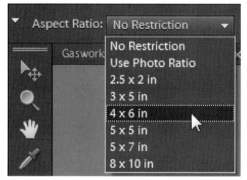

F Use the Aspect Ratio drop-down menu to choose common photo dimensions.

G The Width and Height fields let you specify a custom aspect ratio.

To resize an image to specific dimensions using the Crop tool:

1. Follow steps 1–3 on the previous page to specify an area to crop.

2. From the Aspect Ratio drop-down menu, choose a common photo size F.

   Or, in the options bar, enter a size in the Width and Height fields G. The double-arrow button between the fields swaps values, making it easy to turn a horizontal crop area into a vertical one, and vice-versa.

3. If you need to change the image's resolution, edit the Resolution field; you can define it in pixels per inch or pixels per centimeter using the associated drop-down menu. However, see the sidebar on the next page for important information.

4. Double-click within the selection, press Enter, or click the Commit button to crop the photo.

TIP If you're planning to print your photos using a commercial print service, be sure to crop your images to a standard size first. The images that digital cameras create don't match standard photo aspect ratios, which can lead to prints with black bars around the edges.

TIP You can define color and opacity options for the Crop tool shield (the dimmed area that surrounds your cropped selection) in the Display and Cursors area of the Preferences dialog. The default color is black, and the default opacity is 75 percent.

To crop an image using the Rectangular Marquee tool:

1. Select the Rectangular Marquee tool from the toolbox, or press M.

2. In the image window, drag to define the area of the image you want to keep 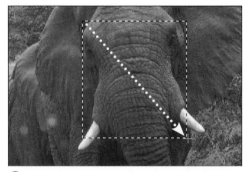.

3. From the Image menu, choose Crop. The image is cropped to the area you selected.

H Drag with the Rectangular Marquee tool to define the part of the image you want to crop.

The Crop Tool Size and Resolution Options

Used together, the Crop tool's Aspect Ratio and Resolution options can lead you down a slippery slope, introducing unexpected image quality problems—foremost among them, unwanted resolution upsampling, which creates a fuzzy, ghosted, and generally out-of-focus effect. For more information on upsampling, see the "Downsampling vs. Upsampling" sidebar in Chapter 3.

As an example, open a 4 x 5-inch image with a resolution of 150 pixels per inch. Select the Crop tool, choose "4 x 6 in" from the Aspect Ratio drop-down menu, and enter 150 in the Resolution field. Define the area you want to crop (which by definition will be a smaller area than the original 4 x 5 image), and then crop.

The area you crop from the original image, no matter the selected size, will be forced up to 4 x 6, and will introduce upsampling .

You can use the Aspect Ratio drop-down menu to control the Width and Height ratios of your cropping selection; just leave the Resolution text field blank, and use the Image Size dialog (after you crop) to set the image resolution.

I Be cautious when using the Crop tool's size and resolution options. Here, an image was cropped with a final size defined that was larger than the original image (top). During cropping, the image was *upsampled,* sacrificing image quality (bottom). Both detail boxes are shown at 100 percent.

(A) The Straighten tool.

(B) With the Straighten tool, you simply click and drag within a tilted photo (top) to align it perfectly (bottom).

(C) A scanned image (top) is automatically straightened (center) or straightened and cropped (bottom).

Straightening a Crooked Photo

Sometimes even your most carefully composed photos may be just a little off angle, with a not-quite-level horizon line or tilted portrait subjects. The nifty Straighten tool makes short work out of getting your crooked photos back into alignment.

Or, perhaps you've scanned an image that shifted when you closed the scanner cover. Elements can automatically straighten it, with the option of cropping it to a clean rectangle.

To use the Straighten tool:

1. Select the Straighten tool from the toolbox, or press P (A).

2. Using a horizon line or other subject as a point of reference, click and drag from one side of the photo to the other.

   When you release the mouse button, your image rotates and aligns along the new horizontal plane you defined (B).

3. Use either the Crop or Marquee Selection tool to remove any extra border area introduced while straightening.

To straighten a scanned image:

From the Image menu, choose one of the following:

- Rotate > Straighten and Crop Image.

- Rotate > Straighten Image.

  The Straighten and Crop Image command will do its best to both straighten the image and delete the extra background surrounding the image. The Straighten Image command simply straightens without cropping (C).

continues on next page

Both methods have their own sets of limitations. Rotate and Straighten works best if there is a space of at least 50 extra pixels or so surrounding the image. If this surrounding border is much smaller, Elements can have a difficult time distinguishing the actual photograph from the border and may not do a clean job of cropping.

Although you'll still need to manually crop your image after using the Straighten Image command, this method is probably a better choice, because you avoid the risk of Elements indiscriminately cropping out areas of your image you may want to keep.

For the surest control, however, straighten your images using the Crop tool as described in the next procedure.

D After you define a preliminary cropping selection (top), rotate the selection so it aligns with your image border (bottom).

To straighten a scanned image using the Crop tool:

1. Select the Crop tool from the toolbox.

2. In the image window, drag to select the area of the image you want to crop and straighten.

3. Move the pointer outside the edge of the selection area until it changes to a rotation pointer **D**.

4. Drag outside of the selection until its edges are aligned with the image border.

5. Drag the selection handles, as necessary, to fine-tune the positioning; then press Enter **E**.

   The image is cropped and automatically straightened.

E Make final adjustments to your cropping selection (top) before Elements automatically crops and straightens the image.

Ⓐ With just a little patience and the Healing Brush and Clone Stamp tools, imperfections caused by a poor scan or dust on the camera lens can be easily removed or repaired.

Repairing Flaws and Imperfections

Little maladies, such as torn edges, water stains, scratches, even specks of dust left on a scanner's glass or the camera's sensor, are the bane of the photo-retouch artist, and are problems all too common when you set to the task of digitizing and restoring old photographs. Even if you're shooting digitally, dust on the lens or the camera sensor can cause unwanted pixels and flaws. To the rescue come three similar but distinctly different repair and retouch tools.

The Spot Healing Brush tool is the perfect tool for removing small imperfections like dust or tiny scratches. With a single click, the Spot Healing brush samples (copies) pixels from around the area of a trouble spot and creates a small patch that covers up the flaw and blends in smoothly with its surrounding area.

The Clone Stamp tool is versatile not just for cleaning up and restoring photos, but for any number of special effects and enhancements. It works on the simple principle of copying and duplicating (cloning) image pixels from one part of an image to another. Although ideal for repairing tears or holes in photographs, it can also be used to add or duplicate objects in a photograph. For example, you can create a hedgerow from one small bush or add clouds to a cloudless sky.

The Healing Brush tool operates like a combination of the Clone Stamp and Spot Healing Brush tools. As with the Clone Stamp tool, it first samples pixels from one area of your image to another. Then, like the Spot Healing Brush tool, it blends those pixels seamlessly with the area you want to repair Ⓐ.

To clean up small areas with the Spot Healing Brush tool:

1. Select the Spot Healing Brush tool from the toolbox, or press J .

2. On the options bar, select a healing method from the radio buttons.

   ▸ Proximity Match samples pixels from around the edge of your brush shape to create the patch over the area you want to repair.

   ▸ Create Texture uses the pixels directly beneath the brush shape to create a soft, mottled texture.

   ▸ Content-Aware uses advanced algorithms to intelligently fill the affected area (see the sidebar on the next page for more information).

3. On the options bar, select a brush size using the brush Size slider.

   Try to size your brush to fit snugly around the flaw you're covering.

4. Click and release the mouse button to apply the patch **C**.

B The Spot Healing Brush tool.

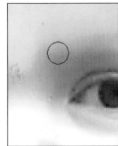

C With a single mouse click, each dust speck is removed.

TIP Alternately, click and drag through a slightly larger area with the Spot Healing Brush tool.

Clone and Healing Overlays

Photoshop Elements has an interesting retouching tool in its arsenal: the overlay. When using the Healing Brush or the Clone Stamp tools, set the origin point and then press Alt+Shift. A translucent overlay of the image appears; the mouse pointer remains fixed on the origin point, so you can see what will be drawn when you click the mouse button **D**. With this approach, you don't have to click blindly and hope that the edit you're about to make is the one you envisioned.

To make the overlay appear whenever the tool is selected, click the Overlay Options button in the options bar (just to the right of the All Layers checkbox) and enable the Show Overlay checkbox.

D The overlay lets you preview what will be drawn (left) when you start drawing (right).

Making Content-Aware Repairs

The Spot Healing Brush tool utilizes one of the best new features in Photoshop Elements 9: content-aware fill. Using technology borrowed from Photoshop CS5, the Spot Healing Brush can not only sample surrounding pixels to make repairs, but can also reconstruct areas based on the image's content.

E I painted over the power line (just once) using the Spot Healing Brush set to Content-Aware.

In most cases, the practical benefit is less time spent making repairs, because Photoshop Elements is applying more "thought" to how to fix an area. You don't need to go over it several times with the Clone Brush as you would have in the past.

For example, when removing power lines from a photo, the Spot Healing Brush also intelligently fills in more complicated areas of the landmark as well as the blue sky **E**.

You can also attempt more dramatic content-aware repairs successfully **F** and **G**. (Of course, results will vary depending on the content of the image.)

TIP If a repaired area doesn't look right, hit it again with the Spot Healing Brush. For example, in **F**, for example, I'd want to clean up the grass clumps that appeared where the girl's shadow had been.

F Painting over the girl and her shadow...

G ...fills the space with content that wasn't there before.

To retouch an image with the Clone Stamp tool:

1. Select the Clone Stamp tool from the toolbox, or press S .

2. On the options bar, select a brush size using the brush Size slider.

   The brush size you choose will vary depending on the area you have available to clone from and the area you're trying to repair. Larger brush sizes work well for larger open areas like skies or simple, even-toned backdrops, whereas smaller brushes work well for textured surfaces or areas with a lot of detail.

3. Move the pointer over the area of your image you want to clone (the pointer becomes a circle, representing the brush size you've specified), and then hold down the Alt key.

   The pointer becomes a target 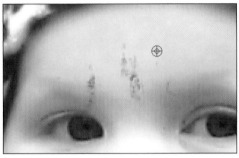.

4. Click once to select the area you want to sample; then, release the Alt key and move the pointer to the area to which you want the clone applied 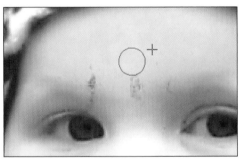.

5. Hold down the mouse button, and drag to "paint" the cloned portion over the new area.

   The original image is replaced with a clone of the sampled image.

🄷 The Clone Stamp tool.

🄸 Clearly, someone needs to clean his scanner! Once you've found an area of your image you want to clone, hold down the Alt key; your pointer turns into a bull's-eye target. Click to set that area as the origin.

🄹 Drag the Clone Stamp tool over the portion of the image you want to replace. As you drag, crosshairs appear, providing a constant reference point of the cloned pixels as you paint over the image.

K The Aligned option gives you control over where the Clone Stamp tool samples image pixels.

L Using the image on the left as a source, the image in the middle was cloned with the Aligned option selected. Although the mouse button was released and depressed several times, the image was still copied *relative* to the initial sampling point. The image on the right was cloned with the Aligned option deselected. Notice that each time the mouse button was released and depressed, the clone again *started* from the initial reference point.

M The Clone tool provides a controlled method for combining parts of one image with another.

To copy images from one picture to another with the Clone Stamp tool:

1. Select the Clone Stamp tool from the toolbox and then select a brush size from the options bar.

2. Still on the options bar, check that the Aligned option is selected **K**.

   With the Aligned option selected, the Clone Stamp tool will always copy pixels relative to the initial sampling point, even if you release the mouse button and press it again to continue. With the Aligned option deselected, each time you release the mouse button and press to resume cloning, you will copy pixels starting from the initial sampling point **L**.

3. Holding down the Alt key, click in the first picture to select the area you want to sample.

4. Click the second picture's image window to make it active, and then drag to paint a clone of the sampled image.

5. The original image in the second picture is replaced with a clone of the sampled image from the first **M**.

TIP Before experimenting with the Clone tool, it's good practice to first create a new, blank image layer. Creating a separate layer not only protects your original image by leaving it unchanged, but it gives you more creative flexibility. You can apply different cloned areas to different layers and then compare the effect of each by turning the layer visibility settings off and on. And if you apply different cloned areas on separate layers, you can experiment further by applying different blending mode and opacity settings to each clone. See Chapter 8, "Working with Layers."

To remove flaws with the Healing Brush tool:

1. In the toolbox, select the Healing Brush tool from beneath the Spot Healing Brush tool .

2. From the Mode drop-down menu on the options bar, check that Normal is selected .

    Normal mode blends sampled pixels with the area you're repairing to create a smooth transition with the area surrounding the repair. Replace mode does little more than duplicate the behavior of the Clone Stamp tool. For information on the other effect modes available from the drop-down menu, see "About Opacity and Blending Modes" in Chapter 8.

3. On the options bar, select a brush size using the brush Size slider.

    The brush size you choose will vary depending on the area you have available to sample from and the area that you're trying to repair.

4. Move the pointer over the area of your image you want to sample and hold down the Alt key. The pointer becomes a target 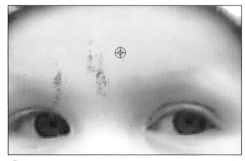.

5. Click once to select the area you want to sample; then release the Alt key and move the pointer to the area you want to repair.

6. Hold down the mouse button and drag to "paint" the sampled image over the new area 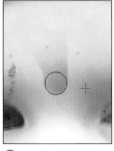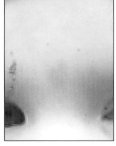.

    The sampled image blends with the repair area to cover any flaws and imperfections.

N The Healing Brush tool.

O Although several healing modes are available, most often the Healing Brush tool works best in Normal mode.

P Once you've found an area of your image to use as a patch, hold down the Alt key and click to select it. Your pointer turns into a bull's-eye target.

Q As you draw, the Healing Brush picks up the pixels relative to the origin point, just like the Clone Stamp tool (left). After you release the mouse button, Elements blends the values in the area (right).

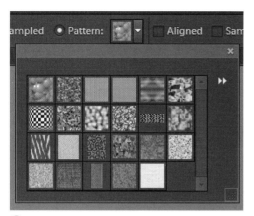

A The Paint Bucket tool.

B You can choose from a variety of patterns in the pattern picker on the options bar.

C Click the Paint Bucket tool in any large area where you want to apply a pattern. Here, a floral pattern was selected to create brand-new living room wallpaper.

Applying Patterns

Although some of Photoshop Elements' patterns can be a little gimmicky, others, like many of the fabric and rock textures, can be useful when you're trying to repair or retouch a damaged or aged photograph. For example, you might use one of the abstract stone patterns to camouflage a particularly damaged background in an old photo that would be difficult to salvage by any other method. The pattern sets provide objects as varied as flowers, stone faces, and textured artist's surfaces, and can be applied using two methods. If you have a large area of the same tonal value or color, you can use the Paint Bucket tool. On the other hand, if you have a smaller area made up of varying colors or textures, use the Pattern Stamp tool.

To apply a pattern to a selected area with the Paint Bucket tool:

1. Select the Paint Bucket tool from the toolbox, or press K A.

2. On the options bar, click the Pattern checkbox.

3. Still on the options bar, click to open the pattern picker B.

4. Click to choose from the list of default patterns, or click the down-arrow button to the right of the thumbnail image to open the Pattern palette menu.

5. Select from the list of pattern sets in the bottom section of the menu.

   The pattern picker displays the new pattern library.

6. Return to the image window and click in the area where you want to apply the pattern. The pattern is painted in the image C.

To apply a pattern with the Pattern Stamp tool:

1. In the toolbox, select the Pattern Stamp tool from beneath the Clone Stamp tool.

   If you hold the Alt key while clicking the Clone Stamp tool in the toolbox, you can toggle between the Clone Stamp and Pattern Stamp tools. Or, if the Clone Stamp tool is already selected, you can select the Pattern Stamp tool from the options bar.

2. On the options bar, select a brush size using the brush Size slider.

   If you like, you can also make opacity and blending changes.

3. Pick a pattern by following steps 3 through 5 in the previous procedure.

4. Once you've chosen a pattern, return to the image window, hold down the mouse button, and then drag to paint the pattern in your image 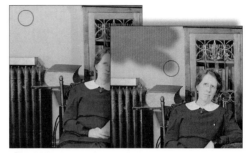.

TIP The Paint Bucket tool fills areas based on tonal value and color, so you'll have the most success filling areas composed of similar values, such as blank walls or clear, cloudless skies. You can adjust the behavior of the Paint Bucket tool by entering different values in the Tolerance text field on the options bar, but the results are a little unpredictable, and the process involves some trial and error.

TIP In addition to the Pattern panel's default mode of Small Thumbnail, you can view patterns as Text Only, Large Thumbnail, Small List, or Large List. As a further aid, if Show Tool Tips is selected in the General Preferences dialog, simply hover over any pattern thumbnail for a second or two to reveal a small pop-up descriptive name of that pattern.

D Position the pattern brush anywhere in your image to paint a pattern.

Mount a Photo on Canvas

You can create an interesting textured effect for almost any photo by using patterns from the Artist Surfaces set.

1. In the Layers panel, create a new layer above your original photo layer.

2. From the Pattern panel menu in the options bar, choose the Artist Surfaces pattern set, and then choose from one of the artist surfaces.

3. With the pattern layer selected, apply a blend mode (try Multiply) to combine the photo and pattern layers.

4. If you like, adjust the pattern layer's opacity setting.

Your photo will appear to be printed on the textured artist surface **E**.

E Any photo can be made to appear rendered on a variety of fine art surfaces.

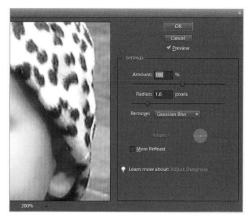

A The Adjust Sharpness dialog's sliders adjust the degree of sharpening you apply.

Original

Amount: 80%

Original

Amount: 150%

B The Amount slider controls the percentage of sharpness applied to your image. The difference here is most pronounced around the eyelid and in the pattern on the hat. Also, the sharpening appears too aggressive in the 150 percent version when zoomed-in so close, but at normal size may look just fine. Feel free to experiment quite a bit to achieve your desired image.

Sharpening Image Detail

Generally speaking, you probably want most of your photos to be in focus—which can be surprisingly difficult to achieve, depending on surrounding movement, zoom level, or even just plain shaky fingers (maybe cut back on the caffeine). Even then, photos may not quite "pop" the way you'd like them to. In addition, any time you resize an image by resampling, pixels may be lost in the process, and so you also lose some degree of image detail.

Elements offers an Auto Sharpen command, but you may want more control. Look to the Adjust Sharpness command, which finds pixels with different tonal values and slightly increases the contrast between those adjoining pixels, creating a sharper edge. The resulting correction can help to enhance detail and bring blurred or fuzzy areas throughout an image into clearer focus.

To sharpen an image:

1. From the Enhance menu, choose Adjust Sharpness to open the Adjust Sharpness dialog A.

2. Make sure the Preview box is checked; then drag the following sliders to adjust the image's sharpness:

   ▸ The Amount slider sets the percentage of contrast applied to the pixels and so determines the degree of sharpness you apply. For high-resolution images (those above around 150 pixels per inch), set the Amount slider to between 150 and 200 percent. For low-resolution images, use settings somewhere around 30 to 80 percent B.

continues on next page

- The Radius slider determines the number of pixels surrounding the contrasting edge pixels that will also be sharpened. Although the radius can be set all the way to 64, you should never have to enter a value much higher than 2, unless you're trying to achieve a strong, high-contrast special effect .

- The More Refined checkbox offers higher quality, but requires more processing time and power. If you're experimenting with the settings, keep this option disabled until you reach the level of sharpening you want.

- The Remove drop-down menu offers three types of correction: Gaussian Blur applies the effect to the entire image; Lens Blur detects edges in its sharpening; and Motion Blur works to reverse the blur caused by camera movement. If Motion Blur is enabled, adjust the Angle setting to match the angle of the movement .

- Use the preview area to see a detailed view of your image as you apply the changes. You can move to a different area of an image by holding down the mouse button and dragging with the hand pointer in the preview screen. You can also zoom in or out of an area using the minus and plus buttons below the preview.

3. When you're satisfied with the results, click OK to close the dialog and apply the changes.

Original   *Amount: 80%*
             Radius: 10.0 pixels

C The Radius slider controls the number of pixels included in any sharpened edge. Smaller numbers include fewer pixels, and larger numbers include more pixels (exaggerated here for effect).

D If the blur is caused by movement of the camera or subject, Motion Blur can compensate.

Adjust Sharpness vs. Unsharp Mask

If you've used Photoshop or another image editor in the past, you may be familiar with the Unsharp Mask command (under the Enhance menu). It provides the same controls as the Remove: Gaussian Blur option of the Adjust Sharpness dialog, and I suspect Adobe kept it in Elements for people who've been using that feature for years. The Adjust Sharpness feature, however, adds compensation for motion blur, which I find to be more common. Depending on the severity of the blur, Adjust Sharpness can salvage a shot that otherwise would have to be rejected.

A The Blur tool.

Original   *After Blur tool applied*

B Drag the brush through the area you want to blur. You can resize the brush as you work on larger and smaller areas.

Enhancing Image Detail

The Adjust Sharpness command works best on entire images or large portions of images. A couple of other tools are better suited for making sharpening and focus adjustments in smaller, more specific areas of an image. Not surprisingly, the Blur tool softens the focus in an image by reducing the detail, and the Sharpen tool helps bring areas into focus. For instance, you can create a sense of depth by blurring selected background areas while keeping foreground subjects in focus, or enhance the focus of a specific foreground subject so that it better stands out from others.

To blur a specific area or object:

1. Select the Blur tool from the toolbox, or press R **A**.

2. On the options bar, select a brush size using the brush Size slider.

   If you want, you can also select a blend mode and enter a Strength percentage. The higher the percentage, the more the affected area is blurred.

3. Move the brush pointer to the area of your image you want to blur; then hold down the mouse button and drag through the area **B**.

   As you drag, the area is blurred.

TIP Working on a portrait? Another tool to consider is the Surface Blur filter (Filter > Blur > Surface Blur), which smooths surface areas like skin without blurring edges. It's an easy way to minimize wrinkles and other sharp details in faces.

To sharpen a specific area or object:

1. Select the Sharpen tool from the tool-box, or press R to toggle through the enhance tools to the Sharpen tool .

2. On the options bar, select a brush size.

   If you prefer, choose a blend mode and enter a Strength percentage. The higher the percentage, the more the affected area is sharpened.

3. Move the brush pointer to the area of your image you want to sharpen; then hold down the mouse button and drag through the area .

   As you drag, the area is sharpened.

TIP Use the Blur and Sharpen tools together when you want to draw attention to a particular person or object. First, use the Blur tool to soften the focus and detail of the subjects you want to appear to recede into the background. Then use the Sharpen tool to bring the subject of primary interest into sharp focus.

C The Sharpen tool.

Original *After Sharpen applied*

D I can pull more detail out of the girl's hair and coat by dragging the Sharpen tool over that area.

A The Smudge tool.

B The Smudge tool can easily do more harm than good, so use it sparingly.

Smudge, not Sludge

The Smudge tool tends to produce a more artificial effect than the other retouching tools, so use it with moderation. Unless your intent is to create a wet paint effect in a large portion of your image, limit use of the Smudge tool to repairing or smoothing small, unobtrusive areas. You don't want a small repair to become the focus of attention.

Blending with the Smudge Tool

The Smudge tool is one of those specialty tools that's a little hard to classify. It's grouped with the Blur and Sharpen tools in the toolbox and is often used for retouching tasks. The Smudge tool's closest cousin may be the Blur tool, because it can also be used to soften edges and transitions in an image. But its real strength lies in its ability to push and pull image pixels around in your picture. Drag the tool through an area, and its pixels smear and blend with the adjacent pixels as if you were pulling a brush through freshly applied paint. Use the Smudge tool in backgrounds and other areas where you may need to smooth flaws or imperfections and where retaining detail isn't critical. With a little practice, you can also create some convincing painterly effects by varying the length and direction of the brushstrokes.

To use the Smudge tool:

1. Select the Smudge tool from the tool-box, or press R to toggle through the enhance tools to the Smudge tool A.

2. On the options bar, select a brush size using the brush Size slider.

   Just as with the Blur and Sharpen tools, you can select a blend mode and enter a Strength percentage. The higher the percentage, the more the affected area is smudged.

3. Move the brush pointer to the area of your image you want to smudge; then hold down the mouse button and drag through the area B.

   As you drag, the area is softened and blended.

Using the Tonal Adjustment Tools

In traditional photography, technicians control darkness and lightness values on specific parts of an image by masking one area of film while exposing another. In the process, selected areas are either burned in (darkened) or dodged (lightened). The Burn and Dodge tools replicate this effect without the bother of creating masks. Drag an adjustable tool's brush pointer through the area you want to affect. If one portion of an image is dramatically overexposed or washed out, and another portion is underexposed, the Dodge and Burn tools can be used to target and correct just those specific problem areas.

The Sponge tool increases or decreases the intensity of the color. Use the Sponge tool to bring colors back to life in badly faded, older photographs; or, work in the opposite direction, pulling the color out of a newer photo to create an antique effect.

To lighten a portion of an image with the Dodge tool:

1. Select the Dodge tool from the toolbox, or press O to toggle to the Dodge tool  Ⓐ.

2. On the options bar, select a brush size using the brush Size slider. Choose a size appropriate to your image (between 20 and 40 pixels is a good start).

   Using the Range and Exposure settings, you can also select a specific tonal range to lighten (shadows, midtones, or highlights) and control the amount of lightness applied Ⓑ.

3. Move the brush pointer to the area of your image you want to lighten; then hold down the mouse button and drag through the area Ⓒ.

Ⓐ The Dodge tool.

Ⓑ Select the part of the tonal range you most want to affect with Photoshop Elements' tonal adjustment tools. With both the Dodge and Burn tools, you can choose to limit your changes to just the shadow, midtone, or highlight areas.

Ⓒ Drag the Dodge or Burn brush through any area to lighten or darken the pixels while preserving image detail. Here, I've used the Dodge tool to lighten the child and chair, keeping the tones in the window (which would get blown out if I were to lighten the entire image).

D The Burn tool.

E In this image, the leopard is washed out and blends into the background (top). The Burn tool added some much needed form and dimension by darkening the pixels in the shadow and midtone areas (bottom).

F On the options bar, choose whether you want the Sponge tool to add or subtract color.

To darken a portion of an image with the Burn tool:

1. Select the Burn tool from the toolbox, or press O to toggle through the tonal adjustment tools to the Burn tool **D**.

2. In the options bar, select a brush size using the brush Size slider.

   If you like, you can also select a specific tonal range to darken (shadows, midtones, or highlights) and control the amount of darkness applied with the Exposure setting.

3. Move the brush pointer to the area of your image you want to darken; then hold down the mouse button and drag through the area **E**.

To adjust the color saturation with the Sponge tool:

1. Select the Sponge tool from the toolbox, or press O to toggle through the tonal adjustment tools to the Sponge tool.

2. On the options bar, select a brush size using the brush Size slider.

3. From the Mode drop-down menu on the options bar, select whether you want to saturate (add) or desaturate (subtract) color **F**.

   You can also adjust the amount of color to be added or subtracted using the Flow percentage slider.

4. Move the brush pointer to the area of your image where you want to change the color's intensity; then hold down the mouse button and drag through the area.

Erasing Backgrounds and Other Large Areas

The Background Eraser tool is an intelligent (and really quite amazing) feature. Not only does it remove the background from around very complex shapes, but it does so in a way that leaves a natural, softened, anti-aliased edge around the foreground object left behind. Additionally, because the Background Eraser tool always erases to transparency, if you use it to remove the background from even a flattened layer, it automatically converts that layer to a floating, transparent one. This allows you to easily place a new background behind a foreground image, or to move it into a different photo composition altogether.

To use the Background Eraser tool:

1. Select the Background Eraser tool from beneath the Eraser tool in the toolbox .

   Alternatively, you can press E to select the Eraser tool and then press E again to toggle to the Background Eraser tool.

2. On the options bar, select a size using the brush Size slider.

3. From the Limits drop-down menu, select one of the limit modes B.

   Contiguous mode erases any pixels within the brush area that are the same as those currently beneath the crosshairs, as long as they're touching one another.

   Discontiguous mode erases all pixels within the brush area that are the same as those beneath the crosshairs, even if they're not touching one another.

4. Select a Tolerance value using the Tolerance slider C. The value controls which pixels are erased according

Ⓐ The Background Eraser tool.

Ⓑ The Limits drop-down menu controls which pixels beneath the brush are sampled and erased.

Ⓒ Use the Tolerance slider to increase or decrease the number of pixels sampled based on their similarity to one another.

 Begin by placing the crosshairs of the brush in the background portion of the image (top), then drag the brush along the outside edge of the foreground object to erase the background (bottom). Continue around the edge of the foreground object until it's completely separated from the background.

to how similar they are to the pixels beneath the eraser crosshairs. Higher Tolerance values increase the range of colors that are erased, and lower values limit the range of colors erased.

5. In the image window, position the eraser pointer on the edge where the background and foreground images meet, and then drag along the edge.

The background portion of the image is erased, leaving behind the foreground image on a transparent background **D**. The brush erases only pixels similar to those directly below the crosshairs, so the entire background can be completely erased while leaving the foreground image intact.

TIP It's okay if the circle (indicating the brush size) overlaps onto the foreground image, but be sure to keep the crosshairs over just the background area. The Background Eraser tool, of course, doesn't really know the difference between background and foreground images, and is simply erasing based on the colors selected, or sampled, beneath the crosshairs. If the crosshairs stray into the foreground image, that part of the image will be erased, too.

TIP There's a third eraser tool—the Magic Eraser tool—that I've chosen not to cover here because, frankly, it doesn't work very well. It operates on the same principle as the Magic Wand tool by deleting like pixels based on color or tonal value. That's all well and good, but you're not given any feedback or opportunity to modify your selection. You just click, and poof—a large area of color is gone. Since the erasure typically is either not quite enough or a little too much, you undo, reset the tolerance, try again, undo—well, you get the idea.

Removing a Foreground Image from Its Background

The Magic Extractor works much the same way as the Background Eraser tool, but distinguishes itself with speed and added control. Using brushes, mark and identify first the foreground image you want to save, and then the background image you want to delete. A set of additional tools helps you to fine-tune your foreground and background selections.

To use the Magic Extractor tool:

1. From the Image menu, choose Magic Extractor to open the Magic Extractor dialog Ⓐ.

2. From the tool area on the left side of the dialog, select the Foreground Brush tool Ⓑ.

3. Use the brush Size slider, if necessary, to adjust the size of your brush, and then use the brush to mark the foreground area of the image—the area of the image you want to preserve.

   You can mark the foreground with a series of either dots or scribbles, or a combination of the two. The idea is to use the brush to get a good cross-sampling of all the different pixel colors and tones in the foreground Ⓒ.

4. Select the Background Brush tool, and in the same manner, mark the area of the image you want to remove.

5. Click the Preview button to see the results of your work Ⓓ.

   Use the Zoom and Hand tools to get a closer look at the transitions between the foreground image and the background.

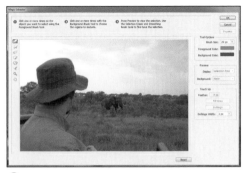

Ⓐ Open the Magic Extractor dialog.

- Foreground Brush
- Background Brush
- Point Eraser
- Add to Selection
- Remove from Selection
- Smoothing Brush
- Zoom
- Hand

Ⓑ The Magic Extractor tool set.

Ⓒ Identify the foreground area with a series of dots and scribbles.

D Click Preview to see the changes you've made to your image in the preview window.

E The Magic Extractor identified the foreground and background areas of the image, and then deleted the background.

6. If necessary, use one of the touch-up tools to modify or clean up the transitions between the foreground image and background:

   ▸ The Point Eraser tool removes portions of marks you've made. When you remove a portion of a mark from the background area, for instance, you're telling the Magic Extractor that you don't want to erase pixels of a particular tonal or color range.

   ▸ The Add to Selection tool allows you to paint back in areas of the foreground image that may have been mistakenly removed along with the background.

   ▸ The Remove from Selection tool works like an eraser to remove areas of the foreground image.

   ▸ The Smoothing Brush softens the transition between the foreground image and transparent background by adding a halo of deleted background color to the edge of the foreground image.

7. If necessary, use the options in the Touch Up area of the dialog to further refine the foreground image.

8. Click OK to finish E.

TIP In the Magic Extractor dialog, you can only Undo (Ctrl+Z) the action of two tools: the Remove from Selection tool and the Smoothing Brush tool. But if you're not happy with the results you're getting, you can start over by either clicking the Reset or Cancel buttons. Clicking the Reset button will undo every action in the Preview window, but will leave the dialog open, whereas clicking Cancel will exit the dialog altogether without applying any changes.

Removing Objects from a Scene

You've probably seen the photo on the Web or forwarded via e-mail from a friend: A couple in full wedding attire are exchanging vows on the beach, the ocean meeting the sky in the background, and...what's that? Yes, a topless sunbather is walking into the frame, ruining an otherwise romantic wedding photo. In Elements, however, that photo would be easily salvageable.

The Photomerge Scene Cleaner lets you take a collection of similar images and selectively "paint out" objects you'd prefer weren't in the photo. Select two or more images that contain an element you want to remove; scenes where people are moving are ideal, because Elements takes areas from the background and superimposes them over the person you wish to hide. (In fact, the early name for Scene Cleaner was "Tourist Remover.")

To remove objects from a scene:

1. Open two or more photos of the scene you want to clean in the Editor, and select them in the Project Bin.

2. Choose File > New > Photomerge Scene Cleaner; or, go to the Guided Edit pane and click Scene Cleaner under the Photomerge heading.

   The first image appears in the Source pane on the left, with an empty Final pane on the right.

3. Choose the image that will be the basis for the finished photo and drag it to the Final pane 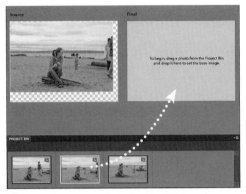.

4. Click a photo in the Project Bin that contains background in the area where you want to remove an object from the Final image .

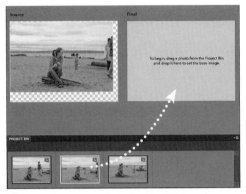

Ⓐ Drag the photo you want to use as a base into the Final pane.

Ⓑ I need to remove the little girl from the Final image, so I click a photo that has a corresponding empty area—in this case, a shot after she's taken a few steps—to load into the Source pane.

C Drawing over the girl in the Final image at right grabs the corresponding pixels from the Source, removing her.

D Two people appeared at the edge of the Final photo, so here I click a third photo (with the blue outline) and paint them out in the Source image. With regions visible, you can see which portions are being copied.

E I've cropped the final photo to remove artifacts left over from blending the images.

5. With the Pencil tool selected, draw over the object to be removed in the Final image C. Elements copies that area from the selected Source image to make the object vanish.

   Repeat steps 4 and 5 to remove other objects from the scene. (Move the mouse pointer off the Final image to preview it without pencil strokes.) The ink color corresponds to the outline surrounding each source image, so you can easily tell which areas are being used. You can also click the Show Regions checkbox to view the patch-work Elements created D.

6. To fine-tune the effect, you may need to use the Eraser tool to erase some of your pencil marks in the Final image.

7. Click Done. Elements saves the image in a new layered file.

TIP Depending on how well the source images lined up, you may need to crop the final image to remove blending irregularities E.

TIP Elements attempts to align the source images based on their contents, but sometimes things end up a little off. If that's the case, click the Advanced Options expansion triangle to reveal the Alignment tool, which you can use to mark three points the images share. Click the Align Photos button to realign them.

TIP Click the Pixel Blending checkbox to get a higher-quality, but slower and more processor-intensive, result.

TIP A tool like Photomerge Scene Cleaner is a great reason to take multiple shots of a scene while you're shooting. With digital photography, you can fire off lots of exposures and end up with plenty of choices.

Recomposing a Scene

When you're taking photos, especially photos of groups, it's not always possible to line people up the way you'd like them to appear. The Recompose tool can help by shifting objects that you choose while retaining a workable background. Like the Photomerge Scene Cleaner, the tool lets you paint areas of an image to choose which objects to retain and which to merge or remove.

Unlike the Photomerge tools, however, the Recompose tool doesn't sport its own interface. It's a cousin to the Crop tool, and performs its magic when you adjust an image's borders.

To recompose a scene:

1. Choose the Recompose tool from the toolbox, or press C . The image gains control handles as if you were using the Crop tool.

2. Drag a handle to resize the image . The tool calculates which areas can be removed or compressed.

   If you like the end result, click the Commit button to finish. If the effect needs more attention, click the Cancel button (or press Esc) and continue to the next step.

3. To gain greater control over which areas are preserved, use the marking tools in the options bar. With the Mark for Protection brush, paint areas that should remain intact . Use the Mark for Removal brush to specify areas that should definitely be removed.

A The Recompose tool.

B We want to bring the man and baby closer together. Drag a handle to recompose the scene. In this case, however, the man's face is compressed.

C The Mark for Protection Brush preserves its painted pixels.

D Areas marked for protection are left unharmed, while the background gets compressed.

E Highlight Skin Tones marks people (or people-colored things) for protection.

4. Drag a handle again to resize the image **D**. You may need to fine tune the marked areas to get a smoother result.

5. Click the Commit button to apply the edit.

TIP You'll probably want to switch to the Crop tool after committing the edit to remove the area that's no longer used in the image.

TIP Is something unwanted in the middle of your scene? Use the Mark for Removal tool to completely paint it out; Elements removes those pixels first.

TIP Choose a size from the Preset menu in the options bar to restrain how the image is resized (for example, to keep the original aspect ratio).

TIP Figuring that this feature would get the most use in bringing people together (or moving them apart), Adobe added a button on the options bar: Highlight Skin Tones. Click it to apply the Mark for Protection brush to areas matching skin tones **E**.

Compositing Images

Combining multiple images to create a single merged image is called compositing. You can combine different digital photos or scanned images to create effects that range from subtle to spectacular to silly. For example, you can replace a landscape's clear blue sky with a dramatic sunset; create complex, multilayered photo collages; or replace the face of the Mona Lisa with that of your Uncle Harold.

To replace part of an image with another image:

1. Open an image that contains an area you want to replace. I'll call this the "target" image.

   In this example, the sky isn't as dynamic as it could be **A**. Since the edges are well defined, the image is a good candidate for the Background Eraser tool.

2. From the toolbox, select the Background Eraser tool; then adjust its brush size and tolerance values.

3. Position the Background Eraser tool along the outside edge of the foreground shape (the tower). Making sure the brush crosshairs are over the background (sky), drag along the edge to erase the background. Continue to erase the background until the area is completely transparent **B**.

4. Open the image you want to use to replace the transparent pixels in your original image. I'll call this the "source" image.

A I'll enhance this image by replacing its background with something more dynamic.

B Use the Background Eraser tool to remove the sky and create a transparent background.

C Drag the source image (the sky) into the target image (the tower).

D Move the sky layer below the tower layer on the Layers panel and adjust the position in the image window.

5. Select the Move tool and drag the source image into the target image **C**.

   In the example, the sky image is larger than the empty background area, which allows flexibility in positioning the new sky in the composition.

   If you like, you can also use the selection tools to select just a portion of the source image, then drag just that selection into the target image.

6. On the Layers panel, drag the source layer below the target layer **D**. (For more information about layers, see Chapter 8.)

7. In the image window, use the Move tool to adjust the position of the source image until you're satisfied with the composition.

TIP It's always good to save a copy of your composition retaining the layers in case you want to make further adjustments. Layered files should be saved as Photoshop Elements (PSD) files.

TIP Instead of using the Background Eraser tool, you could have just as easily used the Magic Extractor in Step 3 to clear the background.

Merging Portions of Multiple Photos

My instructions were simple: Get a good photo of my niece and nephew together. It sounds easy, but you can't assume that a five-year-old and his little sister will sit still. If it weren't for my camera's ability to shoot three frames per second, I think I'd still be trying to get the shot.

Elements makes that quandary much easier with Photomerge, an impressive feature that lets you combine areas of multiple photos into one nearly seamless composition.

To merge portions of multiple photos:

1. Open two or more similar photos in the Editor.

2. Select the photos you want to use in the Project Bin. (If you don't initially, Elements will ask you to do so.)

3. Choose File > New > Photomerge Group Shot; or, in the Edit pane, click the Guided heading and then click Group Shot under Photomerge .

   The first image appears in the Source pane on the left, with an empty Final pane on the right.

4. Drag one of the images to the Final pane . This image is the end result, so it should have the fewest imperfections (such as people's heads turned away from the camera, motion blur, or other issues).

5. Click to select a photo in the Project Bin that contains an element (a better facial expression, for example) you want merged into the Final pane. The photo appears in the Source pane .

Ⓐ Choose the feature in the Guided Edit pane.

Ⓑ Drag the photo you want to use as a base into the Final pane. In this case, the boy's facial expression is my favorite of the three, so I'm building on the first image.

Ⓒ I like the girl's expression in the third image, so I've clicked it in the Project Bin to load it into the Source pane. Elements uses colored borders to help you track which photo is which.

D Elements calculates the pixels surrounding the areas I've drawn and merges them into the Final image.

E I drew over the boy's legs from the second image to merge them into the Final image. I've also enabled the Show Regions option to see how Elements has patched the photo together.

F In the previous figure, the girl's left arm ended up deformed as a result of the merge. To remedy, I used the Eraser tool to shave some of the blue line on the boy's right arm.

6. Select the Pencil tool (if it's not already selected) and, in the Source pane, draw over the area you want to transfer to the Final image **D**. When you release the mouse button, Elements incorporates that area into the Final image.

   Repeat Steps 5 and 6 for other areas you want to merge **E**.

7. Elements does an amazing job of automatically merging images, but it's not perfect. If you need to adjust some areas, use the Eraser tool to edit the drawing lines in the Source pane **F**.

8. Click Done to exit the Photomerge interface. Elements saves the image in a new layered file.

> **TIP** After you exit Photomerge, you may still need to perform some clean-up editing on the image in the Full Edit mode. The merged image appears on a new layer above the Source image. Use the Clone Stamp tool (or the other tools covered in this chapter) to fine-tune the image.

> **TIP** Elements attempts to align the source images based on their contents, but sometimes things end up a little off—due to different image sizes, slightly different camera angles, and so forth. If that's the case, click the Advanced Options expansion triangle to reveal the Alignment tool, which you can use to mark three points the images share. Click the Align Photos button to realign them.

> **TIP** Click the Pixel Blending checkbox to get a higher-quality, but slower and more processor-intensive, result.

> **TIP** The Faces option under Photomerge works similarly to Group Shot, but requires you to set alignment points first. It's great rainy-day fun!

Using the Smart Brush

In Chapter 4, I touched on the Touch Up edits found in the Guided Edit mode, which let you select an area and apply common fixes such as intensifying a blue sky or brightening a person's teeth (see "Making Touch Up Edits"). Those tools are simplified front ends for the Smart Brush found in Full Edit mode.

The Smart Brush applies many more effects—called Smart Paints—than the four offered in the Guided Edit pane, and you can also edit the appearance of a Smart Paint effect after you've applied it.

What's behind the magic? Each Smart Paint application is a new adjustment layer; a layer mask defines the area where the effect is applied (see Chapter 8 for more on working with layers).

To apply a Smart Paint effect:

1. With an image open in Full Edit mode, select the Smart Brush tool from the toolbox Ⓐ or press F.

2. In the Smart Paint menu that automatically appears, choose an effect; click the drop-down menu at top to list categories of effects Ⓑ, and then click a Smart Paint style to use it.

3. Paint over an area of your photo. Elements creates a selection and applies the Smart Paint effect Ⓒ.

    You can adjust the brush size using the Brush pop-up menu in the options bar.

> **TIP** When you apply a new Smart Paint to an image, a new selection is created. To switch easily between multiple Smart Paint areas, click the layer pin that appears. Right-clicking the pin brings up options for refining the area, deleting the effect, or hiding the selection border.

Ⓐ The Smart Brush tool.

Ⓑ The Smart Paint menu and category drop-down menu list the various Smart Brush effects.

Adjustment layer pin

Ⓒ Paint the area to be affected by the Smart Paint effect (Reverse–Black And White shown here).

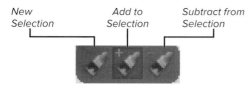

New Selection   Add to Selection   Subtract from Selection

D The selection tools appear above the Smart Paint area.

E Use the Detail Smart Brush tool to draw directly on the layer mask for a more precise selection.

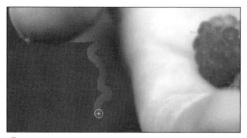

F Smart Paints are actually just adjustment layers.

G The Blue Skies Smart Paint effect applies a gradient fill to the selected area, which you can edit (but please, not like this, I beg you).

To edit a Smart Paint selection area:

- Once you start painting, the brush is in Add to Selection mode so additional areas you paint are added to the selection.

- To apply the Smart Paint to a different area of the image, click the New Selection button and begin painting.

- To deselect part of the Smart Paint area, click the Subtract from Selection button in the Options bar or in the floating toolbar that accompanies the selection **D**.

- Click the Refine Edge button on the options bar to feather, contract or expand, or smooth the edge. The Inverse checkbox inverts the selection.

- To fine-tune the selection, switch to the Detail Smart Brush tool (press F again). The selection border disappears, letting you add to, or subtract from, the mask that defines the area **E**.

To change Smart Paint settings:

In the Layers panel, double-click the adjustment layer that corresponds with the Smart Paint effect **F**.

The dialog that appears depends on the effect you chose; for example, Blue Skies applies a gradient to the area, so the Gradient Fill dialog appears. You can then edit the gradient **G**.

TIP Some Smart Paints, such as the Black and White Yellow Filter, are not editable. Double-clicking the layer reveals that the effect was created in the full version of Photoshop. That actually means Elements has no interface or capability to edit the effect, even though the program is clearly capable of applying it.

Matching the Style of Another Image

One of the best ways to improve one's photography is to emulate what other people have done. I may not have a burning desire to become a landscape photographer (which requires getting up *really* early in the morning for the best light), but when I'm in the right environment you can bet I'm thinking, "I want this shot to look like something Ansel Adams would have made."

Alas, I'm not Ansel Adams, but with the help of Photoshop Elements, I can get my images a little closer to his style. The Photomerge Style Match feature examines a source image and attempts to replicate its style to one of your images.

Adobe provides a handful of source images, but you can also use one of your own (or one you downloaded from the Internet).

To match the style of another image:

1. Open the image you want to edit in the Editor.

2. Choose File > New > Photomerge Style Match, or click the item under Photomerge in the Guided Edit pane.

3. Drag a style image from the Style Bin below the previews **A**. Elements analyzes the source and does its best to apply the same style to your image.

4. To match the coloring of the style image, such as a black-and-white or sepia image, click the Transfer Tones checkbox **B**.

A Adobe provides a few source photos in the Style Bin. Drag one to the Style Image area.

B Enabling the Transfer Tones option carries over custom coloring, such as a black and white image.

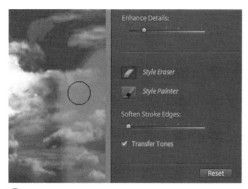

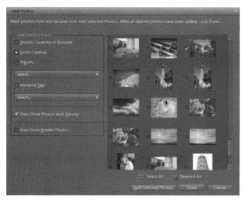

C The style is applied to the entire image, but you can erase areas to further control how the effect appears.

D Use your own images as style sources.

TIP There is no Undo command when erasing selected areas, so you need to repaint them to get the style back (or just click Reset and then reapply the style image).

TIP I find the Style Match feature to be heavy-handed at times; it often posterizes images and blows out highlights. For this reason, I typically reduce the Enhance Details slider. You can also pull back on the Style Intensity amount, but that also minimizes the Transfer Tones feature.

5. Adjust how the effect is applied by manipulating the following sliders:
   - Style Intensity affects the overall amount of the matched style.
   - Style Clarity adjusts the contrast level of the style.
   - Enhance Details adjusts the sharpness of the effect.
6. If you don't like the effect, click the Reset button or select a different photo as the style image.
7. Click Done to apply the effect.

To apply a style to selected areas:

1. After applying the style to the entire image, click the Style Eraser button.
2. Paint the areas where you want the original image to show through **C**. The brush size and intensity is controlled on the options bar.

   Use the Style Painter brush to reapply the style to areas where needed.
3. To feather the edges of your area, drag the Soften Stroke Edges slider.

To add style source images:

1. In the Style Bin, click the Add (+) button
2. From the drop-down menu, choose Add Style Images from Organizer to bring up the Add Photos dialog. (Choosing the hard disk option presents a regular Open dialog to let you find a file.)
3. Click the checkbox next to images you want to add to the Style Bin **D**. To narrow the number of options, use the filters in the Add Photos From area.
4. Click the Add Selected Photos button to add the pictures, then click Done.

Creating Panoramas

With Photoshop Elements, you can create wide, panoramic images that would be difficult to capture with a single shot from a standard camera. The Photomerge Panorama command analyzes your individual photos and assembles them into a single panoramic image Ⓐ.

Taking pictures for panoramas

If you're getting ready to snap some scenic photos and know you want to assemble them into a panorama later, making a few camera adjustments will make it easier to assemble a seamless panorama.

- Use a consistent zoom level when taking the pictures.

- Use a consistent focus. If your subject matter is far away, set your camera's focus to infinity, if the option is available.

- Use consistent exposure. A panorama with widely varied lighting will be difficult to merge seamlessly. Set your camera's exposure manually or lock the exposure setting if possible. Photomerge Panorama can make slight adjustments for images with different exposures, but it is not as effective when the image exposure varies greatly.

- If possible, use a tripod. You can take pictures for a panorama with a handheld camera, but you might find it difficult to keep all of the images perfectly level.

- Overlap sequential images by about 15 to 40 percent Ⓑ. Photomerge looks for similar detail in the edges of your images to match consecutive pictures. Try to capture as much detail throughout the frame to give Photomerge more reference points to match up.

Ⓐ Photomerge combines several separate photos into a single panoramic picture.

15%   40%

Ⓑ The more your images overlap, the better your chances of successfully merging them. Try for an overlap of between 15 and 40 percent.

TIP Try taking *two* versions of panorama images: one with the camera held horizontally and one with the camera held vertically. See which option makes a better panorama.

TIP You're not limited to creating horizontal panoramas. You can also create vertical panoramas of tall subjects, such as skyscrapers or redwood trees.

TIP Some digital cameras include a feature that helps you compose multiple overlapping photos when you shoot.

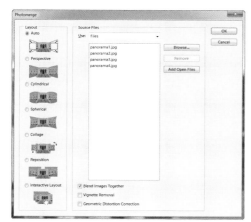

C Browse for photos to merge in the Photomerge dialog.

D When you click OK, your merged images open in a new Elements file.

E Choose to fill in the edges using content-aware technology.

F The edges are filled in (with varying levels of success due to the image contents, especially at the bottom).

Assembling images into a panorama

To create a panoramic image, select the images you want to merge and then let Photomerge work its magic.

To create a panorama:

1. Open the images you want to merge.

   If you want to make any adjustments, such as tonal corrections or cropping, make your corrections first, before you begin assembling the images.

2. From the File menu, choose New > Photomerge Panorama. The Photomerge dialog appears C.

3. Click the Add Open Files button to use the images from Step 1. If you need to delete a file from the list, select it and then click the Remove button.

   If you want to add more images, click the Browse button to open the Open dialog; then navigate to the folder containing the images you want to merge.

4. Choose a panorama style from the Layout column based on your source images. For example, you'd choose Cylindrical if you shot a 360-degree revolution around one point.

   The Interactive Layout option works differently than the rest, as you'll see on the following pages; for now, don't choose it.

5. When you have all of the images you want in the Source Files list, click OK.

   Photoshop Elements automatically merges them into a single image D.

6. Elements can attempt to fill in the empty area using its content-aware technology. In the dialog that appears, choose whether to apply the fix (E and F).

continues on next page

G After creating the panorama, you can use the Crop tool to trim the image.

TIP You may see an alert message telling you that some images can't be assembled. If Photomerge can't find enough common details in your images, it will ignore those files. See the next page for a solution.

TIP Once you click OK to create your panorama, there's no returning to the Photomerge dialog to make further adjustments. If you're not happy with the way the panorama rendered, you'll need to start over. Refer to the following topics for further instruction on how to make additional adjustments to your panorama before you click the OK button.

TIP If seams are still visible in the panorama, try touching up the areas with the Clone tool.

TIP Use the Crop tool to remove those rough edges and give your panorama a nice, crisp rectangular border **G**.

TIP Before you print your final panorama, take the time to examine its size in the Image Size dialog (from the File menu, choose Resize > Image Size). Depending on the size and resolution of the images you've used, your panoramas can quickly grow to exceed the standard paper stock sizes for your printer (which are usually no larger than 8.5 x 14 or 11 x 17 inches). Once you've determined the final image dimensions, use either the Image Size dialog or the controls in the Print Preview dialog to resize your image so it will fit on whatever paper stock you have available.

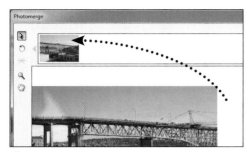

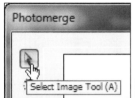

H Drag an image in the work area to the Lightbox.

I The Select Image tool.

J When you drag one image over another, the top image becomes semitransparent, allowing you to align the images.

Adjusting images using the Interactive Layout

When you choose the Interactive Layout option in the initial Photomerge dialog, Elements merges the selected images, but then opens a new window where you can fine-tune the composition.

To reposition images in the panorama:

1. If you want to remove an image from the panorama before repositioning it, drag it from the work area into the Lightbox (just above the main preview area) **H**.

2. Check that the Select Image tool is highlighted in the Photomerge dialog **I**.

3. Drag the image over the image with which it should merge. As you drag, the image becomes partially transparent so you can more easily line it up with the one below it **J**.

4. When the two images match up, release the mouse button.

   If Snap to Image is selected in the dialog, any two overlapping images will automatically try to match up with one another. If Snap to Image is not selected, Photomerge allows you to align the overlapping image manually.

   Turning off Snap to Image allows you to move the images in small increments if they are not matching up exactly. You may also need to rotate an image slightly to make it match up with its neighbor correctly.

continues on next page

5. Select the Rotate Image tool, and then drag to rotate the selected image if needed .

The Photomerge dialog offers several options for moving through its work area while composing your panoramas, including its own built-in navigator.

6. To navigate through the work area, do one of the following:

▸ Select the Move View tool (the hand icon) in the dialog and drag in the work area.

▸ In the Navigator, drag the view box. This changes the view in the work area ⓛ.

▸ Use the scroll bars at the bottom and right edges of the work area.

7. To change the zoom level in the work area, do one of the following:

▸ Select the Zoom tool in the dialog and click in the work area to zoom in.

▸ Hold down the Alt key while clicking to zoom out.

▸ Move the slider under the thumbnail in the Navigator.

▸ Click the Zoom icons under the thumbnail in the Navigator section of the dialog.

TIP You may see some tonal variation as a result of merging the images in the Interactive Layout (as in the images on the next page). However, Elements smooths those when the final panorama is constructed.

Ⓚ You can rotate images to help align them in the work area.

Ⓛ Drag the view box in the Navigator to change the view in the work area.

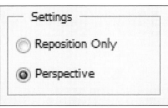

M Click the Perspective radio button to add exaggerated perspective to your merged composition.

N When you select the Perspective setting, Photomerge adjusts and distorts the images to create the illusion of a vanishing point. Here, the vanishing point image is identified by the light blue outline.

O When you change the Vanishing Point image, the other images adjust and distort in response to change the perspective.

Enhancing perspective

Even the most sophisticated camera lenses tend to flatten what little depth or perspective is present in the landscapes or objects they capture. Photomerge Panorama lets you restore that lost perspective to create a more natural-looking panoramic image. In addition, you can adjust the vanishing point (the point where natural perspective recedes into the distance) to help draw attention to a specific area or object in the panorama.

To add perspective to a panorama:

1. In the Settings section of the dialog, select the Perspective option **M**.

   The outside edges of the panorama are distorted, creating a more dramatic, and sometimes more realistic, perspective view **N**. The middle of the center image is designated as the vanishing point, and the outside images appear to recede into its center. The vanishing point image is identified by a blue outline when it's selected.

2. To make a different image the vanishing point image, first select the Set Vanishing Point tool.

3. Click a different image in the work area. The panorama changes the perspective to make it look as if the other images now recede into the new Vanishing Point image **O**.

4. If the perspective option doesn't give you the effect you'd hoped for, select the Reposition Only option in the Settings section of the dialog to return your panorama to its original state.

   You can also remove the perspective from your panorama by dragging the Vanishing Point image to the Lightbox.

Correcting Red Eye

When you're in an indoor or darkened space, your pupils grow larger to let in more light. The pupils can't shrink fast enough to compensate for a camera's flash, so when that light reflects off the back of the eye, it causes red eye. Many cameras pre-flash before the picture is actually snapped, giving the subject's pupils a chance to contract and greatly reduce the effects of red eye. But chances are you still have some older photos lying around you'd like to repair. The Red Eye Removal tool offers an effective way to remove red eye, simply by changing pixels from one color to another.

To remove red eye from a photo:

1. Select the Red Eye Removal tool from the toolbox, or press Y .

2. On the options bar, set the Pupil Size slider to match the proportional size of the pupil (the red part of the eye that you want to turn black) to the colored portion of the eye. Then, use the Darken Amount slider to control the darkness of the retouched pupil ⓑ.

   Although these settings are not inconsequential, the defaults of 50 percent work fine in most cases I've tried.

3. If necessary, zoom in on the area you want to correct; then click and drag to draw a selection over the colored portion of one eye ⓒ.

4. Release the mouse button to remove the red eye effect. If you're not quite satisfied with the results the first time, press Ctrl+Z to undo the operation, and then repeat steps 2 through 4, revising the option bar settings or changing the size of the selection before you click and drag.

Ⓐ The Red Eye Removal tool.

Ⓑ Two sliders on the options bar help you to adjust red eye removal.

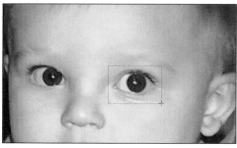

Ⓒ To remove red eye, draw a selection around the eye and release the mouse button.

Changing and Adjusting Colors

Almost any photograph can benefit from some simple color or lighting corrections. For example, you might find that a vivid sunset you photographed ends up looking rather dull and ordinary, or that a portrait taken outdoors is too dark to discern any details. Luckily, you're never stuck with a roll of inferior images. Photoshop Elements provides a powerful set of color correction tools, with both manual and automatic adjustments, so you can fine-tune your images as much as you want.

In this chapter, I'll review Photoshop Elements' color-correction tools and discuss which tools you may want to use, and when you'll most likely want to use them. I'll also show you how to help colors display and print accurately (also known as *color management*) and how to correct colors and tonal values in your images. Along the way, I'll shed some light on why what may appear to be the most obvious color-enhancement options are not always the best choices for improving the color in an image.

In This Chapter

About Color Models and Color Modes

No matter how your images got into the computer, whether from a scanner, a digital camera, or copied from a stock art CD, the version of the image stored on your hard disk can only approximate the colors of the original scene. A computer is only capable of dealing with numbers, so it somehow has to come up with numerical equivalents of the colors perceived by our eyes.

Computers use number systems, called color models, to display and reproduce color. One of the most common is the RGB color model. In this model, the color of each pixel is described as combinations of different amounts of the colors red, green, and blue. These colors were chosen because the cells in our eyes that respond to color (called cones) come in three types; some are sensitive to red, some to green, and some to blue. Therefore, the RGB model tries to characterize colors in a way that's similar to the way the human eye perceives them.

Color Modes

A color *mode* specifies which color model will display and print your images. Elements includes four color modes—RGB, Grayscale, Bitmap, and Indexed. (Another common mode, CMYK, is not supported; it's primarily used for print publishing.)

- RGB mode. RGB stands for red, green, and blue, which are the three color channels your eyes perceive . These are also the three color phosphors used in your computer monitor to display color. The combination of these channels creates the full-color image you see. Many selection and correction options allow you to adjust these colors independently.

Red

Green

Blue

 An RGB image is made up of three separate color channels: Red, Green, and Blue. (Each channel contains only its color's hues, which are represented in grayscale when viewed separately like this.)

B Grayscale mode converts the color channels to shades of gray.

C You can convert any grayscale image to a bitmapped image (here enlarged to 100 percent to show the texture).

D Converting from RGB to Grayscale discards the color information.

- Grayscale mode. A grayscale image is made up of 256 unique shades of gray B. Converting from RGB to Grayscale reduces the image to just one color channel, so the resulting image file size is about one third of the RGB version. If you're looking to create a black and white photo, however, see "Converting to Black and White," later in this chapter.

- Bitmap mode. A bitmap image really is a black-and-white image, because during the conversion, each pixel is rendered as black or white C.

- Indexed mode. The indexed color version of an image is limited to a maximum of 256 colors, and is used when you're preparing images strictly for viewing on computer monitors. In most cases you won't convert photos to this mode but will instead use the Save for Web dialog (see Chapter 12).

To change color mode:

1. From the Image menu, select Mode and choose one of the color modes. The Bitmap and Indexed Color options present you with conversion options; the Grayscale option displays a dialog asking if you want to discard the color information D.

2. Click OK.

TIP Before converting your file to another color mode, it's a good idea to save a "master" version of your photo first. That way, no matter what changes you make to your image, you always have the original, unaltered version.

Managing color

You've learned some color basics, but before going any further, you may want to take a couple of steps to ensure that the color you see on your monitor will be reasonably accurate when you decide to print or send images to the Web. Fortunately, color management in Elements is simple and doesn't require any labor-intensive chores on your part.

You should first make sure the colors you see on the monitor are reasonably accurate and represent what others will see on their monitors. Calibrating your monitor is a particularly good idea if you have an older monitor or have inherited it from a friend or relative (you don't know what they might have done to the monitor settings). If you have a newer monitor, it probably came with an accurate calibration from the factory.

Windows includes a color calibration tool in the Displays control panel. Or, turn to tools such as Datacolor's Spyder (spyder. datacolor.com).

If you prefer, you can also choose color settings optimized for either Web graphics or color printing.

Color Management Is an Imperfect Science

As you start selecting and adjusting colors in Photoshop Elements, it's important to understand that the term *color management* can be a little misleading.

Color management operates under the assumption that we're creating artwork at our calibrated monitors under specific, controlled lighting conditions, and that our desktop printers work at peak performance at all times. In other words, it assumes controlled, uncompromised perfection.

At the time of this writing, the late afternoon sun is casting some lovely warm reflections off the blinds of the window and onto the wall directly behind my computer monitor, and is competing for attention with the glow from the 40-watt, soft-white bulb in my desk lamp. Therein lies the problem: The vast majority of Photoshop Elements users are working in similarly imperfect conditions.

In addition to trying to make a perfect science out of a host of imperfect variables, color management all but ignores one of the most imperfect sciences of all: our very human, very subjective perception. I may print out an image I find perfectly acceptable, whereas you may look at the same image and decide to push the color one way or another to try to create a different mood or atmosphere. That's what makes everything I create so different. That's what makes it art. And that's (at least in part) what makes color management an imperfect science. So, as you read through this chapter, keep in mind that your images will never look precisely the same when viewed by different users on different monitors. And that's perfectly all right.

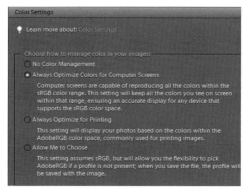

Choose a color management option best suited to the final output of your image.

About Color Profiles

The choices you make in the Color Settings dialog affect only the display of an image onscreen and won't affect how an image is printed. The Always Optimize for Printing option, for instance, will simulate the AdobeRGB color spectrum on your monitor but will not assign the AdobeRGB color profile to an image. A color profile is information embedded in an image and stored in the background until it's required (usually by a printer). The color profile helps to interpret the RGB color information in an image and convert it to a color language that a printer can understand, and so reproduce the most accurate color possible. You can assign a color profile to an image at any time regardless of the option you've set in the Color Settings dialog. With an image open, simply choose Convert Color Mode from the Image menu. From the Convert Color Profile submenu, you can Remove an unwanted profile (sRGB, for example) and apply the profile more suitable for printing: AdobeRGB.

To choose color settings:

From the Edit menu, choose Color Settings.

The Color Settings dialog appears with three color management options plus the option to choose No Color Management **E**.

- Always Optimize Colors for Computer Screens displays images based on the sRGB (standard RGB) color profile and is the default setting. It's a good all-around solution, particularly if you are creating images to be viewed primarily onscreen.

- Always Optimize for Printing displays color based on the AdobeRGB profile. Although the image you see onscreen may display with only subtle color differences (as compared to sRGB), you will generally get truer, more accurate color when you send the image to print.

- Allow Me to Choose will default to sRGB, but if the image contains no color profile, you'll have the option of choosing AdobeRGB.

Converting to Black and White

Taking a color photograph and making it black and white (well, technically *grayscale*) can involve more than just draining the color. The RGB values can be adjusted to highlight different tones in the final image and the contrast can be changed—edits you could perform separately later. But the Convert to Black and White dialog rolls them into one place and throws in some handy presets, too.

To convert an image to black and white:

1. Open the image you want to convert.

2. From the Enhance menu, choose Convert to Black and White (or press Ctrl+Alt+B) to open the similarly-named dialog 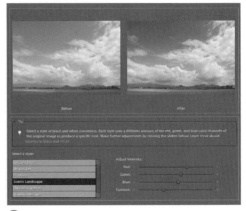.

3. Optionally, choose a preset from the Select a style list that matches the type of image you're editing **B**.

4. If you want to change the black and white photo's appearance, use the Adjust Intensity sliders **C**.

5. When you're satisfied with the result in the preview, click OK. The photo is converted to black and white **D**.

> **TIP** Duplicate the layer the image is on in the Layers panel before you open the Convert to Black and White dialog, and then apply the command to that layer. The feature applies only to the active layer, not the entire image as if you had switched to Grayscale mode.

A The Convert to Black and White dialog includes many adjustments you likely would have made anyway.

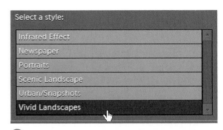

B Elements includes several preset styles that can get you started.

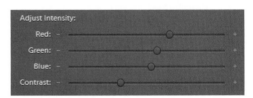

C Experiment with the Adjust Intensity sliders to get the look you want.

D You may not be Ansel, but you're getting there.

A Select the area you want to convert to grayscale.

B The color in the selection is removed.

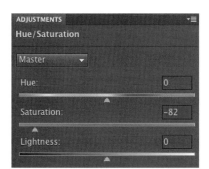

C Use the Saturation slider in the Hue/Saturation dialog to control the amount of color you remove from an image.

Removing Color

Unlike converting to black and white (which removes all color information from an image), you can use the Remove Color command to remove color from just a portion of an image. This feature can be used to great effect for highlighting or dimming specific areas, creating neutral fields in which to place type, or as a first step before applying a colorization or color tint effect.

To apply the Remove Color command:

1. Using any of the selection or marquee tools, select the area of your image from which you want to remove the color **A**.

2. From the Enhance menu, choose Adjust Color > Remove Color, or press Ctrl+Shift+U.

   All color is removed from the selected areas of the image and replaced by levels of gray **B**.

TIP You can control how much color to remove from an image or selection by decreasing saturation. In the Layers panel, create a new Hue/Saturation adjustment layer. (See "Making Color and Tonal Changes with Adjustment Layers" in Chapter 8 for more information.) Then, move the Saturation slider to the left until you achieve the desired effect **C**. The value 0 on the saturation scale represents normal color saturation, whereas −100 (all the way to the left) represents completely desaturated color, or grayscale.

About Tonal Correction

Tonal correction tends to be one of the least understood (and most intimidating) features of Elements. Mention levels and histograms and white points to even some seasoned graphics professionals, and you'll see their eyes begin to glaze. That's a shame, because there's really no magic involved.

In plain terms, correcting tonal range simply comes down to adjusting brightness and contrast. Elements offers several ways to make automatic brightness and contrast adjustments. But the most precise and intuitive method is by using the Levels dialog, and the heart of the Levels dialog is the histogram.

Understanding histograms

The histogram is a graphic representation of the tonal range of an image. The lengths of the bars represent the number of pixels at each brightness level: from the darkest on the left to the lightest on the right. If the bars on both sides extend all the way to the left and right edges of the histogram box, the darkest pixels in the image are black, the lightest pixels are white, and the image is said to have a full tonal range 🅐. If, as in many images, the bars stop short of the edges, the darkest and lightest pixels are some shade of gray, and the image may lack contrast. In extreme circumstances, the bars may be weighted heavily to the left or right, with the tonal range favoring either the shadows or highlights 🅑. Whatever the tonal range, the brightness and contrast of an image can be adjusted using sliders located beneath the histogram in the Levels dialog (see "Adjusting Levels Manually," later in this chapter).

🅐 A photo displaying full tonal range and its accompanying histogram. Note how the histogram extends all the way to the left and right, indicating that pure blacks are present in the darkest shadow areas and pure whites are present in the lightest highlight areas. The fairly uniform peaks and valleys throughout the middle portion of the histogram also indicate sufficient pixel data present in the midtones.

🅑 Here's the same image, this time too bright and with insufficient contrast. Note the lack of data on the left end, indicating a lack of black pixels, and the abundance of data on the right, indicating very light tones.

A Camera Raw gives you an opportunity to adjust the raw, unedited image data.

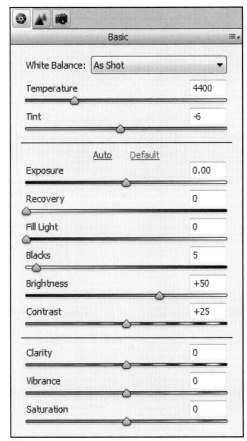

B The Camera Raw dialog contains many adjustment tools for correcting an image before it's opened in Elements.

Adjusting Camera Raw Photos

Many digital cameras save photos in camera raw format, which is the unedited data captured by the camera's image sensor; each manufacturer uses its own proprietary specifications, so you'll see files ending in .NEF, .CRW, or others. Camera raw gives you more options for adjusting an image—the camera hasn't already made choices for sharpening or tonal balance for you.

Unlike changes made in Photoshop Elements, however, the modifications you make in the Camera Raw dialog are saved alongside your image, so you can go back and tweak the raw settings later if you want.

To adjust camera raw images:

1. Open an image. If the file is in camera raw format, the Camera Raw dialog appears A.

2. If you want to give the dialog first crack at the image, click Auto above the adjustment sliders. Otherwise, edit the settings by dragging each slider B. Here's a breakdown of what they do:

   ▸ White Balance. The Temperature and Tint sliders make the photo warmer or cooler. (The Auto button doesn't apply to White Balance settings.)

   ▸ Exposure brightens or darkens the image.

   ▸ Recovery pulls detail out of blown-out (very bright) areas.

   ▸ Fill Light brightens midtones without overexposing the image.

   ▸ Blacks pushes darker areas to black.

continues on next page

- Brightness raises or lowers the overall illumination.
- Contrast applies contrast to the image's midtones.
- Clarity sharpens the image by detecting and working on edges, as opposed to sharpening everything.
- Vibrance applies saturation but doesn't allow colors to become clipped (blown out).
- Saturation increases or decreases the color intensity as a whole.

More controls are available in the detail tab (click the icon with two triangles):

- Sharpening offers the same type of controls discussed in Chapter 6; the settings are applied to the entire image.
- Noise Reduction works to remove the digital spottiness caused by shooting in low-light situations or at high ISO settings. The Luminance slider applies to grayscale noise, while the Color slider affects chroma noise, or noise made up of multiple colors.

3. The Camera Raw dialog also includes several tools found in Elements **C**; if you need to rotate the image, for example, you may as well do it here.

4. Click the Open Image button to apply the adjustments and open the file in Elements **D**.

TIP The clipping indicators can warn if areas are too white or too black **E**.

TIP If you're planning to apply sharpening in Elements later, don't make those adjustments in the Camera Raw dialog.

TIP Hold Alt and click Open Image to save a new copy with the raw edits applied.

C The following tools are available if you want to make the adjustments here (left to right): Zoom, Move, Eyedropper (for identifying white point), Crop, Straighten, Fix Red-Eye, Preferences (for the Camera Raw dialog), and Rotate counter-clockwise and clockwise.

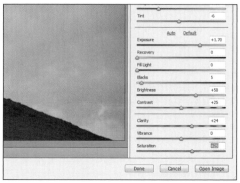

D When you're happy with the results, click the Open Image button.

Shadow clipping warning   *Highlight clipping warning*

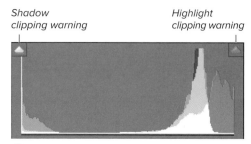

E The clipping icons warn when darks or whites are too heavy; click an icon to view the affected areas in the image.

 The photo on the top lacks sufficient tonal range, particularly in the highlight and lighter midtone areas. The photo on the bottom, corrected with the Auto Levels command, reveals more detail in both the shadow and highlight areas because the pixels have been distributed across the full tonal range.

Get Smart

Finessing an image's levels and other settings gives you an enormous amount of power to correct tonal ranges—but maybe you don't have the time or desire to be a slave to the sliders. The Auto Smart Fix command under the Enhance menu does it all for you. If you don't like the result, build from there or start over and tackle each setting yourself.

Adjusting Levels Automatically

Photoshop Elements gives you the option of applying a quick fix to image levels and contrast with the Auto Levels and Auto Contrast commands. Although I recommend working with the histogram in the Levels dialog, the auto commands can be a good jumping-off point before launching into more controlled, manual image correction. The auto commands tend to be most successful when applied to a photograph that contains an average tonal range; one where most of the image detail is concentrated in the midtones. Midtones are those tonal values that fall about halfway between the darkest and lightest values. Midtone areas tend to contain more image information— more visible detail, that is—than extremely dark or light areas. Photos with predominant midtones—whether in grayscale or in color—are usually the best candidates for auto correction. Severely overexposed or underexposed images may be beyond help. If the camera or scanner didn't capture the detail in the first place, it's not there to be corrected.

To apply Auto Levels to an image:

1. From the Enhance menu, choose Auto Levels, or press Ctrl+Shift+L.

   Photoshop Elements instantly adjusts the image's tonal range .

2. If you're not happy with the result, select Edit > Undo Auto Levels, or press Ctrl+Z.

To apply Auto Contrast to an image:

1. From the Enhance menu, choose Auto Contrast, or press Alt+Ctrl+Shift+L .

   Photoshop Elements instantly adjusts the image's contrast **C**.

2. To undo, choose Edit > Undo Auto Contrast, or press Ctrl+Z .

TIP As mentioned earlier, the auto commands work best in specific circumstances (as when the image's tonal range favors the midtones) and should be used sparingly. The Auto Levels command, in particular, can yield surprising and unexpected color shifts. In some instances it seems to overcompensate by swapping out one undesirable color cast for another, whereas in others it may ignore the color altogether and throw the contrast way out of whack. Give these auto commands a try, but be prepared to commit that Undo keyboard shortcut to memory.

TIP If you're looking for adjustments without all the detail, the Quick Fix environment groups a cross-section of some of the more commonly used commands and functions into one convenient, interactive workspace. See Chapter 4 for more information.

B Choose Enhance > Auto Contrast to apply an instant contrast fix to your image.

C The photo on the top lacks sufficient contrast, so detail is lost in both the shadow and highlight areas. The photo on the bottom, corrected with Auto Contrast, reveals detail not present in the original.

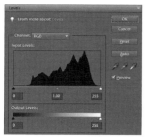

A The Levels dialog.

Black levels

B Moving the left slider underneath the left edge of the histogram spreads the darker pixels more evenly into the dark areas of the midtones and shifts the darkest pixels to black.

White levels

C The right slider affects the lightest pixels in the image. Moving the right slider underneath the right edge of the histogram spreads the lighter pixels more evenly into the light areas of the midtones and shifts the lightest pixels to white, resulting in more detail in the highlight areas.

Adjusting Levels Manually

The Levels dialog can do more to improve the overall tonal quality of your image than any other workspace in Elements. Many images, whether scanned or imported from a digital camera, don't contain the full tonal range, and as a result lack sufficient contrast. That lack of contrast translates into loss of detail, usually most noticeably in the shadow and highlight areas. Using the histogram and sliders in the Levels dialog, you darken the darkest pixels and lighten the lightest ones to improve contrast, then adjust the brightness levels in the midtones.

To adjust the tonal range:

1. From the Enhance menu, choose Adjust Lighting > Levels, or press Ctrl+L to open the Levels dialog A.

2. Select the Preview box and drag the slider on the left until it rests directly below the left edge of the histogram B. The image darkens as the darkest pixels in the image move closer to black.

3. Drag the slider on the right until it rests directly below the right edge of the graph C. The image lightens as the lightest pixels move closer to white.

4. Drag the middle slider to the left or right to adjust the brightness level of the pixels that fall in the midtones.

5. Click OK to close the Levels dialog.

> **TIP** **What about the Brightness/Contrast command? I never use it. Unlike Levels, which affects pixels in specific tonal ranges, Brightness/Contrast indiscriminately lightens or darkens pixels across the entire tonal range, typically creating more problems than it solves.**

Adjusting Lighting

Overexposed background images and underexposed foreground subjects are a common problem for most amateur photographers. Much like the Levels command, the Shadows/Highlights dialog operates on pixels in specific tonal ranges while leaving the other tonal ranges alone.

To lighten detail in shadow:

1. From the Enhance menu, choose Adjust Lighting > Shadows/Highlights.

   The Shadows/Highlights dialog appears .

2. In the Shadows/Highlights dialog, do one or all of the following:

   ▸ Drag the Lighten Shadows slider to the right to lessen the effect of the shadows, or to the left to introduce shadow back into the image.

   ▸ Drag the Darken Highlights slider to the right until you're satisfied with the detail in the foreground or other brightly lit areas.

   ▸ Drag the Midtone Contrast slider to the right to increase the contrast, or to the left to decrease the contrast.

3. Click OK to close the Shadows/Highlights dialog and apply the changes .

> **TIP** I've found in many (if not most) images imported from a digital camera, the Shadows/Highlights dialog defaults work surprisingly well on their own, requiring just minor slider adjustments.

> **TIP** In any case, use the Midtone Contrast slider sparingly. A little goes a long way, and adjustments of more than plus or minus 10 percent can quickly wash out or flatten an image's details.

A The Shadows/Highlights dialog.

B The top photo is underexposed in the foreground, so detail in the girl's face is hidden in shadow. In the bottom photo, making adjustments with the Lighten Shadows and the Midtone Contrast sliders selectively brightens and enhances detail in both her face and shirt.

C I shot three different exposures to capture detail in the foreground and the background.

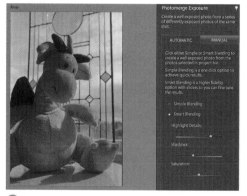

D The automatic merge did a pretty good job, but the colors are a bit too saturated.

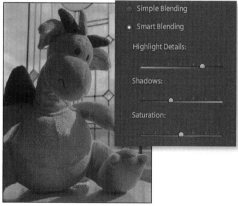

E Adjust the blend settings to balance highlights, shadows, and saturation.

Fixing lighting using Photomerge Exposure

Another way to deal with photos that contain over- or under-exposed areas is to run them through the Photomerge Exposure feature. When you're shooting, especially in difficult lighting situations, put your camera into its *bracketing* mode, which captures successive shots and applies a different level of exposure compensation for each; typically, you'll get three shots with EV (Exposure bias Value) settings of –1, 0, and +1. Capture them in burst mode to minimize movement between shots.

To fix lighting using Photomerge Exposure (Automatic mode):

1. Open two or more related images with different exposures C and select them in the Project Bin.

2. Choose File > New > Photomerge Exposure. Or, switch to the Guided Edit mode and click Exposure under the Photomerge heading.

   Elements examines the files and opens the Photomerge Exposure interface in Automatic mode D.

3. Use the following controls to adjust the appearance E:

   ▸ Highlight Details adds more details to highlight areas, which can make the image darker.

   ▸ Shadows lightens or darkens shadow areas.

   ▸ Saturation boosts or tones down the colors.

   You can also switch from Smart Blending to Simple Blending, but doing so disables the additional controls.

4. Click Done.

To fix lighting using Photomerge Exposure (Manual mode):

1. If you're not happy with the automatic results, or you want more control over how the feature is applied, click the Manual tab.

2. In the Project Bin, click a photo that has a good foreground exposure.

3. Drag a photo with good background exposure to the Background pane .

4. With the Selection Tool active, paint the foreground area you want to appear against the background image . Use the Eraser Tool to clean up edges of your selection.

5. Use the Transparency slider to control how much the areas are blended—this is helpful if the foreground image is too bright, for example.

6. Click the Edge Blending checkbox to smooth the areas that overlap in the final image.

7. Click Done to create a new merged image .

TIP For best results, mount your camera on a tripod to take shots destined for the Photomerge Exposure tool.

TIP When taking pictures of people, a fast burst rate is essential; differences in body position between images creates a blurred, ghosting effect.

TIP In the Manual mode, click Advanced Option to reveal controls for aligning the images by hand.

F The image with the yellow border here has a better sky, so I'm using it as the background.

G Paint an area from the foreground image to selectively choose what appears in the final image.

H The final image retains the dramatic background and sheds more light on the poor soul who woke up early to capture this photo.

Adjusting Color

A Choose Auto Color Correction from the Enhance menu to automatically remove color cast from your image.

Color cast refers to a general shift of color to one extreme or another: An image can be said to have a yellow or red cast, for instance. Although sometimes introduced into images intentionally (to create a certain mood or effect), color casts are usually unhappy accidents. They can result from any number of circumstances, from a scanner in need of calibrating to tired chemicals in a film developer's lab. Even light from a fluorescent bulb can create unwanted color shifts in photographs.

Thankfully, Elements gives you several ways to deal with color cast: a wonderful little automatic menu command, a dialog that allows you to manually color-correct an image by adding and subtracting color values in small increments, a dialog for adjusting color curves, and a feature that can dramatically improve skin tones.

To adjust color with the Auto Color Correction command:

From the Enhance menu, choose Auto Color Correction, or press Ctrl+Shift+B **A**.

That's it. Photoshop Elements performs some elegant, behind-the-scenes magic, examining the image's color channels and histogram and performing a little math, and voilà—no more color cast.

> **TIP** I use this feature all the time before applying any other image correction. I'm constantly amazed at how well this simple menu command works, and usually give it a try even if I don't perceive a color cast. It almost always offers some degree of improvement to the color.

To adjust color using color curves:

1. From the Enhance menu, choose Adjust Color > Adjust Color Curves to open the Adjust Color Curves dialog.

2. To go with one of Elements' suggestions, click one of the styles at left 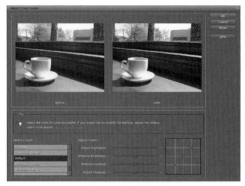. You can also drag the sliders under Adjust Sliders to manually tweak highlights, midtone brightness and contrast, or shadows. The points on the color curve to the right represent each setting.

3. Click OK to apply the color changes.

B The Adjust Color Curves feature provides one more way of fine-tuning an image's color.

To adjust color in an image based on skin tones:

1. From the Enhance menu, choose Adjust Color > Adjust Color for Skin Tone to open the Adjust Color for Skin Tone dialog.

2. Check that the Preview checkbox is selected, and then move the cursor onto the photo until it becomes an eyedropper. Click with the eyedropper on any part of a person's skin .

   Photoshop Elements adjusts the color in the entire image, but pays special attention to the skin tones.

3. If you're not satisfied with the results, click a different area of skin, or use the sliders to fine-tune the color change 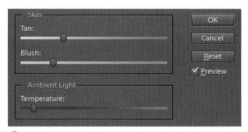.

4. Click OK to close the dialog and set the color changes.

C The eyedropper samples skin tones in a photo and then makes a best-guess color correction.

D Use dialog sliders to make manual skin tone corrections.

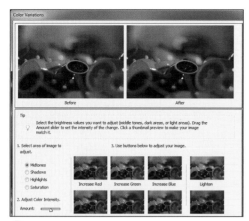

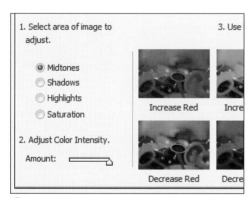

E The core of the Color Variations dialog is the lower, thumbnail button area. Each time you click a thumbnail you apply a slight color shift to your image. The thumbnails can be clicked any number of times and in any combination.

F The Amount slider is a bit of a brute force mechanism, but it works well with trial and error.

To remove color cast with the Color Variations dialog:

1. From the Enhance menu, choose Adjust Color > Color Variations.

2. Determine the color cast of your image.

   Because Elements doesn't offer any help in determining color cast, you're pretty much on your own here. Look for clues to color cast in objects or areas you are familiar with and can make good, educated guesses on. Ask yourself if that bright blue sky is looking a little yellow, or if those leafy greens have a little pink tinge to them, and then work from there.

3. In the lower portion of the dialog, click the thumbnail with the description that best describes what you need to do (Increase Red, Decrease Blue, and so on) while referring to the After view in the top half of the dialog **E**.

4. Continue to click any combination of thumbnails, as many times as necessary, until the After view looks satisfactory.

5. Click OK to close the Color Variations dialog and view your corrected image.

> **TIP** To a large degree, using the Color Variations dialog is a matter of trial and error, and to a lesser degree a rather subjective process **F**. And as much as I'd like to provide some little hints or formulas, experience and experimentation are the real keys to success with this dialog.

> **TIP** If you find yourself completely lost, or just want to start over, click the Before thumbnail in the upper-left corner, or the Reset Image button along the right side to reset the entire dialog.

Replacing Color

The Replace Color command does just what you would expect it to do, and does it very well indeed. In a nutshell, it allows you to select a specific color, either across an entire image or in an isolated area of an image, and then change not only the color but its saturation and lightness values as well. Eyedropper tools let you add and subtract colors to be replaced, whereas a slider control softens the transition between the colors you choose and those around them. I've seen this used to great effect on projects as varied as experimenting with different color schemes before painting a house's trim to changing the color of a favorite uncle's tie so that it no longer clashes with his suit.

To replace color across an entire image:

1. From the Enhance menu, choose Adjust Color > Replace Color.

2. In the Replace Color dialog, click the Selection radio button under the image preview box **A**.

   When the Replace Color dialog is open, your pointer will automatically change to an eyedropper tool when you move it over your image.

3. With the eyedropper tool, click in the image to select the color you want to change **B**.

   The color selection appears as a white area in the image preview of the Replace Color dialog **C**.

4. To expand the selection and include similar colors, drag the Fuzziness slider to the right. To contract the selection and exclude similar colors, drag the Fuzziness slider to the left.

A Options under the image preview box let you choose whether to view your color selections or just the image.

B Click the actual image in the image window to make a color selection.

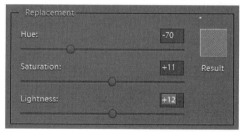

C The image preview area of the Replace Color dialog shows selected colors as white or shades of gray.

D Drag the Hue, Saturation, and Lightness sliders until you capture the right color effect. You may have to experiment a little until you get it just right.

You may want to expand or contract your selection beyond the limits of the Fuzziness slider. If parts of a selection fall too heavily in shadow or highlight, or have very reflective surfaces, you may need to make additional color selections or deletions.

5. To add a color to the selection, Shift-click the eyedropper tool in another area of the image. To subtract a color from the selection, press Alt and click.

   The dialog contains separate add and subtract eyedropper tools, but the keyboard shortcuts provide a much more efficient way to modify your color selections.

6. With the Preview checkbox selected, drag the Hue, Saturation, and Lightness sliders **D** until you achieve the desired color effect.

   These sliders operate just like the ones in the Hue/Saturation dialog. The Hue slider controls the actual color change; the Saturation slider controls the intensity of the color, from muted to pure; and the Lightness slider controls the color's brightness value, adding either black or white.

7. Click OK to close the Replace Color dialog and view your corrected image.

To replace color in a specific area of an image:

1. In the image window, make a selection around the area to which you want to apply the color change **E**.

2. From the Enhance menu, choose Adjust Color > Replace Color.

3. In the Replace Color dialog, click the Image button under the image preview. A detail view of your selection appears. When the Replace Color dialog is open, your pointer automatically changes to an eyedropper tool.

4. With the eyedropper tool, click in the image preview box of the Replace Color dialog to select the color you want to change **F**.

5. Click the Selection radio button to toggle to the Selection view.

6. To add or subtract a color from the selection, click the Image button to toggle back to that view; then use the keyboard shortcuts, as described in the previous procedure, to adjust the selection.

7. Use the Fuzziness slider to further fine-tune your selection **G**.

8. With the Preview checkbox selected, drag the Hue, Saturation, and Lightness sliders until you achieve the desired color.

9. Click OK to apply your changes.

> **TIP** If you prefer, you can always choose to make your color selection in the actual image in the image window, just as I did in the previous procedure. But if the selections you're making are small, relative to the total size of your image, it's often easier to work within the confines of the Replace Color dialog.

E Any selections you make are reflected in the Replace Color dialog.

F Click the image within the Replace Color dialog to make a color selection.

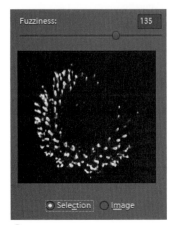

G Increasing Fuzziness expands the selection area.

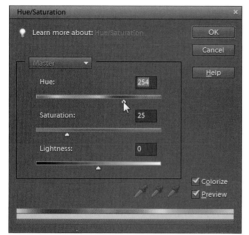

A Click the Colorize checkbox to add a colored tint to any image.

B The position of the Hue slider determines the color your tinted image will be.

Adding a Color Tint to an Image

Using a technique called colorization, you can add a single color tint to your images, simulating the look of a hand-applied color wash or the warm, antique glow of an old sepia-toned photograph. You can apply the effect to any image, even if it was originally saved as grayscale, as long as you first convert it to RGB. In addition to colorizing an entire image, you can use layers and layer modes to tint specific areas or objects. Because the shades of color you apply are determined by the image's original tonal values, photographs with good brightness and contrast levels make the best candidates for colorizing.

To colorize an area of an image:

1. Using any of the selection or marquee tools, select the area of your image you want to colorize. If you want to colorize an entire image, it's not necessary to make a selection.

2. From the Enhance menu, choose Adjust Color > Adjust Hue/Saturation, or press Ctrl+U to open the Hue/Saturation dialog.

3. With the Preview checkbox selected, click the Colorize checkbox **A**. Clicking the Colorize checkbox converts all the color in the image to a single hue.

4. Drag the Hue slider right or left until you arrive at the color you like **B**.

5. Drag the Saturation slider to adjust its values. Dragging to the left moves the color's saturation value closer to gray, whereas dragging to the right moves its value closer to a fully saturated color.

continues on next page

6. Drag the Lightness slider to adjust the color's brightness values.

Dragging to the left dims the color's brightness value, shifting it closer to black, whereas dragging to the right brightens its value, shifting it closer to white.

7. Click OK to close the Hue/Saturation dialog. Your image (or selection) is now composed of different values of the single color hue you selected.

TIP When you're applying a color tint to just a portion of your image, I recommend making a selection and then creating a new Hue/Saturation adjustment layer in the Layers panel **C**. See "Making Color and Tonal Changes with Adjustment Layers" in Chapter 8 for more information.

Hue/Saturation adjustment layer

C When selectively colorizing your image, you'll get more flexibility by using an adjustment layer.

Working with Layers

Photoshop Elements allows you to work on individual image layers, a feature that lets you make edits that don't permanently alter your original image. You can create and name new layers, and then reorder, group, and even merge selected layers.

In this chapter, you'll learn how layers are created, and then explore several methods and techniques to help you take advantage of one of Elements' most powerful and creative features.

The chapter concludes with a look at the Undo History panel. This helpful panel tracks and displays a record of every action you make (from selections, to layer creation, to retouching), and then lets you easily undo any action and return to different states in the history of your image creation.

In This Chapter

Understanding Layers

When you first import or scan an image into Photoshop Elements, it consists of one default layer. In many cases, you'll probably want to make a few simple changes to your photo and will have no need for multiple layers. But when you begin working with some of the more involved and complex image manipulation and retouching tools, you'll find that layers can make things a whole lot easier.

Layers act like clear, transparent sheets stacked one on top of another, and yet, when you view a final image, they appear as one unified picture 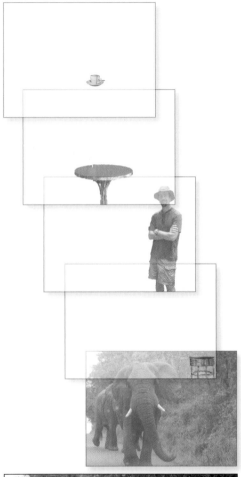. As you copy and paste selections, you may notice these operations automatically create new layers in your image. You can edit only one layer at a time, which allows you to select and modify specific parts of your photo without affecting the information on other layers. This is the real beauty of layers: the ability to work on and experiment with one part of your image while leaving the rest of it completely untouched. One exception is the adjustment layer, which lets you make color and tonal corrections to individual or multiple layers without changing the actual pixels.

Layers appear in your image in the same order as they appear in the Layers panel. The top layer of your image is the first layer listed on the Layers panel, and the background layer is positioned at the bottom of the list.

A Layers act like clear acetate sheets, where transparent areas let you see through to the layers below. (It's a good thing I showed the layers, or you might think the photo was undoctored!)

Show or hide layers — Fully locked

Active layer — More button

LAYERS

Normal — Opacity: 100%

Coffee Cup

Table

Jeff

Stool

Background

Lock:

New Layer — Create Adjustment Layer — Lock — Delete Layer

Add Layer Mask — Transparent pixels locked

A The Layers panel shows stacked layers exactly as they're arranged in your image. This panel gives you complete control over the stacking order of your layers, whether they're visible or hidden.

Layers Panel Options

Thumbnail Size

None

OK

Cancel

Thumbnail Contents

Layer Bounds

B Change thumbnail views from the Layers Panel Options menu.

Using the Layers Panel

When you launch Photoshop Elements for the first time, the Layers panel automatically appears in the lower-right corner of your screen in the panel bin. You can use the Layers panel from within the panel bin, or drag it out into the work area.

You can select which layer to make the active layer, display and hide layers, and lock layers to protect them from unintentional changes **A**. You can also change layer names, set the opacity (transparency) of individual layers, and apply blending modes.

The panel menu offers quick access to many of the same commands found on the Layer menu, plus options for changing the appearance of the panel thumbnails.

To view the Layers panel:

Do one of the following:

- Choose Window > Layers.

- Double-click the Layers panel tab in the panel bin.

- Choose Window > Reset Panels to return all the panels to their default locations, including Layers, which appears in the lower right.

To view the Layers panel menu:

Click the More button in the top-right corner of the Layers panel.

Once the Layers panel menu is open, you can select a command from the menu.

TIP To change the appearance of the layer thumbnail views, choose Panel Options from the Layers panel menu and click the size you want **B**. The smaller the icon, the more layers you're able to view at one time on the panel.

Layer Basics

To begin working with layers, you need to master just a few fundamental tasks. Start by creating and naming a new layer, and then add an image (or portion of an image) to it.

Once you've constructed an image file of multiple layers, you need to select the individual layer before you can work on that layer's image. Keep in mind that any changes you make will affect only the selected (active) layer, and that only one layer can be active at a time.

To create a new layer:

1. From the Layer menu or from the Layers panel menu, select New > Layer, or press Ctrl+Shift+N.

2. In the New Layer dialog, choose from the following options:

   ▸ Rename the layer with a more meaningful and intuitive name. The default names are Layer 1, Layer 2, Layer 3, and so on 🅐.

   ▸ Choose a blending mode for the layer.

     The default blending mode is Normal, meaning that no change will be applied to the layer. You can experiment with other blending modes directly from the Layers panel.

   ▸ Choose the layer's level of opacity.

     Opacity can also be adjusted at any time from the Layers panel.

   ▸ Apply a clipping mask over a previous (or lower) layer.

     The lower layer acts as a window for the upper layer's image to show through. For a detailed description of layer grouping, see "Creating Clipping Masks," later in this chapter.

🅐 Default layer names are Layer 1 for the first layer you create, Layer 2, Layer 3, and so on. You can enter a new name when creating a layer, or you can rename it later.

New Layer button

🅑 Click the New Layer icon to quickly create a new, blank layer.

TIP You can also quickly create a new layer by clicking the New Layer icon near the bottom of the Layers panel 🅑. The new layer appears as the top layer in the panel with the default blending and opacity modes applied. To rename the new layer, double-click its name in the Layers panel and enter a new name.

TIP To work more easily on your image, you can choose to show or hide any of its layers from the Layers panel menu.

C Click the layer name or thumbnail to make it the active (editable) layer.

D When you click a layer image in the image window, a bounding box appears to show you that it is the selected, active layer.

Visible   *Hidden*

E Click the eye icon to hide a layer; click again to make the layer visible.

To select a layer:

Do one of the following:

- On the Layers panel, click the Layer thumbnail or name to make that layer active **C**.

  If you've imported an image from a digital camera, by default it will have only one layer—the background layer, which is selected automatically.

- Select the Move tool and click directly on a layer image in the image window. A border with selection handles appears around the layer image to indicate that it's selected **D**.

To show or hide a layer:

On the Layers panel, click the eye icon to hide the layer (the eye disappears). Click again and the eye reappears, making the layer visible again in the image window **E**.

TIP When you try to select or make changes to an area in your image, you might encounter weird and unexpected results. For example, your selection can't be copied, or you apply a filter but nothing happens. More often than not, this is because you don't have the correct layer selected. Just refer to the Layers panel to see if this is the case. Remember that the active layer is always highlighted in the Layers panel.

TIP Quickly show or hide multiple layers by clicking and dragging through the eye column.

TIP To quickly display just one layer, Alt-click its eye icon. The other layers become hidden. Alt-click again to show all layers.

To delete a layer:

1. Select a layer on the Layers panel.

2. Do one of the following:

   ▸ With the layer selected, click the Trash icon on the Layers panel 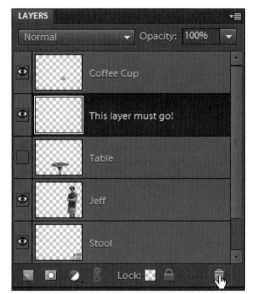 and then click Yes in the dialog that appears.

   ▸ From the Layer menu or from the Layers panel menu, choose Delete Layer.

   ▸ Drag the layer to the Trash icon on the Layers panel.

F Clicking the Trash icon also removes the selected layer.

Background Layers

When you open a photo imported from a digital camera or scanner, the photo appears on the background (or base) layer in Photoshop Elements. In fact, when you open an image file from just about any source, chances are it has been flattened and contains only a background layer. This layer cannot be reordered (that is, its relative position or level cannot be moved), and it cannot be given a blending mode, or assigned a different opacity.

When you create a new image and choose Transparent for its background, the bottom layer is called Layer 1. This layer can be reordered, and you can change its blending mode or opacity just as with any other layer.

A simple background layer can never be transparent, but that's okay if you're not concerned with changing opacity or applying blending modes. However, if you want to take advantage of the benefits transparency offers, start by creating an image with transparent background contents, or convert an existing background layer to a regular layer.

See "Converting and Duplicating Layers," later in this chapter, for details on turning background layers into regular layers (and vice-versa).

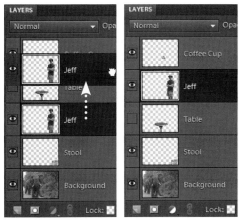

A Drag a layer up or down on the Layers panel to change its stacking order.

Changing the Layer Order

The layer stacking order determines which layers are on top of others, and plays a big role in determining how your image looks. As you build a composition, you may decide you want to change the layer order, either to help you work more easily on a particular layer, or to get a particular result or effect. The actual, visible overlapping of elements is determined by the layer order, so you may need to reorder layers frequently when you work on complex images.

Elements provides two main ways to change the stacking order of your layers. The most common and versatile approach is to drag the layer within the Layers panel. The second way is to select the Layer > Arrange menu and then choose commands such as Bring to Front and Send to Back— a method similar to what you use to arrange objects in a drawing program.

To change the layer order by dragging:

1. On the Layers panel, select the layer you want to move.

2. Drag the layer up or down in the Layers panel **A**.

   You will see a thick double line between the layers, indicating the new layer position.

3. Release the mouse button when the layer is in the desired location.

To change the layer order by arranging:

1. Select the layer you want to move on the Layers panel.

2. From the Layer menu, choose Arrange, and then select one of the following options from the submenu; or use the keyboard shortcuts noted for each 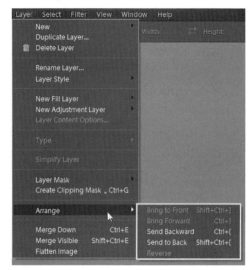.

   ▸ Bring to Front (Ctrl+Shift+]) moves the layer to the top of the Layers panel and the image .

   ▸ Bring Forward (Ctrl+]) moves the layer up by one step in the stacking order .

   ▸ Send Backward (Ctrl+[) moves the layer down by one step in the stacking order.

   ▸ Send to Back (Ctrl+Shift+[) makes the layer the bottom layer on the Layers panel.

   You can also Shift-click to select two layers in the Layers panel, and select Reverse to swap their order in the layer stack.

TIP If your image contains a background layer and you choose the Send to Back command, you'll find that the background layer stubbornly remains at the bottom of your Layers panel. By default, background layers are locked in place and can't be moved. To get around this, just double-click and rename the background layer to convert it to a functional layer. Then you can move it wherever you like.

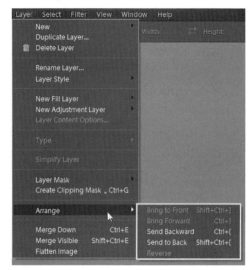

B You can also change a layer's position using the options on the Layer > Arrange menu.

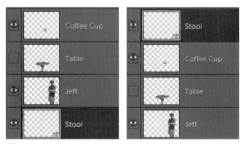

C The Bring to Front command moves the layer to the top level in your image.

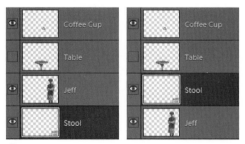

D The Bring Forward command moves the layer up just one level.

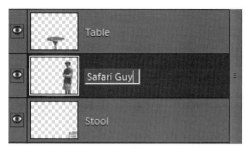

A To rename a layer, just double-click its name on the Layers panel.

Link icon

B Link icons indicate which layers are linked together.

Managing Layers

As you add layers to an image, Elements assigns them a default numerical name (Layer 1, Layer 2, and so on). As your image becomes more complex, it's much easier to find a cloud image on a layer called "Clouds" than it is to remember that it's on "Layer 14," for example.

You can also link layers together, so that any changes, such as moving and resizing, happen to two or more layers together.

And you can protect layers from unwanted changes by locking them. All layers can be fully locked, so that no pixels can be changed, or you can lock just the transparent pixels, so that any painting or other editing happens only where opaque (non-transparent) pixels already are present. This partial locking is useful if you've set up your image with areas that you know you want to preserve as transparent (like for a graphic you want to incorporate into a Web page). And locking an image protects it in other ways, too: You can move a locked layer's stacking position on the Layers panel, but the layer can't be deleted.

To rename a layer:

1. Double-click the layer's name on the Layers panel to display the text cursor and make the name editable **A**.

2. Enter a new name for the layer and press the Enter key. The new name appears on the Layers panel.

To link layers:

1. Ctrl-click to select the layers in the Layers panel that you want to link.

2. Click the Link button. The link icon appears in each linked layer, to the right of the layer name **B**.

To lock all pixels on a layer:

1. Select the layer on the Layers panel.

2. Click the Lock All button.

   The Lock All icon appears to the right of the layer name on the Layers panel **C**.

To lock transparent pixels on a layer:

1. Select the layer on the Layers panel.

2. Click the Lock Transparent Pixels button.

   The Lock Transparent Pixels icon appears to the right of the layer name on the Layers panel **D**.

Lock All

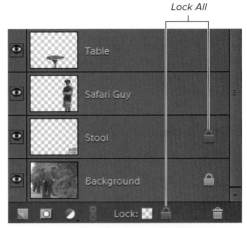

C The Lock All icon indicates that the layer's pixels are completely locked.

Lock Transparent Pixels

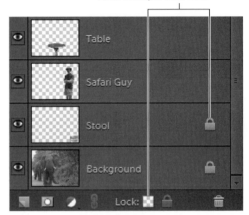

D The Lock Transparent Pixels icon indicates that the transparent pixels are locked.

A The top image is a composite of a number of layers from a 3D rendering program: a background layer, the pole, the sign's shadow on the pole, and three layers for the sign itself. To simplify the file, the three sign layers were merged into a single layer, and the pole and the shadow were combined (lower right). The finished image will look the same, but because it's composed of fewer layers, its file size will be significantly smaller.

B Combine a single layer with the layer below it by using the Merge Down command.

Merging Layers

Once you begin to create projects of even moderate complexity, the number of layers in your project can add up fairly quickly. Although Elements lets you create an almost unlimited number of layers, there are a couple of reasons why you may want to consolidate some or all of them into a single layer **A**. For one thing, it's just good housekeeping. It doesn't take long before the Layers panel begins to fill, and you find yourself constantly scrolling up and down in search of a particular object or text layer. And every layer you add drains a little more from your system's memory. Continue to add layers, and, depending on available memory, you may notice a decrease in your computer's performance.

Photoshop Elements offers three approaches to merging image layers. You can merge just two at a time, merge multiple layers, or flatten your image into a single background layer.

To merge one layer with another:

1. On the Layers panel, identify the two layers you want to merge, and then select the topmost of the two.

   Photoshop Elements will merge two layers only when one is stacked directly above the other. If you want to merge two layers that are separated by one layer or more, you'll need to rearrange their order in the Layers panel before they can be merged.

2. From the More menu on the Layers panel, choose Merge Down **B**, or press Ctrl+E. The two layers are merged into one.

To merge multiple layers:

1. On the Layers panel, identify the layers you want to merge, checking that the Visibility (eye) icon is on for just the layers you want to merge.

2. From the More menu on the Layers panel, choose Merge Visible , or press Ctrl+Shift+E.

   All of the visible layers are merged into one layer.

TIP You can create a new layer and then place a merged copy of all of the visible layers on that layer by holding the Alt key while choosing Merge Visible from the Layers panel's More menu. The visible layers themselves aren't merged and so remain separate and intact **D**. This technique offers you a way to capture a merged snapshot of your current file without actually merging the physical layers. It can be a handy tool for brainstorming and comparing different versions of the same layered file. For instance, take a snapshot of a layered file, change the opacity and blending modes of several layers, and then take another snapshot. You can then compare the two snapshots to see what effect the different settings have on the entire file.

C Only the three visible layers will be merged into one using the Merge Visible command.

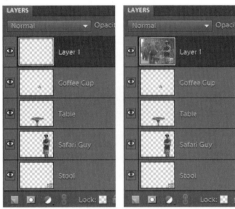

D On the left, a new layer has been created at the top of the Layers panel. If you hold the Alt key while selecting Merge Visible from the panel menu, all visible layers are merged and copied to the new layer, as shown on the right.

E Use the Flatten Image command to combine all the layers in a project into a single layer.

To flatten an image:

1. In the Layers panel, click the More button to open the panel menu.

2. From the panel menu, select Flatten Image.

3. If any layers are invisible, a warning box appears asking if you want to discard the hidden layers. If so, click OK.

   The entire layered file is flattened into one layer **E**.

TIP If there's any chance you may eventually want to make revisions to your layered image, always create a duplicate file before flattening so the layers are safely preserved in your original. Once you've flattened, saved, and closed a file, there's no way to recover those flattened layers.

Removing a Halo from an Image Layer

Often when you create a new image layer from a selection, you'll find you've inadvertently selected pixels you didn't want to include. This is a particularly common problem when you're trying to remove an image from its background using the Magic Wand or Quick Selection tools. On close inspection, what you thought was a clean selection actually includes a halo of colored background pixels.

Once you've pasted your selection into its new layer, choose Adjust Color from the Enhance menu, and then choose Defringe Layer from the Adjust Color submenu. In the Defringe dialog, enter a pixel width to control how much of the border of your image you want to affect—for high-resolution images, I usually start around 5. Then, just click OK to see the results in the image window **F**. If you're not happy with the results, undo the operation by pressing Ctrl+Z, then repeat the steps, entering a new pixel width in the Defringe dialog.

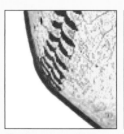 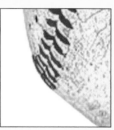

F When zoomed in, it's apparent that the old, weathered baseball I've cut and pasted carried with it a halo of the background it was resting on (left). After applying Defringe, the colored halo has disappeared (right).

Converting and Duplicating Layers

You now know you can create a new layer using the Layer > New command; in addition, Elements creates layers in all sorts of sneaky ways. For example, whenever you copy and paste a selection into an image, it's automatically added to your image on a brand new layer.

When you start editing an image, you'll often find it convenient to create a selection and convert it to a layer to keep it isolated and editable within your photo. It's also quite easy to duplicate a layer, which is useful when you want to copy an existing layer as is, or use it as a starting point and then make additional changes.

The background layer is unique and by default can't be moved, but sometimes you will need to move it, change its opacity, or apply a blending mode. To do any of those things, you'll need to convert it to a regular layer. And sometimes you'll want to convert an existing layer to the background.

To convert a selection to a layer:

1. Make a selection using any of the selection tools .

2. From the Layer menu, choose New; then perform one of the following commands:

   ▸ Layer via Copy (Ctrl+J). The selection is copied to a new layer, leaving the original selection unchanged **B**.

   ▸ Layer via Cut (Ctrl+Shift+J). The selection is cut to a new layer, leaving a gaping hole in the original layer, with the current background color showing through **C**.

A Select an area to convert to its own layer.

B Copying a selection to a new layer leaves the original selection unchanged.

C The Layer via Cut command cuts the selected pixels to a new layer. (The new layer has been hidden here to demonstrate that it's actually cut, not copied.)

Use the Duplicate Layer dialog to rename your new duplicate layer.

You can also duplicate a layer by dragging any existing layer to the New Layer button.

The new layer appears right above the original layer on the Layers panel.

To duplicate a layer:

1. Select the layer on the Layers panel.

2. Duplicate the layer using one of the following methods:

   ▸ If you want to create a new name for the layer, choose Layer > Duplicate Layer.

   The Duplicate Layer dialog appears, where you can rename the layer . Note that you can also get to this dialog from the Layers panel menu.

   ▸ If you're not concerned with renaming the layer right now, just drag the selected layer to the New Layer icon on the Layers panel .

   The new layer appears above the original layer with a "copy" designation added to the name .

TIP Perhaps this is because of the way I originally learned it, but I always duplicate layers by dragging them to the New Layer button. I then double-click the layer's name to type a new name.

To convert a background to a layer:

1. From the Layer menu, choose New > Layer from Background.

2. If desired, type a new name for the layer and click OK 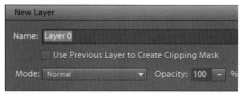.

To convert a layer to a background:

1. Select a layer on the Layers panel.

2. From the Layer menu, choose New > Background From Layer .

3. The new background appears at the bottom of the Layers panel .

TIP You can also convert the background by double-clicking it on the Layers panel, which brings up the same New Layer dialog.

TIP The Type and Shape tools also each automatically generate a new layer when you use them, keeping those elements isolated on their own unique layers.

TIP The Background From Layer command won't work if you already have an existing background layer in your Layers panel. Why? Because no image can have two background layers at the same time. To get around this, convert the current background to a regular layer. Then, follow the steps to convert a regular layer into a background.

G You can convert the background to a layer and rename it during the conversion.

H You can convert a layer to a background by choosing Layer > New > Background From Layer.

I New background layers always appear at the bottom of the Layers panel.

A To copy a layer, just drag it from the Layers panel and drop it directly onto another image.

B The new layer appears directly above the previously selected (active) layer in the destination image and in the Layers panel.

Copying Layers Between Images

It's extremely easy to copy layers from one Elements document to another. If you're used to the drag-and-drop technique, you'll be glad to know this method works well for copying layers as well as selections. Remember, as you copy and paste selections they end up on their own layers. So, layers often contain unique objects you can easily share between photos.

To drag and drop a layer from the Layers panel:

1. Open the two images you plan to use.

2. In the source image, select the layer you want to copy by clicking it in the Layers panel.

3. Drag the layer's name from the Layers panel into the destination image **A**.

   The new layer appears both in the image window and on the Layers panel of the destination image **B**. When you drag a layer from one image into another, the original, source image is not changed. The layer remains intact.

To drag and drop a layer using the Move tool:

1. Open the two images you plan to use.

2. Select the Move tool, and then in the source image window, select the layer you want to copy by clicking it.

   You can also select the layer by clicking its thumbnail in the Layers panel.

3. With the Move tool still selected, drag the actual image layer from the source image window to the destination image .

   The copied layer appears on the Layers panel immediately above the previously active layer.

To copy and paste a layer between images:

1. In the source image, select the layer you want to copy from by clicking it either in the Layers panel or the image window.

2. Choose Select > All to select all of the pixels on the layer, or press Ctrl+A.

3. Choose Edit > Copy to copy the layer to the clipboard, or press Ctrl+C.

4. In the destination image, choose Edit > Paste, or press Ctrl+V.

   The contents of the copied layer appears in the center of the destination image.

TIP In some cases, the layer in your source image may be larger than the destination image, in which case not all of the layer will be visible. Just use the Move tool to bring the desired area into view.

TIP If you're viewing open documents in tabbed view, drag an item to the tab of the file to which you want it added.

C The Move tool lets you copy a layer from one image window to another.

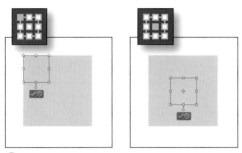

A Precise scale and rotation values can be entered for any shape.

B Both of these squares are being reduced in size by about half. The one on the left is scaled toward its upper-left corner, and the one on the right is scaled toward its center.

 C The Commit Transform button scales the layer image to the size you define.

Transforming Layers

You can also scale (resize), rotate, and distort layer images. They can be altered either numerically, by entering specific values on the options bar, or manually, by dragging their control handles in the image window. Constrain options, such as proportional scaling, are available for most transformations, and a set of keyboard shortcuts helps to simplify the process of adding distortion and perspective.

To scale a layer image:

1. Click a layer in the Layers panel to activate it; then from the Image menu, choose Transform > Free Transform, or press Ctrl+T. The options bar displays the scale and rotation text fields and the reference point locator **A**.

2. On the options bar, click to set a reference point location **B**.

   The reference point determines what point your layer image will be scaled to: toward the center, toward a corner, and so on.

3. If you want to scale your layer image proportionately, click the Constrain Proportions checkbox.

4. Enter a value in either the height or width text field. The layer image is scaled accordingly.

5. At the lower-right corner of your layer image, click the Commit Transform button **C**, or press Enter.

TIP You can scale a layer image manually by selecting it with the Move tool and then dragging any one of the eight handles on the selection border. Constrain the scaling by holding down the Shift key while dragging one of the four corner handles.

To rotate a layer image:

1. Click a layer in the Layers panel; then from the Image menu, choose Rotate > Free Rotate Layer .

   The options bar changes to show the scale and rotation text fields and the reference point locator.

2. On the options bar, click to set a reference point location **E**.

3. Enter a value in the rotate text field.

   The image will rotate accordingly.

4. Click the Commit Transform button, or press Enter.

TIP To rotate the image in 90- or 180-degree increments or to flip it horizontally or vertically, choose Image > Rotate; then choose from the list of five menu commands below the Free Rotate Layer command.

TIP You can rotate a layer image manually by selecting it with the Move tool and then moving the pointer outside of the selection border until it becomes a rotation cursor **F**. Drag around the outside of the selection border to rotate the image. In addition, you can constrain the rotation to 15-degree increments by holding down the Shift key while dragging the rotation cursor.

TIP If you simply want to reposition a layer image in the image window, click anywhere inside the image with the Move tool and then drag the image to its new position.

D You can apply any of the layer rotation menu commands to a layer image.

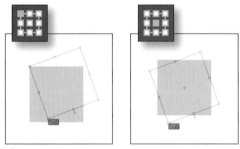

E Both of these squares are being rotated about 20 degrees. The one on the left is rotated around its upper-left corner, and the one on the right is rotated around its center.

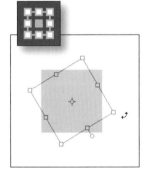

F Rotate any layer image manually by dragging it around its reference point with the rotation pointer.

G Choose one of the three specific transformation commands.

H The same square layer image transformed using Skew (left), Distort (center), and Perspective (right).

Before

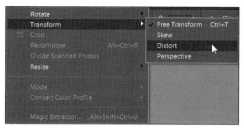

After

I You can align or distribute objects on different layers.

To distort a layer image:

1. Click a layer in the Layers panel to make it active. From the Image menu, choose Transform; then choose Skew, Distort, or Perspective **G**.

2. On the options bar, check that the reference point location is set to the center.

   The reference point can, of course, be set to any location, but the center seems to work best when applying any of the three distortions.

3. Drag any of the layer image's control handles to distort the image.

   Dragging the control handles will yield different results depending on the distort option you choose **H**.

4. On the options bar, click the Commit Transform button, or press Enter.

5. Click the Commit Transform button a second time (or press Enter) to deselect the image layer and hide the selection border.

To align or distribute layer objects:

1. Select two or more layers in the Layers panel; the Distribute command requires three or more selected layers.

2. Select the Move tool from the toolbox.

3. From the options bar, click the Align or Distribute drop-down menu and choose how you'd like the layer objects repositioned **I**.

About Opacity and Blending Modes

One of the most effective and simple ways to enhance your layered image is to create the illusion of combining one layer's image with another by blending their pixels. This differs from merging layers because the layers aren't actually combined, but rather appear to mix together. Photoshop Elements provides two easily accessible tools at the top of the Layers panel that can be used alone or in tandem for blending multiple layers: the Opacity slider and the Blending Modes drop-down menu. The Opacity slider controls the degree of transparency of one layer over another. If a layer's opacity is set at 100 percent, the layer is totally opaque, and any layers beneath it are hidden. If a layer's opacity is set to 30 percent, 70 percent of any underlying layers are allowed to show through .

Blending modes are a little trickier. Whereas Opacity settings strictly control the opaqueness of one layer over another, blending modes act by mixing or blending one layer's color and tonal value with the one below it. The Difference mode, for example, combines one layer's image with a second, and treats the top layer like a sort of negative filter, inverting colors and tonal values where dark areas blend with lighter ones .

Ⓐ Two separate layers (top) compose this image of me and a giant coffee cup. The lower-left image displays the top layer with an opacity setting of 100 percent. The lower-right image displays the top layer with an opacity setting of 50 percent.

Ⓑ The image on the left contains no blending modes; the image on the right displays the top layer with the Difference blending mode applied.

C The top layer is selected on the Layers panel. Its opacity is set at 100 percent.

Opacity slider

D You can change a layer's opacity from 0 to 100 percent by dragging the Opacity slider.

To set a layer's opacity:

1. On the Layers panel, select the layer whose opacity you want to change **C**.

2. To change the opacity, do one of the following:

   ▸ Enter a percentage in the Opacity text field, which is located at the top of the Layers panel.

   ▸ Click the arrow to activate the Opacity slider and then drag the slider to the desired opacity **D**.

TIP You can change the opacity settings in 10-percent increments directly from the keyboard. With a layer selected on the Layers panel, press any number key to change the opacity: 1 for 10 percent, 2 for 20 percent, and so on. Also, pressing two number keys in rapid succession will work—for example, 66 percent. If this technique doesn't seem to be working, make sure you don't have a painting or editing tool selected in the toolbox. Many of the brushes and effects tools can be sized and adjusted with the number keys, and if any of those tools are selected, they take priority over the Layers panel commands.

TIP A background layer contains no transparency, so you can't change its opacity until you first convert it to a regular layer (see "To convert a background to a layer," earlier in this chapter).

To apply a blending mode to a layer:

1. On the Layers panel, select the upper-most layer to which you want to apply the blending mode.

   Remember, blending modes work by mixing (blending) the image pixels of one layer with the layers below it, so your project will need to contain at least two layers in order for a blending mode to have any effect.

2. Select the desired blending mode from the Blending Mode drop-down menu **E**.

   The image on the layer to which you've applied the blending mode will appear to mix with the image layers below.

TIP You can apply only one blending mode to a layer, but it's still possible to apply more than one blending mode to the same image. After assigning a blending mode to a layer, duplicate the layer and then choose a different blending mode for the duplicate. There are no hard-and-fast rules to follow, and the various blending modes work so differently with one another that getting what you want is largely an exercise of trial and error. But a little experimentation with different blending mode combinations (and opacities) can yield some very interesting effects that you can't achieve any other way.

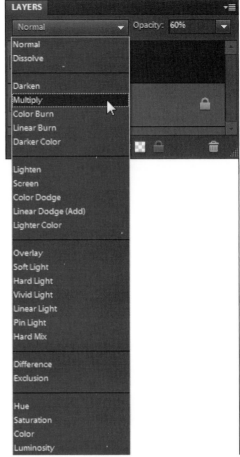

E Select a blending mode from the Layers panel's Blending Mode menu.

This project is composed of two layers: a photo of clouds and the CLOUDS text layer. The photo completely covers the text layer in the image at top, but when made a clipping mask, the clouds peek through only where the text is visible.

In this figure, the CLOUDS text layer serves as the base layer. It will soon be grouped with the Sky layer, which is directly above it.

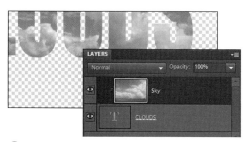

A clipping mask appears indented.

Creating Clipping Masks

Any object placed on a layer, including photographic images and lines of editable text, can be used as the basis for masking any number of layer objects above it. Think of the lower, or base layer, as a window through which the upper layers are allowed to show through. So, for example, you could have a photograph of the sky placed within the word "CLOUDS" Ⓐ. Once applied, any layer mask can be repositioned independently of the others, or all masks can be linked and moved as a group.

To create a clipping mask:

1. On the Layers panel, identify the layer you want to use as your base layer Ⓑ. Your layers must be arranged so that the layer you want to mask is directly above the base layer.

2. Still on the Layers panel, select the layer above the base layer; then from the Layer menu choose Create Clipping Mask, or press Ctrl+G. The two layers are now grouped, and the upper layer is visible only in those areas where the base layer object is present.

   On the Layers panel, the base layer's name is underlined, and the masked layer is indented Ⓒ.

To remove a clipping mask:

1. On the Layers panel, select the base layer.

2. From the Layer menu, choose Release Clipping Mask, or press Ctrl+G.

TIP For a faster way to create a layer group, Alt-click the space between the two layers.

Using Layer Masks

In several examples in this chapter, objects (such as the coffee cup or table) have been removed from their backgrounds. In those cases, I made a selection, then deleted the surrounding pixels. The problem, of course, is that I can't get those pixels back without returning to the unedited source files.

Photoshop Elements 9 offers a better way. Instead of deleting pixels, you can hide them using a layer mask. That enables you to edit what appears at any point, keeping your precious pixels intact.

Layer masks are always grayscale: black pixels hide content, white pixels reveal it. Gray pixels, however, become transparent depending on how dark they are, opening up all sorts of possibilities for compositions.

To create a layer mask:

1. Make a selection of the area in your image you want to keep visible.

2. Click the Add Layer Mask button in the Layers panel. A mask is created to the right of the image thumbnail 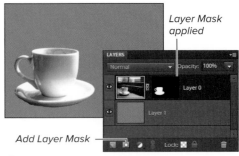.

   To reverse the mask (make the selection transparent), Alt-click the Add Layer Mask button.

To edit a layer mask:

1. Click the layer mask thumbnail for the layer you want to edit.

2. Use the editing tools to change the contents of the mask. For example, paint with the brush tool set to black to make more areas transparent **B**.

> **TIP** Since a mask is just a grayscale image, you can apply filters and other interesting effects to it **C**.

Layer Mask applied

Add Layer Mask

A The black areas of the mask hide the layer's pixels without deleting them.

B Painting with black in the layer mask "erases" the visible portion of the image.

C To achieve this halftone highlight effect, I duplicated the image, created a circular gradient within the mask, and then applied the Color Halftone effect to the mask. To punch up the contrast, I changed the color of the underlying layer (which shows through the dark portions of the mask) to white.

Link disabled

D With the mask unlinked, moving its contents shifts the visible portion of the image, not the image itself.

Mask disabled

E It's often helpful to turn off a mask without deleting it when you need to view the full image.

To unlink a layer mask:

Click the link icon between the image thumbnail and the mask thumbnail.

The mask can be repositioned independently of the image **D**.

To disable a layer mask:

With the layer selected, choose Layer > Layer Mask > Disable. A red X appears over the mask to indicate that it's not currently active **E**.

To turn it back on, choose Layer > Layer Mask > Enable.

To delete a layer mask:

Select the layer and choose Layer > Layer Mask > Delete. The mask is removed, leaving the image untouched.

To apply a layer mask:

If you want to make the mask permanent, choose Layer > Layer Mask > Apply. Transparent pixels are erased from the image on that layer.

TIP The layer mask commands are also available by right-clicking and choosing them from the contextual menu that appears. I much prefer this approach, since my cursor is usually already there within the Layers panel.

TIP Ctrl-click a layer mask to select its contents without needing to make a new selection.

TIP Photoshop Elements has had layer masks for several revisions, but the feature wasn't as accessible as it is now. For example, when you make a selection in an image and apply an adjustment layer (described later in this chapter), Elements creates a layer mask so the effect is applied only to the selection.

Applying Effects with Layer Styles

With Layer styles, you can add editable effects to individual layers within an image, and you can be as conservative or as wild as your heart desires. For example, you can add a subtle drop shadow to an object, or you can go in the opposite direction and set your friend's hair ablaze with the Fire layer style. Beveled edges, glowing borders, and even custom textures can all be applied to any object or text layer. The Layer Styles options in the Effects panel contain a series of style sets, grouped as galleries and accessed from the panel's drop-down menu. Once you've applied a layer style, you can choose to keep it as an active element of a layer and return to and adjust it at any time; or you can choose to merge the layer object and style together to simplify the layer.

To apply a layer style:

1. On the Layers panel, choose the layer to which you want to apply the style  Ⓐ.

2. To open the Effects panel (if it's not already visible), do one of the following:
   - From the Window menu, choose Effects.
   - Double-click the Effects panel tab in the panel bin.

3. Click the Layer Styles icon at the top of the panel Ⓑ.

4. From the Library drop-down menu, choose a style set Ⓒ. The set you choose presents a gallery from which you can select a specific style.

5. In the style gallery, click the style you want to apply to your layer.

Ⓐ Select a layer to apply a layer style.

Layer Styles icon

Ⓑ The Effects icons allow you to select Filters, Layer Styles, and Photo Effects (or All) from the same panel.

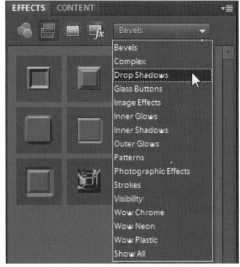

Ⓒ Layer styles are divided into different style sets.

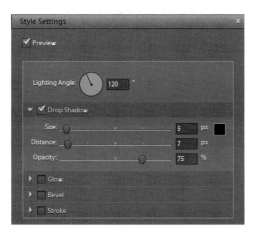

D Choose a style from the panel gallery and click Apply to make the style active.

Layer Style icon

E When a layer style is applied, a Layer Style icon appears to the right of the layer name.

F Use sliders in the Style Settings dialog to modify the shadow, glow, bevel, and stroke styles.

6. Click the Apply button (or double-click the chosen style). The style is applied to the layer object D, and a Layer Style icon appears next to the layer name on the Layers panel.

To remove a layer style:

From the Layer menu, choose Layer Style > Clear Layer Style. The command removes all styles from the layer, no matter how many have been applied.

To edit a layer style:

1. On the Layers panel, double-click the Layer Style icon E. The Style Settings dialog opens.

2. Make sure the Preview box is selected; then refer to the image window while dragging the Size, Distance, and Opacity sliders F.

TIP Multiple layer styles can be assigned to a single layer; however, only one layer style from each set can be assigned at a time. In other words, you can assign a drop shadow, bevel, and outer glow style to the same layer all at once, but you can't assign two different bevel styles at the same time.

TIP Layer styles can be applied only to images or text on a regular, transparent layer. If you try to apply a style to a background layer, a warning box asks if you want to first make the background a layer. Click OK and the background is converted to a layer; the layer style will be applied automatically.

TIP Elements allows you to apply a layer style to a blank layer, but the layer style won't have any effect until text or an image is placed on the layer. When you place something on a layer with a previously assigned layer style, it will display with the layer style's attributes: drop shadow, beveled edge, and so on.

The Style Settings Dialog

Not all of the layer styles can be adjusted, but, using a series of sliders, a wheel, checkboxes, and radio buttons, you can make adjustments to drop shadows, inner and outer glows, bevels, and stroke styles. Here's a quick tour of the Style Settings dialog controls 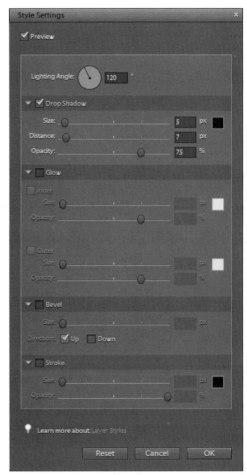.

Except for Lighting Angle and Bevel, each section contains a slider to determine how opaque the effect appears, as well as a color well for changing the effect's color. The distance and size slider values are all based on units of pixels. Click a style's checkbox to enable it.

- The Lighting Angle wheel controls the direction of the light source when a bevel or shadow style is applied. Changing the light angle will change which beveled surfaces are in highlight and which are in shadow, and will also control where a drop shadow falls behind an object B.

- The Drop Shadow's Distance slider controls the distance that a drop shadow is placed from an object. The larger the number, the more shadow is exposed from behind an object. If the distance is set to 0, the shadow is centered directly under the object and isn't visible. The Size slider determines how large the shadow appears.

- The Inner Glow Size slider lets you increase or decrease the amount of glow radiating in from the edges of an object.

- The Outer Glow Size slider lets you increase or decrease the amount of glow radiating out from the edges of an object.

Ⓐ Please, please, please, never use all of these effects at once! I'm just showing all options.

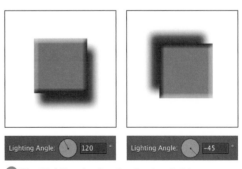

Ⓑ The Lighting Angle wheel sets a light source for any bevel or drop shadow styles you apply, and can be set to light any object from any angle.

 When the bevel direction is set to Up, the object bevel appears to come forward (left). When the bevel direction is set to Down, the object bevel appears to recede into the distance (right).

- The Bevel Size slider controls the amount of beveled edge on your object. An inside bevel of 3 will be almost imperceptible, whereas larger values create an increasingly more pronounced bevel effect.

- The Bevel Direction radio buttons control the appearance of a bevel style. If the Up button is selected, the bevel will appear to extrude or come forward; if the Down button is selected, the bevel will appear to recede .

- The Stroke effect draws a solid line around elements on the layer. The size slider sets the line's width.

Once you've applied a layer style, you can return to it at any time to modify it, but you also have the option of merging the layer style with its layer by simplifying. In effect, simplifying is like flattening an individual layer. Simplifying a layer permanently applies a layer style to its layer and can help to reduce the complexity and file size of your project.

To simplify a layer:

1. On the Layers panel, click to select the layer you want to simplify.

2. From the panel menu on the Layers panel, choose Simplify Layer.

   The layer style is merged with the layer, and the Layer Style icon disappears from the layer on the Layers panel.

Making Color and Tonal Changes with Adjustment Layers

Adjustment layers let you make color and tonal adjustments to your image (much like the commands discussed in Chapter 7, "Changing and Adjusting Colors") without changing the actual pixels in your image. Adjustment layers work like filters, resting above the actual image layers and affecting any image layers below them. They can be especially useful when you want to experiment with different settings or compare the effects of one setting over another.

Because you can apply opacity and blending mode changes to adjustment layers (just as you would to any other layer), they offer a level of creative freedom not available from their menu-command counterparts. For instance, you can create a Levels adjustment layer above an image, and then change the opacity of that adjustment layer to fine-tune the amount of tonal correction applied.

To create an adjustment layer:

1. On the Layers panel, identify the topmost layer to which you want the adjustment layer applied, and then select that layer.

   Remember that the adjustment layer affects all layers below it on the Layers panel, not just the one directly below it.

2. At the top of the Layers panel, click the Create Adjustment Layer button **A**.

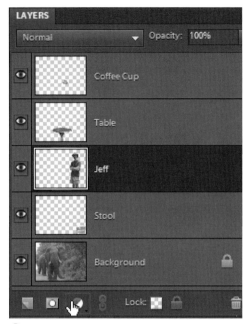

A Once you've selected a layer, click the Create Adjustment Layer button.

About Fill Layers

The Create Adjustment Layer drop-down menu includes not only tonal correction options such as Levels, but a list of three layer fill options: Solid Color, Gradient, and Pattern. Follow my lead and ignore these options. They don't do anything that can't be accomplished by simply creating a new layer and applying a fill or pattern—except that they do it with more overhead, because adjustment layers require more processing power and create larger files than regular layers.

B Choose an adjustment command from the drop-down menu.

C The edits you make in the adjustment dialog apply to all layers below the adustment layer, but do not change those layers' pixels.

D The adjustment layer has been grouped with the object layer directly below it.

3. From the drop-down menu, choose from the list of adjustment layer options **B**.

   When you choose an adjustment layer option, its dialog opens and a new adjustment layer is created above the selected layer **C**.

4. Use the sliders to adjust the settings, and then click OK to close the dialog.

   If you want to return to the adjustment layer dialog later, just double-click its layer thumbnail on the Layers panel.

   By default, an adjustment layer affects all the layers below it in the Layers panel. But if you create a clipping mask, the effects of the adjustment layer will be limited to one specific layer.

To apply an adjustment layer to a single layer:

1. In the Layers panel, move the adjust-ment layer directly above the layer to which you want it applied.

2. With the adjustment layer still selected in the Layers panel, choose Create Clipping Mask from the Layer menu, or press Ctrl+G.

   The adjustment layer and the one directly below it are grouped, and the effects of the adjustment layer are applied only to that single layer **D**.

TIP A much faster way to create a clipping mask is to Alt-click the space between the two layers.

Using the Undo History Panel

The Undo History panel lets you move backward and forward through a work session, allowing you to make multiple undos to any editing changes you've made to your image. Photoshop Elements records every change and then lists each as a separate entry, or state, on the panel. With one click, you can navigate to any state and then choose to work forward from there, return to the previous state, or select a different state from which to work forward.

To navigate through the Undo History panel:

1. To open the Undo History panel, choose Undo History from the Window menu.

2. To move to a different state in the Undo History panel, do one of the following:

   ▶ Click the name of any state.

   ▶ Drag the panel slider up or down to a different state .

Ⓐ Use the panel slider to move to virtually any point in time in the creation of your project.

TIP The default number of states that the Undo History panel saves is 50. After 50, the first state is cleared from the list, and the panel continues to list just the 50 most recent states. The good news is you can bump the number of saved states up to 1000, provided that your computer has enough memory. In the Photoshop Elements preferences, choose Performance. In the History & Cache box enter a larger number in the History States field.

TIP If memory is at a premium (and you'd rather Photoshop Elements not clog up your precious RAM by remembering your last 50 selections, brushstrokes, and filter effects), set the number in the Undo History States field to 1. You can still undo and redo your last action as you work along, but for all practical purposes, the Undo History panel is turned off.

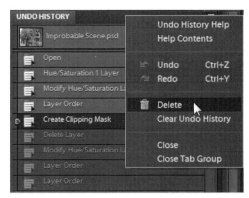

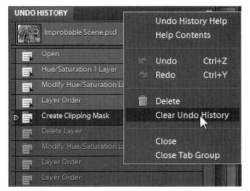

B Delete any state by selecting it and choosing Delete from the panel menu.

C If system memory is a concern, you can periodically clear the panel of all states.

To delete a state:

Click the name of any state, then choose Delete from the panel menu **B**.

The selected state and all states following it are deleted.

To clear the Undo History panel:

Do one of the following:

- From the panel menu, choose Clear Undo History **C**.

  This action can be undone, but it doesn't reduce the amount of memory used by Photoshop Elements.

- Hold down the Alt key, then choose Clear Undo History from the panel menu.

  This action cannot be undone, but it does purge the list of states from the memory buffer. This can come in handy if a message appears telling you that Photoshop Elements is low on memory.

TIP Deletion of a state can be undone, but only if no changes are applied to the image in the interim. If you make a change to the image that creates a new state on the panel, all deleted states are permanently lost.

TIP Sometimes—when you're working on an especially complex piece, for instance—the Undo History panel may become filled with states that you no longer need to manage or return to, or that begin to take their toll on your system's memory. At any time, you can clear the panel's list of states without changing the image.

9

Filters and Effects

For decades, photographers have used lens filters to improve and alter the look of their photographs when shooting—to change the intensity of color values, or lighten certain tones and darken others. For more creative effects, they would also rely on darkroom and printing techniques.

Thanks to the advancements of digital technology, though, you don't have to fiddle with chemicals or additional camera equipment to enhance your photographs. The filters and effects included in Photoshop Elements go far beyond what's been possible in traditional photography. Many of these filters (such as the Blur filters) allow you to make subtle corrections and improvements to your photos, whereas other filters (such as Artistic, Stylize, and Sketch) can transform an image into a completely new piece of artwork. Photoshop Elements also provides effects you can add to your photos, including striking image effects (lizard skin, anyone?) as well as type effects and unique textures.

Using the Effects Panel

Photoshop Elements offers you almost unlimited possibilities for tweaking and enhancing your images. Most filters include a dialog where you can preview any changes and adjust the settings for either a subtle or dramatic effect. And some of the filters (such as the Liquify filter) are so comprehensive, they seem like separate applications within Photoshop Elements.

Effects work a bit differently than filters. When you apply an effect, Elements runs through a series of automatic actions in which a number of filters and layer styles are applied to your image. Effects are a bit more complex than filters. If you want to add a drop shadow, picture frame, or brushed-metal type to a photo, browse through the Effects panel to see what's available.

To view the Effects panel:

1. In the Editor, choose Window > Effects (if the panel isn't already visible).

2. Click either the Filters or Photo Effects icon at the top of the Effects panel Ⓐ.

Filters   *Photo Effects*   *Library drop-down menu*

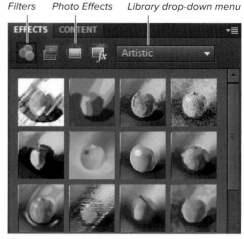

Ⓐ Access filters and photo effects from the Effects panel.

Filter and Effect Plug-ins

Plug-ins provide a nifty way to extend your Photoshop Elements experience. Want to add some sophisticated 3D shadows or translucent effects to your photos? If you can't find the effect or filter you want in Photoshop Elements, chances are good that a plug-in might do the trick. Most of the plug-ins designed for Photoshop will work just as well in Photoshop Elements, since both applications use the same file format (PSD). Some plug-in packages, clearly meant for professionals and creative types, don't come cheap—they can cost a few hundred dollars. But many plug-ins are available free of charge. One of the best places to start looking for filter and effect plug-ins is at the Adobe Exchange site (www.adobestudioexchange.com), where you can download and share filters, effects, and other plug-in goodies with other Photoshop and Photoshop Elements users.

B When you select Show All from the Library drop-down menu, all filters or effects in their respective libraries are displayed at once.

C Select Show Names from the panel menu to display filters or effects with their names.

To change the number of filters or effects displayed in the panel:

Do one of the following:

- Click the Show All button to the right of the Photo Effects button.

- If it's not already selected, choose Show All from the Library drop-down menu to see all filters or effects **B**.

- Select a set of filters or effects from the Library drop-down menu to see just the ones in that set.

To change the panel view:

Do one of the following:

- From the More menu, choose Small, Medium, or Large Thumbnail View to change the size of the filters or effect previews. Medium is the default.

- From the More menu, choose Show Names to view the filters or effects with their identifying names **C**.

TIP Filter plug-ins created by third-party developers usually appear at the bottom of the Filters panel menu.

Applying Filters and Effects

Effects don't include a preview window, but you'll find useful examples of each effect on the Effects panel. For many filters and effects, a good approach is to select a small area of your image and apply the change to see the results—that way, you don't waste a lot of time waiting for your computer to process changes to the entire image. The exceptions are effects like Frames, where the effect is designed to be applied to your entire image. A few effects (such as the Cutout and Recessed frame effects) require you to make a selection before you can apply the effect.

To apply a filter:

1. To apply a filter to an entire layer, select the layer on the Layers panel to make the layer active. To apply a filter to just a portion of your image, select an area with one of the selection tools 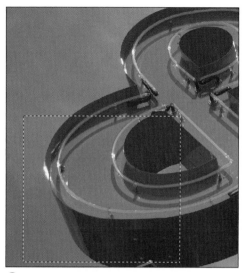.

2. Do one of the following:

   ▶ To immediately apply the filter or effect, double-click its button on the Effects panel; or, drag any filter from the Effects panel onto your image in the image window.

   ▶ If you want to control how the effect appears, go to the Filter menu and choose a filter from one of the submenus. The Filter Options dialog appears ⓑ. Continue following the next steps.

3. In the Filter Options dialog, experiment with the available values and options until you get the look you want.

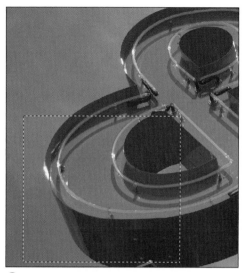

ⓐ Filters and effects can be applied to an entire layer or to a selection.

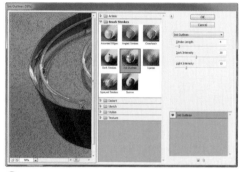

ⓑ The Filter Options dialog includes a large preview window and sliders you can use to adjust a filter's settings.

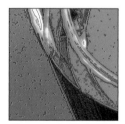 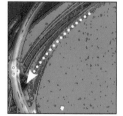

ⓒ To move around (or pan) the preview image, just click and drag to move the image.

D After you click OK, the filter is applied to your image.

The Filter Dialogs

Given the sheer number of filters in Photoshop Elements, there's no way to cover the specific steps for each filter in the space of this book. Fortunately, the vast majority of these filters work the same way. So once you've used a couple of them, you can figure out the rest pretty easily. Most filters use the same Filter Options dialog with a preview window and slider bars that allow you to control the level and intensity of the filter. When using a filter for the first time, you should preview the default filter setting and apply it by clicking OK. Not what you wanted? Just press Ctrl+Z to undo your changes and start over. When you're back in the filter's dialog, you can experiment by adjusting the sliders to preview more (or less) dramatic results in your photo.

4. In the dialog preview window, you can change the view by doing one of the following:

   ▸ To zoom in or out, click either the Zoom In (plus sign) or Zoom Out (minus sign) button.

   ▸ To see a specific area of your image, click and drag within the preview window **C**.

5. Click OK. The filter is applied to your image **D**. If you're not happy with the result, choose Edit > Undo or select the previous state from the Undo History panel.

TIP Filters with additional options include ellipses (...) after their names.

TIP The list in the lower-right corner of the Filter Options dialog lets you add multiple filters before applying them to your image. Click the New Filter Layer button (the document icon) and choose another filter to see how it affects the image.

TIP As you add filters, you'll notice that you're presented with two different types of Option dialogs. The Add Noise filter, for instance, opens to a dialog specific to just that filter. But filters contained in the Artistic, Brush Strokes, Distort, Sketch, Stylize, and Texture groups open to an Option dialog where you can not only adjust the settings for the filter you've selected, but also choose a completely different filter from a filter set menu in the center of the dialog. Just click any of the filter set names to open them, and then choose a new filter by clicking its thumbnail. A preview window changes to reflect the new filter you've selected.

To apply effects:

1. To apply an effect to an entire layer, select the layer to make it active. To apply an effect to just a portion of the image, select an area using one of the selection tools.

2. In the Effects panel, double-click the chosen effect 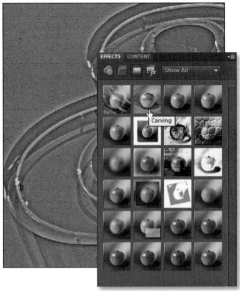.

If you prefer, you can also drag any effect from the Effects panel directly onto your image.

When you apply an effect, it creates one or more new layers immediately above the selected layer **F**.

TIP To reduce the visible impact of an effect, change the opacity of the effect layer using the Opacity slider on the Layers panel.

TIP Sometimes the filter and effect names, and their thumbnails, don't represent the variety of results you might get by applying them to an image. Experiment by pushing the filter and effect options to extreme limits. You'll often be surprised by the results. Print a copy of your image for future reference and to use on other photos. It's also a good idea to rename the layer with a descriptive name related to the effect you used: for instance, Blizzard 30%.

TIP To change the look of an effect, experiment with the various blend modes on the Layers panel.

E Double-click any effect in the Effects panel to apply it to an image or selection. You can also drag an effect or filter from the panel into the image window.

F When you apply an effect, it generates one or more layers above the selected layer. The number of new layers depends on the series of actions required to create the specific effect.

A You can apply the Motion Blur filter to an entire layer or to a selection, as I'll do in this photo.

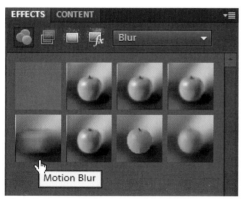

B Once you've chosen a layer or selection, double-click the Motion Blur thumbnail.

Simulating Action with the Blur Filters

Photoshop Elements includes a few blur filters that can create a sense of motion where none exists. In many cases, you'll want to select a specific area in your photo when using these filters, so that the motion or movement is applied to one object, such as a person, your dog, or a pair of shoes.

The Motion Blur filter blurs a layer or selection in a specific direction and intensity. The result simulates the look of taking a picture of a moving object with a fixed exposure or of panning a camera across a still scene.

The Radial Blur filter creates the impression of a camera zoom or of an object moving toward or away from you. You can also create the impression of an object spinning at variable rates of speed. In either case, the Radial Blur filter lets you control the center of the effect and the amount of blurring or motion.

To add a motion blur to an image:

1. Select the desired layer to make it active. To create a feeling of motion in just a portion of your image, select an area with one of the selection tools **A**.

2. Do one of the following:

   ▶ To apply the default settings, choose Blur from the Library drop-down menu on the Effects panel, and double-click the Motion Blur filter **B**.

   ▶ To customize the settings, go to the Filter menu and choose Blur > Motion Blur. The Motion Blur dialog appears with options for the motion angle and distance.

continues on next page

3. Set the Angle and Distance options to get the look you want ⑥. You can refer to the preview window in the dialog, and if the Preview option is checked, you can also see the results in the main image window.

By default, the Angle option is set to 0°, meaning that the pixels will be blurred along the horizontal axis as shown next to the Angle text field. So, the impression of motion will be right to left (or left to right) across your screen. You can change the angle by dragging the line on the Angle icon or by entering a number of degrees in the Angle text box.

The Distance option determines the number of pixels included in the linear blur, with the default set to 10 pixels (a moderate amount of blurring). When you reach the upper limits of this option (999 pixels), the objects in your photo may become barely recognizable.

4. When you are satisfied with the effect, click OK to apply it to your image ⑩.

TIP It may look more realistic if you feather your selection before applying the blur (choose Select > Feather). See Chapter 5 for more on feathering selections.

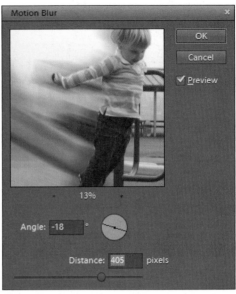

⑥ The Motion Blur dialog includes options for the angle and distance of the effect.

⑩ Click OK to see the Motion Blur filter applied to your image. If you want to back up and try again, just choose Edit > Undo and experiment with different settings.

E The Radial Blur dialog does not include a preview, but the Quality options include Draft, which you can use to quickly apply and view the effects of the filter on your image.

Spin   *Zoom*

F To change the center point, drag the preview in the Blur Center window.

To add a circular blur to an image:

1. Select the desired layer to make it active. To create a feeling of radial motion in just a portion of your image, select an area with one of the selection tools.

    A circular (elliptical) selection works especially well when you want to create a circular effect.

2. Select the Radial Blur by doing one of the following:

    ▸ To apply the effect's default settings, double-click the Radial Blur filter on the Effects panel.

    ▸ To specify the settings, got to the Filter menu and choose Blur > Radial Blur. The Radial Blur dialog appears, with options for amount of blur, blur center, blur method, and quality **E**.

3. Set the Amount and Blur Center values.

    The two Blur Method options are Spin and Zoom **F**. Choose Spin to blur along circular lines or Zoom to blur along lines radiating from the center, as if you were zooming in or out of an image.

4. Select a Quality option for the filter.

    Draft quality produces a quicker rendering of the filter, but with slightly coarse results. The Good and Best options both take a bit longer to render, but provide a smoother look; there's not a big difference between the latter two options.

5. When you are satisfied with the effect, click OK to apply it to your image.

> **TIP** The Radial Blur filter doesn't include a preview window, so if you aren't happy with the results and want to try different settings, just click the Edit Undo button (or press Ctrl+Z) to try again.

The Blur Filters

I've covered the steps for using a couple of my favorite blur filters, but the others can be just as effective. Here's a summary of how the blur filters work and when you might want to use them.

Blur softens the look of an image or selected area and is great for retouching photos where there's a harsh edge or transition. The results are similar to what you get with the Blur tool.

Blur More works like the Blur filter, but with much greater intensity—it's like using the Blur filter three times on the same image. The results are often too dramatic for minor photo retouching, but are great for blurring one particular area of an image (like the border), thereby emphasizing the untouched areas. Keep in mind that the Blur and Blur More filters don't include a dialog or preview window. Just select a layer or area and apply the filter to see the results.

Gaussian Blur allows you a greater amount of control over the blur effect, and you can use this filter to make anything from minor to major adjustments to your image. For most simple photo retouching, the Blur filter works well, but if you're not happy with your results and want to tweak a bit, try Gaussian Blur.

Motion Blur can be used to simulate a moving object or the panning of a camera.

Radial Blur results in either a zooming or spinning motion, depending on the option you choose.

Smart Blur lets you build customized blurs, with complete control over the blur radius (the area affected by the blur effect) and threshold (the number of pixels within a given area affected by the blur). Smart Blur is useful for softening an image or for times when you want a more subtle blur effect.

Surface Blur softens broad areas while keeping edges sharp. Surface Blur can be helpful on portraits where you want to minimize the appearance of wrinkles and minor imperfections. It's not the same as the retouching you'll find in any glossy magazine at the grocery store checkout stand, but it can smooth out common skin issues without resorting to touch-up tools such as the Healing Brush tool.

The Liquify Tools

Warp lets you push pixels around as you drag with the mouse.

Turbulence is similar to the Warp tool, but it incorporates some actions of the other Liquify tools to create random variations, or turbulence. You can change the amount of turbulence with the Turbulence Jitter slider in the tool options.

Twirl Clockwise and **Twirl Counterclockwise** rotate pixels in either direction.

Pucker moves pixels toward the center of the brush area.

Bloat moves pixels away from the brush center and toward the edges of your brush.

Shift Pixels moves pixels perpendicular to the direction of your brush stroke.

Reflection copies pixels to the brush area, allowing you to create effects similar to a reflection in water.

Reconstruct restores distorted areas to their original state. As you brush over areas with this tool, your image gradually returns to its original state, undoing each change you've made with the Liquify tools. You can stop the reconstruction at any point and continue from there.

The **Zoom** and **Hand** tools work just like those on the Photoshop Elements toolbar.

Distorting Images

The Distort filters include an amazing array of options that let you ripple, pinch, shear, and twist your images. Experiment with all of the Distort filters to get a feel for the different effects you can apply to your images. One filter in particular stands above the others in its power and flexibility: Liquify.

The Liquify filter creates amazing effects by letting you warp, twirl, stretch, and twist pixels beyond the normal laws of physics. You've probably seen plenty of examples of this filter, where someone's face is wildly distorted with bulging eyes and a puckered mouth. However, you can also use the Liquify filter to create more subtle changes and achieve effects that would be impossible with any other tool.

The Liquify filter is unique in that it includes a dialog with its own complete set of image manipulation tools. And because the Liquify filter works within its own dialog box, you can't undo specific changes with the Edit > Undo command or Undo History panel. Fortunately, the Liquify filter offers its own Reconstruct tool to restore any area to its original (or less contorted) state. The Reconstruct tool allows you to "paint" over your image and gradually return to the original version, or stop at any state along the way. If you just want to go back and start over, clicking the Revert button is the quickest method.

To distort an image with the Liquify filter:

1. Select an entire layer, or make a selection of the area you want to change.

2. From the Filter menu, choose Distort > Liquify; or, on the Effects panel, choose Distort from the Library drop-down menu and double-click the Liquify filter.

   If your image includes a type layer, you will be prompted to simplify the type to continue. This means the type layer will be flattened into the rest of your image's layers. Be aware that if you click OK, the type will no longer be editable.

   The Liquify dialog appears, including a preview of the layer or selection area. The Warp tool is selected by default, with a brush size of 64 and a pressure of 50 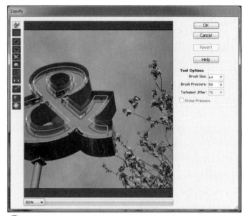.

   You'll probably want to change the brush size and pressure during the course of your work.

3. To change the brush settings, do one of the following:

   ▸ To change the brush size, drag the slider or enter a value in the option box. The brush size ranges from 1 to 600 pixels.

   ▸ To change the brush pressure, drag the slider or enter a value in the option box. The brush pressure ranges from 1 to 100 percent.

4. Distort your image with any of the Liquify tools located on the left side of the dialog **B** until you achieve the look you want. To use any tool, simply select it (just as you do tools on the main toolbar) and then move your pointer into the image **C**.

A The Liquify dialog includes its own set of distortion tools as well as options for changing the brush size and pressure.

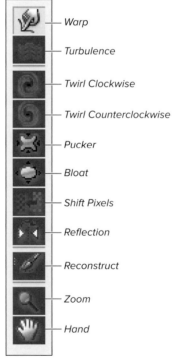

- Warp
- Turbulence
- Twirl Clockwise
- Twirl Counterclockwise
- Pucker
- Bloat
- Shift Pixels
- Reflection
- Reconstruct
- Zoom
- Hand

B The Liquify tool set.

 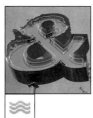

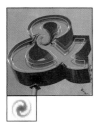 

 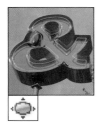

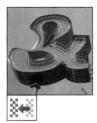 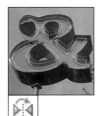

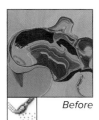 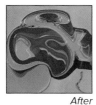

Before　　　　　　　*After*

C The best way to become familiar with the Liquify distortion tools is to experiment with them on a variety of images, as in this series of photos.

To undo changes:

In the Liquify dialog, click the Reconstruct tool. Then, while holding down your mouse button, "brush" over your image to gradually undo each change you've made.

To undo all Liquify changes:

In the Liquify dialog, click the Revert button to return the image to its original state.

TIP Here's another way to undo Liquify changes: In the Liquify dialog, hold down the Alt key. The Cancel button changes to Reset. Click the Reset button to undo any changes you've made with the Liquify tools. The Revert and Reset buttons work the same way, but the Reset button, true to its name, also resets the Liquify tools to their original settings.

TIP The Reflection tool can be a little hard to master. You may find it works better if you use a large brush size and 100 percent pressure. Also, the direction of your stroke determines which way the image is reflected.

Correcting Camera Distortion

Most cameras may be digital these days, but it's still an optical medium, and every camera has tradeoffs; for example, some lenses offer incredible zoom, but at the expense of introducing barrel distortion around the edges. The Correct Camera Distortion filter provides tools to compensate.

To correct camera distortion:

1. Select a layer or make a selection to edit.

2. From the Filter menu, choose Correct Camera Distortion. The dialog of the same name appears .

3. Apply the following controls based on the distortion found in your image:

   ▸ Remove Distortion. Drag the slider to the left to bloat the image or to the right to pinch it 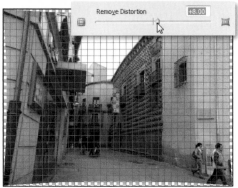.

   ▸ Vignette. To add or remove a vignette (such as found in old photographs), drag the Amount slider to match the vignette area. Use the Midpoint slider to adjust the vignette's size.

   ▸ Perspective Control. Drag the Vertical and Horizontal Perspective sliders to tilt the image. The Angle control rotates the image.

   ▸ Edge Extension. After using the controls above, you may want to scale the image with Edge Extension to crop unwanted blank areas caused by the adjustments.

4. Click OK to apply the changes.

TIP As with most adjustment dialogs, hold Alt and click the Cancel button if you want to reset the dialog's settings.

A Correct Camera Distortion fixes many common photographic gaffes.

B The corner of the building on the left curves due to lens distortion (top), so I've applied a small amount of Remove Distortion to pinch the image slightly and straighten the curve (bottom).

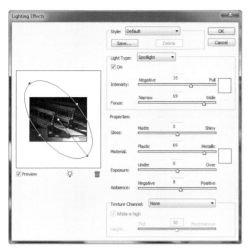

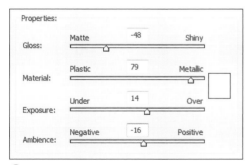

A When you first open the Lighting Effects dialog, it may seem a bit intimidating. But it only takes a little experimentation with the settings to see the range of effects possible with this filter.

B The Properties area offers an almost infinite combination of settings you can use to change the appearance and intensity of the lighting.

C The Triple Spotlight filter has been applied to this image.

Creating Lights and Shadows

Lights and shadows add drama to almost any photograph. It's always best to plan your lighting before you take your picture, but there are times when you just can't control these factors. Elements includes some nifty filters to help you enhance the lighting after the fact. The Lighting Effects filter lets you create a seemingly infinite number of effects through a combination of light styles, properties, and even a texture channel. It's almost like having your own lighting studio.

To add lighting effects to an image:

1. Select the desired layer to make it active. To confine the lighting effect to just a portion of your image, select an area using one of the selection tools.

2. Select the Lighting Effects filter by doing one of the following:

   ▸ To apply a default effect, go to the Effects panel, choose Render from the Library drop-down menu and double-click the Lighting Effects filter.

   ▸ To adjust the settings, go to the Filter menu and choose Render > Lighting Effects. The Lighting Effects dialog appears **A**.

3. Choose a predefined Style, or create your own using the following controls:

   ▸ Choose a Light Type from the drop-down menu, which includes Directional, Omni, and Spotlight options. Each lighting style is based on one of these three light types.

   ▸ Set light properties **B**.

4. When you are satisfied with the effect, click OK to apply it to your image **C**.

Light styles and types

The Lighting Effects dialog offers a mind-boggling number of properties, light types, and styles, making it more than a little difficult to figure out where to start. Here's a list of some of the most useful lighting styles and types.

Lighting styles

- Flashlight focuses a direct spotlight on the center of the image, with the rest of the image darkened. It's set at a medium intensity with a slightly yellow cast.

- Floodlight has a wider focus and casts a white light on your image.

- Soft Omni and Soft Spotlight provide gentle lightbulb and spotlight effects respectively, and work well for many different kinds of images.

- Blue Omni adds a blue overhead light to your image and offers insight into how lighting styles and types work together. If you select this light type, you'll see a blue color box in the Light Type area of the dialog. If you click on this box, the Color Picker appears 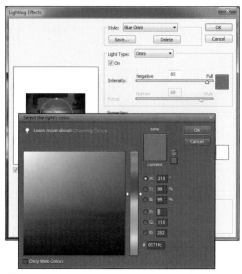, letting you change the color to anything you want. Once you've chosen a new color, click OK to apply your custom lighting style to your photo.

- Most of the remaining lighting styles create more dramatic and special-ized effects (for example, RGB Lights consists of red, green, and blue spot-lights), but are worth exploring.

Light types

- Directional creates an angled light that shines from one direction across your photo .

Ⓓ Some lighting styles, such as Blue Omni, include colored lights. Change the color by clicking the lighting color box, which opens the Color Picker.

Lighting Direction

Ⓔ The Directional light produces a light source that shines in one direction across your photo, as indicated by the line in the image preview window.

F The Omni light creates the impression of a light shining directly onto your photo. To change the size of the lit area, drag one of the boundary handles.

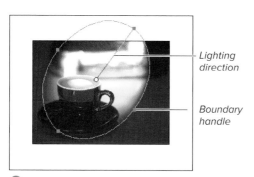

G The Spotlight is represented by an elliptical boundary in the preview. Drag a handle to change the area being lit, and drag the lighting direction line to change the direction of the light source.

- Omni produces a light that shines down on your image from above **F**.

- Spotlight creates a round spotlight in the center of your image. In preview mode, you'll see that the boundaries of the light look like an ellipse. You can change the size of the ellipse by dragging any of the handles. To change the direction of the light, just drag to move the line **G**.

When you select a light style, it automatically defaults to whichever light type best supports that look—so, for example, the Floodlight style uses the Spotlight type.

Light properties

Once you've chosen a light style and type, you have complete control over four different lighting properties.

- Gloss establishes how much light reflects off your image and can be set from Matte (less reflection) to Shiny (more reflection).

- Material determines the surface properties of your image. It can be set from Plastic to Metallic. As you move the setting toward Plastic, the highlights scatter across the surface more; with Metallic, the highlights are more contained.

- Exposure increases or decreases the light. If you click through the light types, you'll notice that most of them leave this setting at, or close to, 0. This is one setting you may just want to leave as is or make only subtle changes to since it has such a pronounced impact on the light.

- Ambience refers to ambient lighting, or how much you combine the particular lighting effect with the existing light in your photo. Positive values allow in more ambient light, and negative values allow less.

To add a lens flare:

1. Select the desired layer to make it active. To confine the lighting effect to just a portion of your image, select an area using one of the selection tools.

2. Select the Lens Flare filter by doing one of the following:

   ▸ To apply a default setting, go to the Effects panel, choose Render from the Library drop-down menu, and double-click the Lens Flare filter.

   ▸ To specify settings, got to the Filter menu and choose Render > Lens Flare. The Lens Flare dialog appears, with options for the brightness, flare center, and lens type .

3. Set the brightness option by dragging the slider to the right to increase or to the left to decrease the brightness.

4. To move the flare center, just click the image preview to move the crosshairs to another location.

5. Set the Lens Type options as desired, and when you're happy with what you see, click OK to apply the filter to your image ⒤.

   The options include settings for three common camera lenses (50–300mm Zoom, 35mm, and 105mm), plus Movie Prime, and the filter creates a look similar to the refraction or lens flare you'd get with each one ⒥.

Flare Center

Ⓗ The Lens Flare dialog adjusts the brightness, flare center, and lens type.

Ⓘ I applied the Lens Flare filter with the default brightness and lens type options.

35mm Prime   *105mm Prime*   *Movie Prime*

Ⓙ The lens options can be subtle.

10

Painting and Drawing

A lifetime ago (in computer years, anyway) a little company just south of San Francisco introduced a small beige box with a tiny 9-inch keyhole of a monitor and a mouse resembling a bar of soap. It could display and print only in black and white, was incapable of reproducing even remotely convincing photographic images, and was strictly limited to a resolution of 72 pixels per inch. And yet, graphic artists smiled a collective smile, because bundled in its modest software suite, alongside its stunted little word processor, Apple's Macintosh gave the world MacPaint.

Painting and drawing programs have jumped by leaps and bounds since taking those first, early baby steps, but one feature remains the same: They're still so much fun to use!

In this chapter, you'll learn how to use Photoshop Elements' built-in drawing and painting tools to create original artwork or to enhance your digital photos—whether you're filling parts of your image with color, adding a decorative stroked border to a logo or design element, or "painting" a photo with Impressionist-style brushstrokes.

In This Chapter

About Bitmap Images and Vector Graphics

Photoshop Elements' painting and drawing tools render artwork in two fundamentally different ways.

The painting tools, including all the varied fills, gradients, brushes, and erasers, work by making changes to pixels—adding them, removing them, or changing their colors. A bitmap image is composed entirely of tiny pixels; and digital photos, the mainstay of Photoshop Elements, are bitmap images. Although you can apply paintbrushes, color fills, special effects, and filters to bitmaps, they simply don't resize well. If you try to enlarge a digital photo, for example, you'll see that its image quality suffers as the pixels get bigger, resulting in a blurry mess.

The drawing tools (shape creation tools, really) form images not by manipulating pixels but by constructing geometric paths based on precise mathematical coordinates, or vectors. Images created with these drawing tools, known as vector graphics, hold one decided advantage over their bitmap cousins: They can be scaled up or down, virtually infinitely, with no loss of detail or resolution A. Elements' scalable fonts, for example, are based on vector shapes, so they can be stretched, warped, and resized to your heart's content. Vector graphics files also tend to be smaller than comparable bitmap image files, since a path shape requires less information for your computer to process and render than a similar shape constructed of pixels.

Although designed to work with different kinds of graphics, the painting and drawing tools are equally easy to use, and work well together if you want to combine vector and bitmap graphics—such as adding type or custom shapes to a favorite photo.

A A photographic bitmap image is constructed of pixels (top). Any attempt to zoom in on or enlarge a portion of the image can make the pixels more pronounced and the image more pixelated. A vector image (bottom) is drawn with a series of geometric paths rather than pixels. Vector graphics can be enlarged or reduced with no loss of detail or resolution.

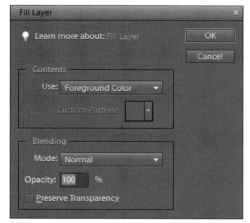

 **A** Clicking the foreground or background color swatch in the toolbox opens the Color Picker.

B The Fill Layer dialog offers several options for filling a layer or selection with color.

C The Use drop-down menu contains various sources from which to choose a fill color. Choose the Foreground Color option to apply a specific color chosen from the Color Picker or Swatches panel.

Filling Areas with Color

You have two primary ways of filling areas with a solid color. With the Fill dialog, you can quickly blanket an entire layer or a selected area of a layer with color. The Paint Bucket tool operates in a more controlled manner, filling only portions of areas based on properties that you set on the options bar. Either method works especially well for those times when you want to cover large, expansive areas with a single color.

To fill a selection or layer with color:

1. Using any of the selection or marquee tools, select the area of your image you want to fill with color.

   If you want to fill an entire layer, it's not necessary to make a selection.

2. To select a fill color, do one of the following:

   ▸ Click either the current foreground or background color swatch at the bottom of the toolbox **A** to open the Color Picker; then select a color.

   ▸ From the Swatches panel, click any color to select it.

3. From the Edit menu, choose either Fill Selection or Fill Layer to open the Fill Layer dialog **B**.

4. From the Use drop-down menu, choose a source for your fill color **C**.

   In addition to the foreground and background colors, you can use the Fill command to fill a selection or area with a pattern or with black, white, or 50-percent gray. Or you can choose Color to open the Color Picker and select a different color altogether.

continues on next page

5. From the Blending area of the dialog, select a blending mode and opacity for your fill. (For more information on blending modes, see "About Opacity and Blending Modes" in Chapter 8.)

6. Click the Preserve Transparency checkbox if you want to preserve a layer's transparency when you apply the fill.

7. Click OK to close the dialog.

   The selection or layer is filled with the color and properties you specified .

D In this example, an area of the Background layer is selected (left), then filled with a color using the Fill dialog (right).

TIP To save time, use simple keyboard shortcuts to fill a selection or layer with either the current foreground or background color. Alt+Delete will fill a selection or layer with the current foreground color, and Ctrl+Delete applies the current background color.

TIP To swap the foreground and background color swatches in the toolbox, press X.

TIP To convert the foreground and background color to black and white (the defaults), press D.

About Preserving Transparency

The Preserve Transparency checkbox works just like the Lock Transparent Pixels button on the Layers panel. If the checkbox is highlighted and you fill a layer that has both opaque and transparent pixels, the transparent areas will be locked (or protected), and only the opaque areas of the layer will be filled . If you check Preserve Transparency and then try to fill an empty layer (one containing only transparent pixels), the layer remains unfilled. That's because the whole layer, being transparent, is locked. If you fill a flattened layer, like Photoshop Elements' default background layer, the checkbox is dimmed and the option isn't available because a background layer contains no transparency.

E When a layer (left) is filled using the Preserve Transparency option, the transparent areas of the layer remain protected and untouched, and only the layer object accepts the fill color (right).

F The Paint Bucket tool.

G The Paint Bucket tool takes advantage of all of Photoshop Elements' blending modes and opacity options.

H The options bar contains several settings that fine-tune the Paint Bucket's fill properties.

I The Paint Bucket tool fills areas based on their tonal values. Here it automatically selects and fills just the light-colored background area.

To apply fill color with the Paint Bucket tool:

1. Select the Paint Bucket tool from the toolbox (or press K) **F**.

2. Select a foreground color from either the Color Picker or the Swatches panel.

3. On the options bar, select a blending mode and opacity setting, if desired **G**.

4. Still on the options bar, set a Tolerance value; then specify whether you want the colored fill to be anti-aliased, to fill only contiguous pixels, or to affect all layers **H**.

   For more information on these options, see the sidebar "How Does that Paint Bucket Tool Work, Anyway?" on the next page.

5. Click the area of your image where you want to apply the colored fill.

   The selected color is painted into your image **I**.

How Does that Paint Bucket Tool Work, Anyway?

If you're familiar with other painting and drawing programs, Photoshop Elements' Paint Bucket tool may leave you scratching your head. In many paint programs, the Paint Bucket tool does little more than indiscriminately dump color across large areas of an image. But Elements' Paint Bucket tool is much more intelligent and selective about where it applies color. Depending on the parameters you set in the options bar, it fills areas based on the tonal values of their pixels.

The Tolerance slider determines the range of pixels the Paint Bucket fills. The greater the value, the larger the range of pixels filled.

Click Anti-alias to add a smooth, soft transition to the edges of your color fill.

Click Contiguous to limit the fill to pixels similar in color or tonal value that touch, or are contiguous with, one another. If you're using the Paint Bucket tool to switch your car's color from green to blue, this ensures that only the car's green pixels are turned blue—not all the green pixels within the entire image.

If you select the Use All Layers checkbox, Photoshop Elements recognizes and considers pixel colors and values across all layers, but the fill is applied only to the active layer. This means if you click the Paint Bucket tool in an area of any inactive layer, the fill will be applied to the current active layer **Ⓐ**.

Ⓐ If the All Layers checkbox is selected and you click the Paint Bucket tool in an inactive layer (top), the fill for that specific area is applied to the active layer (bottom).

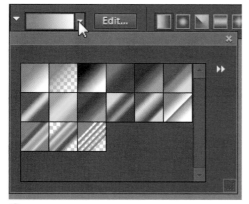

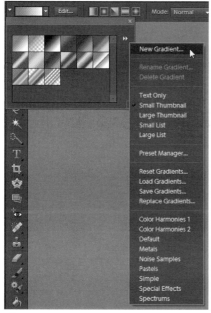

Ⓐ The Gradient tool.

Ⓑ Open the gradient picker to select from sets of gradient thumbnails.

Ⓒ The gradient picker's menu offers several picker display options plus access to a variety of gradient sets.

Filling Areas with a Gradient

The Gradient tool fills any selection or layer with smooth transitions of color, one blending gradually into the next. It can be rendered as an opaque fill or seamlessly incorporated into a layered project using any of Elements' blending modes and opacity settings. Use a gradient to create an effective background image for a photo; to screen back a portion of an image; to create an area on which to place type; or apply it to any shape or object to simulate the surface texture of metal or glass.

To apply a gradient fill:

1. Using any of the selection or marquee tools, select the area of your image where you want to apply the gradient.

   If you want to fill an entire layer, you don't need to make a selection.

2. Select the Gradient tool from the tool-box (or press G) **Ⓐ**.

3. On the options bar, click to open the gradient picker **Ⓑ**.

4. Click to choose from the list of default gradients, or if you want to view additional gradient sets, click the More button (the triangles to the right of the thumbnail images) to open the gradient picker menu **Ⓒ**.

   Gradient sets are located in the bottom-most section of the menu. When you select a new gradient set, it replaces the set displayed in the gradient picker.

   continues on next page

5. On the options bar, click to choose a gradient style 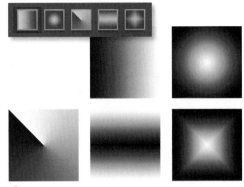.

    Choose from five gradient styles: Linear, Radial, Angle, Reflected, and Diamond.

6. In the image window, click and drag in the area where you want to apply the gradient ⓔ.

    The selection or layer is filled with the gradient.

TIP **Hold down the Shift key to constrain a gradient horizontally, vertically, or at a 45-degree angle.**

ⓓ Click a gradient style button on the options bar to draw one of five gradient styles.

ⓔ Drag from the center to the edge to create a halo effect with the Radial gradient.

Gradient Types

You can create two gradient types from the Gradient Editor: Solid and Noise.

Solid is the default gradient type. When creating or editing a gradient in Solid mode, you can add color and opacity stops and adjust the smoothness of the transition between colors with a percentage slider. You can also change the location of the Color and Opacity stops and their midpoints.

Noise is, well, largely useless. Noise creates random bands of color based on either the RGB or HSB color model, and although there must be some good application for it somewhere, I have yet to stumble on what it might be. Feel free to experiment with this gradient, but you probably won't end up using it much.

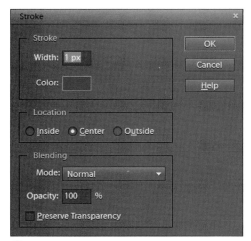

A Draw lines around selections using the Stroke dialog.

Selected

Inside

Centered

Outside

B Once an object is selected, you can stroke it either inside, centered on, or outside of the selection.

Adding a Stroke to a Selection or Layer

Photoshop Elements' Stroke command adds a colored rule or border around any selected object or layer. With the Stroke command, you can easily trace around almost anything, from simple rectangle or ellipse selections to complex typographic characters. Because you can control both the stroke's thickness and where the stroke is drawn in relation to a selection (inside, outside, or centered), you can create everything from delicate, single-ruled outlines to decorative, multiple-stroked borders and frames.

To apply a stroke:

1. Using any of the selection or marquee tools, select the area of your image to which you want to add a stroke.

   If you're adding a stroke to an object on its own transparent layer, there's no need to make a selection. Instead, just check that the layer is active on the Layers panel.

2. From the Edit menu, choose Stroke (Outline) Selection to open the Stroke dialog **A**.

3. In the Width text field, enter the stroke width, in pixels.

   There's no need to enter the pixel abbreviation (px) following the number value.

4. Change the stroke color by clicking the Color box and opening the Color Picker.

5. Select the location of the stroke. The location determines where the stroke is drawn: inside, outside, or centered directly on the selection **B**.

continues on next page

6. Ignore the Blending portion of the dialog for now.

7. Click OK to apply the stroke to your selection or layer .

TIP Photoshop Elements uses the foreground color for the stroke color unless you change the color in the Stroke dialog. So if you want to pick a stroke color from the Swatches panel, click the Swatches panel to assign the foreground color before anything else; then choose Stroke from the Edit menu. The color you choose from the Swatches panel will appear as the stroke color in the dialog.

C Select an object (left), and then choose the Stroke command to apply a stroke (right).

Creating a Stroke Layer

It's a good habit to create a new layer before applying strokes to your image. That way, you can control attributes such as opacity and blending modes right on the Layers panel. You can even turn strokes off and on by clicking the stroke layer's visibility icon. If you're adding a stroke to a selection, simply create a new layer and then follow the steps in the task "To apply a stroke." If you're stroking an object on a transparent layer and want its stroke on a separate layer, you need to perform a couple additional steps:

1. Identify the object to which you want to add a stroke; then press Ctrl and click once on the layer on the Layers panel. The object is automatically selected in the image window **D**.

2. Create a new layer by clicking the New Layer button at the top of the Layers panel.

3. With the new layer selected on the Layers panel, choose Stroke (Outline) Selection from the Edit menu; then follow steps 3 through 7 of "To apply a stroke."

A stroke is created for the object, but placed on its own layer.

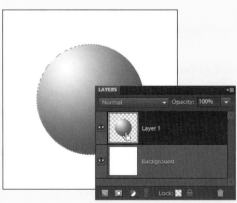

D Ctrl-click the Layers panel to create a selection around a layer object.

E The first step in creating a multiruled border is to create a thick stroke. Here, I used a stroke of 15 pixels.

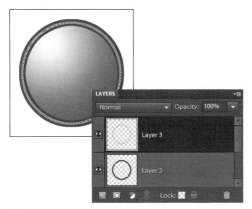

F Placing a narrow stroke of a different color over the broad first stroke creates an attractive three-ruled border.

To create a decorative border:

1. Make a selection, either by using one of the selection or marquee tools, or by selecting an object on a transparent layer as described in the "Creating a Stroke Layer" sidebar.

2. Create a new layer; then apply a wide stroke to the selection **E**.

   In this example, I used a stroke of 15 pixels.

3. With the selection still active, create a new layer above the first.

4. Apply a stroke narrower than the first and in a contrasting color or value **F**.

5. Continue to add stroke layers until you achieve the desired result.

TIP You can create different effects by adding inside and outside strokes.

Using the Brush Tool

The Brush tool is a near limitless reservoir of hundreds of different and unique brushes. You can apply painted brushstrokes directly to the surface of any photograph, or open a new file to serve as a blank canvas upon which you can create an original work of fine art. The dozen preset brush libraries offer selections as varied as Calligraphic, Wet Media, and Special Effect, and any brush can be resized from 1 pixel to a staggering 2500 pixels in diameter. You can paint using any of Photoshop Elements' blending modes and opacity settings, and you can turn any brush into an airbrush with a single click of a button. So whether you're a budding Van Gogh, would like to add a color-tint effect to an antique black-and-white photograph, or just enjoy doodling while talking on the phone, Photoshop Elements' brushes can help to bring out your inner artist.

To paint with the Brush tool:

1. To select a paint color, do one of the following:

   ▸ Click the current foreground color swatch at the bottom of the toolbox to open the Color Picker.

   ▸ Choose a color from the Swatches panel.

2. Select the Brush tool in the toolbox (or press B) .

3. On the options bar, click to open the Brush Presets panel **B**.

4. Click to choose from the list of default brushes, or select a different brush set from the Brushes drop-down menu **C**.

A The Brush tool.

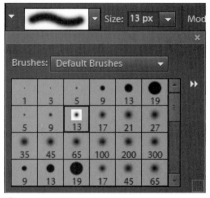
B Open the Brush Presets panel to select from sets of different brushes.

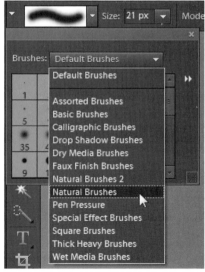
C The Brushes drop-down menu gives you access to a variety of brush sets.

D Use the brush Size slider to resize your brush.

E Create realistic brush effects simply by dragging through the image window.

F Click the Airbrush button on the options bar to give a brush the characteristics of an airbrush.

Once you've selected a brush, you can use it at its predefined size, or you can resize it using the brush Size slider on the options bar **D**.

5. Again on the options bar, select a blend mode and opacity setting.

6. In the image window, drag to paint a brushstroke **E**.

TIP You can easily resize brushes on the fly using simple keyboard shortcuts. Once a brush of any size is selected, press the] or [key to increase or decrease the current brush size to the nearest unit of 10 pixels. Thus, if you're painting with a brush size of 23 pixels and press the] key, the brush size increases to 30 pixels and then grows in increments of 10 each subsequent time you press]. Conversely, a brush size of 56 pixels is reduced to 50 pixels when you press the [key, and the brush continues to shrink by 10 pixels each time thereafter that you press [.

TIP When any tool that uses a brush-type pointer is selected (the Eraser, Blur, Sharpen, and Clone tools, for instance), use the same keyboard shortcuts above.

TIP Almost any brush can be made to behave like an airbrush by clicking the Airbrush button on the options bar **F**. With the Airbrush activated, paint flows more slowly from the brush and gradually builds denser tones of color. The Airbrush option is most effective when applied to soft, round brushes or to brushes with scatter and spacing properties. (For more information on scatter and spacing properties, see the sidebar "Understanding the Brush Dynamics Panel" later in this chapter.)

Creating and Saving Custom Brushes

With so many different brushes and brush sets at your disposal, you may be surprised to discover you can change not only the size of brushes, but other characteristics such as flow, shape, and color. Photoshop Elements provides you with all the tools you need to modify existing brushes and create your own from photographs or scanned objects, such as leaves or flower petals. Once you've created a new brush, you can store it temporarily in an existing brush set or save and organize it into a new brush set of your own. Any new brush sets you create are then accessed and loaded from the Brushes drop-down menu on the Brush Presets panel.

To create a custom brush:

1. Select the Brush tool from the toolbox (or press B).

2. From the list of preset brushes on the options bar, click to select a brush you want to customize 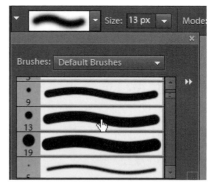.

3. On the options bar, click the More Options button to open the Brush Dynamics panel **B**.

4. Use the sliders on the panel to modify the Fade, Hue Jitter, Scatter, Spacing, and Hardness properties of the brush.

    For more information on these slider controls, see the "Understanding the Brush Dynamics Panel" sidebar later in this chapter.

5. You can also adjust the angle and roundness of the brush **C**.

A To create a new brush, select an existing brush and customize its properties.

B The Brush Dynamics panel contains sliders to modify a brush shape.

C The lower portion of the Brush Dynamics panel offers controls for angle and roundness.

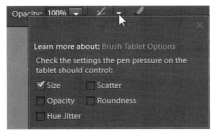

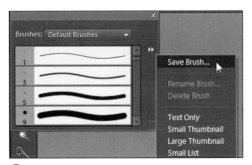

As you move the sliders, or enter angle and roundness values, refer to the brush presets preview on the options bar to see the effects of your changes. All but the Hue Jitter property will be reflected in the preview on the options bar **D**.

6. If you have a pressure-sensitive digital tablet connected to your computer, you can control how the pen's pressure will affect your brush settings.

   On the options bar, click the Tablet Options button, then check the boxes for the brush settings you want the pen pressure to control **E**.

7. When you're satisfied with your changes, click anywhere on the options bar to close the panel.

8. On the options bar, use the brush Size slider to size your brush.

9. Still on the options bar, open the Brush Presets panel; then select Save Brush from the panel options menu **F**.

   The Brush Name dialog opens.

10. Type a name for your new brush and click OK.

    Your new brush appears at the bottom of the current brush presets list on the Brush Presets panel **G**.

D The Brush Presets preview area here shows an original brush (top) and the same brush customized on the Brush Dynamics panel (bottom).

E Tablet options give you control over how pen pressure affects certain brush settings.

F Save your customized brushes on the Brush Presets panel menu.

G The new brush appears at the bottom of the panel list.

To create a brush from a photographic object:

1. Open an image that contains an object or area from which you want to create a new brush.

2. To select an object from the image, do one of the following:

   - Using one of the selection tools, select the object or portion of a photograph you want to make into a brush. The Selection Brush and Magnetic Lasso tools both work well for this kind of selection .

   - If you already have an object on its own transparent layer, hold down Ctrl and click on the layer thumbnail in the Layers panel.

3. From the Edit menu, choose Define Brush from Selection. The Brush Name dialog opens with a representation of your new brush in its preview box .

4. Enter a name for the brush and click OK to close the dialog.

5. Select the Brush tool from the toolbox; then from the options bar, open the Brush Presets panel. Your new brush appears at the bottom of the current brush presets list 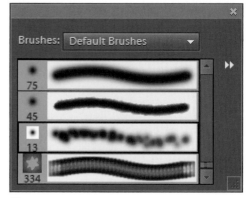.

6. Click to select the new brush; then on the options bar, click the More Options button to open the Brush Dynamics panel.

7. Use the sliders on the panel to modify the brush attributes; then click anywhere on the options bar to close the panel.

TIP Images with high contrast generally work best as brush shapes. Remember that you're not saving any color information—just the object's shape and its tonal values—so you'll want to use shapes with as much defined detail as possible.

H A custom brush can be made out of virtually any selected object. In this example, I've selected a large flower.

I The selection appears in the brush preview of the Brush Name dialog.

J Once saved, your new brush appears in the brush presets list.

Understanding the Brush Dynamics Panel

With a bit of exploration, you'll find the Brush Dynamics panel to be a useful tool for creating new brushes and modifying existing ones.

The Spacing slider controls the spacing of the brush shape and is based on a percentage of the brush's current size **K**. The default for most round brushes is 25 percent; 5 percent seems to be the optimum for most of the fine-art brushes such as Chalks, Pastels, and Loaded Watercolor.

The Fade slider sets the number of steps a brush takes to fade to transparent and can simulate the effect of a brush running out of paint as it draws across a surface. One step is equal to a brush width, so the fade effect is dependent on Spacing **L**.

The Hue Jitter slider determines how randomly the brush renders color, based on the foreground and background colors. The lower the jitter percentage, the more the foreground color is favored. If the percentage is set to the maximum of 100, the foreground and background colors (and mixtures of the two colors combined) are represented in equal measure throughout the brushstroke.

The Hardness slider controls the hardness or softness of a brushstroke's edges. A Hardness value of 100 percent creates a solid brushstroke with no soft edges **M**.

The Scatter slider determines how much a brush shape is spread around with each stroke. The higher the percentage, the more brush shapes are scattered and spread. Lower percentages create almost no scatter at all **N**.

The Angle value allows you to rotate a brush shape to any angle, and the Roundness value can be used to flatten or squish a brush shape.

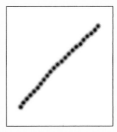

K A brush spacing value of 25 percent (left) and 75 percent (right).

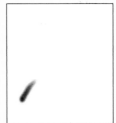

L A brush fade value of 0 (left) and 15 (right).

M A brush hardness value of 0 percent (left) and 100 percent (right).

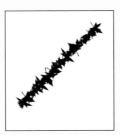

N A brush scatter value of 0 percent (left) and 30 percent (right).

Managing brush sets

Managing brushes is no different than managing other presets (such as gradients and patterns). When you create a new brush, it's saved in the presets file. But once you reset the brushes on the Brush Presets panel or select a different brush set, any new brushes you've created will be lost. Use the Preset Manager to create and save new brush sets.

To create a new brush set:

1. Create as many new brushes as you like, as described in the previous procedures.

2. From the Brush Presets panel menu, choose Preset Manager.

   The Preset Manager dialog opens to the current brush set displayed on the Brush Presets panel 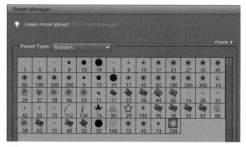.

3. Scroll through the thumbnail views until you find the brushes you want to include in your new set.

4. In the thumbnail area, Ctrl-click to select all of the brushes you want to include 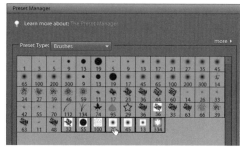.

   If you select a brush by mistake, you can deselect it by holding down Ctrl and clicking the thumbnail a second time.

5. Click the Save Set button to open the Save dialog.

6. In the File name text field, enter a new name to describe your brush set and click Save . Your brush set is saved with the brushes you selected in step 4, but it won't appear on either the More menu in the Preset Manager or the Brushes drop-down menu on the Brush Presets panel until after you quit and then restart Photoshop Elements.

O The Brushes Preset Manager.

P Select brushes you want included in your new brush set.

Q Name your new brush set in the Save dialog.

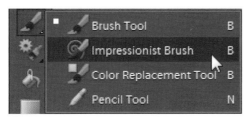

A The Impressionist Brush tool.

B The brush size can have quite an impact on the way the Impressionist Brush tool affects your photograph. In the top photo, I painted with a brushstroke of 10 pixels. In the bottom photo, I changed the brushstroke to 20 pixels.

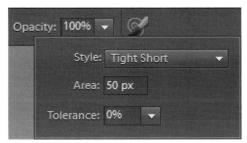

C The Impressionist Brush Options panel has controls for different brush styles and the amount of image area they affect with each brushstroke.

Creating Special Painting Effects

The Impressionist Brush tool adds a painterly look to any photographic image. Although similar in effect to some of the Artistic and Brush Stroke filters, the Impressionist Brush tool allows you to be much more selective about which areas of an image it's applied to. That's because it uses the same scale-able, editable brushes as the Brush tool. You can use the Impressionist Brush to create compelling works of art from even the most mundane of photographs.

To paint with the Impressionist Brush tool:

1. Open the image to which you want to apply the Impressionist Brush effect.

2. Select the Impressionist Brush tool from beneath the Brush tool in the toolbox **A**.

   Alternatively, you can press B to select the Brush tool and then press B again to toggle to the Impressionist Brush tool.

3. On the options bar, select a brush from the Brush Presets panel.

   You can, of course, use any brush with the Impressionist Brush tool, but the round, soft-sided brush that Photoshop Elements picks as the default works especially well.

4. Again on the options bar, select a size with the brush Size slider **B**.

   You can also select a mode and an opacity option, although in most cases the defaults of Normal and 100 percent are fine.

continues on next page

5. Still on the options bar, click the More Options button to open the Impressionist Brush Options panel 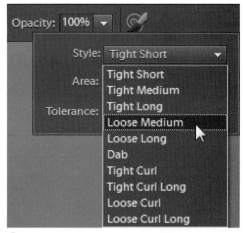.

6. From the Style drop-down menu, select a brush style **D**.

I tend not to stray much beyond the top three Styles (Tight Short, Medium, and Long), although the Dab style also creates some pretty effects.

7. In the Area text field, enter a value, in pixels, for the amount of area you want to affect with each stroke of the brush.

For example, say you start with a brush that makes a single brush mark 10 pixels wide, and then select an Area value of 80 pixels. As you move the brush through the image—and depending on the brush style you chose—it will swoosh around an area of 80 x 80 pixels, distributing the paint in 10-pixel dollops.

8. If desired, select a Tolerance setting to determine the range of pixels affected.

You may want to keep the Tolerance slider set at 0 percent and leave it alone. In use with the Impressionist brush, this setting seems wildly erratic and not worth the trouble.

9. In the image window, drag the brush through your image. The image takes on a painterly look wherever the brush is drawn through it **E**.

TIP Images with resolutions of 150 pixels per inch and higher make the best candidates for the Impressionist Brush tool, because the higher resolution helps to preserve detail when the effect is applied.

TIP Stick to using smaller brush sizes, particularly on low-resolution images. Although any rules of thumb vary from image to image, a good starting place is a brush size between 6 and 10 pixels and an Area setting between 30 and 50.

D Brush styles vary from subtle (Dab) to extravagant (Loose Curl Long).

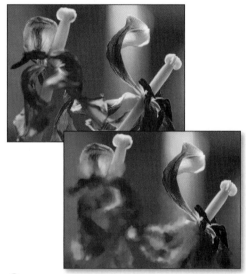

E Simply drag the brush through your photo to create a work of art.

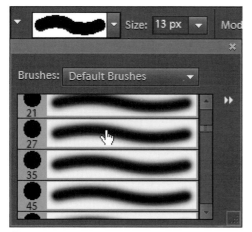

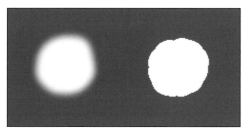

Erasing with Customizable Brush Shapes

The images or brushstrokes you choose to remove from a photograph are often as important as those you decide to add or leave behind. The basic Eraser feature is a powerful tool for cleaning up and fine-tuning your images, taking full advantage of every brush style and size that Elements has to offer. Not only can you perform routine erasing tasks such as rubbing away stray pixels, you can also customize an eraser's brush and opacity settings to create unique texture, color, and pattern effects.

(A) The Eraser tool.

(B) The same brush presets are available for the Eraser tool as for the Brush tool.

(C) An eraser in Brush mode (left) and in Pencil mode (right).

To use the Eraser tool:

1. Select the Eraser tool from the toolbox (or press E) **(A)**.

2. On the options bar, select a brush from the Brush Presets panel **(B)**.

3. Again on the options bar, select a size using the brush Size slider.

4. From the Mode drop-down menu, select one of the three eraser modes (Brush, Pencil, or Block).

    If you select a soft, anti-aliased brush and then choose Pencil from the mode menu, the eraser will become coarse and aliased **(C)**.

5. Still on the options bar, select an opacity using the Opacity slider.

6. In the image window, drag the eraser through your image.

    The image is erased according to the attributes you've applied to the eraser.

Erasing on Flattened vs. Layered Images

The Eraser tool functions in a fundamentally different way, depending on whether it's erasing on a flattened image, such as Photoshop Elements' default background, or on a layer of a multilayered file. When erasing on a flattened image, the Eraser tool doesn't really erase at all. Instead, it replaces the image with the current background color displayed in the toolbox. In other words, it simply paints over the image with the background color  **D**.

On the other hand, when erasing a portion of an image from a layer, the Eraser tool actually removes the pixels from the layer, creating a transparent hole and exposing the image on the layer directly below it **E**.

TIP You're not limited to round or square brush shapes for your erasers. Any brush, even pictorial ones (for instance, Maple Leaves and Dune Grass) or photographic ones (like Scattered Leaves) can be used as erasers. Try experimenting with different brush shapes and opacity settings to create unusual textures and patterns in your photographs.

D On a flattened image layer, the Eraser tool paints with the current background color wherever the eraser is dragged.

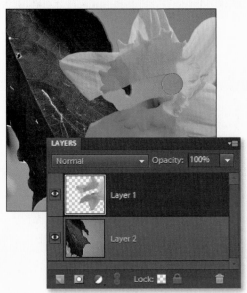

E When erasing on a layer with transparency, the Eraser tool actually removes image pixels (here, the center of the flower layer) and exposes the image on the layer below (the leaf).

Understanding Shapes

In Photoshop Elements, you create shapes not by rendering them with pixels, but by constructing them from vector paths, which are actually vector masks. I'll use some simple circle and square shapes to illustrate what that means.

Each time you draw a shape with one of the shape tools, Photoshop Elements is performing a little behind-the-scenes sleight of hand. Although it may appear that you're drawing a solid, filled circle, for instance, what you're really creating is a new layer containing both a colored fill and a mask with a circle-shaped cutout **A**. When you move, reshape, or resize a shape, you're actually just moving or reshaping the cutout and revealing a different area of the colored fill below it **B**. When you add to or subtract from a shape by drawing additional shapes, you're simply revealing or hiding more of the same colored layer **C**.

Every time you create a new shape, a new shape layer is added to the Layers panel. A shape layer is represented in the panel thumbnails by a gray background (the mask) and a white shape (the mask cutout, or path). Since a shape's outline isn't always visible in the image window—if you deselect it, for instance—the Layers panel provides a handy, visual reference for every shape in your project **D**. And as with any other layered image, you can use the Layers panel to hide a shape's visibility and even change its opacity and its blending mode.

A When you draw a shape, you're actually drawing a shape mask.

B Moving a shape really means moving the cutout portion of the mask.

C Adding a shape to a layer masks off another portion of the colored fill below it, in this case giving the illusion that the circle has a square hole in its center.

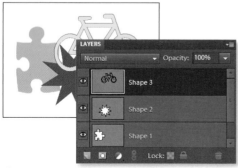

D Shapes appear on their own layers.

Drawing Basic Shapes

In Photoshop Elements, you can draw five basic geometric shapes (a shape selection tool and a tool for creating custom shapes are discussed in detail later in this chapter). Shapes can be drawn freely by clicking and dragging, or they can be constrained according to your specification of size, proportion, and special characteristics. You can use the shape tools to create logos or geometric designs; or, because a new layer is created with every shape you draw, you can draw shapes directly over any photo or scanned image without fear of damaging the image.

To draw a shape:

1. Select a shape tool from the toolbox (or press U) 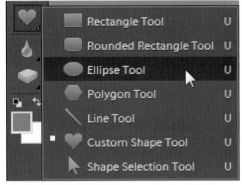.

   To cycle through the shape tools, press U again until you arrive at the shape you want.

2. To select a shape color, do one of the following:

   ▸ Click the current foreground color swatch at the bottom of the toolbox, or click the color box on the options bar to open the Color Picker.

   ▸ Choose a color from the Swatches panel.

3. If they're available for the tool you've selected, you can set special properties for your shape before you draw. On the options bar, enter values specific to the shape you've chosen .

   For the Rounded Rectangle tool, you can enter a corner radius. For the Polygon tool, you can enter the number of sides. For the Line tool, you can enter a pixel weight.

Ⓐ The Ellipse shape tool.

Ⓑ Some shape tools, such as the Polygon tool, have properties you can set on the options bar.

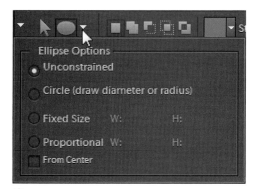

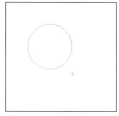

C Every shape tool has its own particular set of geometry options.

D Drawing a shape is as simple as clicking and dragging.

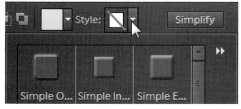

E When any of the shape tools are selected, the shape tool style picker appears on the options bar.

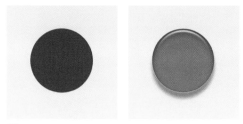

F A simple circle drawn with the ellipse shape tool (left) is transformed into a glossy button (right) using a style from the style picker.

4. On the options bar, click the arrow next to the shape buttons to open the Geometry Options panel C.

In the Geometry Options panel, select from the available options for that particular shape or leave the options set to the default of Unconstrained.

5. In the image window, click and drag to draw the shape D.

If you like, you can add a style to your shape from the Shape tool's built-in style picker.

6. On the options bar, click the icon or arrow to open the style picker E.

7. Choose from the list of available styles or click the arrows to the right of the thumbnail images to open the Style panel menu. The style picker displays the new style set.

8. Click a style in the style picker to apply it to your shape F.

9. To deselect the shape and hide the path outline, press Enter.

TIP If you decide to remove a style from a shape, you have two options. With the shape layer selected in the Layers panel, either open the Style panel menu in the style picker and then choose Remove Style; or, right-click the Layer Style icon on the desired layer in the Layers panel and choose Clear Layer Style.

Transforming Shapes

You're not limited to just creating shapes in Photoshop Elements. You can also scale (resize), rotate, and distort them to your liking. Shapes can be altered either numerically, by entering specific values on the options bar, or manually, by dragging their control handles in the image window. Constrain options, such as proportional scaling, are available for most transformations, and a set of keyboard shortcuts helps to simplify the process of adding distortion and perspective.

To scale a shape:

1. Select the Shape Selection tool by doing any of the following:

   ▸ Choose the Shape Selection tool from beneath the current shape tool in the toolbox 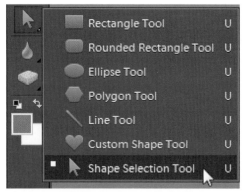.

   ▸ Press U to select any shape tool and then press U again until you toggle to the Shape Selection tool.

   ▸ Select any shape tool in the toolbox, and then choose the Shape Selection tool from the options bar (it looks like an arrow).

2. In the image window, select the shape with the Shape Selection tool.

3. From the Image menu, choose Transform Shape > Free Transform Shape, or press Ctrl+T.

   The options bar changes to show the scale and rotation text fields, and the reference point locator .

4. On the options bar, click to set a reference point location. The reference point determines what point your shape will be scaled to: toward the center, toward a corner, and so on 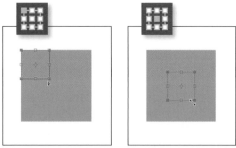.

Ⓐ The Shape Selection tool.

Ⓑ Precise scale and rotation values can be entered for any shape.

Ⓒ These squares are both being reduced in size by about half. The one on the left is scaled toward its upper-left corner, and the one on the right is scaled toward its center.

D The Commit Transform button scales the shape to the size you define.

5. If you want to scale your shape proportionately, click the Constrain Proportions checkbox.

6. Enter a value in either the height or width text field. The shape is scaled accordingly.

7. Click the Commit Transform button **D**, or press Enter.

TIP You can scale a shape manually by selecting it with the Shape Selection tool and then dragging any one of the eight handles on the selection border. Constrain the scaling by holding down the Shift key while dragging one of the four corner handles.

TIP If you want to simply reposition a shape in the image window, click anywhere inside the shape with the Shape Selection tool and then drag the shape to its new position.

About the Shape Geometry Options Panels

Each shape tool (with the exception of the Shape Selection tool) has its own unique Geometry Options panel. The two rectangle tools and the Ellipse and Custom Shape tools all offer similar options for defining size, proportions, and constraint properties; and the Polygon and Line tools each have their own unique sets of options **E**. The Polygon tool's most distinctive option is the Star checkbox. When Star is selected, you're presented with a couple of indent properties that fold the polygon in on itself, so that the points of its angles become the tips of a star shape **F**. When the Line tool is selected, you can choose from a small set of Arrowheads options based on the pixel weight of the line.

TIP To constrain the proportions of any shape (to make a rectangle a perfect square or an ellipse a perfect circle, for example) without the aid of the Geometry Options panel, hold down the Shift key as you drag.

E The Polygon tool's geometry options and the Line tool's arrowhead options.

F Using the Polygon tool's Star option, a six-sided polygon (left) can be changed into a six-point star (right).

To rotate a shape:

1. Select the Shape Selection tool from the toolbox or options bar.

2. In the image window, select the shape with the Shape Selection tool.

3. From the Image menu, choose Rotate > Free Rotate Layer 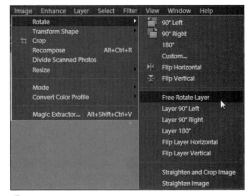.

   The options bar changes to show the scale and rotation text fields, and the reference point locator.

4. On the options bar, click to set a reference point location.

   The reference point determines the point around which your shape will be rotated 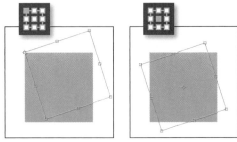.

5. Enter a value in the rotate text field.

   The shape will rotate accordingly.

6. Click the Commit Transform button, or press Enter.

TIP **To rotate your shape in 90- or 180-degree increments or to flip it horizontally or vertically, choose Image > Rotate; then choose from the list of five menu commands below the Free Rotate Layer command.**

TIP **You can rotate a shape manually by selecting it with the Shape Selection tool and then moving the pointer outside of the selection border until it becomes a rotation cursor** 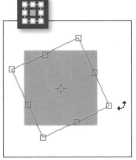**. Drag around the outside of the selection border to rotate the shape. In addition, you can constrain the rotation to 15-degree increments by holding down the Shift key while dragging the rotation cursor.**

G You can apply any of the layer rotation menu commands to your shapes.

H These squares are both being rotated about 20 degrees. The one on the left is rotated around its upper-left corner, and the one on the right is rotated around its center.

I Rotate any shape manually by dragging it around its reference point with the rotation pointer.

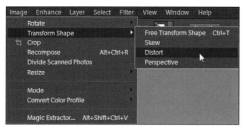

J Choose one of the three specific transformation commands.

K The same square shape transformed using Skew (left), Distort (center), and Perspective (right).

Distortion Shortcuts

With a few keyboard shortcuts, you can avoid having to return to the Image menu each time you want to apply a different distortion.

From the Image menu, choose Transform Shape > Free Transform Shape; then use the following shortcuts while dragging the shape handles in the image window:

To Distort: Ctrl

To Skew: Ctrl+Alt

To create Perspective: Ctrl+Alt+Shift

To distort a shape:

1. Select the Shape Selection tool from the toolbox.

2. In the image window, select the shape with the Shape Selection tool.

3. From the Image menu, choose Transform Shape; then choose Skew, Distort, or Perspective **J**.

4. On the options bar, check that the reference point location is set to the center.

   The reference point can, of course, be set to any location, but the center seems to work best when applying any of the three distortions.

5. Drag any of the shape's control handles to distort the shape.

   Dragging the control handles will yield different results depending on the distort option you choose **K**.

6. Click the Commit Transform button, or press Enter.

Creating Custom Shapes

Once you've gained a basic understanding of working with Elements' geometric shapes, you can begin combining those shapes together to create even more interesting and intricate shapes. Shape option buttons allow you to perform a little vector path magic by creating brand-new shapes out of the intersections and overlapping portions of the rectangle, ellipse, and polygon shapes.

The Custom Shape tool is in a world unto itself, working from a library of nearly 400 complex vector graphics grouped into categories as diverse as ornaments, music, fruit, symbols, and nature—far beyond the relatively simple icons and graphics you can build with the basic geometric shape tools.

To add a shape to an existing shape:

1. Follow steps 1 through 5 in the task "To draw a shape," earlier in this chapter.

   Make sure that this first shape's path remains selected . This technique will only work when both shapes are being drawn to the same layer.

2. From the toolbox, select the shape tool for the next shape you want to add.

   You can use the same shape more than once, if you wish.

3. On the options bar, set color, value, and geometry options as desired.

4. Still on the options bar, click to select one of the shape area options **B**.

5. In the image window, click and drag to draw the new shape **C**.

6. To deselect the shapes and hide their path outlines, press Enter.

A When a shape is selected, its path outline is visible (left). The path disappears when the shape is deselected (right).

B The shape area options define how one shape reacts with another.

C As the new shape is drawn, only its outline is visible (left). When the new shape is completed, it's filled according to the preset shape area option (right). In this case, the option was set to Intersect Shape.

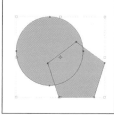

D Shift-click to select the shapes you want to combine.

E The Combine button groups multiple shapes.

To combine multiple shapes:

1. Select the Shape Selection tool from the toolbox.

2. In the image window, click to select the first shape; then Shift-click to select the additional shapes you want to group **D**.

3. On the options bar, click the Combine button **E**. The shapes are combined into one complex shape.

TIP The Layers panel can be a useful tool when working with the shape tools. Its layer thumbnails provide good visual feedback, particularly when you're building complex shapes and want to verify that the new shapes you create are being placed on the correct layers.

continues on next page

TIP You can only combine shapes that appear on the same layer on the Layers panel, like those I created in the previous procedure. However, if you've created shapes on separate layers and then decide you want to combine them, all is not lost. With the Shape Selection tool, select one of the shapes. Then from the Edit menu, choose Cut (Ctrl+X). In the Layers panel, click to select the shape layer you want to combine the "cut" shape with, and then from the Edit menu, choose Paste (Ctrl+V). The shape will be pasted into the selected layer along with the other shape. From there, just follow the steps to combine multiple shapes.

TIP When selecting multiple shapes, work from the inside out. In other words, if you have a large shape with a smaller cutout or intersecting shape inside it, select the smaller, inside shape first. Photoshop Elements doesn't assign any stacking order per se to multiple shapes on a layer, but if a larger, outside shape is selected first, the selection sort of covers up any smaller shapes inside, making them next to impossible to select.

TIP Up until the moment multiple shapes are grouped together with the Combine button, they can be selected individually and then scaled, rotated, distorted, and even duplicated with the Copy and Paste commands.

About the Shape Area Options Buttons

Photoshop Elements gives you five options to choose from when creating a new shape or modifying an existing one **F**.

Create New Shape Layer does just that; it draws a new shape on its own, separate layer.

Add to Shape Area draws a new shape on the same layer as the existing shape.

Subtract from Shape Area adds a shape to the same layer as the existing shape, creating a cutout or hole.

Intersect Shape Areas adds a shape to the same layer as the existing shape and causes only those areas where the two shapes overlap to be visible.

Exclude Overlapping Shape Areas does just the opposite of Intersect Shape Areas, creating a cutout or hole where the two shapes overlap.

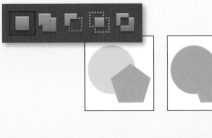

F On the options bar, click to select one of five shape area options.

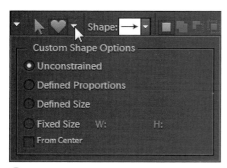

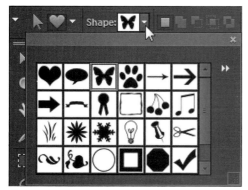

G The Custom Shape tool offers geometry options similar to those for the Ellipse and Rectangle tools.

H Open the custom shape picker to select from sets of complex shape thumbnails.

I You draw a custom shape just as you would any other shape: simply by clicking and dragging. Here, I clicked to apply the butterfly shape (left) and then dragged with the mouse to enlarge it (right).

To draw a custom shape:

1. Select the Custom Shape tool by doing one of the following:
   ▸ Select the Custom Shape tool from beneath the current shape tool in the toolbox.
   ▸ Press U to select any shape tool; then press U again to toggle to the Custom Shape tool.

2. To select a shape color, do one of the following:
   ▸ Click the current foreground color swatch at the bottom of the toolbox, or click the color box on the options bar to open the Color Picker.
   ▸ Choose a color from the Swatches panel.

3. On the options bar, click the arrow next to the Custom Shape button to open the Custom Shape Options panel G. Select from the available options or leave the options set to Unconstrained.

4. Still on the options bar, click to open the custom shape picker H.

5. Click to choose from the list of default shapes, or select a different shape set from the Custom Shapes drop-down menu.

6. In the image window, click and drag to draw the selected shape I.

7. Press Enter to deselect the shape.

TIP Custom shapes can be used in combination with other shapes and with the shape area options just like any of the basic geometric shapes.

If you ever want to paint on a shape or apply any filter effects to it, you'll first need to convert the shape from a vector path to a bitmap.

To convert a vector shape to a bitmap:

1. To open the Layers panel, do one of the following:
   - From the Window menu, choose Layers.
   - Click the arrow on the Layers panel tab in the panel bin.

2. On the Layers panel, click to select the layer containing the shape (or shapes) you want to convert to bitmaps 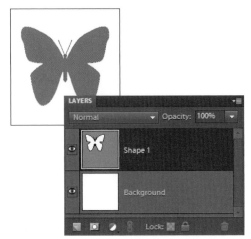.

3. From the More menu on the Layers panel, select Simplify Layer **K**.

   The vector shape is converted to a bitmap, and instead of showing the shape's path, the layer thumbnail displays the shape's image on a transparent background **L**.

J Use the Layers panel to select a custom shape's layer.

K The Simplify Layer command converts a custom shape's vector path to a bitmap graphic.

L The vector path layer thumbnail (left) and the converted bitmap thumbnail (right).

(A) The Cookie Cutter tool.

(B) The Cookie Cutter tool uses the same shape libraries as the Custom Shape tool.

Using the Cookie Cutter Tool

The Cookie Cutter tool isn't exactly a painting or drawing tool, although right up to the moment you press the Commit Transform button, it behaves in exactly the same way as the Custom Shape tool. The Cookie Cutter tool uses the Custom Shape tool's libraries of shapes to create distinctive masked versions of image layers. The difference between the two (and it's a biggie) is that whereas the Custom Shape tool creates vector shapes, the Cookie Cutter tool creates a raster image. So, although you can initially scale, rotate, and otherwise distort a Cookie Cutter shape just like a vector graphic, once you commit the shape to your image, the final result is still a raster (or bitmap) image layer. Once you understand the Cookie Cutter's limitations, it can still be a fun and useful tool.

To mask an image with the Cookie Cutter tool:

1. From the toolbox, click to select the Cookie Cutter tool, or press Q (A).

2. On the options bar, click the Shape Options button to open the Cookie Cutter Options panel.

   Select from the available options or leave the options set to Unconstrained.

3. Still on the options bar, click to open the Cookie Cutter shape picker (B).

4. Click to choose from the list of default shapes, or select a different shape set from the Custom Shapes drop-down menu.

continues on next page

5. In the image window, click and drag over an image layer to draw the selected shape.

The image now appears only within the Cookie Cutter shape, leaving the rest of the layer transparent .

If you apply the Cookie Cutter tool to a flattened, background layer, it automatically converts the layer to a working layer with transparency.

6. To reposition the shape in the image window, place the cursor anywhere inside the shape bounding box, and then click and drag.

Notice that as you drag the shape, different areas of the original image are revealed, as if you were moving a window around on a solid wall .

7. To scale, rotate, or otherwise transform the shape, refer to the section "Transforming Shapes," earlier in this chapter.

8. When you're satisfied with the size and position of your masked shape, click the Commit Transform button, or press Enter .

Once you commit the shape to the image layer, you can apply blending modes, opacity changes, and filters just as you would on any other raster image layer.

TIP For a similar effect that affords you more flexibility (namely, the ability to transform your layer mask indefinitely), create a shape with the Custom Shape tool, and then follow the steps in the section "Creating Clipping Masks," in Chapter 8.

C When you draw a shape with the Cookie Cutter tool, any underlying images are visible only within the shape.

D You can position, scale, rotate, and otherwise transform a Cookie Cutter shape right up to the moment you commit the shape to the image layer.

E Once you commit the shape, its bounding box disappears.

Working with Type

When you think about all of the sophisticated photo retouching, painting, and drawing you can do in Photoshop Elements, manipulating type may not be a priority on your to-do list. However, you can create some amazing projects with the type tools, including greeting cards, posters, announcements, and invitations—and you don't have to fire up another software application.

This chapter covers the text formatting options and special type effects you can create with Photoshop Elements. If you've had any experience with word processing programs, the basic text formatting options will be familiar to you. But unlike a word processor, Photoshop Elements lets you create myriad special effects, using the type warping and masking tools and layer styles.

Creating and Editing Text

When you use the type tools, your text is automatically placed on a new, unique layer. Since the text exists on its own layer, you can modify your text every way layers allow, including moving, applying blending modes, and changing the opacity. Also, having text on its own layer allows you to go back and edit it whenever you want.

You'll likely want to adjust the position of your text, and this is done just as easily as moving an object on any other layer. If you want to paint on your text or apply filters or effects to it, you'll need to simplify the layer by converting it to a standard bitmap. But remember: After a type layer has been simplified, it becomes part of the image, which means you can no longer edit the text. Fortunately, as long as you don't close the file, the Undo History panel will let you go back to the state your type was in before it was simplified. And you can always save a separate version of your file prior to simplifying the type layer.

To add text to an image:

1. With an image open, click to select the Horizontal Type or Vertical Type tool on the toolbar (or press T) 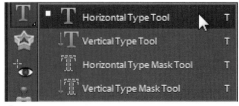.

   Your pointer changes to an I-beam, as in many other text-editing programs .

2. In the image window, move the pointer to the area where you want to insert your text, and then do one of the following:

   ▸ Click to create a text insertion point. This method is perfect if you're setting just a single line of text, or a simple two- or three-line title or heading.

Ⓐ Click the type tool icon to choose from four different type tools.

Ⓑ When using one of the type tools, your pointer changes appearance to look like an I-beam. The text entry point is indicated by a vertical line whose height is based on the type size.

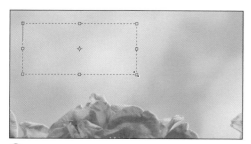

C Alternatively, drag the I-beam to create a paragraph text box.

D After you click once to establish the insertion point of your type, just start entering text. Press the Enter key to move to a new line.

E To make changes to existing text, click the appropriate layer on the Layers panel.

- ▸ If you want to set a long text paragraph, click and drag to create a paragraph text box **C**.

3. Type your text **D**. If you want to start a new line, press Enter.

If you've created a paragraph text box, the text automatically flows to a new line when it bumps up against the border of the text box.

4. To confirm the text you've entered, do one of the following:

- ▸ Press the Enter key on the numeric keypad.
- ▸ Click anywhere in your image, click a panel, or click a tool on the toolbar.

A new type layer is created and is visible on the Layers panel. The layer name is the text you entered.

To edit text:

1. Click a type layer on the Layers panel to make it active **E**.

2. In the image window, click in the text and edit as you would in any basic word processor.

3. Confirm your edits by clicking anywhere in your image.

TIP Consider changing the font size before you begin typing (which I describe shortly); 12-point text is easily lost in a high-resolution photo.

TIP If you want to add more text to a different part of your image, simply click elsewhere in the image and start typing. The new text is added to its own separate layer.

TIP Your image must be in grayscale or RGB mode if you want to add type to it. Elements' two other image modes, bitmap and index, don't support type layers.

To move text:

1. On the Layers panel, click the type layer you want to move.

2. Click the Move tool on the toolbar.

   When you click the Move tool, your type is surrounded by a selection bounding box, allowing you to move the type as a single object anywhere on your image.

3. In the image window, drag your text to a new location .

To simplify a type layer:

1. Choose a type layer on the Layers panel by clicking on it.

2. From the Layer menu or from the Layers panel menu, choose Simplify Layer.

   The layer ceases to be a type layer and the text is treated as pixels instead.

> **TIP** You can also move a type layer with the Type tool selected: Hold Ctrl and click the layer; then drag it into position.

> **TIP** When you simplify a type layer, does its icon in the Layers panel look empty? The tiny thumbnail may not appear to display your text if the type is small in relation to the full image size. Try this: Click the More drop-down menu and choose Panel Options. In the dialog that appears, click Layer Bounds in the Thumbnail Contents section, and then click OK. The layer's thumbnail icon displays only the text, not the entire image.

F Because text exists on its own separate layer, you can move it to different areas in the image by using the Move tool.

A The type formatting tools are all available on the text options bar.

B To select your text, drag across it with the text pointer.

C Double-click within a word to select it.

D Triple-click anywhere in a line of type to select the entire line.

Thursday through Saturday Only!

E Quadruple-click anywhere in a paragraph to select the entire paragraph.

Changing the Look of Your Type

You should be comfortable using the type formatting tools—font family, font style, and font size—because they're very similar to those found in most word processing programs. You can also change the text alignment and text color. All of these options are available on the text options bar **A**.

To change any of these attributes, you first need to select the text characters you want to change. Most of the time, you'll want to select and apply changes to an entire line of text, but you can also select individual words or even individual characters.

To select text:

1. Click the type layer you want to edit on the Layers panel, or click on the type itself with the Move tool.

2. Select a type tool.

3. To select the text, drag across the characters to highlight them **B**, or do one of the following:

   ▸ Double-click within a word to select the whole word **C**.

   ▸ Triple-click to select an entire line of text **D**.

   ▸ Quadruple-click to select an entire paragraph of text **E**.

TIP You can select all the text on a layer without even touching the text with your pointer. Just select the type layer on the Layers panel and double-click the T icon.

To choose the font family and style:

1. Select the text you want to change.

2. From the options bar, choose a font from the font family menu 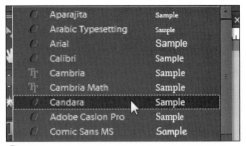.

3. Still on the options bar, choose a style from the font style menu **G**.

   If the font family you selected doesn't include a particular style, you can click the Faux Bold or Faux Italic button to change the look of your text **H**.

TIP If you haven't memorized the look of each and every font on your computer (and who has?), Photoshop Elements' font family menu displays an example of each font next to its font name. You can change the size of font samples or turn the display of the samples off by choosing Edit > Preferences > Type and then using the drop-down menu in the Type Options section of the Type Preferences dialog **I**.

F All available fonts are listed on the font family menu.

G Many fonts allow you to select a style from the font style menu.

H If a font doesn't include style options, you can apply a bold or italic format with the icons on the options bar.

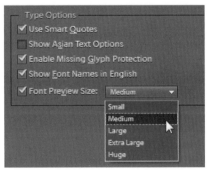

I Options in the Type Preferences dialog let you control the display of font previews in the font family menu.

J Use the type size menu to adjust the size of your type. To use a size not listed, just enter it in the text field.

K Hold down the Shift key to quickly increase your type size in 10-point increments.

To change the font size:

1. Select the text you want to change.

2. Choose a size from the type size menu on the options bar **J**.

   To change to a type size not listed on the menu, just enter a new value in the type size text field.

TIP Quickly adjust the type size up and down using keyboard shortcuts. Just select your text and then press Ctrl+Shift+. (period) to increase the size in 2-point increments. To reduce the size of the text, press Ctrl+Shift+, (comma).

TIP You can also adjust the type size up and down in 1- or 10-point increments. Select your text and then select the type size in the type size menu on the options bar. Next, use the up and down keys on your keypad to size the type up and down in 1-point increments. If you hold down the Shift key while pressing the up or down keys, the type will adjust in 10-point increments **K**.

TIP To change the default measurement unit for type, go to the Photoshop Elements Preferences and choose Units and Rulers. Here you can select among pixels, points, and millimeters (mm).

To change the line spacing:

1. Select the lines of text you want to change.

2. Choose a value from the line space menu on the options bar .

   To change to a line spacing value not listed on the menu, enter a new value in the line space text field.

To apply underline or strikethrough:

1. Select the text you want to change.

2. Click either the Underline or Strikethrough icon on the options bar to apply that style to your text **M**.

> **TIP** The default line spacing value for any type size (Auto) serves as a good starting point, but it's surprising that something as simple as increasing or decreasing line spacing can have a dramatic visual impact **N**.

> **TIP** If your type layer is set to a vertical orientation, the underline appears on the left side of the type.

L Use the line space menu to select line spacing for your type. You can also enter a line spacing value in the menu text field.

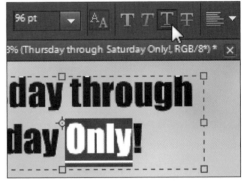

M Apply underline and strikethrough from the options bar.

N Default line spacing (top), and the same type size but with smaller line spacing (bottom).

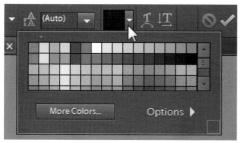

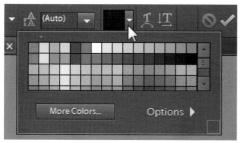 Aligning text within a paragraph box: Left Align (top); Center (middle); Right Align (bottom).

 Change the text color by clicking the color selection drop-down menu.

To change the alignment:

1. Select the text you want to change.

2. From the options bar, choose an alignment option ⓞ.

   The type shifts in relation to the origin of the line of text, or in the case of paragraph text, in relation to one side of the text box or the other. For point and click type, the origin is the place in your image where you first clicked before entering the type.

   ▸ Left Align positions the left edge of each line of type at the origin, or on the left edge of the paragraph text box.

   ▸ Center positions the center of each line of type at the origin, or in the center of the paragraph text box.

   ▸ Right Align positions the right edge of each line of type at the origin, or on the right edge of the paragraph text box.

To change the text color:

1. Select the text you want to change.

2. Click the color selection drop-down menu on the options bar and choose a color from the panel ⓟ. Or, click inside the box to open the Color Picker.

3. Click OK to apply the new color to your text.

> **TIP** You can also change the color of all text on a text layer without selecting the text in the image window. With the Text tool selected in the Tools panel, click to select a text layer in the Layers panel to make it the active layer, then follow the procedure to change the text color.

Working with Vertical Text

Most of the time, you'll use the standard Horizontal Type tool. But you can also change your type to a vertical orientation whenever you want. One of the reasons Elements includes both horizontal and vertical type is to accommodate the needs of the Asian-language versions of the product, such as Korean, Japanese, and Chinese.

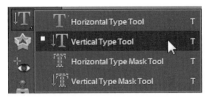

A The Vertical Type tool is located directly under the Horizontal Type tool.

To create vertical text:

1. With the image window open, click the Vertical Type tool on the toolbar **A**.

   The pointer changes to an I-beam.

2. Move the pointer to the area where you want to insert your text, and then do one of the following:

   ▸ Click to create a text insertion point.

   ▸ Click and drag to create a paragraph text box.

3. Type your text on the image **B**. The characters appear in descending order on your image.

4. To start a new line that will appear to the left of the first line, press Enter **C**.

   If you've created a paragraph text box, the text automatically flows to a new line when it bumps up against the bottom of the text box.

   To create and control the position of another line of vertical text, reselect the Vertical Type tool and create a separate, independent vertical type layer.

B When you use the Vertical Type tool, your text appears in descending order (from the top down) on your image.

C When you press Enter, another line of vertical type is added to the left of the first line.

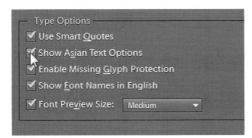

D Switch between horizontal and vertical type by clicking the Change text orientation icon on the options bar.

To change the orientation of the text:

1. Select a type layer on the Layers panel.

2. Select the Type tool on the toolbar and then click the Change text orientation icon on the options bar **D**.

   The text changes to the opposite orientation: If your text is horizontal, it flips to vertical orientation—and vice versa.

   TIP If you have Asian language fonts installed on your computer and you want to use the Asian type formatting options, choose Edit > Preferences > Type and select Show Asian Text Options **E**.

E If your system supports Asian text options, you can work with them by selecting this feature in the Preferences > Type dialog.

Anti-aliasing Type

You can choose to smooth the edges of, or anti-alias, your type, just as you can with image selections as discussed in Chapter 5, "Making Selections." In most cases, you'll use Photoshop Elements to create fairly large, display-size text. For this reason, you'll normally want to anti-alias your text so it doesn't appear to be jagged **A**.

The exception is in cases where you are using smaller font sizes, such as 14 points or less, and are planning to use the image for onscreen viewing on the Web. At smaller sizes, anti-aliasing actually makes your text less readable, and the smoothing effect looks more like blurring **B**. Also, in the process of anti-aliasing, many more colors are generated, and not all Web browsers support all of these colors, so some unwanted color artifacts may appear around the edges of your type. By default, anti-aliasing is turned on.

To turn anti-aliasing off and on:

1. Select a type layer on the Layers panel.

2. Do one of the following:
- ▸ Click the Anti-aliasing icon on the options bar. To reselect anti-aliasing, click the icon again **C**.
- ▸ From the main menu, choose Layer > Type > Anti-Alias Off, or Layer > Type > Anti-Alias On.

A You'll usually want to anti-alias your type, especially when using larger type sizes. This example shows 60-point type viewed at 200 percent.

B When using type sizes of about 14 points or less, you may want to turn off anti-aliasing so your text doesn't become blurry. This example shows 10-point type viewed at 200 percent.

C Turn anti-aliasing off and on with this icon on the options bar.

B The Horizontal and Vertical orientation options create radically different results.

C In this example, the Bend slider helps to dramatically exaggerate the fish shape.

A Click the Create Warped Text icon on the options bar to experiment with various type distortions.

Warping Text

Photoshop Elements lets you distort text easily using the Warp tool. You can choose from 15 different warping options in the Warp Text dialog. In this dialog, you can adjust the amount of the bend in the type, as well as the horizontal and vertical distortion.

Even after you've warped your text, it's still completely editable, and you can make additional formatting changes to it at any time. But because the warp effect is applied to the entire type layer, you can't warp individual characters—it's all or nothing.

To warp text:

1. Select a type layer on the Layers panel.

2. From the toolbar, select a type tool (so that the type options appear on the options bar) and click the Create Warped Text icon **A**.

   The Warp Text dialog appears.

3. Choose a warp style from the drop-down menu.

4. Choose either Horizontal or Vertical orientation for the effect **B**.

5. You can also modify the amount of Bend and Horizontal or Vertical distortion using the sliders **C**.

6. Click OK to apply the effect.

To remove text warp:

1. On the Layers panel, select a type layer that's been warped.

2. Select a type tool and click the Create Warped Text icon on the options bar.

3. Choose None from the Style drop-down menu 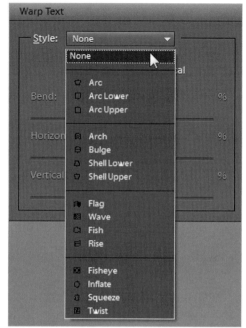.

4. Click OK to remove the effect.

TIP As you experiment with the various warping options, your text can undergo some pretty dramatic changes. For this reason, you might want to move your text around to see how it looks in different parts of your image. Luckily, you can do this without closing the Warp Text dialog. If you move your pointer into the image area, you'll see that it automatically changes to the Move tool so you can move your text around while adjusting the warping effect.

D To remove text warp, select None from the Style drop-down menu.

A To create a type mask, first select the layer on which you want it to appear.

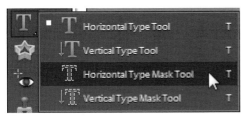

B You can choose either the Horizontal or Vertical Type Mask tool.

C Your type appears reversed out of the colored mask.

Creating Text Effects Using Type Masks

Sometimes the text effects you want to create are better done with a type selection, not the actual, editable type. The Horizontal and Vertical Type Mask tools let you enter text, which is automatically converted to a selection in the shape of type. Since it's a selection, you can do everything you can do to any other selection—you can paint or fill the type or transform its geometry by skewing it or applying perspective. Unlike the previous type tools discussed, the type mask tools do not create a unique layer. The type selection appears on whichever layer is active at the time you use the tool. The bottom line: A type selection is just like any other selection, but in the shape of text.

To create a selection with the type mask tools:

1. Make sure your active layer is the one where you want the text selection to appear **A**.

2. Select either the Horizontal or Vertical Type Mask tool **B**.

3. Set the type options (such as font, style, or size) on the options bar.

4. Enter text on the image by either clicking or clicking and dragging and then typing your text.

   The text appears reversed out of the colored mask overlay **C**.

continues on next page

5. Commit your text selection by clicking outside the selection or pressing Enter.

Your text area is selected .

You can now apply additional changes to the selection.

To fill a text selection with an image:

1. Create a text selection following the steps in the preceding task.

Be sure to position the selection over the image you want to show through the text.

2. Copy the selection to the clipboard by choosing Copy from the Edit menu, or by pressing Ctrl+C.

3. From the File menu, choose New > Image from Clipboard 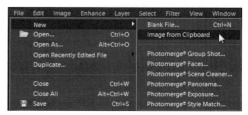.

Your text selection appears in its own file, with the image peeking through .

TIP Up until the moment you commit the text, you can edit your type masks (change their font, size, line spacing, and alignment) just as you would any other line or paragraph of type.

TIP You can move a text selection around in the image window as if it were any other selection. Once you click the Commit icon, select any of the marquee selection tools from the toolbox. Move the cursor over your text selection until it becomes the Move Selection icon. Then you can click and drag to reposition your text selection.

D After you commit the type, it appears as a selection with the typical selection border.

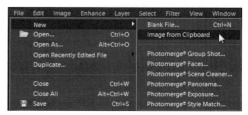

E When you select File > New > Image from Clipboard, a new file is created that contains your text selection.

F You can create all sorts of interesting text effects by filling type with images.

G To fill text with a gradient, start by making a type selection.

H Click the Gradient tool on the toolbar and then choose a gradient.

I Drag in the direction you want the gradient to appear inside your type.

NIGHT

J This example uses the Linear gradient.

To apply a gradient to a text selection:

1. Create a text selection following the steps in the task "To create a selection with the type mask tools" G.

2. Click the Gradient tool on the toolbar and choose any gradient style on the options bar H.

3. Drag across your text selection to establish the direction of the gradient I.

4. Deselect the text selection.

   Your text appears with the gradient fill J.

Applying Layer Styles to Type

Since the Horizontal and Vertical Type tools create a unique text layer, you can use layer styles to make all sorts of unusual and interesting changes to your type. The significant advantage of using layer styles with your text (as opposed to using type masks) is that your text remains editable.

To apply a layer style to type:

1. Enter text in your image using either the Horizontal or Vertical Type tool 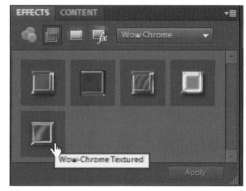.

2. Make sure the appropriate type layer is selected on the Layers panel; then, on the Effects panel, choose a style from the Layer Styles panel list **B**.

3. Click the Apply button to apply the style to your text **C**.

> **TIP** When choosing a font, it's a good idea to go with bolder sans-serif typefaces. This way, your type is more likely to remain readable after you've applied the style.

> **TIP** If you're not quite getting the look you want, remember that you can set lighting angle, shadow distance, and other options by selecting Layer Style > Style Settings from the Layer menu, or by double-clicking the Layer Style icon to the right of the layer name in the Layers panel.

NIGHT

A To use layer styles with your type, first enter text with one of the type tools.

B You can use any of Photoshop Elements' dozens of layer styles on your type.

NIGHT

C Sophisticated effects that would be difficult to create manually are easily applied to text.

Preparing Images for the Web

If you take digital photos, you may want to post them to a Web page or a social-networking site. Whether you decide to post a snapshot of an old push mower to eBay or just want to share vacation photos with your Aunt Ruth, the considerations are much the same.

Size and speed influence most decisions regarding image preparation for the Web, and they are the central themes of this chapter. While broadband is now widely available worldwide, it's still a good idea to optimize the size of your digital images: the smaller the image file size, the more quickly it appears, even with the fastest Internet connection.

I'm not abandoning aesthetics—after all, there's little purpose in uploading a photograph that's too fuzzy or distorted to be seen clearly. This chapter's focus is also about creating compact files that look good.

If you're looking to post a gallery of photos instead of optimizing and saving images one at a time, see Chapter 14.

Understanding Image Requirements for the Web

Preparing images for the Web presents a set of challenges distinct from commercial and ink-jet printing. Even with abundant broadband worldwide, a significant percentage of Web users have dial-up or relatively slow broadband connections. This means your images need to be small enough to download quickly while retaining color and clarity comparable to your original image.

Photoshop Elements offers some digital sleight of hand through a process called optimization. Optimization pares down and streamlines an image's display information based on settings you can choose among and preview to determine the best combination of values.

By limiting the number of colors in an image, or by selectively discarding pixels that are less critical than others, Elements removes information from an image and reduces the associated file size. Once an image has been streamlined in this way, it is optimized .

Photoshop Elements offers four file format options for optimizing an image: JPEG, GIF, PNG-8, and PNG-24. Generally speaking, JPEG and PNG-24 are most appropriate for images that contain subtle transitions of tone and color (like photographs), while GIF and PNG-8 are best for graphics or illustrations containing a lot of flat color or typography .

A The original illustration (top) contains a great deal of detail and subtle gradations of tone and color. The over-optimized version (bottom) is greatly simplified and contains far less color and image information.

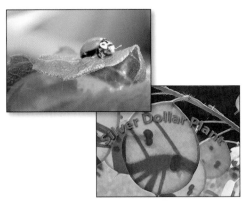

B The photograph on the left, with its subtle and varied tones and color, is a good candidate for JPEG optimization, whereas the flat, bold colors and use of typography in the illustration on the right make it more appropriate for GIF optimization.

About the Save for Web Dialog

The Save for Web dialog might be more appropriately called the "Prepare Web Images" or "Optimization" dialog. Within it, you'll find all the tools, drop-down menus, and text fields necessary to transform any digital photograph, painting, or illustration into a graphic that will work well in a Web browser.

The original and optimized image previews, the heart of this dialog, provide instant visual feedback whenever setting adjustments are made. Information fields below the image previews constantly update to reflect the current optimization format, file size, and download times. And at any time in the optimization process, you can preview and verify exactly how your image will appear in any Web browser loaded on your computer.

Choosing File Formats

- JPEG: JPEG is the most common file format for images on the Web. Because it supports 24-bit color (which translates to over 16 million colors), it's the ideal format for optimizing photos without sacrificing too much image quality. However, because it's a lossy format—meaning that it doesn't provide as much fidelity as the original information by selectively reducing quality to reduce image file size—it's not the best choice for images where detail and sharpness are critical, such as scanned line art, vector graphics, or images containing a lot of type.

- GIF: If you want to keep the detail in your images as sharp as possible, try using the GIF format. The GIF format sacrifices subtle gradations of tone and color, but retains the sharpness and image detail that can be lost with the JPEG format, making it a good choice for animations, images with transparency, vector graphics, and images with type.

- PNG: PNG comes in two main flavors, both supported by Elements: PNG-8, which is similar to GIF, and PNG-24, which is similar to JPEG. PNG is a newer image format than both GIF or JPEG, and it wasn't until 2002 or 2003 that you could rely on browsers to display PNG images correctly.

  Versions of Internet Explorer earlier than IE 7 still may have problems with features like transparency. If you're creating images that will mostly be viewed by people who have newer browsers, PNG is a reasonable choice; if your audience is mostly using old computers and browsers, it's not so good.

  Although in some cases PNG-8 images can be slightly smaller than comparable GIF images, PNG formats (particularly PNG-24) tend to produce images markedly larger than their GIF and JPEG counterparts. Keeping with the goal of controlling file size, stick with GIF and JPEG formats for optimizing your images.

Optimizing an Image for the Web

With the Save for Web command, Photoshop Elements provides a simple, automated method that saves an optimized copy of your original image. You may want to experiment with the custom optimization settings, but the predefined settings should satisfy the requirements of most of your optimization tasks.

To save an image for the Web:

1. Open the image you want to optimize.

2. From the File menu, choose Save for Web 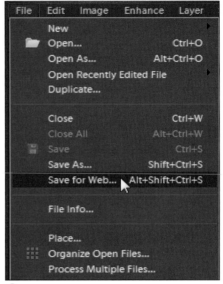, or press Ctrl+Alt+Shift+S. The Save for Web dialog opens on top of the active image window, displaying the image in side-by-side original and optimized previews 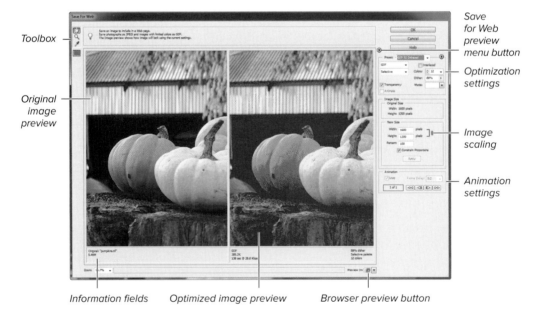.

Ⓐ Open the Save for Web dialog from the File menu.

Toolbox

Original image preview

Information fields   Optimized image preview   Browser preview button

Save for Web preview menu button

Optimization settings

Image scaling

Animation settings

Ⓑ The Save for Web dialog. The image on the left shows the original image. The image on the right shows a preview of what the same image will look like after it's been optimized.

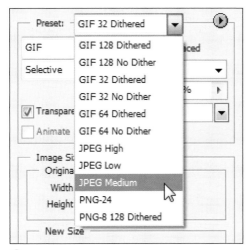

C Choose from the list of predefined settings for JPEG, GIF, or PNG optimization formats.

D Once you've chosen a predefined optimization setting, the rest of the options change accordingly. Here, the options have automatically changed to reflect the Medium JPEG optimization format.

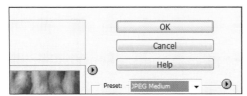

E Click OK to save your optimized image.

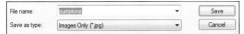

F Enter a name and destination for your optimized file in the Save Optimized As dialog.

3. From the Preset drop-down menu, choose a predefined optimization setting C.

   The various drop-down menus within the Preset portion of the dialog change to reflect the setting you've selected D, as does the optimized preview in the center of the dialog.

4. Click the OK button E.

5. In the Save Optimized As dialog, type a new name for your file and verify that the file type matches the optimization format you chose in the Save for Web dialog F.

6. Choose a location for your file and then click Save.

   The Save Optimized As and Save for Web dialogs automatically close, and your optimized image is saved to the location you specified.

The Save for Web Preview Menu

The Preview menu , which you can find by clicking the triangle button to the right of the optimized image in the Save for Web dialog, is one of those easy-to-overlook tools in a space already packed with checkboxes, panels, and drop-down menus.

As its name implies, the Preview menu works with the image preview (the optimized side of the image preview, to be exact) and establishes parameters for the way that the image preview is displayed. Depending on the color space you select in the top portion of the Preview menu, you can view your image as it would appear in a browser on your own monitor or on a standard Macintosh or PC monitor; or, you can see a preview of how it would appear if it were saved with its color profile.

The bottom portion of the menu offers a variety of standard dial-up and high-speed Internet connection settings. Whichever connection speed you choose here determines the estimated connection speed value displayed in the information box below the optimized preview image . So, by doing nothing more than selecting from a handful of menu options, you can get a good idea of how much time it will take anyone, with any number of connection speeds, to download and display your image.

None of the settings you choose from the Preview menu affect the actual image file in any way. They're for the purpose of previewing only and are completely independent of the attributes you actually apply to an image in the Settings portion of the dialog. There's no way to include a setting for connection speed with an image, since connection speed depends on the type of Internet service each individual uses.

A It's a little hard to find, but the Preview menu controls the appearance of the optimization preview and the information displayed below it.

B After you've chosen a connection speed from the preview menu, the Save for Web dialog uses that input, along with the optimization format you've selected, to estimate the size the file will be when optimized and the time it will take to download. That information is displayed below the optimized preview.

About Color Models and Color Lookup Tables

Although you certainly don't have to be proficient in Web color theory to save images for the Web that look good, a little background information on the different color models will help you make more informed decisions as you choose colors for your Web images. When you optimize an image using the GIF format, Photoshop Elements asks you to pick a color model from the Color Reduction Algorithm drop-down menu. Since GIF images are limited to just 256 colors, color models help to define which colors—from the vast spectrum of millions of colors—will be used in any individual optimized image. Sets of colors are given priority over others depending on the color model chosen, as follows:

- Perceptual color leans toward colors to which the human eye is most sensitive.

- Selective color draws from the largest possible range of colors, incorporating colors from the Web-safe panel as much as possible. Selective is the default option.

- Adaptive color favors those colors that appear most often in a particular image. For instance, a seascape may contain colors primarily from the blue spectrum.

- Restrictive (Web) is limited to the standard 216 Web colors and typically produces color the least true to the original image. Virtually all browsers and personal computer monitors are capable of displaying in thousands and millions of colors; Web colors are an artifact of a time in which 8-bit (256-color) video cards were common, nearly a decade ago.

After you've selected a color model and chosen a maximum number of colors from the Colors drop-down menu, Photoshop Elements builds a color lookup table specific to the image you're optimizing.

A color lookup table can be thought of as a panel of color swatches. If an original image contains more colors than you specify for its GIF version's color lookup table, any missing colors will be re-created as best they can, using the existing number of colors in the color panel. If the original image contains fewer colors than you've specified, the color lookup table will shrink and will contain only the colors in the image.

Either way, no unnecessary color information is included in the color lookup table, meaning that your image's file size is kept to a minimum.

Adjusting Optimization Settings

You're not limited to using predefined settings to optimize your images. Fine-tune the settings further by using the collection of drop-down menus, checkboxes, and sliders available in the Settings portion of the Save for Web dialog. For example, if you want your JPEGs to retain a little more image quality, you can change the default quality setting for a Medium JPEG image from 30 to 45, improving its sharpness and detail without increasing its size much. As you make adjustments, refer to the optimized image preview where you can see how your changes affect the image, as well as view its current potential file size and download time.

To apply custom JPEG optimization settings to an image:

1. Open the image you want to optimize, then choose File > Save for Web to open the Save for Web dialog.

2. From the Preset drop-down menu, choose one of the predefined JPEG settings 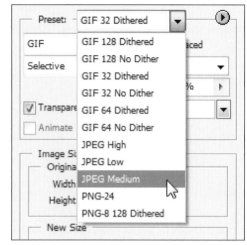.

   You don't have to choose one of the presets, but they can serve as a good jumping-off point for building your own settings. For instance, if you decide small file size and quick download time are priorities, you might want to start with the predefined JPEG Low setting and then customize the settings from there.

3. Verify that JPEG is selected from the Optimized file format drop-down menu, or if you've decided to skip step 2, choose JPEG from the Optimized drop-down menu .

A If you like, choose one of the predefined JPEG settings to use as a baseline for your own custom settings.

B Optimization formats can be changed at any time from the drop-down menu.

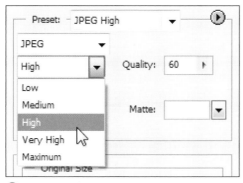

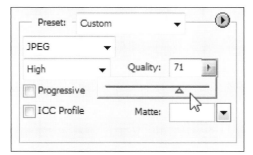

C Choose from five basic quality options for JPEG images.

D Once a quality option has been selected, use the slider control to fine-tune it.

☑ Progressive

E The Progressive feature draws your JPEG image incrementally on a Web page as it downloads, eventually displaying the image in its final state.

4. To set the image quality, do one of the following:
   - From the compression quality drop-down menu, select a quality option **C**.
   - Drag the Quality slider while referring to the optimized preview **D**.

   The Quality slider has a direct impact on the Quality drop-down menu, and vice versa. Remember that a setting in the Very High or Maximum range will create a file six to eight times larger than one saved in the Low range.

5. Select the Progressive checkbox if you want your image to build from a low-resolution version to its final saved version as it downloads in a Web browser **E**.

   This option is more critical for large, high-quality images with download times in the tens of seconds. Rather than leaving a blank space, the low-res image appears almost immediately, giving your Web page visitors something to look at until the complete file is downloaded.

6. Select the ICC Profile checkbox if you've previously saved a color profile with your image and want that information preserved in your optimized image.

   Unless your photo or art contains some critical color (a logo with a very specific corporate color, for instance), leave this box unchecked. Not all browsers support color profiles, and the inclusion of the information can increase file size significantly.

continues on next page

7. If your original image contains transparency, see "Making a Web Image Transparent" later in this chapter.

8. Click the OK button in the Save for Web dialog to rename and save your optimized image.

To apply custom GIF optimization settings to an image:

1. Open the image you want to optimize, then choose File > Save for Web to open the Save for Web dialog.

2. From the Preset drop-down menu, choose one of the predefined GIF settings, or choose GIF from the Optimized file format drop-down menu 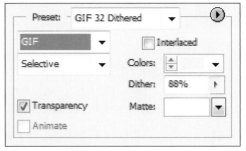.

3. From the Color Reduction Algorithm drop-down menu, choose a color lookup table to apply to your image 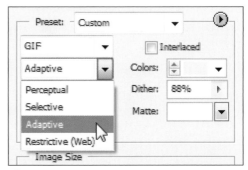. (See the sidebar "About Color Models and Color Lookup Tables," earlier in this chapter.)

4. From the Colors drop-down menu, choose the maximum number of colors that will appear in your image 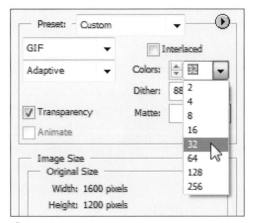.

   You can choose from the list of eight standard color panel values, use the arrows to the left of the text field to change the values in increments of one, or simply enter a value in the text field and press Enter.

   When formatting GIF images, the number of colors you specify will have a larger impact on final file size and download time than any other attribute you set. Naturally, the fewer colors you select, the smaller the image file size will be, so experiment with different values, gradually reducing the number of colors, until you arrive at a setting you find acceptable ❶.

F Choose the GIF setting to optimize illustrations, vector art, or type.

G The GIF format offers several schemes for interpreting and displaying the color in your image.

H A GIF image can contain from 2 to 256 colors.

 This illustration was optimized with three GIF color panels containing progressively fewer colors. From left to right, the illustrations were saved with panels of 16, 8, and 4 colors, creating file sizes of roughly 88K, 72K, and 50K, respectively.

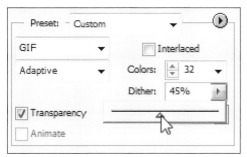

 Since diffusion is the default dither option for any GIF image you create in the Save for Web dialog, you can control the amount of dithering that occurs: from 0 to 100 percent.

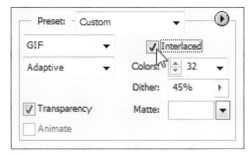

 The Interlaced feature works like JPEG's Progressive option to draw your image incrementally on a Web page as it downloads.

5. Use the Dither slider to specify a percentage for the dither .

Higher percentages create finer dither patterns, which tend to preserve more detail in images where limited color panels have been specified.

Although not accessible from the Save for Web dialog, Photoshop Elements gives you the option to save a GIF image with one of three different Dither options. (For more information, see the sidebar "Choosing Dithering Options.")

6. If you want your image to build from a low-resolution version to its final saved version as it downloads in a browser, select the Interlaced checkbox .

Interlacing a GIF image works in much the same way as applying the Progressive option to a JPEG image. If you choose not to select the interlace option, your image won't display on a Web page until it's completely downloaded.

7. If your original image contains transparency, see "Making a Web Image Transparent" later in this chapter.

8. Click the OK button to rename and save your optimized image.

TIP If you want to save an image in the PNG-8 format, you'll notice it uses all the same options as for GIF, and the procedures for applying custom PNG-8 settings will be exactly the same as those for GIF. The only options available for PNG-24 are transparency and interlacing.

Choosing Dithering Options

Because a GIF image works with a limited color panel, it's impossible to reproduce most of the millions of colors visible to the human eye, much less subtle gradations of tone and color. GIF optimization employs a little visual trick called dithering to fool the eye into perceiving more colors and softer transitions than are actually there. By reorganizing pixels of different hues and values, dithering can do a surprisingly good job of simulating thousands of colors with a panel of a hundred colors or less Ⓐ. Dithering involves placing colors adjacent to one another in a small checkerboard pattern of pixels to create the illusion of another color. Blue and yellow pixels mixed together will blend to create green. Black and white pixels mixed in varying proportions will simulate a graduated fill or soft-edged drop shadow. (Dithering is related to halftoning, which uses dots of different sizes to show varying shades of gray or colors.)

Dithered GIFs created via Save for Web use a diffusion dither. But if you save an image from the Save As dialog (File > Save As) and select CompuServe GIF from the Format drop-down menu, Photoshop Elements offers you a choice of three dithering options.

Diffusion is the default scheme for any of the predefined GIF settings; it creates a random pattern that usually yields the most natural-looking results. Diffusion is the only option that allows you to control the percentage of dither present in your image.

Pattern, as its name implies, lays down pixels in a uniform grid pattern. It can have the effect of a very coarse halftone screen such as you might see in low-resolution newspaper photography.

Noise creates a random pattern similar to Diffusion, but attempts to blend color transitions further by allowing color from one area to spill over slightly into an adjoining area. It occasionally produces an interesting effect, but will rarely be your first choice.

Ⓐ The original image (left) relies on thousands of subtle tonal and value changes to define shapes, shadows, and highlights. The GIF-optimized version (right) shows the close-up results of dithering. Since GIF optimization uses a limited panel of colors, it gathers together pixels of whatever colors are available to reproduce an approximation of the original image.

Optimizing Images to Specific File Sizes

Photoshop Elements has yet one more little optimizing trick. There may be times when image quality isn't as critical as the data size of your files. Perhaps you want to e-mail a weekend's worth of photos to some friends, but don't want to clog up their mailboxes with megabytes of image files. You can send a batch of mediocre-quality images, and then let them pick out the ones they'd like you to create high-resolution copies or prints of.

On the right side of the Save for Web dialog, just next to the main optimization settings drop-down menu, is the Optimize to File Size arrow button. Click the button, and then select Optimize to File Size 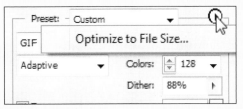.

In the Optimize to File Size dialog, type in the size you want your file to be 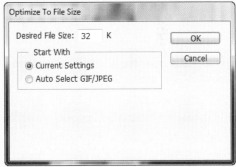. In the Start With area of the dialog, you can also choose from Current Settings, which tells Elements to do its best with your Save for Web settings; or Auto Select, which allows Elements to choose the format that will work best for your image, given the file size constraints.

A Choose Optimize to File Size for additional optimization control.

B In the Optimize to File Size dialog, you can choose to have file size take priority over image quality.

Making a Web Image Transparent

In just a few simple steps, you can preserve the transparency of any image using options available in the GIF formatting settings. Once transparency has been set, an image of any shape (even one with a transparent cutout) can be placed on a Web page and made to blend seamlessly—matted—with its background.

To apply transparency to an image:

1. Open the image you want to make transparent.

2. By default, Elements creates a single layer for an image called Background . In the Layers panel, double-click the Background layer, change its name in the Name field to something like "Regular Layer" , and then click OK.

3. Using any combination of selection tools you choose, select the part of the image that you want to be transparent. (See Chapter 5, "Making Selections.")

4. Choose Edit > Delete to remove those selected parts of the image. A checkerboard pattern fills those areas, indicating they're now transparent 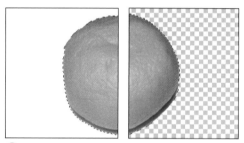.

5. Choose File > Save for Web to open the Save for Web dialog.

6. Select any one of the GIF formats from the Preset drop-down menu.

7. If it's not already selected, click to select the Transparency checkbox.

    The image in the optimized preview area will be displayed against a transparency grid pattern 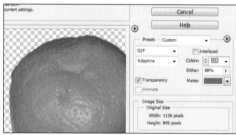.

Ⓐ The Background layer is created by default when an image is opened, but it doesn't allow transparency.

Ⓑ Rename the background layer so you can create transparency in the image.

Ⓒ Select the parts of the image to remove, and use Delete to create a transparent background.

Ⓓ GIF optimization offers the added bonus of preserving transparency in your Web-bound images.

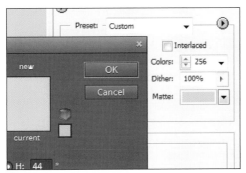

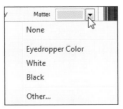

E Choose a matte color from the Color Picker to match your intended Web page background.

F Choose an option from the drop-down menu to use a preset color.

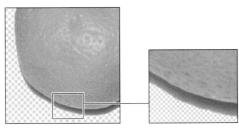

G The color you select from the Matte drop-down menu or color box fills in the semitransparent pixels around your image, helping to maintain a smooth edge and creating a seamless transition when the image is placed on a Web page of the same color.

8. To select the color that will be used to blend, or matte, your image with the Web page background color, choose one of these two options:

▸ Click the Matte color box to open the Color Picker; then select a color from the main color window or enter color values in either the HSB, RGB, or Web color space text fields **E**.

▸ From the Matte drop-down menu, choose a color option **F**.

Only the semitransparent pixels around the edges of the image are filled with the matte color. If the matte color matches the color of the Web page background, the transition between the transparent image and its background will be seamless **G**.

TIP JPEG doesn't support true transparency, but you can set transparent areas in your source image with the background of the Web page for which the JPEG image is intended. Follow the steps in the earlier task, "To apply custom JPEG optimization settings to an image," and then click the Matte color box to open the Color Picker. Select a color; then click OK. The transparent areas fill with the matte color.

TIP If your Web page will use a patterned background, set the matte color to None; otherwise, you'll get a distracting halo of color around the image.

TIP The Eyedropper Color option is helpful only if the color of your Web page background also happens to be present in your image. The Other option simply opens the Color Picker. You're better off using the Matte drop-down menu only when selecting the White, Black, or None options.

Identifying Web Page Background Colors

You'll need to do a little homework to identify the color of your Web page background if you didn't choose that value yourself (or haven't made a note of it) before you can precisely assign a matte color to your transparent GIF images in Photoshop Elements.

The most accurate method of determining the color of the Web page is to identify the color values in the Web page's source code. This isn't nearly as intimidating as it sounds. Open any Web page, then from the browser's menu, find the command to view the source code. (In Internet Explorer, you simply choose View > Source; in Mozilla Firefox, View > Page Source.) A window will open, with code describing everything from the location of graphics and text to the background color.

Once you have the source code window open, scan down the entries for the one that begins with **<body>** near the top of the page. In the same line, directly to the right, it will say, **bgcolor**= followed by either a 6-digit Web color code (something like #663300) or RGB color values . The "bgcolor" stands for background color with the number corresponding to that color. Simply jot down the color values from the Web page source code, and then return to Photoshop Elements and enter those same values in the bottom field of the Color Picker to assign the matte color.

If the site uses Cascading Style Sheets (CSS) to define a background color, look for an area near the top of the page that reads **body { color: #number**, and use the code that appears instead of **number**.

Sometimes CSS styles are linked to another file. Look for a line near the top of the source code that reads in part, **<link href="stylesheet.css"**. Open that file via your browser (enter the filename after the domain name), and look for the **body { color:** information there.

A In this example, I'm viewing the source code for a page from a Web site. On the **<body>** line is the color code for the Web page background—**bgcolor="#663300"**—which translates to brown.

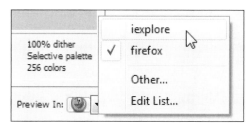

A You can open your optimized image directly in a browser for previewing.

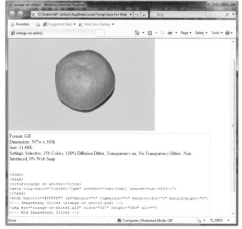

B When your image opens in a browser, it's accompanied by all of the settings you specified in the Save for Web dialog.

Previewing an Image

Before you commit to saving your optimized image, you should see exactly how it will appear in a Web browser window. Although the Save for Web optimized preview gives you a good approximation of how the final image will look, there's no substitute for seeing the image displayed in its natural environment.

Additionally, you can remain within the Save for Web dialog to preview your image as if it were viewed on an older, lower-end system, limited to just 256 colors (rare, but still out there). This can be helpful, because it allows you to design primarily for most current computer systems while giving you the opportunity to fine-tune your settings to accommodate the limited display capabilities of older systems. Note that this is only a preview and in no way affects your actual image file or its settings.

To preview an image in a Web browser:

1. Open the image you want to preview, then choose File > Save for Web to open the Save for Web dialog.

2. At the bottom of the Save for Web dialog, choose a Web browser or click the current browser icon on the Preview In drop-down menu **A**.

   The browser opens displaying the optimized image plus its dimensions and the settings you specified **B**.

3. Close the browser window to return to the Save for Web dialog.

To preview an image as it would display on older monitors:

1. From the preview menu in the Save for Web dialog, choose Browser Dither 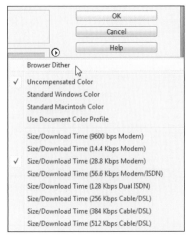.

   The image in the optimized preview window appears just as it would on an 8-bit (256-color) monitor, allowing you to anticipate what this image will look like on older computer systems **D**.

2. To turn off the browser dither preview, choose Browser Dither again from the preview menu.

C Select Browser Dither from the preview menu if you want to view your image using a limited Web-safe panel.

D When you select Browser Dither, the optimized preview changes to display your image as it would appear on an older, 256-color monitor.

Saving and Printing Images

Photoshop Elements can save images in a number of file formats, each with its own set of specialized uses and limitations. In this chapter, I'll begin with a discussion of formatting options and then move on to other considerations for saving your image files and preparing them for printing. I'll look at how to format and save multiple images (known as *batch processing*) and then look at tools you can use to lay out, organize, and catalog your image files. In addition, I'll look closely at the steps necessary to get the best prints from your digital images, whether you're printing them at home or uploading your files to an online photo service.

In This Chapter

Understanding File Formats

Photoshop Elements lets you save an image in many different file formats, from the native, information-rich Photoshop format to optimized formats for the Web, such as GIF and JPEG. Among these is an extremely specialized collection of formats (PCX, PICT Resource, Pixar, PNG, Raw, Scitex CT, and Targa) you'll rarely need to use and won't be discussed here. What follows are descriptions of the most common file formats.

Photoshop

Photoshop (PSD) is the native file format of Photoshop Elements, meaning that the saved file will include information for any and all of Elements' features, including layers, styles, effects, typography, and filters. As its name implies, any file saved in the PSD format can be opened not only in Photoshop Elements, but also in Adobe Photoshop. Conversely, any Photoshop file saved in its native format can be opened in Photoshop Elements. However, Photoshop Elements doesn't support all the features available in Photoshop, so although you can open any file saved in the PSD format, some of Photoshop's more advanced features (such as layer sets) won't be accessible to you within Photoshop Elements.

A good approach is to save every photo you're working on in the native Photoshop format and then, when you've finished editing, save a copy in whatever format is appropriate for that image's intended use or destination. That way, you always have the original, full-featured image file to return to if you want to make changes or just save in a different format.

Choosing Compression Options

As you save images in the various formats available, you're presented with a variety of format-specific dialogs, each containing its own set of options. One of those options is a choice of compression settings. Compression (or optimization) makes an image's file size smaller; the file downloads faster when you post it to a Web page, for example. Following is a brief rundown of the compression schemes.

JPEG: JPEG works best with continuous-tone images like photographs. It compresses by throwing away image information and slightly degrading the image, and is therefore a lossy compression.

LZW: This is the standard compression format for most TIFF images. Although it works best on images with large areas of a single color, LZW helps reduce file sizes at least a little for nearly any image to which it's applied. Since it works behind the scenes, throwing out code rather than image information (and so doesn't degrade the image), LZW is a lossless compression.

RLE: This is a lossless compression similar to LZW, but it's specific (in Elements) to BMP compressed files. It's particularly effective at compressing images containing transparency.

ZIP: This compression scheme is also similar to LZW, but it has the advantage of adding a layer of protection to files that makes them less susceptible to corruption if they're copied between systems or sent via e-mail. Zip files are common on the Windows platform, and Mac OS X can open them; however, some older Macintosh systems can open them only if Stuffit Expander is installed.

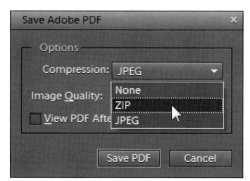

A When you save your work as a PDF file, you can apply JPEG or ZIP compression.

Photoshop EPS

Photoshop EPS is actually a format you don't want to use. Although EPS (Encapsulated PostScript) files are compatible with a host of graphics and page layout programs, they're not the best choice for saving bitmap images, which are what Photoshop Elements creates.

The EPS format adds layers of PostScript code to describe everything from the way an image appears in preview to the way it is color managed, which translates into overhead in the form of bloated file size and slower display time. Any advantage this format holds for displaying and printing vector art and typography is lost on Photoshop Elements' raster art.

JPEG and GIF

The two major Web file formats (JPEG and GIF) are covered in detail in Chapter 12, so I'll look at them just briefly here. Of particular note is the fact that you can use the Save As command to save an image as a GIF or JPEG file, with virtually all of the same file options as in the Save for Web dialog—so the obvious question is: Why use one saving method over the other when saving for the Web?

The Save for Web dialog offers several features the individual GIF and JPEG Save As command dialogs don't. For one, Save for Web provides a wonderful before-and-after preview area.

No less valuable is the flexibility you have to change and view different optimization formats on the fly. An image just doesn't appear the way you expected in GIF? Try JPEG. Additionally, with the click of a button, you can open and preview your optimized image in any browser present on your system.

Photoshop PDF

Portable Document Format (PDF) is the perfect vehicle for sharing images across platforms or for importing them into a variety of graphics and page layout programs. PDF is also one of only three file formats (native Photoshop and TIFF are the other two) that support an image file's layers; layer qualities (like transparency) are preserved when you place a PDF into another application like Adobe Illustrator or InDesign. The real beauty of this format is that a PDF file can be opened and viewed by anyone using Adobe's free Acrobat Reader software. PDF offers two compression schemes for controlling file size: ZIP and JPEG **A**.

TIFF

Tagged Image File Format (TIFF) is a work-horse among the file formats. The format was designed to be platform independent, so TIFF files display and print equally well from both Windows and Macintosh machines. Additionally, any TIFF file created on one platform can be transferred to the other and placed in almost any graphics or page layout program.

You can optimize TIFF files to save room on your hard drive using one of three compression schemes, or you can save them with no compression at all . Of the three compression options, LZW is the one supported by the largest number of applications and programs.

The Pixel Order option should be left at the default of Interleaved. The Byte Order option encodes information in the file to determine whether it will be used on a Windows or Macintosh platform. On rare occasions, TIFF files saved with the Macintosh option don't transfer cleanly to Windows machines. But since the Mac has no problem with files saved with the IBM PC byte order, I recommend you stick with this option.

Checking the Save Image Pyramid check-box saves your image in different tiers of resolution, but since not many applications support the Image Pyramid format, leave this box unchecked.

Checking the Save Transparency checkbox ensures transparency will be maintained if you place your image into another application like Illustrator or InDesign.

If your image contains layers, choose from two Layer Compression schemes, or choose to discard the layers altogether and save a copy of your image file.

B Although the TIFF format offers several compression schemes, LZW is usually the most reliable.

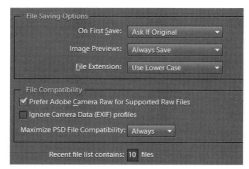

A The Saving Files window of the Preferences dialog.

B The On First Save drop-down menu lets you control when the Save As dialog appears.

C Use the File Extension drop-down menu to determine how you want filename extensions displayed.

Setting Preferences for Saving Files

The Saving Files portion of the Preferences dialog provides a number of ways to control how Elements manages your saved files.

To set the Saving Files preferences:

1. From the Edit menu, choose Preferences > Saving Files. The Preferences dialog opens with the Saving Files window active **A**.

2. From the On First Save drop-down menu, you can choose when you want to be prompted with the Save As dialog **B**.

3. From the Image Previews drop-down menu, choose an option to either save or not save a preview with the file.

4. From the File Extension drop-down menu, choose whether file extensions should be upper or lower case **C**.

5. In the File Compatibility portion of the dialog, set the Maximize PSD File Compatibility drop-down menu to Always. This gives you the maximum number of compatibility options.

6. If you're pre-processing Raw files in another program, deselect the Prefer Adobe Camera Raw for Supported Raw Files option.

7. To assign your own color profile to images, select the Ignore Camera Data (EXIF) profiles checkbox.

8. In the text field labeled Recent file list contains, enter a number from 1 to 30.

9. Click OK to close the dialog and apply your preferences settings.

Adding Personalized File Information in the Editor

With any Photoshop Elements file open, choose File Info from the File menu to open the File Info dialog **A**. Within this dialog, you can add personalized information specific to any file, including title, author, description, and copyright information. Although most of the information entered here is accessible only by opening the dialog from within Photoshop Elements, some of it does have practical uses both inside and outside the application. Entries from the Document Title, Author, Description, and Copyright Notice text fields can be included when you create a Picture Package discussed later in this chapter.

Also, the Description field can be included with any saved image (see "Setting additional printing options" later in this chapter). And if you select Copyrighted from the Copyright Status drop-down menu, a copyright symbol appears in the Image Window title bar, alerting anyone who receives a copy of your file that it's copyright protected **B**.

The File Info dialog is useful for retrieving information, too. Many digital cameras include EXIF annotations (such as date and time, resolution, exposure time, and f-stop settings) for each digital photo. To access this information, click the Camera Data tab. Any EXIF information imported with the photo from your digital camera is displayed **C**. You can use this information to note settings from your more successful photos—a handy reference for future outings. You can also view EXIF annotations in the Properties panel in the Organizer.

A Use the File Info dialog to add title, copyright, and other information to any specific file.

B When a file is assigned copyright status in the File Info dialog, a copyright symbol appears next to the filename at the top of the image window.

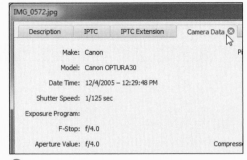

C The File Info dialog displays EXIF information included with photos imported from digital cameras.

A You can save groups of files from a number of different sources.

B Select a folder containing all the images you want to save at one time.

Formatting and Saving Multiple Images

You've just finished a prolific day of shooting pictures, and as a first step to sorting through all those images, you'd like to convert them to Elements' native Photoshop format and then change their resolution to 150 dpi. You could, of course, convert them individually, but the Process Multiple Files command can do all that tedious, repetitive work for you.

To batch process multiple files:

1. From the File menu, choose Process Multiple Files to open the dialog of the same name.

2. From the Process Files From drop-down menu **A**, do one of the following:

   ▸ To select images within a folder on your hard drive, choose Folder, click the Browse button, and then locate and select the folder containing the images you want to convert **B**. If you spot folders within the folder you select that also contain files you want to convert, click the Include All Subfolders checkbox in the Process Multiple Files dialog.

   ▸ To select images stored in a digital camera, scanner, or PDF, choose Import; then select the appropriate source from the From drop-down menu. The choices in the From drop-down menu will vary depending on the hardware connected to your computer.

   ▸ To select files that are currently open within Photoshop Elements, choose Opened Files.

continues on next page

3. Click the Destination Browse button; then locate and select a folder to save your converted files.

   In the Browse for Folder dialog that appears, you're also offered the option of creating a new folder for your converted files.

4. If you want to add a file-naming structure to your collection of converted images, select the Rename Files checkbox; then select naming options from the two drop-down menus 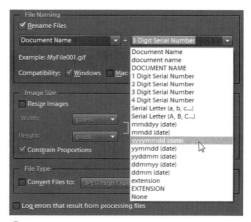.

   Refer to the Example text (located below the Rename Files checkbox) to see how the renaming changes will affect your filenames.

5. Select the Compatibility checkboxes for whichever platforms you want your filenames to be compatible with.

   A good approach is to select all three of these, just to be on the safe side. Notice that the Windows platform is preselected and dimmed.

6. If you want to change either the physical dimensions of your image or its resolution, click the Resize Images checkbox, then do one or both of the following:

   ▸ To convert all of your images to a specific size, first select a unit of measure from the units drop-down menu, then enter the width or height in the appropriate text field, making sure that the Constrain Proportions checkbox is selected .

   ▸ From the Resolution drop-down menu, choose a resolution in dots per inch (dpi) to change the resolution of all your images .

C Choose from a number of file-naming options to arrange your images in consecutive order.

D You can resize entire groups of images to the same width or height dimensions.

E Choose a resolution to apply to all of the files in your selected group.

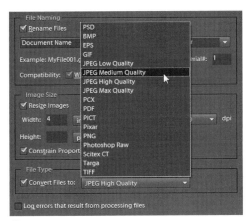

F Choose a formatting option to apply to all the files in your selected group.

The resolution setting in this dialog is in dots per inch (print resolution) rather than pixels per inch (screen resolution), so changing just the resolution here will do nothing to alter your image, or change its file size. It changes only the dimensions of the final printed image and has no effect on the size it displays onscreen. (For more information on image resizing, see "Changing Image Size and Resolution" in Chapter 3.)

7. From the Convert Files to drop-down menu, choose the desired format type **F**.

8. Click OK to close the dialog and start the batch process. The selected files are opened, converted in turn, and then saved to the folder you've chosen.

   If you've chosen one of the import options, an additional series of dialogs appears, guiding you through the selection of images to import.

TIP Using a little simple math can help you to convert pixel dimensions to inches. Just multiply the resolution you've selected by the number of inches (of either height or width) that you want your final image to be. For example, if you've selected a resolution of 72 dpi, and you want the width of your images to be 4 inches; simply multiply 72 by 4, then enter the total (288) in the width text field.

Creating a Contact Sheet

You may have lots of photos downloaded from your digital camera, but with unhelpful filenames like 102-0246_IMG.JPG, organizing and sorting them can be a difficult task. And although the Organizer lets you view and sort through your images, sometimes it's nice to have a printed hard copy to study and mark up. In traditional photography, contact sheets are created from film negatives and provide a photographer or designer with a collection of convenient thumbnail images organized neatly on a single sheet of film or paper. The Contact Sheet feature works in much the same way.

To make a contact sheet:

1. Do one of the following:
   - In the Organizer, select the photos you would like to include.
   - In Photoshop Elements, open the files you want, or select them in the Project Bin.

2. Click the Create tab in the Panel Bin.

3. Click the Photo Prints button.

4. From the options that appear, click the Print Contact Sheet button . The Prints dialog opens.

5. Specify the printer, and optionally select printer settings and paper size.

6. If you want to add more images to the contact sheet, click the Add button in the lower-left corner of the Print Photos dialog . Otherwise skip to Step 10.

   The Add Media dialog opens .

Ⓐ The option to create a contact sheet is found within the Photo Prints category.

Ⓑ Add more photos to the contact sheet.

Ⓒ The Add Media dialog lets you bring in photos you hadn't previously included.

D Control the number of thumbnails that appear on each page of your contact sheet.

Choosing Paper

A wide range of papers is available for your inkjet printer. For most photos, you'll want to print on either photo paper or glossy photo paper (glossy photo paper is thicker, and a little more durable). Quality matte paper is often preferred for high-resolution photographs, and you can even find archival-quality paper that won't fade for 100 years. If you just want to print a quick proof, your regular inkjet printer paper will do in a pinch.

Before you start buying paper, it's a good idea to review the documentation that came with your printer (or check out your printer manufacturer's Web site) to see a list of recommended paper choices.

7. In the Add Media From area, select from one of the following options:

   ‣ Media Currently in Browser displays all of the photos currently visible in the Organizer's Browser window.

   ‣ Entire Catalog displays every photo you've imported into the Organizer.

   ‣ Album displays photos that you've organized into a single photo album.

   ‣ Keyword Tag displays photos to which you've assigned a specific attribute tag.

8. If you choose the Album or Keyword Tag option, choose a photo group from the Select drop-down menu.

   The Add Media dialog updates to display all photos from the option you selected in the Add Media From area.

9. Click to select the photos you want to include on your contact sheet, and then click Done.

   The preview window in the center of the Print Photos dialog now includes all the photos you have selected.

10. Click the arrows to the right of the Columns text field to designate the number of columns per page your photo thumbnails will occupy **D**.

11. Click Show Print Options to select the type of text information you would like to have appear below each photo thumbnail.

12. Click Print to send the completed contact sheet to your printer.

Creating a Picture Package

Photoshop Elements' Picture Package creates a page with multiple copies of the same image, just like the kind you'd receive from a professional photographer's studio.

To make a picture package:

1. Do one of the following:

   ▶ In the Organizer, select the photo you would like to print.

   ▶ In Photoshop Elements, open the file you want, or select it in the Project Bin.

2. Click the Create tab in the Panel Bin.

3. Click the Photo Prints button.

4. From the options that appear, click the Print Picture Package button. The Picture Package dialog opens **A**.

5. From the Select a Layout drop-down menu, choose the layout and dimensions for your picture package.

6. Click the Fill Page With First Photo checkbox to include as many copies of the image as will fit **B**.

7. Click Print to send your completed picture package to the printer.

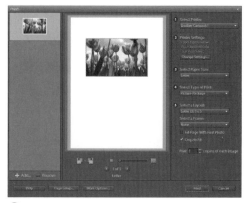

A A picture package creates pages that you can print and cut out for framing.

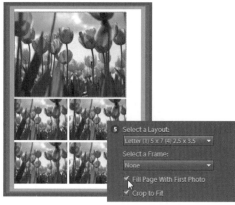

B Mark the Fill Page With First Photo option to group the prints onto the page.

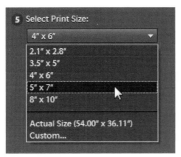

A The Photoshop Elements Print dialog.

B Choose the size the photo will be on the printed page.

Cropping in the Print Dialog

One frustration with printing photos is that the standard aspect ratios of photo prints are different than the ratio used by most cameras. You can pre-crop the image in Elements, but that involves creating a duplicate and cropping the duplicate. Blech.

Instead, after selecting a print size, apply the cropping in the Print dialog. Click the Crop to Fit checkbox to let Elements frame the new size. If that's not quite what you're looking for, drag the image in the preview to move it within the frame (indicated by a blue box). You can also drag the size slider below the preview to further adjust how the image is framed.

Printing an Image

Whether you're printing final photos for clients or just some snapshots for family, you can print to a local printer from within Photoshop Elements.

To print an image:

1. Do one of the following:
   - ▸ In the Organizer, select the photos you would like to print.
   - ▸ In Elements, open the files you want, or select them in the Project Bin.

2. Click the Create tab in the Panel Bin.

3. Click the Photo Prints button.

4. From the options that appear, click the Print with Local Printer button. The Print dialog opens **A**.

5. Select a printer and optionally adjust settings specific to it from the Select Printer and Select Paper Size options.

6. Click the Select Print Size drop-down menu and choose the size at which the image will print **B**. The page preview reflects the page size in proportion to the image you want to print.

   Choosing Custom opens the More Options dialog (see the next page).

7. Specify the number of copies of each page to print.

8. Click the Print button to send the job to the printer.

Setting more printing options

Elements offers optional print settings for adding more information to your prints. They can be helpful when printing drafts or outputting images for other projects.

To set more printing options:

1. Before you print, click the More Options button and, in the dialog that appears **C**, do one of the following:

   ▸ In the Photo Details area, click the checkboxes to display an image's date, caption, or file name. If a document title or description has been entered for the image in the File Info dialog, it will be represented in the page preview as gray bars **D**. (See the sidebar "Adding Personalized File Information," earlier in this chapter.)

   ▸ In the Border area, click the Thickness checkbox and specify a width for a line if you want one **E**. Click the small color swatch to the right to select the border's color. You can also set a background color for the page.

   ▸ If you're making transfers for t-shirts, click the Flip Image checkbox under Iron-on Transfer to invert the image horizontally. (If your printer's driver has an invert image option, make sure that's not selected—otherwise, the image will flip back to its original orientation when printed.)

   ▸ Under Trim Guidelines, click the Print Crop Marks button if you want to include crop marks **F**.

2. Click the Apply button to view the changes in the preview without leaving the More Options dialog. Or, click OK to return to the Print dialog.

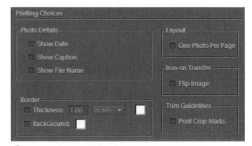

C The More Options print dialog.

D Photo details appear as simple gray bars in the preview window.

E Select a measurement unit and size for your border.

F Crop marks positioned at the corners.

A Create a photo prints order.

B The Review Order screen lists the photos you've chosen along with other ordering options.

Ordering Prints

In the past, you'd shoot a roll of film, take it to a photo developer, and after a few days (or a few hours) you'd have prints of all your images. Now, you can order prints directly from within Photoshop Elements—and order just the images you want, rather than everything shot on the roll.

To order prints:

1. In the Organizer, select one or more photos to print. Or, in the Editor, choose open image files from the Project Bin.

2. Click the Create tab and then click the Photo Prints button **A**.

3. Click the Order Prints from button. Elements prepares the images and then brings up an order dialog **B**.

4. Enter your login information if you already have an account with the vendor; otherwise, you can sign up for a new account within the order screen.

5. A single 4 x 6 print is selected for each image. Change quantities for any of your photos by editing the number fields.

6. Click Next to specify recipients for the order.

7. Click Next to review the order.

8. Click Next to enter your credit card information and billing address, and then click the service's Place Order button.

   The images are uploaded, printed on photo paper, and mailed in a few days.

Sharing Your Images

If you're shooting photos and making compositions within Photoshop Elements, it's a safe bet that you want to share them with others. In the past, you'd make prints and either carry them everywhere or send them through the mail. Now, you can make your own slideshow (without the cumbersome projector), build an online gallery for friends and family to view, upload photos to social media sites like Flickr and Facebook, and e-mail photos directly.

Making Your Own Slide Show

With Photoshop Elements, you can create a self-contained, portable slide show—a useful and elegant way to share your photos and images with friends and family.

Although Elements can output a slide show as a movie (.wmv) or even burn it to a DVD, in this exercise I'll focus on creating a slide show as an Adobe Acrobat PDF (Portable Document Format) file. The operative word here is portable. You can view a PDF file on nearly any Windows or Macintosh computer, as long as Adobe's Acrobat Reader is installed.

When you open the PDF file in Acrobat Reader, the slide show automatically opens in full-screen mode. Slides can change with a transition you select when creating the PDF  . In an automatic slide show, the slides change at preset intervals you set when you generate the file. Alternatively, if you prefer to advance each slide manually, you can create a slide show that changes slides with keyboard commands.

A When you create a slide show, you can specify how your slide show transitions from one image to the next. This slide show displays the Wipe Down transition, where a new image rolls down over the previous image's slide.

To create a PDF slide show:

1. In the Organizer, select one or more photos that will appear in the slide show.

2. In the Task Pane, click the Create tab. A list of items you can create appears.

3. Click Slide Show **B**. The Slide Show Preferences dialog opens, where you select the different options for your slide show. Here you can apply transition effects, change the background color, crop photos to fit a landscape or portrait format, and set quality options **C**.

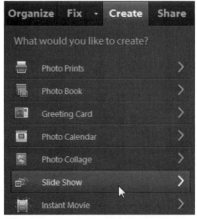

B The Create tab leads to a variety of creations.

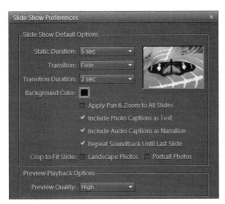

C Set options before you create your slide show in the Slide Show Preferences dialog.

D The Slide Show Editor.

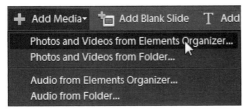

E The Slide Show Editor features a set of controls to help you play and navigate through your slide show during its creation.

F Add photos, video, and even audio to a slide show from the Organizer or from a folder.

4. Select the options you would like to apply to your slide show, then click OK to close the dialog. The Slide Show Editor window opens D.

5. To preview your slide show, first click the Rewind and then the Play button below the Slide Show preview E.

To add photos to the slide show:

1. Click the Add Media button above the preview window, and then choose a source for your photos from the menu F.

   Note that you can also add video and audio files to a slide show.

2. Click to select the photos you want to include in your slide show, and then click Done (or click Open, if your source was a folder). The Slide Show Bin at the bottom of the Slide Show Editor is populated with all of the photos and video you selected, complete with the transitions you chose from the Slide Show Preferences dialog.

TIP You can return to the Slide Show Preferences dialog at any time during the creation of your slide show by choosing Slide Show Preferences from the Edit menu.

TIP A variation of a slide show is a flipbook, which creates a movie out of images; click the Create tab and choose Flipbook from the More Options menu.

To reorder slides:

1. In the Slide Show Bin, click to select the slide you want to move .

2. Hold down the mouse button and drag the slide to a different location in the Slide Show Bin.

   When you release the mouse button, the slide and its transition snap into place in the new location .

   Alternately, you can click the Quick Reorder button above the Slide Show Bin so that you can see all of the slides in your slide show at once. Click and drag to move slides in the Quick Reorder window just as you do in the Slide Show Bin.

G Select a slides in the Slide Show Bin.

H Click and drag a slide in the Slide Show Bin to move it to a different spot in your slide show (top). When you release the mouse button, the slide and its transition snap into place.

To edit slide transitions:

1. In the Slide Show Bin, click the transition between the two slides you would like to change .

2. From the Transition drop-down menu, select a new transition **J**.

   If you'd like, you can also change the duration of the transition—the amount of time it takes to transition from one slide to the next.

3. From the Duration drop-down menu, select a time, in seconds.

I Click any transition to edit its properties.

> **TIP** You can apply new transition effects to more than one slide at a time by selecting multiple transitions at once. Click to select the first transition you want to change, and then Ctrl-click to select subsequent transitions. Alternately, if you want to select every transition in your slide show, choose Select All Transitions from the Slide Show Editor Edit menu.

J The Slide Show Editor offers a myriad of transitions.

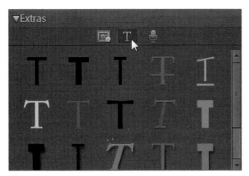

K The Slide Show Editor offers a collection of type styles to choose from.

L Drag to add a text placeholder to a slide.

Edit Text   ×

An Exciting
Adventure

OK   Cancel

M As you type, the text appears immediately in the Preview.

N You can use the Slide Show Editor's default type styles, or use the type controls to customize your type manually.

To add text to a slide:

1. In the Slide Show Bin, click to select the slide onto which you want to apply text.

   The slide appears in the Slide Preview.

2. Click the Text button in the Extras pane to open the default text collection K; then scroll to find the text style you would like to use.

3. Drag the selected text directly onto the slide in the Slide Preview L.

4. Double-click the default text in the Slide Preview to open the Edit Text box.

5. Type the text you would like to appear on your slide and then click OK M.

6. Use the controls in the Properties area of the Slide Show Editor to change the font, size, color, and orientation of the text N.

7. You can reposition the type by clicking anywhere within its bounding box and dragging it to a new location.

TIP If you want to add some whimsy to your slides, feel free to drag elements from the Graphics section of the Extras pane to the slide preview area.

TIP The Narration button in the Extras pane enables you to record audio narration that will accompany the currently selected slide.

To save a slide show:

1. Click the Save Project button (you can also choose Save Slide Show Project from the File menu, or press Ctrl+S).

2. In the Save dialog, type a name for your slide show and click Save .

   Your slide show is saved to the Organizer's Photo Browser.

3. To close the Slide Show Editor, do one of the following:

   ▸ From the File menu, choose Exit Slide Editor, or press Ctrl+Q.

   ▸ Click the close button in the Slide Show Editor window.

   ▸ If you want to output a slide show right away, leave the Slide Show Editor open and proceed to the next task.

To output a slide show:

1. Click the Output button near the top of the Slide Show Editor ⓟ.

   The Slide Show Output window opens.

2. To output the slide show, first check that Save As a File is selected in the options column on the left side of the window ⓠ.

3. Choose the Movie File (.wmv) radio button to create a movie slideshow; this option retains transitions, videos, and any Pan & Zoom settings.

   Or, click the PDF File radio button in the center of the window.

4. Choose the image size and other settings you would like to apply to your slide show ⓡ.

5. Click OK. Then, in the Save As dialog, navigate to the location where you would like to save your slide show, rename it if you would like, and click Save.

ⓞ The Slide Show Editor has its own unique Save dialog.

ⓟ The Output button is the first step to creating a PDF.

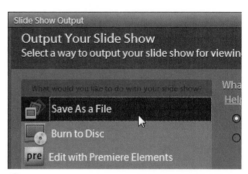

ⓠ The Slide Show Output window offers several different ways to export your slide show.

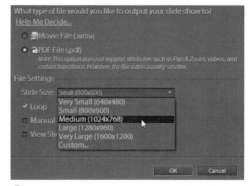

ⓡ You can export a slide show as either a PDF or a movie file.

⑤ Play a movie slideshow from the Organizer.

6. After creating the output file, you're asked if you would like to import the file into your catalog; click Yes or No.

If you selected View Slide Show after Saving in the Slide Show Output dialog, Acrobat Reader launches automatically and plays your slide show.

To view a movie slide show:

To view a movie slideshow, double-click it in the Organizer (if you opted to import it there; otherwise, open the file in Windows Explorer). The file opens, where you can play it and apply keyword tags **⑤**.

To view a PDF slide show:

1. Make sure Adobe Acrobat Reader is installed on your computer. If it's not, install it from the Photoshop Elements installation disc, or download it free from www.adobe.com.

2. In Acrobat Reader, open the PDF slide show you created.

The slide show appears, taking up the full screen. If the slide show is set to run automatically, each image will be displayed for the time you set in the Slide Show dialog.

3. To navigate through your slide show, use the following keyboard commands:

   ▸ Move forward one slide by pressing Enter or the right arrow key.

   ▸ Move back one slide by pressing Shift+Enter or the left arrow key.

   ▸ Exit Full Screen view and access Acrobat Reader's interface by pressing Ctrl+L.

Creating an Online Album

Preparing a gallery of photos for use on the Web can be repetitive, tedious work. You have to resize and format each image, one at a time—a lengthy process. Photoshop Elements eliminates this drudgework with its Online Album feature. When you create an Online Album, Elements guides you through the steps to building a Flash-based slideshow that can be published to Photoshop.com, to a CD or DVD, or uploaded directly to a Web server via FTP (File Transfer Protocol).

To create an Online Album:

1. In the Organizer, select one or more photos that will appear in the album.

2. In the Task Pane, click the Share tab.

3. Click the Online Album option Ⓐ.

4. If you want to share an album you've already set up, click the Share Existing Album option and then jump to step 9. Or, click Create New Album to build one from scratch.

5. Choose where you'd like to share the album (Photoshop.com or Export to Hard Disk) by clicking one of the radio buttons under the Share To heading. Click Next to continue.

6. Give the album a title in the Album Name field, and optionally specify an album category Ⓑ. Thumbnails of your selected photos appear in the Task Pane.

7. To add more photos, select them in the Catalog pane and click the Add (+) button in the Task pane. To remove photos from the album, select them in the Task Pane and click the Remove (–) button.

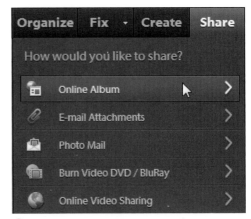

Ⓐ Choose Online Album from the Share tab.

Ⓑ Create a new Online Album.

C Elements displays an animated preview of the Online Album.

D Choose how to share the album.

E The Share button in the Album list is a speedy way to publish an album's photos online.

8. Click the Sharing tab to continue. Photoshop Elements builds a preview of the album **C**.

9. If you'd like to change the album style, click one of the template icons above the preview; double-click a thumbnail to preview the appearance.

   More templates are available from the Select a Template drop-down menu.

   The rest of the steps on this page apply to publishing to Photoshop.com.

10. Click the Share to Photoshop.com checkbox **D**. If you're sharing to the hard disk, click the Done button to build the album.

    The files Photoshop Elements creates can be uploaded to your Web server; or, click the index.html file to view the album.

11. To make the album viewable to anyone, enable the Display in My Gallery option.

    An album can also be shared only with a few people; choose their names in the Send E-mail To field. (Click the icon above the field to set up your contact book if no names appear; see "Sending Images by E-mail," later in this chapter.)

    The Allow Viewers to options apply to both public and private shared albums.

12. Click the Done button to publish the album. Elements builds the album and uploads it to Photoshop.com.

TIP A faster method of creating an Online Album is to click the Share icon that appears to the right of an album **E**. This approach skips steps 3 through 8.

To edit a shared album:

1. Select the shared album in the Albums pane.

2. Add or remove photos by doing one of the following:

   ▸ Click the Edit Album button at the top of the pane to display the Album Details pane, then add or remove photos using the Add (+) or Remove (–) buttons.

   ▸ Add photos to the album by dragging them from the Catalog pane.

3. Click the Done button. Elements uploads new images if needed and modifies the slide show.

   Or, click the Sharing tab to change the album name, template, or privacy options.

To stop sharing an album:

Locate the shared album in the Albums pane and click the Stop Sharing button **F**.

Although the album will no longer be available as a published slide show, the photos will remain at Photoshop.com.

F Click the Stop Sharing button to remove the album's online slide show.

(A) Popular photo-sharing options are available.

(B) Upload directly to Flickr from the Organizer.

Start with Compatible Files

Elements won't convert your images when uploading to a third-party service, as it does for Photoshop.com. For example, Flickr accepts JPEG files but not camera raw files. If you typically shoot in raw, you'll need to first save your image as JPEG (choose File > Save As) before uploading to the service.

Uploading to a Photo Sharing Service

Photoshop.com is deeply tied into Photoshop Elements, but it wasn't the first photo sharing service on the scene. If you already have an account with another service, such as Flickr or Facebook, you can upload photos directly from within Elements. I'll use Flickr in my example below.

To upload to a photo sharing service:

1. In the Organizer, select one or more photos you wish to upload.

2. Click the Share tab of the Task Pane.

3. Click the Share to Flickr button (A).

   The first time you do so, you'll need to authorize Elements as a legitimate sharing service within Flickr. Click the Authorize button in the Share to Flickr dialog, which takes you to Flickr's site on the Web. Return to the Share to Flickr dialog and click the Complete Authorization button. The Upload to Flickr interface appears (B).

5. The photos you selected appear in the Items field; click the Add (+) or Remove (–) buttons if you want to change which images are uploaded.

6. If you wish to include the photos in a set, click the Upload as a set checkbox and specify a photoset you've previously set up at Flickr or create a new one by typing its title in the Set Name field.

7. Specify the photos' privacy settings under the heading Who can see these photos?

8. Type keyword tags in the Tags field.

9. Click the Upload button to publish the photos.

Sending Images by E-mail

With the E-mail feature, Elements stream-lines the process of sending digital photos to family and friends. If your photo is too large or is in the wrong file format, Elements can automatically resize your image, if you prefer.

To attach a simple photo to e-mail:

1. In the Organizer, select the photo or image you want to send.

2. Click the Share tab in the Task Pane and click the E-mail Attachments button .

3. From the Maximum Photo Size drop-down menu, you can choose to change the size of your attachment or leave it unchanged.

   If you choose an option other than Use Original Size, use the Quality slider to control the size and download speed of your attachment **B**.

   If the source image is not a JPEG file, you also have the option of converting the outgoing file. Click Next.

4. Type a personal note in the Message field.

5. Choose a name (or names) from the Select Recipients list.

   If you're using the E-mail function for the first time, your Select Recipients window will probably be empty, and you'll want to create a recipient list. See the steps on the next page.

6. Click Next. Elements converts the images and attaches them to an outgoing message in your default e-mail program.

A From the Share tab, choose E-mail Attachments.

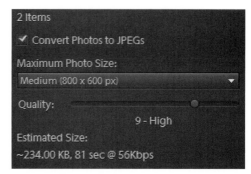

B The Quality slider allows you to make size and quality adjustments to your image, just as you can in the Save for Web dialog.

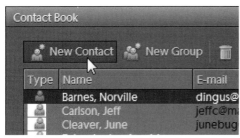

© It's easy to add new contacts to your list.

To add or edit recipients:

1. To create a new contact/recipient, or to edit a recipient's contact information, click the Edit Contacts button at the recipients screen. You can also choose Edit > Contact Book.

2. In the Contact Book dialog, click New Contact ©; or, select an existing contact, and then click the Edit button.

3. In the New Contact or Edit Contact window, add detailed telephone and mailing address information.

4. When you've finished adding or editing your contact information, click OK to close the window. Then click OK again to close the Contact Book dialog.

Editor Keyboard Shortcuts

TO CHOOSE A TOOL

Tools

Move	V
Zoom	Z
Hand	H
Eyedropper	I
Marquee	M
Lasso	L
Magic Wand	W
Selection Brush	A
Type & Type Mask	T
Crop	C
Cookie Cutter	Q
Straighten	P
Red Eye Removal	Y
Healing Brush	J
Clone Stamp	S
Eraser	E
Brush	B
Smart Brush	F
Pencil	N

TO CHOOSE A TOOL

Tools *(continued)*

Paint Bucket	K
Gradient	G
Shape	U
Blur	R
Sponge	O

TO CYCLE THROUGH TOOLS

Marquee tools	M
Lasso tools	L
Type & Type Mask tools	T
Healing Brush tools	J
Clone Stamp tools	S
Eraser tools	E
Brush tools	B
Smart Brush tools	F
Shape tools	U
Blur & Sharpen tools	R
Dodge & Burn tools	O

Marquee Tool

Draw marquee from center	Alt-drag
Constrain to square or circle	Shift-drag
Draw from center and constrain to...	Alt+Shift-drag

Move Tool

Constrain move to 45°	Shift-drag
Copy selection or layer	Alt-drag
Nudge selection or layer 1 pixel	Arrow key
Nudge selection or layer 10 pixels	Shift+arrow

Lasso Tool

Add to selection	Shift-click, then draw
Delete from selection	Alt-click, then draw
Intersect with selection	Alt+Shift-click, then draw
Change to Polygonal Lasso	Click, then Alt-drag

Polygonal Lasso Tool

Add to selection	Shift-click, then draw
Delete from selection	Alt-click, then draw
Intersect with selection	Alt+Shift-click, then draw
Draw using Lasso	Alt-drag
Constrain to 45° while drawing	Shift-drag

Magnetic Lasso Tool

Add to selection	Shift-click, then draw
Delete from selection	Alt-click, then draw
Intersect with selection	Alt+Shift-click, then draw
Add point	Single click
Remove last point	Backspace or Delete
Close path	Double-click or Enter

Magnetic Lasso Tool *(continued)*

Close path over start point	Click on start point
Close path using straight line segment	Alt-double-click
Switch to Lasso	Alt-drag
Switch to Polygonal Lasso	Alt-click

Crop Tool

Rotate crop marquee	Drag outside crop marquee
Move crop marquee	Drag inside crop marquee
Resize crop marquee	Drag crop handles
Resize crop box while maintaining its aspect ratio	Shift-drag corner handles

Shape Tools

Constrain to square or circle	Shift-drag
Constrain Line tool to 45°	Shift-drag
Transform shape	Ctrl+T
Distort	Ctrl-drag
Skew	Ctrl+Alt-drag
Create Perspective	Ctrl+Alt+Shift-drag

Type Tool

Select a word	Double-click in text
Select a line	Triple-click in text
Select a paragraph	Quadruple-click in text
Select all characters	Ctrl+A
Left align text	Ctrl+Shift+L
Center text	Ctrl+Shift+C
Right align text	Ctrl+Shift+R
Increase by 2 points	Ctrl+Shift+ . (period)
Decrease by 2 points	Ctrl+Shift+ , (comma)
Scroll through fonts	Select font in menu+up/down arrow

WORKING WITH TOOLS

Paint Bucket Tool

Change color of area	Shift-click outside canvas

Brush and Pencil Tool

Decrease or increase size by 10 pixels	[or] (bracket keys) (or by 1 pixel when size is less than 10 pixels)

Smudge Tool

Smudge using Foreground color	Alt-drag

Eyedropper Tool

Choose Background color	Alt-click

DISPLAY SHORTCUTS

Change View

Zoom In	Ctrl+Spacebar-click/drag or Ctrl++ (plus)
Zoom out	Alt-Spacebar-click/drag or Ctrl+− (minus)
Zoom to 100% / Actual pixels	Double-click Zoom tool or Ctrl+Alt+0 (zero)
Zoom to fit window / Fit on screen	Double-click Hand tool or Ctrl+0 (zero)
Show/hide edges of selection	Ctrl+H
Show/hide ruler	Ctrl+Shift+R

Hand Tool

Toggle to zoom in	Ctrl
Toggle to zoom out	Alt
Fit image on screen	Double-click tool

DISPLAY SHORTCUTS

Zoom Tool

Zoom out	Alt-click
Actual size	Double-click tool

Move Image in Window

Scroll up one screen	Page Up
Scroll down one screen	Page Down
Scroll left one screen	Ctrl+page up
Scroll right one screen	Ctrl+page down
Scroll up 10 pixels	Shift+page up
Scroll down 10 pixels	Shift+page down
Scroll left 10 pixels	Ctrl+Shift+page up
Scroll right 10 pixels	Ctrl+Shift+page down
Move view to upper left	Home key
Move view to lower right	End key

MENU SHORTCUTS

File Menu

New	Ctrl+N
Open	Ctrl+O
Open As	Ctrl+Alt+O
Close	Ctrl+W
Close All	Ctrl+Alt+W
Save	Ctrl+S
Save As	Ctrl+Shift+S
Save for Web	Ctrl+Alt+Shift+S
Print	Ctrl+P
Print Multiple Photos	Ctrl+Alt+P
Exit	Ctrl+Q

Edit Menu

Undo	Ctrl+Z
Redo	Ctrl+Y
Cut	Ctrl+X
Copy	Ctrl+C
Copy Merged	Ctrl+Shift+C
Paste	Ctrl+V
Paste Into Selection	Ctrl+Shift+V
Color Settings	Ctrl+Shift+K
Preferences > General	Ctrl+K

Image Menu

Free Transform	Ctrl+T
Image Size	Ctrl+Alt+I

Enhance Menu

Auto Smart Fix	Ctrl+Alt+M
Auto Levels	Ctrl+Shift+L
Auto Contrast	Ctrl+Alt+Shift+L
Auto Color Correction	Ctrl+Shift+B
Auto Red Eye Fix	Ctrl+R
Adjust Smart Fix	Ctrl+Shift+M
Adjust Lighting > Adjust Levels	Ctrl+L

MENU SHORTCUTS

Enhance Menu *(continued)*

Adjust Color > Adjust Hue/ Saturation	Ctrl+U
Adjust Color > Remove Color	Ctrl+Shift+U

Layer Menu

New > Layer	Ctrl+Shift+N
New > Layer via Copy	Ctrl+J
New > Layer via Cut	Ctrl+Shift+J
Create Clipping Mask	Ctrl+G
Arrange > Bring to Front	Ctrl+Shift+]
Arrange > Bring Forward	Ctrl+]
Arrange > Send Backward	Ctrl+[
Arrange > Send to Back	Ctrl+Shift+[
Merge Down	Ctrl+E
Merge Visible	Ctrl+Shift+E

Select Menu

All	Ctrl+A
Deselect	Ctrl+D
Reselect	Ctrl+Shift+D
Inverse	Ctrl+Shift+I
Feather	Ctrl+Alt+D
Nudge selection marquee 1 pixel	Arrow key
Nudge selection marquee 10 pixels	Shift+Arrow key

Filter Menu

Last Filter	Ctrl+F
Adjustments > Invert	Ctrl+I

Liquify Filter

Warp tool	W
Turbulence tool	T
Twirl Clockwise tool	C
Twirl Counterclockwise tool	L

MENU SHORTCUTS

Liquify Filter *(continued)*

Pucker tool	P
Bloat tool	B
Shift Pixels tool	S
Reflection tool	M
Reconstruct tool	E
Zoom tool	Z
Hand tool	H
Reverse direction for Shift Pixels	Alt+tool and Reflect tools
Increase/decrease brush pressure by 1	Up/down arrow key
Increase/decrease brush size by 1	Up/down arrow key

Organizer Keyboard Shortcuts

MENU SHORTCUTS

File Menu

Get Photos and Videos > From Camera or Card Reader	Ctrl+G
Get Photos and Videos > From Scanner	Ctrl+U
Get Photos and Videos > From Files and Folders	Ctrl+Shift+G
Catalog	Ctrl+Shift+C
Make a CD/DVD	Ctrl+Alt+C
Copy/Move to Removable Disk	Ctrl+Shift+O
Backup Catalog	Ctrl+B
Duplicate	Ctrl+Shift+D
Rename	Ctrl+Shift+N
Move	Ctrl+Shift+V
Export As New File(s)	Ctrl+E
Print	Ctrl+P
Exit	Ctrl+Q

MENU SHORTCUTS

Edit Menu

Undo	Ctrl+Z
Redo	Ctrl+Y
Copy	Ctrl+C
Select All	Ctrl+A
Deselect	Ctrl+Shift+A
Delete from Catalog	Delete key
Rotate 90° Left	Ctrl+Left
Rotate 90° Right	Ctrl+Right
Auto Smart Fix	Ctrl+Alt+M
Auto Red Eye Fix	Ctrl+R
Adjust Date and Time	Ctrl+J
Add Caption	Ctrl+Shift+T
Update Thumbnail	Ctrl+Shift+U
Set as Desktop Wallpaper	Ctrl+Shift+W
Visibility > Mark as Hidden	Alt+F2
Stack > Automatically Suggest Stacks	Ctrl+Alt+K
Stack > Stack Selected Photos	Ctrl+Alt+S
Stack > Reveal Photos in a Stack	Ctrl+Alt+R

MENU SHORTCUTS

Edit Menu *(continued)*

Stack > Collapse Photos in Stack	Ctrl+Alt+Shift+R
Color Settings	Ctrl+Alt+G
Preferences > General	Ctrl+K

Find Menu

Set Date Range	Ctrl+Alt+F
Clear Date Range	Ctrl+Shift+F
By Caption or Note	Ctrl+Shift+J
By Filename	Ctrl+Shift+K
All Version Sets	Ctrl+Alt+V
All Stacks	Ctrl+Alt+Shift+S
By Media Type > Photos	Alt+1
By Media Type > Video	Alt+2
By Media Type > Audio	Alt+3
By Media Type > Projects	Alt+4
By Media Type > PDF	Alt+5
By Media Type > Items with Audio Captions	Alt+6
Items with Unknown Date or Time	Ctrl+Shift+X
Untagged Items	Ctrl+Shift+Q
Unanalyzed Content	Ctrl+Shift+Y
Find People for Tagging	Ctrl+Shift+P

View Menu

Refresh	F5
Media Types > Photos	Ctrl+1
Media Types > Video	Ctrl+2
Media Types > Audio	Ctrl+3
Media Types > Projects	Ctrl+4
Media Types > PDF	Ctrl+5
Details	Ctrl+D

MENU SHORTCUTS

Window Menu

Timeline	Ctrl+L
Properties	Alt+Return

Help Menu

Photoshop Elements Help	F1

Display Drop-Down Menu

Thumbnail View	Ctrl+Alt+1
Import Batch	Ctrl+Alt+2
Folder Location	Ctrl+Alt+3
Date View	Ctrl+Alt+D
View Photos in Full Screen	F11
Compare Photos Side by Side	F12

NAVIGATING IN THE PHOTO BROWSER

Move Selection up/down/left/right	Up/Down/Left/Right
Show full-size thumbnail of selected photo	Return

VIEWING PHOTOS IN FULL SCREEN MODE

Start slide show	Spacebar
Show next slide	Right/Down
Show previous slide	Left/Up
Pause slide show	Spacebar
End slide show	Esc

Index

Single Photo View button, 30, 33

skewing, 201, 263

skies, brightening, 88

skin tones, 174

slide shows, 48, 54, 324–330, 332, 344

Small Thumbnail button, 30

smart albums, 52–53

Smart Blending mode, 171

Smart Blur filter, 226

Smart Brush tool, 4, 146–147

Smart Fix slider, 87

Smart Paint effect, 146–147

Smart Tags, 42

Smooth command, 112

Smudge tool, 131, 339

snapping to images/objects, 82, 97, 153

Soft Omni lighting style, 232

Soft Spotlight lighting style, 232

Solid gradients, 242

sorting

    albums, 48, 50

    photos, 54

    thumbnails, 30

spacing, 251, 278

Spacing slider, 251

special effects. *See* effects

Sponge tool, 4, 133

Spot Healing Brush tool, xiv, 119, 120

Spotlight lighting type, 233

Spyder tool, 160

squares, 95

stacking photos, 22, 58–59

Standard dialog, 20–22

star ratings. *See* rating photos

status bar, 15

Straighten and Crop Image command, 117

Straighten Image command, 118

Straighten tool, 4, 117, 166

straightening images, 4, 117–118, 166

strikethrough style, 278

stroke color, 244

Stroke command, 243–244

Stroke effect, 211

stroke layers, 244, 245

Style Match feature, 148–149

Style Settings dialog, 209, 210–211

style source images, 148–149

styles

    applying to images, 149

    CSS, 304

    layer, 208–211, 288

    lighting, 231, 232

    matching, 148–149

    text, 278

Stylus Pressure option, 99

stylus tablet, 99, 249

subcategories, 45–47

subfolders, 21, 313

Surface Blur filter, 129, 226

Switch Colors tool, 4

synchronization

    backups, 64–68

    photos between computers, 64

    photos with Photoshop.com, 67–68

    resolving problems, 68

    settings for, 64–68

T

tabbed windows, 79, 80

Tag Cloud, 41

tagged photos, 44–47, 54. *See also* keyword tags

tags. *See* keyword tags

teeth, whitening, 88

text. *See also* type

    aligning, 279

    captions, 33, 34, 68, 320

    color, 279

    editing, 272, 273

type mask tools, 285–287
type masks, 285–287
Type tool, 4, 338

U

UnCheck All button, 23
underline style, 278
Undo command, 86, 137
Undo History panel, 214–215
undoing changes, 86, 137, 229
Units & Rulers command, 277
units of measure, 77, 78, 81
Unsharp Mask command, 128
upsampling, 74, 75, 116
Use All Layers option, 240

V

vector graphics, 236, 264
vector shapes, 268, 269
version sets, 6, 67, 344
vertical text, 280–281
Vibrance slider, 165
video, 27, 343
video cards, 295
View menu, 76, 84, 344
viewing images. *See also* previews
    at 100%, 15
    displaying areas of, 16
    in Organizer, 22
    on screen, 74–75
views, display shortcuts, 339
Vignette effect, 111
vignetting, 111, 230

W

Warp tool, 227, 228
warping text, 283–284
Watch Folders, 25
Web browsers, 291, 297, 305
Web images, 289–306. *See also* images
    color, 295, 297–300, 303–306
    file formats, 291
    optimizing, 160, 290–301
    previewing, 294
    requirements for, 290
    in Web Photo Gallery, 33, 34, 48
Web pages, 70, 73
Web Photo Gallery, 33, 34, 48
Welcome Screen, 2
White Balance slider, 165
Whiten Teeth tool, 88
whitening teeth, 88
Width option, 99
Window menu, 10, 344
windows
    arranging, 79–80
    moving images in, 339
    multiple views, 79–80
    resizing to fit, 15
WMV files, 27
work area, 2–4, 28–30
workspaces, 12, 19, 28, 62

X

x coordinates, 77

Y

y coordinates, 77
Yahoo! Maps, 60
Year view, 57

Z

zero point, 81
ZIP compression, 308, 309
Zoom field, 84
Zoom In button, 13, 14
Zoom Out button, 14
Zoom slider, 13, 84
Zoom text box, 13, 15
Zoom tool, 4, 13–16, 166, 228, 339
zooming in/out, 13–16, 80, 84, 339
zoom-percentage text box, 14

WATCH
READ
CREATE

Meet Creative Edge.

A new resource of unlimited books, videos and tutorials for creatives from the world's leading experts.

Creative Edge is your one stop for inspiration, answers to technical questions and ways to stay at the top of your game so you can focus on what you do best—being creative.

All for only $24.99 per month for access—any day any time you need it.

peachpit.com/creativeedge